D0974933

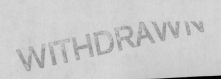

OXFORD ENGLISH DRAMA

General Editor: MICHAEL CORDNER

Associate General Editors: PETER HOLLAND · MARTIN WIGGINS

EIGHTEENTH-CENTURY WOMEN DRAMATISTS

WOMEN wrote some of the most engaging and celebrated comedies produced on the Restoration and eighteenth-century London stage and in the process offered a decidedly female perspective on the theatre's traditional marriage plot. This volume introduces modern readers to four censored, neglected, or lost jewels of our dramatic tradition written by four of this era's most prominent comic playwrights. **Mary Pix** (1666–1709), a 'female wit' of the 1690s championed by William Congreve, provided vehicles for the greatest acting talents of her day. **Susanna Centlivre** (1669?–1723), one of the most successful playwrights of the century, gave David Garrick and Kitty Clive their favourite roles. **Elizabeth Griffith** (1727–93), a celebrated novelist, wrote plays that reflected contemporary continental ideas about the nature and purpose of the theatre. **Hannah Cowley** (1743–1809), hailed for her sparkling dialogue and comic portraiture, proved popular on both sides of the Atlantic. The four comedies selected for this volume showcase lively, independent, and thoroughly original heroines negotiating their ways through a London made up of oppressive guardians, ingenious con artists, and a variety of mercenary, jealous, ambivalent, and rakish suitors—and doing so with consummate wit and resourcefulness.

MELINDA C. FINBERG holds degrees from Yale and Princeton Universities and has held an appointment as a Lecturer at Princeton University. Prior to entering academia, she was an actress in New York City. She has been a frequent speaker at scholarly conferences across the United States on eighteenth-century women writers and is a contributor to a CD Rom program for teaching Shakespeare to US secondary school students. For nearly twenty years she has been a writer and editor, with a particular interest in the theatre, and currently she is an independent scholar.

MICHAEL CORDNER is Reader in the Department of English and Related Literature at the University of York. He has edited George Farquhar's *The Beaux' Stratagem*, the *Complete Plays* of Sir George Etherege, *Four Comedies* of Sir John Vanbrugh, and, for Oxford English Drama, *Four Restoration Marriage Plays* and Sheridan's *The School for Scandal and Other Plays*. He is writing books on *The Comedy of Marriage* and *Shakespeare and the Actor*.

PETER HOLLAND is Professor of Shakespeare Studies and Director of the Shakespeare Institute, University of Birmingham.

MARTIN WIGGINS is a fellow of the Shakespeare Institute and Lecturer in English at the University of Birmingham.

OXFORD ENGLISH DRAMA

OXFORD WORLD'S CLASSICS

Eighteenth–Century Women Dramatists

MARY PIX
The Innocent Mistress

SUSANNA CENTLIVRE
The Busybody

ELIZABETH GRIFFITH
The Times

HANNAH COWLEY
The Belle's Stratagem

Edited by
MELINDA C. FINBERG

OXFORD
UNIVERSITY PRESS

OXFORD

UNIVERSITY PRESS

Great Clarendon Street, Oxford OX2 6DP

Oxford University Press is a department of the University of Oxford.
It furthers the University's objective of excellence in research, scholarship,
and education by publishing worldwide in

Oxford New York

Athens Auckland Bangkok Bogotá Buenos Aires Cape Town
Chennai Dar es Salaam Delhi Florence Hong Kong Istanbul Karachi
Kolkata Kuala Lumpur Madrid Melbourne Mexico City Mumbai Nairobi
Paris São Paulo Shanghai Singapore Taipei Tokyo Toronto Warsaw

with associated companies in Berlin Ibadan

Oxford is a registered trade mark of Oxford University Press
in the UK and in certain other countries

Published in the United States
by Oxford University Press Inc., New York

© Melinda C. Finberg 2001

British Library Cataloguing in Publication Data

Data available

Library of Congress Cataloging in Publication Data

Data available

ISBN 978-0-19-955481-2

3

Typeset in Ehrhardt by
RefineCatch Limited, Bungay, Suffolk
Printed in Great Britain by
Clays Ltd, St Ives plc

For

Alexander Everett and Meredith Bronwyn Agran

CONTENTS

ACKNOWLEDGEMENTS

THIS volume would not have been possible without the encouragement, assistance, and expertise of a wide range of colleagues, friends, and institutional supporters. I am especially grateful to the Huntington Library in San Marino, California, and its staff for access to its incomparable holdings, and for the Princeton Graduate Alumni/Mellon Fellowship and Princeton University Women's Studies Program research grant that helped fund my research there; to Beth Harrison and Lee Mitchell of Princeton University's Department of English; to such scholars as Ulrich C. Knoepflmacher, Robert Mack, Marie McAllister, and Rena Lamparska for generously sharing their time and expertise with me; to Derek Hughes and Martha Bowden for their aid on queries that escaped me; to Mary George, head research librarian at Princeton's Firestone Library; to Janice Powell, the head librarian at Princeton's Marquand Library; to R. M. Harvey, principal reference librarian at the Corporation of London Guildhall Library; to Martin Wiggins, Eugene Giddens, and Roberta Barker at the Shakespeare Institute in Stratford; to Lisa Horowitz, Jeanne Raimo, and Emily Neubauer for their research assistance; to Margaret Anne Doody for introducing me to this project, and to Michael Cadden for his unflagging support and his much appreciated editorial suggestions. The errors that remain are solely my responsibility. My especial thanks to my mother, Doris Finberg, and my husband, Raymond Agran, for their love, encouragement, and critical eyes. Lastly I wish to express my deepest appreciation to Michael Cordner, the general editor of this series, and Judith Luna and Frances Whistler at Oxford University Press for their faith in this project, their patience, and the guidance that brought it to fruition, to Dorothy McCarthy for her sensitive copy-editing, and to Elizabeth Stratford for shepherding this volume through production.

Melinda C. Finberg

INTRODUCTION

THE plays contained in this volume are all comedies. All take place among the fashionable society of London, and all are written by women. That women dramatists played an important role in the theatrical history of Restoration and eighteenth-century England is a fact that has been forgotten or ignored for nearly one hundred years, and a fact worth recalling. Female playwrights first gained access to the English stage at the same time as actresses, that is, when the theatres reopened in 1660, after the Restoration.

It would be difficult to address the works of women playwrights of the eighteenth century without looking back to Aphra Behn (1640–89). Behn was the first woman in England to earn her living through her writing, and she wrote poetry, novels, translations, and drama. She produced her first play, *The Forced Marriage*, for the Duke's Company at Lincoln's Inn Fields in 1671,[1] and by the middle of the decade had become one of the most popular contemporary dramatists. The wildness of Behn's life easily rivals that of any of the characters in her plays. Behn emerged from obscure origins, probably spent part of her youth in Surinam, became a spy for the English government during the Anglo-Dutch War in 1666, and was imprisoned for debt in 1667. She was a staunch and active Tory all her life and wrote political propaganda on behalf of her party during the late 1670s and early 1680s. Behn was also an outspoken proponent of sexual freedom for women, and she operated, from at least 1667 to her death, as an independent woman, even recording her love affairs, with members of both sexes, in her poetry.[2] The late twentieth century saw a resurgence of interest in Behn and her work, and revivals of her comedy *The Rover* (1677) have been recently staged to great acclaim on both sides of the Atlantic.

Behn became a complicated role model for the women playwrights

---

[1] Jacqueline Pearson suggests that Behn chose the Duke's Company because it was under the management of a woman, Lady Davenant: Pearson, *The Prostituted Muse: Images of Women and Women Dramatists 1642–1737* (New York, 1988), 145.

[2] A great deal of scholarship is available on Aphra Behn. For more information on her life and career, see Maureen Duffy, *The Passionate Shepherdess* (London, 1977); Angeline Goreau, *Reconstructing Aphra: A Social Biography of Aphra Behn* (Oxford, 1980); and Frederick M. Link, *Aphra Behn* (New York, 1968).

who followed her. The sexual explicitness and unpunished debauchery prevalent in Restoration comedy provoked the ire both of those who believed that the theatre was inherently immoral and of those who believed that its proper purpose was to teach virtue. Many of these moralists objected especially to women writers, and exploited Behn's personal and literary licentiousness as examples of what could be expected from a woman let loose in the public forum of the theatre. During the remainder of the seventeenth century, a woman's play was immediately assumed to be bawdy, and women playwrights laboured under Behn's notorious reputation, regardless of their own personal conduct. None the less, Behn's skill as a writer and her forthright insistence on taking her legitimate place among the celebrated writers of her age inspired an efflorescence of women dramatists between 1660 and 1800. Even in the face of such attacks on the immorality of the contemporary stage and demands for its reform as Jeremy Collier's inflammatory tract, *A Short View of the Immorality and Profaneness of the English Stage* (1698), Mary Pix, Delarivière Manley, Catherine Trotter, and Susanna Centlivre remained open admirers of Behn and viewed themselves as following where she had led. Even Hannah Cowley, whose career began a full century after Behn's, and who lived during a time in which it was more dangerous to acknowledge openly a debt to her, clearly traced her lineage back to this literary forebear and adapted Behn's *The Lucky Chance* (1686) for her own *A School for Greybeards* (1786).

The women playwrights who wrote between the Restoration and the end of the eighteenth century never found acceptance easy, but they produced a large body of estimable work. A combination of influences at the turn of the nineteenth century, including the reconfigurations of London's stages, a corresponding change in dramatic tastes, and increasing pressure on women writers to confine their lives and their works within the limits of a strict moral code, all contributed to the near disappearance of women playwrights in the nineteenth century.

Selecting texts for this volume was both exciting and daunting. So little attention has been given to eighteenth-century women playwrights that any single attempt to redress this neglect runs the risk of condemning those works not included to even deeper obscurity. In the final analysis, the selections in this volume are, to a certain degree, arbitrary, and while they include some of the greatest comedies by women of the period, and perhaps even two of the era's best comedies by any authors, it must be remembered that other wonderful comedies by women, by such noteworthy dramatists as Frances Sheridan and Elizabeth Inchbald among others, are also deserving of our attention and still remain inaccessible to today's directors or students of drama.

Mary Pix

In the anonymous satire *The Female Wits* (1696),[3] Mary Griffith Pix is caricatured as Mrs Wellfed, 'a fat Female Author, a good, sociable, well-natur'd Companion, that will not suffer Martyrdom rather than take off three Bumpers in a Hand.' (*The Female Wits*, sig. a5v). Mrs Wellfed, a foolish, open-hearted character, is able to recognize her own flaws, enjoys good food, wine, and the company of the actors. While Pix's girth and epicurean enjoyment were well known, she was a well respected, and almost universally well liked, member of London's literary community. An admirer of the great Aphra Behn and friend and colleague of Susanna Centlivre, Pix can be seen as a link between women writers of the Restoration and Augustan periods.[4]

Very little is known about the details of Pix's life before her astonishing literary début. She was born in 1666 in Nettlebed, Oxfordshire, and although her father was a country vicar, her mother came from a well-connected family, and there is evidence that Pix was accepted in local polite society and had friends in high places.[5] She married a merchant-tailor, George Pix, in 1684 in London and the marriage produced one child, a son, who died in 1690. In 1696 Pix burst upon the literary world with a tragedy, *Ibrahim, the Thirteenth Emperour of the Turks* (Drury Lane, June 1696), a farce, *The Spanish Wives* (Dorset

---

[3] There is significant dispute as to when the anonymous *The Female Wits* was first produced. It did not appear in print until 1704. The satire could not have appeared until after April 1696, because its setting is a rehearsal of Delarivière Manley's *The Royal Mischief*, which had its première then. The *London Stage* estimates it was produced in September 1696, but other scholars suggest 1697 because of its references to Elkanah Settle's *The World in the Moon*, which was first staged in June 1697. See Emmett L. Avery *et al.*, *The London Stage, 1660–1800* (Carbondale, Ill., 1960–8), i. 467, and a very thorough discussion in Constance Clark, *Three Augustan Women Playwrights* (New York, 1986), 289–91.

[4] Clark, *Three Augustan Women Playwrights*, 217–18. Robert D. Hume uses the term Augustan drama to refer to plays written in the first quarter of the eighteenth century in *The Development of English Drama in the Late Seventeenth Century* (Oxford, 1976), 432.

[5] Clark, *Three Augustan Women Playwrights*, 187–8.

Garden, August 1696); and a novel, *The Inhuman Cardinal; or Innocence Betray'd.*[6]

After her début, Pix quickly became established in London theatrical circles. She emulated Behn's comedies of intrigue with their multiple plots, and her style was further influenced by her mentor, William Congreve. Pix was a friend and supporter of other women writers such as Catherine Trotter, Delarivière Manley, Sarah Fyge-Egerton, and Susanna Centlivre, as well as the actress Elizabeth Barry. Peter Anthony Motteux, a well-known lyricist and playwright, wrote the prologue, epilogue, and at least one song for *The Innocent Mistress*.

Pix moved to the theatre at Lincoln's Inn Fields with *The Innocent Mistress* in 1697. The play was regarded as successful and has been said to show the earliest example of Congreve's influence on her.[7] Her plays became a staple in the repertory of Thomas Betterton's theatre company at Lincoln's Inn Fields and later at the Queen's Theatre. They were vehicles for the talents of Elizabeth Barry, Anne Bracegirdle, and Thomas Betterton, who played Bellinda, Mrs Beauclair, and Sir Charles Beauclair, respectively, in *The Innocent Mistress*.

Following the success of *The Spanish Wives*, and before her move to Lincoln's Inn Fields, Pix sent a copy of her comedy *The Deceiver Deceived* to the actor George Powell in hopes of having his company at Drury Lane produce it. Powell rejected the comedy, but shortly thereafter, in September 1697, produced his own *Imposture Defeated*, which clearly plagiarizes Pix's work. Congreve came to Pix's defence, and *The Deceiver Deceived* was produced at Lincoln's Inn Fields in November of that year with a prologue attacking the theft of Pix's work by the Drury Lane company. Powell replied with a vindictive counterattack on Congreve, Pix, and Trotter in his *Animadversion on Mr Congreve's Late Answer to Mr Collier* (1698).[8] While being caricatured in *The Female Wits* had not distressed Pix enough to affect her

[6] Nancy Cotton points out that Pix's professional début was not as sudden or unprepared as appears. She refers to Pix's dedicatory letter to *The Spanish Wives* (1696) in which Pix writes to Colonel Tipping of Whitfield, 'You have known me from my childhood, and my inclination to poetry.' Cotton suggests that Pix may have built up a reserve of material over the years. See Nancy Cotton, *Women Playwrights in England, c.1361–1750* (Lewisburg, Pa., 1980), 88–9.

[7] Clark, *Three Augustan Women Playwrights*, 258. Clark believes Pix may have modelled Sir Francis Wildlove and Mrs Beauclair on Valentine and Angelica from Congreve's *Love for Love* (1695).

[8] Although published anonymously, this piece is now credited to Powell. See [George Powell,] *Animadversion on Mr Congreve's Late Answer to Mr Collier*, ed. Arthur Freeman (London, 1698; rep. New York, 1972).

work, Powell's malice seems to have caused her to wish to remove herself from public scrutiny, and after 1699 she published her works less openly, even having some printed anonymously.

Despite this unpleasant professional episode, Pix retained the steadfast support of Congreve, Betterton, and the company at Lincoln's Inn Fields, were her steadfast supporters, and even Princess Anne permitted the battle-scarred *Deceiver Deceived* to be dedicated to her. No sexual scandal attached itself to Pix's name, and despite frequent misogynistic lampoons on her supposed ignorance, her works display evidence of significant education in languages and literature. Between 1696 and 1706 Pix wrote six comedies and seven tragedies. A frequent motif in all her works is sexual violence and female victimization. The tragedies abound with graphic rape and murder; the comedies with forcible confinements and threats of rape.[9] Present-day audiences have lost their taste for Augustan tragedy, but Pix's comedies, particularly *The Innocent Mistress*, *The Spanish Wives*, and *Adventures in Madrid* (1706), with their emphasis on farcical intrigue and wily heroines, deserve to be revisited.

The Innocent Mistress is a comedy of intrigue that pays tribute both stylistically and thematically to Aphra Behn. Pix exhibits a masterly sense of choreography, interweaving five comic plots, in a very Behn-like fashion, into a whole that comments on love and courtship and the evils of marriages based on money. The structure of Pix's comedy examines love and courtship from two opposite sides of the spectrum: the witty battle between Sir Francis Wildlove and Mrs Beauclair and the hopeless platonic affair of Sir Charles Beauclair and Mariamne/Bellinda. Offsetting these two pairs of lovers are three plots exploring how three other couples, and their associates, cheat each other into and out of unions of convenience.

At one end of the spectrum is the battle of the sexes between Sir Francis Wildlove and Mrs Beauclair, an incarnation of the witty and sophisticated Restoration 'gay' couple: he an unreformed rake and wit; she a virtuous and very clever woman of fashion. Her ability to outwit him wins him over. The plot is reminiscent of Behn's Hellena and Willmore in *The Rover*. Not only does Mrs Beauclair baffle all of her

⁹ Linda R. Payne suggests that women authors such as Pix often used sexual violence as a way of portraying their ambivalence towards the male-dominated hierachy that allowed them to produce their works while at the same time it constrained and victimized them ('Mary Pix', in Paula R. Backscheider (ed.), *Dictionary of Literary Biography*, 80, *Restoration and Eighteenth-Century Dramatists*, 1st ser. (Detroit, 1989), 180).

lover's assignations with other women as Hellena does, but she also engages in an exploit of transvestism in which she becomes her lover's rival for another woman.

The scene in which the furious and frustrated Sir Francis bursts in on his supposed rival and recognizes Mrs Beauclair in her male garb (4.3) is charged with sexual tension. While before the Restoration and the advent of actresses on the British stage, transvestite plots were a way of getting young male actors out of female attire and into more appropriate dress, after the Restoration these same stage conventions could be used to show off the shapely legs of the actresses that were generally concealed beneath their elaborate skirts. Although an actress raising her skirts would be deemed obscene, an actress revealing herself in close fitting male attire was acceptable. Pix highlights the titillating nature of this transvestism, by confronting Sir Francis with Mrs Beauclair's shapeliness, revealed to him for the first time. He is torn between admiring what he sees and defending himself from her accusations. Mrs Beauclair is sensible of the effect she has created and augments it by announcing her intention of returning to female attire with language that implies further exposure rather than concealment. She tantalizes him by apologizing, 'I must beg your pardon; I'm in haste to unrig,' (4.3.42) that is 'undress.'

At the other end of the spectrum is the platonic love affair of Sir Charles and his innocent mistress, Bellinda, at first blush a plot indebted to the pressure of the reform movement to banish sexual degeneracy and immorality from the stage. Theirs is a platonic love which has no hope of consummation and which draws on models from popular romances of the day, such as those by Madeleine de Scudéry (1607–1701),[10] in which lovers endure horrendous suffering and seemingly endless separations that test and prove the purity of their affections. However, Pix subtly casts doubt on the purity of these supposed exemplars of honour, who continually agonize over the propriety of their actions. Sir Charles is not a total innocent regarding his own unhappiness. Although he was young when married to the current Lady Beauclair, he never speaks of having tried to avoid this pecuniary match. Bellinda would appear to be more courageous in this regard, but her overly romantic language opens her to the mockery even of her friends. When Bellinda describes to Mrs Beauclair how she came to meet and fall in love with Sir Charles, she confesses, 'I blushed and fondly thought this man my amorous stars, in kindness, destined for

---

[10] e.g. *Artamène, ou le Grand Cyrus* (1649–53) and *Clélie, histoire romaine* (1654–60).

my happiness. But oh!'—and earthy Mrs Beauclair cuts off Bellinda's high-flown rhapsody with, 'But oh, he was married, and that spoiled all' (1.2.43).

Beaumont, who has been sent by Lord Belmour to find his wayward daughter, dismisses Bellinda as being corrupted by too much romance literature. He reports that she was

Too studious for her sex, and fell upon the seducers of the women: plays, and romances. From thence she formed herself a hero, a cavalier, that could love and talk like them; whilst her father, without consulting her, provided a husband, rich, but wanting all Scudéry's accomplishments. This man she called monster, and finding the marriage unavoidable, took her jewels and what money was in her power, and in the stage-coach fled to this populous wilderness, if that can be proper, for here we are, in crowds, concealed as well as in a desert. (1.1.163–71)

According to Beaumont, Mariamne is discontented with the mundane life proposed to her and seeks romance, adventure, and freedom by running away. He ridicules her by comparing her tame flight by stage-coach to London, where her money can keep her private and secure, to the narrow escapes from imprisonment or rape of romance heroines who find themselves in dungeons, deserts, or forests, away from civilization. But there is a certain irony inherent in Pix holding up plays and novels, of the kind she herself writes, as the seducers of women and in her suggestion that literacy in women leads to their acting immorally or at least unsuitably. After all, if one strips away Beaumont's mockery, all we know is that Mariamne objected to being forced into a marriage for money, and, having the financial resources to protect herself, escaped. Pix leaves the question open as to whether Mariamne/Bellinda is a laughably quixotic character or a true innocent, as the title of the comedy suggests, hovering between misery and disgrace in the forms of a loveless marriage and a married lover— although the final outcome of her rebellion against a tyrannous father and adherence to her own code of honour does suggest virtue rewarded.

The other three plots explore the issues raised regarding marriage, love, and money and provide a commentary on the major love stories. The saga of Cheatall, Arabella, and Beaumont offers a mock romance juxtaposed to that of Sir Charles and Bellinda, while the machinations of Lady Beauclair, Peggy, and Spendall, an illiterate, countrified mother-and-daughter team and the con artist out to marry the daughter for her money, mock the conventions of polite courtship. It is possible that Peggy, a young, ignorant, country girl who overeats and guzzles wine, is a self-parody of Pix, or at least of her reputation.[11] The turbulent romance of jealous Mr Flywife and the kept mistress posing as his wife makes up the final plot of the comedy. Perhaps in a slight bow to the pressure to reform the theatre, Pix uses these unsavoury characters to act out the adultery and lechery that is hinted at by the actions and passions of the more central characters. Mr Flywife's violence and Mrs Flywife's viciousness provide a counterbalance to the ethereal romance of Bellinda and Sir Charles.

The complexity of this character-driven comedy has implications for its staging. Most of the action is designed to take place on the forestage in front of the proscenium, in close proximity to the audience,[12] and the setting is relegated to a minor role. Sometimes the comedy makes do with stock sets of an interior of a house, exterior of a house, the park, etc. Often Pix does not describe the scene at all; location is established by which characters enter and their dialogue.[13] For example, in 1.2, which begins in Bellinda's apartment, it is established that the Flywifes are her neighbours in the lodging house. When Bellinda and company exit, Mrs Flywife and Jenny enter. The original edition does not indicate a scene break here. It may be that a scene change occurred without an indication or it may be that we have made the transition to the Flywife apartment without a change of scenery; the set for all the action in the lodging house may be merely a stock sitting-room. As Peter Holland points out, when acting primarily takes place on the forestage, 'fluidity of location is achieved without the need of a new set'.[14] The characters enter and exit, and the audience is supposed to accept that the location has changed without attention being focused on that fact. Specifically indicated scene changes in the first edition of Pix's comedy generally involve a move from an interior to an exterior scene (or vice versa) or a drastic change, such as from a house to a tavern 'discovered' behind a set of shutters. The specificity of character dynamics prevents any confusion. At a time when Lincoln's Inn Fields was competing with the larger Dorset Garden stage, Peter Motteux, in his prologue to *The Innocent Mistress*, felt called upon to comment upon the difference between the two theatres:

[11] Clark, *Three Augustan Women Playwrights*, 197.

[12] For a detailed description of the architecture of Pix's stage, see below, 'The Restoration and Eighteenth-Century Stages'.

[13] For the purposes of this edition, some scene locations have been interpolated accordingly.

[14] Peter Holland, *The Ornament of Action: Text and Performance in Restoration Comedy* (Cambridge, 1979), 39.

'Here, scenes well-wrought, and there, well-painted scenes' (l. 12). Motteux compares the skilful writing of such dramatists as Pix at Lincoln's Inn Fields with the emphasis on scenery and spectacle at the larger theatre. Pix's development of her large and delightfully diverse cast of characters and her masterful orchestration of their multiple plots could engross its audience on the simplest stage.

Susanna Centlivre

Susanna Centlivre was one of the most popular and successful playwrights of the eighteenth century. By the end of the nineteenth century, only four non-Shakespearian comedies written before 1750 were regularly produced on the English stage, and two of them, *The Busybody* (1709) and *The Wonder: A Woman Keeps a Secret* (1714), were by Centlivre.[15] Centlivre was a consummate actor's writer; her comedies were favourite choices for actors' benefits[16] throughout the century, and were chosen by both David Garrick and Kitty Clive for their farewell performances. Like Pix, Centlivre traces her literary lineage back to Aphra Behn,[17] and while her plays bow to the more conservative and less licentious tastes of the early eighteenth century, her biography smacks of the romance and notoriety of her predecessor.

The details of Centlivre's early days are sketchy. She was born in about 1670, the daughter of a Mr Freeman of Holbeach in Lincolnshire. Her mother died when she was young; her father remarried, and died when she was 15. For the adventures of her youth, we are indebted to the anecdotes of John Mottley, who knew Centlivre in the latter part of her life and wrote an account of her for *A Compleat List*

[15] See John Wilson Bowyer, *The Celebrated Mrs Centlivre* (Durham, NC, 1952), p. v, and Pearson, *The Prostituted Muse*, 202. The other two plays were *She Would and She Would Not* (1702) by Colley Cibber and *A New Way to Pay Old Debts* (1625) by Philip Massinger.

[16] Part of an actor's contract with a theatre company was a stipulation for a benefit performance, generally in March or April. The receipts from this benefit constituted a substantial part of the actor's income, and so great care was taken by the actor to select a piece to show off his or her talents and to attract a large audience. For more information, see Allardyce Nicoll, *The Garrick Stage: Theatres and Audience in the Eighteenth Century* (Athens, Ga., 1980), 91–5.

[17] Suz-Anne Kinney notes that Centlivre publicly acknowledges her debt to Behn in a letter in *Familiar and Courtly Letters* (1700) and also used Behn's *nom de plume*, Astraea, as an act of homage, as well as appropriation, in her contributions to *Letters of Wit, Politicks and Morality* (1701). See Kinney, 'Confinement Sharpens the Invention: Aphra Behn's *The Rover* and Susanna Centlivre's *The Busie Body*', in Gail Finney (ed.), *Look Who's Laughing: Gender and Comedy* (Amsterdam, 1994), 82.

of all the English Dramatic Poets (1747). Mottley says Centlivre left home after her father's death because she was poorly treated by her stepmother. His history of her adventures is full of images of transvestism: she posed as 'Cousin Jack' to the poet Anthony Hammond when he was still a student at Cambridge, and lived with him for several months, and later spent some time as a strolling player, specializing in male roles.[18]

At 16, Centlivre became romantically involved with a Mr Fox, nephew to Sir Stephen Fox. She lived with him for a year, apparently until his death, and may or may not have been married to him.[19] She is then rumoured to have married a Mr Carroll, a young gentleman in the army, and lived with him also for a year, before he was killed in a duel. She continued to use Carroll's name, publishing her first plays as Susanna Carroll,[20] and passing herself as a widow until her marriage to Joseph Centlivre, a chef to Queen Anne, in 1707. The marriage lasted until her death on 1 December 1723 and was by most reports a happy one.

Jacqueline Pearson points out that Centlivre's life and career contradict many of our stereotypes about early women playwrights: she produced a large number of plays, and these plays remained in the repertories of major theatres; she wrote while enjoying a successful marriage, and she was very generous to her female colleagues.[21] She was close friends, and possibly a collaborator, with Mary Pix, and after Pix's death in 1709, Centlivre organized a production of *The Busybody* as a benefit for Pix's estate. She also gave the actress Frances Maria Knight the publication rights to her play *Love's Contrivance* (1703). Other theatrical friends included Nicholas Rowe, George Farquhar, and Richard Steele.

Of the nineteen plays Centlivre wrote between 1700 to 1722, the most popular were *The Gamester* (1705), *The Busybody* (1709), *The Wonder: A Woman Keeps a Secret* (1714), and *A Bold Stroke for a Wife*

---

[18] Pearson, *The Prostituted Muse*, 205. Pearson wonders whether Mottley's anecdotes are actually true or if they reflect an eighteenth-century biographer's discomfort with portraying an independent young woman. Perhaps it was easier to explain her freedom by placing her in male guise.

[19] Jean Gagen, 'Susanna Centlivre', in Paula R. Backscheider (ed.), *Dictionary of Literary Biography*, 84, *Restoration and Eighteenth-Century Dramatists*, 2nd series (Detroit, 1989), 18.

[20] Gagen, in 'Susanna Centlivre', notes that many catalogues still list these plays under the authorship of Susanna Carroll.

[21] Pearson, *The Prostituted Muse*, 202.

(1718). Her comedies do not easily fit into one category; they combine elements of romantic comedies of intrigue, comedies of manners, and comedies of humours.[22] Some critics, including Robert Hume, have charged Centlivre with a lack of originality because she borrowed and adapted plots from other English and Continental sources, but this judgement is undeservedly harsh. Even Shakespeare is guilty of such stealing, and, as other critics[23] have noted, Centlivre's use of her sources can be quite original, often giving them an ironic twist that casts them in a new political light, and adapting stock conventions to comment on the treatment and condition of women in Augustan society.

Centlivre's plays reveal the transitions under way in the theatre of her time as well as her strong political views. Unlike many of her Restoration predecessors, including her much-admired Behn, who were staunch Tories, Centlivre was an ardent Whig and a supporter of the House of Hanover, and she once even attempted to use her comedy to address contemporary politics directly: *The Humours of Elections* (1715), which was published again later that year as *The Gotham Election*, satirized the electioneering methods of the Tories in the real town of Gotham. The election of 1715 had resulted in violence, and the political atmosphere remained tense. The government, anxious to avoid inflaming the controversy, had even ordered the clergy to avoid expressing political opinions in their sermons. Therefore, because of its subject matter, the Master of the Revels refused to license Centlivre's farce. In her preface to the printed edition, Centlivre expresses her disappointment at being denied the licence to perform, but acknowledges that no previous author had attempted to deal so pointedly with a contemporary political topic.[24]

Centlivre had also eagerly entered the theatrical political fray early in her career by using the preface and epilogue to her first play, *The*

---

[22] The basis for 'comedies of humours' can be found in the traditional medical belief that a person's constitution was controlled by four basic 'humours' or 'liquids'. If one humour predominated over the other three the result would be a lack of balance, in both health and character. An overabundance of yellow bile resulted in a person governed by choler or anger; of blood, generosity and love; of phlegm, dullness or cowardice; and of black bile, melancholy, laziness, or gluttony. The term 'comedies of humours' is mostly applied to early seventeenth-century plays, in particular the satiric comedies of Ben Jonson, such as *Every Man in His Humour* (1598) and *Volpone* (1606).

[23] e.g. Bowyer, *The Celebrated Mrs Centlivre*, 100–3; Jacqueline Pearson, *The Prostituted Muse*, 208–28; Kinney, 'Confinement Sharpens the Invention', 83, 93–5; and Gagen, 'Susanna Centlivre', 40.

[24] Gagen, 'Susanna Centlivre', 34.

Perjur'd Husband (1700), to argue vigorously against the Nonconformist clergyman Jeremy Collier's call for theatrical reform in his *Short View of the Immorality and Profaneness of the English Stage*. Collier held that the proper purpose of theatre should be 'to recommend Virtue, and discountenance Vice; To shew the Uncertainty of Humane Greatness, the suddain Turns of Fate, and the Unhappy Conclusions of Violence and Injustice: 'Tis to expose the Singularities of Pride and Fancy, to make Folly and Falsehood contemptible, and to bring every Thing that is Ill Under Infamy, and Neglect' (p. 1). Centlivre firmly believed that comedy was meant to entertain, not to instruct, and found Collier's proposed reforms undermined that aim. In the epilogue to *The Perjur'd Husband*, Centlivre asserts that the stage is a reflection of society, not a model for it; reforming the stage will not reform society, but if society reforms itself, the stage will follow suit.

Although she recoiled from Collier's prescriptions for the theatre, Centlivre did react to changes in public taste, and her plays, while recalling the wit of the Restoration, eschew its rakish immorality. Her characters are not moral exemplars, but neither are they vicious. Centlivre understood that her financial success depended upon pleasing her audiences, and she bridled against any attempt to limit her comedy beyond her governing principle of entertaining her audience. In the preface to *Love's Contrivance* (1703), she declares,

The Criticks cavil most about Decorums, and cry up Aristotle's Rules as the most essential part of the Play. I own they are in the right of it; yet I dare venture a wager they'll never persuade the Town to be of their Opinion, which relishes nothing so well as Humour lightly tost up with Wit, and drest with Modesty and Air . . . I do not say this by way of condemning the Unity of Time, Place, and Action; quite contrary, for I think them the greatest Beauties of a Dramatick Poem; but since the other way of writing pleases full as well, and gives the Poet a larger Scope of Fancy . . . why should a Man torture, and wrack his Brain for what will be no Advantage to him.

Suz-Anne Kinney notes many of the parallels between Centlivre and her predecessor Aphra Behn. Both were pragmatic and tremendously popular; both were also criticized for writing dangerous and immoral plays.[25] Both also, despite their popularity, had their work attacked, not so much for its content as for the fact that it was written by a woman. In her dedication to *The Platonick Lady* (1707), Centlivre laments:

[25] Kinney, 'Confinement Sharpens the Invention', 83.

A Play secretly introduc'd to the House, whilst the Author remains unknown, is approv'd by every Body: The Actors cry it up, and are in expectation of a great Run; the Bookseller of a Second Edition, and the Scribler of a Sixth Night: But if by chance the Plot's discover'd, and the Brat found Fatherless, immediately it flags in the Opinion of those that extoll'd it before, and the Bookseller falls in his Price, with this Reason, *It's a Woman's*. Thus they alter their judgment, by the Esteem they have for the Author, tho' the Play is still the same.

The frustrations Centlivre felt over her work being slighted, not for its quality but for its author's gender, were to be experienced nearly eighty years later by her dramatic successor, Hannah Cowley, who continued to labour under similar prejudices. Behn, Centlivre, and Cowley were all criticized for exceeding the limits of female respectability in their writing, and were equally outspoken about the injustice of the attacks on them. This triumvirate of female comic genius, whose works span over one hundred years, may have wearied of the constant necessity of defending their talent, but they produced some of their century's best and most enduring comedies.

The Busybody was premièred at Drury Lane on 12 May 1709 and initially ran for thirteen performances. It was such an enormous success that it not only became a staple of Drury Lane's repertory but was also performed at Lincoln's Inn Fields and elsewhere.[26] Bowyer records it was performed over 250 times before 1750 and more than 200 times between 1750 and 1800.[27] *The Busybody* was a favourite choice for benefits and royal command performances at court to the end of the eighteenth century, and it continued to be staged throughout the nineteenth.

Although *The Busybody* is often regarded as Centlivre's best comedy, there has been speculation that it is largely the work of her friend, Mary Pix.[28] This seems highly unlikely. Although it is certainly

---

[26] Gagen, 'Susanna Centlivre', 27.

[27] Bowyer, *The Celebrated Mrs Centlivre*, 103–4.

[28] Bowyer, (*The Celebrated Mrs Centlivre*, 94) and Clark both refer to rumours that Pix and Centlivre collaborated on *The Busybody* and *The Gamester* (1705). Clark cites the contemporary critic Thomas Brown's assertion (*The Works of Mr Thomas Brown. In Prose and Verse: Serious, Moral and Comical*, 4 vols. (London, 1707–11), iv. 237) and notices of the benefit for Pix's estate that appeared in *The London Gazette* and *The Daily Post Boy*, which attribute the 'Greatest part' of the two comedies to Pix. See also Linda R. Payne, 'Mary Pix', 174. Payne offers no other proof of this assertion nor does she say whether she gives the claim any credence.

probable that Pix supported Centlivre's work, and possible that she gave some assistance, the comedy resembles Centlivre's style much more than Pix's. The styles and politics of the two dramatists differ widely. While comparatively restrained, Pix's comedies favour Restoration tastes for rake-taming and prurience. Her plots frequently portray the victimization of women, including confinements, rapes, or threats of rape. Although not overtly political, Pix is uncomfortable with the notion of revolution, and her plays reflect a concern with restoring rightful order. While Centlivre is also concerned with the oppression of women, her female characters are more likely to take matters into their own hands, and her Whig support for the results of the Glorious Revolution makes it easier for Centlivre to advocate throwing off unjust authority. Centlivre's tyrants are also more parodic than vicious, her skill with dialogue is superb, and her focus tends to be on fewer and more fully developed characters and plots. Perhaps it was Centlivre's generosity to her friends that led her to allow Pix posthumous credit for one of her own best works.

The structure of *The Busybody* is fairly conventional.[29] The focus is on two couples, one witty, the other romantic, trying to come together against the wills of one woman's father and the other's guardian. Miranda engages both her lover, Sir George Airy, and her guardian and would-be lover, Sir Francis Gripe, in a battle of wits in order to gain her independence and the marriage of her choice. The woes of Isabinda and her lover, Charles, who is also Sir Francis's son, are modelled on the Spanish comedy of intrigue,[30] a genre characterized by conflicts between love and rigid codes of honour played out by tyrannous fathers (or father-figures) trying to force young women into

---

[29] Many critics have accused Centlivre of stealing the plots and characters of *The Busybody* from other sources, but John Wilson Bowyer does an excellent job of refuting them. Although a number of critics, including Hume, trace the character of Marplot back to Dryden's *Sir Martin Mar-all*, which in turn was based on Molière's *L'Étourdi*, Bowyer points out the significant differences in the characters. Bowyer thinks critics who cite Jonson's *The Devil is an Ass* as a source for Marplot and the dumb scene may be more accurate, but that again Centlivre is original in her adaptation, and that 'except for the two scenes from Jonson, [Centlivre's] borrowings are general and no discredit to her' (Bowyer, *The Celebrated Mrs Centlivre*, 100–3).

[30] This genre was called in Spanish, *la comedia de capa y espada* (literally, 'comedy of cape and sword'; the term also refers to comedy depending more on stage business or intrigue than on scenery). Writers in the genre included Calderón, Lope de Vega, and Tirso de Molina. For more detail, see John Loftis, *The Spanish Plays of Neoclassical England* (New Haven, 1973).

marriages against their will, inventive young women who scheme to outwit these authority figures, and their valiant suitors, and incorporating intricate plots, frequent duels, and mistaken identities. Isabinda's father, Sir Jealous Traffick, fearing the freedom allowed English women will lead to his daughter's ruin and his own dishonour, embraces Spanish customs, including sequestering Isabinda and arranging a marriage for her to a Spanish merchant. The two plots are connected by the friendship of the two women and the misguided interference of the busybody, Marplot.

The role of Marplot, who has been called 'one of the most attractive of literature's simpletons',[31] was a choice role for actors, including David Garrick, and the character was so popular that Centlivre was forced to write a sequel about him, *Marplot: or, The Second Part of the Busybody* (1710).[32] Although some critics have described Marplot as 'desexed'[33] or as a 'curiously unmale figure',[34] he is rather an early eighteenth-century homosexual stereotype, following in the tradition of such characters as Sir Jolly Jumble, the 'old Goat' in Otway's *The Soldier's Fortune* (1680), and the Abbé in *Sir Anthony Love* (1691) by Thomas Southerne, who are also go-betweens and establish a pattern of voyeurism among 'stage sodomites'.[35]

More specifically, Marplot is a successor to the character of Maiden in Thomas Baker's *Tunbridge-Walks, or The Yeoman of Kent* (1703), whom Susan Staves cites as a new type: an obviously homosexual character portrayed as an ultra-effeminate fop.[36] Baker describes Maiden in the list of dramatis personae as 'a Nice-Fellow, that values himself upon his Effeminacies'. Baker's *Tunbridge-Walks* was well-known and popular enough to have been used for actors' benefits,[37] and it is highly significant that Centlivre had Baker write the prologue to *The Busybody* and that the prologue is advertised as 'by the author of *Tunbridge-Walks*'. This prominent selection hardly seems

---

[31] F. W. Bateson, *English Comic Drama 1700–1750* (1929; repr. New York, 1963), 70.

[32] The sequel enjoyed a fair amount of popularity, but never as much as its original. In the sequel Marplot is more camp and farcical and less amiable.

[33] Kinney, 'Confinement Sharpens the Invention', 95.

[34] Pearson, *The Prostituted Muse*, 210.

[35] Laurence Senelick, 'Mollies or Men of Mode? Sodomy and the Eighteenth-Century London Stage', in *Journal of the History of Sexuality*, 1/1 (July 1990), 43–4.

[36] Susan Staves, 'A Few Kind Words for the Fop', *Studies in English Literature*, 22 (1982), 413–28.

[37] Emmett L. Avery, *The London Stage 1700–1729: A Critical Introduction* (Carbondale, Ill., 1968), pp. xc–xci.

coincidental. Rather, it signals that those who enjoyed Baker's comedy may also enjoy Centlivre's, and gives us a clue to the campiness originally used in portraying Marplot.

Although Marplot is not as extreme as Maiden, like Baker's character, he exhibits a number of stereotypically effeminate characteristics: he is cowardly, loves gossip, and fusses over little animals.[38] Upon Marplot's first entrance, Charles points out his sexual ambiguity by remarking how Marplot's injured nose mars his 'beautiful countenance' and by introducing him to Sir George as 'a gentleman that has a passionate desire to kiss your hand'. While Baker's Maiden openly admits that he has neither sexual experience with nor interest in women, Marplot's lack of interest in the opposite sex is conveyed less directly: through innuendo, pun, and the ways in which other men never view him as a sexual threat. Sir George even seems concerned that he may be perceived as too much like Marplot. Marplot's ignorance of heterosexual romantic intrigue leads to his disrupting the plots of his friends, and to Miranda making the telling observation that 'you converse but little with our sex' (4.5.155).

The character of Miranda is another choice part. Clever and vivacious, she casts herself in a number of roles as she plays her rival lovers, Sir George and Sir Francis, against each other. Miranda's ingenuity is brought to the test in the comedy's celebrated 'dumb scene' in which she chooses to be actively silent to subvert the attempts of her lovers to control her.

Sir Francis Gripe is an unusually sympathetic character for an obstructing miser. He loves Miranda not only for her money but for her wit, and his final exit, amidst curses, echoes that of Malvolio in Shakespeare's *Twelfth Night*, an unreconciled, impotent figure, with no role in the marriage celebrations. His counterpart in the secondary love plot, Sir Jealous Traffick, is more parodic than sympathetic. His misguided love of all things Spanish could readily have been understood in 1707 as an anti-Jacobite satire. Sir Jealous's fondness for prescribing fasting and penitence to Isabinda and his swearing by St Iago ('James') lampoon the Roman Catholicism of the court of the dethroned James II. Sir Jealous, like James II, is a father who wishes to choose a Catholic husband for his daughter, but whose daughter prefers a Protestant spouse, and it is a foregone conclusion, according to the historical precedent, that she will usurp him. Sir Jealous's general

---

[38] Pearson, *The Prostituted Muse*, 210.

distrust of women ('For, in our loose country, the women are as dangerous as the men', 2.2.17–18), has a political twist to it, considering he speaks during the reign of Queen Anne through the words of a female Whig playwright.

Many critics[39] have taken exception to Sir Jealous's sudden acceptance of Isabinda and Charles's marriage, and fault Centlivre for failing to provide sufficient preparation for his change of heart. What these critics are missing is the stage business that occurs during the dialogue. The extremes of both Sir Jealous's severity and Isabinda's noble defiance are undercut by the comic physicality of the scene in which Sir Jealous attempts to force Isabinda to marry the Spanish merchant, who unknown to either of them, is Charles. Unlike Sir Francis, whose character is portrayed with some pathos, Sir Jealous is a wholly laughable character, much more English than Spanish, and more concerned with money than honour.[40] Two things occur before Sir Jealous casts a favourable eye on his daughter's marriage: first, he is delighted that Sir Francis has become a victim of a more humiliating deceit; and second, Sir Jealous discovers that, as a result of the successful plot against Sir Francis, rather than being penniless, his new son-in-law is now rich. The language used to convey this information is understated, but this is drama and not a novel, and there is no narrator to point out any irony.

While *The Busybody* ends with the marriages of Miranda and Sir George and Charles and Isabinda, Centlivre's conclusion betrays an ambivalence about the marriage plot other eighteenth-century women dramatists come to share. While Miranda, in the guise of Sir George's incognita, teases him, 'Matrimony! Ha, ha, ha! What crimes have you committed against the god of love that he should revenge 'em so severely to stamp husband upon your forehead?' (1.1.326–8), she is well aware it is the women who are in more danger of experiencing marriage as hardship. A woman's fortune was under the control of her father or guardian before her marriage, and was turned over to her husband upon their union. Miranda has a very brief period of independence between the time Sir Francis signs over the control of her property to her and her scheduled marriage to him. She uses her

---

[39] e.g. Hume, *The Development of English Drama in the Late Seventeenth Century*, 119–20.

[40] For a discussion of this significant difference between Spanish *comedia* and English comedy of manners, see Loftis, *The Spanish Plays of Neoclassical England*, 70–1. Although his discussion concerns Restoration comedy, its ideas may also be applied to Augustan.

fleeting independence to act on behalf of herself and her friend, Isabinda,[41] but the best she can hope is to secure their marriages to men of their own choosing. Amidst the bustle and intrigue of plotting a romantic elopement, Miranda's primary focus is economic. When an enraptured Sir George responds to the coded summons Miranda has sent to him by Marplot, she waves away all of his language of courtship with, 'Prithee, no more of these flights, for our time's but short and we must fall into business' (4.5.20–1). When he proves eager to elope, Miranda requires a short delay because, 'I dare not stir till I hear [Sir Francis is] on the road; then I and my writings, the most material point, are soon removed' (4.5.50–1). Miranda has no romantic illusions about marriage and acknowledges the risks of her actions with the lamentation, 'there's no remedy from a husband but the grave' (5.1.5).

For Miranda and Isabinda, marriage is a necessary evil because it offers the only escape from the tyranny of a guardian or father. Marriage to a man of one's choosing offers them the hope of some liberty, but, in truth, they have no economic independence beyond that permitted by male authority. Other characters are pointedly left single. Patch and Scentwell, maidservants to Isabinda and Miranda, depend on employment rather than marriage for economic security. When Charles makes a grand gesture, inviting his man, Whisper, and Scentwell to join the marriage party, they both turn him down flat in favour of remaining in service. It is a question left open whether Charles is making a general comic assumption that those who are eligible will happily join the fertility rite or whether he is joking, aware that Whisper has been conducting a flirtation with Patch, a flirtation which, now their employers are married, they are left to pursue as they see fit. Scentwell's rejection of Whisper, 'Coxcomb! And I prefer my lady before a footman' (5.4.146), has a class slur to it that may suggest her interest in the other remaining bachelor on the stage: the conspicuously single yet totally ineligible Marplot!

By the prominent exclusion of Marplot from the comic closure of *The Busybody*, Centlivre calls attention to the inadequacy of marriage to tie up all loose ends. This pointed failure to incorporate all the major characters into a comedy's marriage plot recurs in the works of

[41] Gagen calls attention to Miranda's fundamental decency as it is displayed in this instance. She could acquire Charles's property for herself when Sir Francis offers to disinherit him in her favour, but instead goes out of her way to secure Charles's legal papers so that he can claim a long-overdue inheritance. 'Miranda's virtue obviously encompasses far more than her chastity and may be Centlivre's attempt to demonstrate again her idea of what virtue in a woman really is' (Gagen, 'Susanna Centlivre', 30).

the remaining two authors in this volume. Elizabeth Griffith leaves a stageful of eligible unmarrieds, with no prospects, at the conclusion of *The Double Mistake*, and Hannah Cowley leaves her most interesting female character, Bella, in her début production, *The Runaway*, single, with only a last-minute mention of a soon-to-return lover. And while the heroine of *The Belle's Stratagem* may be a reworking of Bella and a redressing of the character's previous neglect, Cowley still manages to leave several other characters conspicuously single at the end of the latter comedy. This ambivalence about the institution of marriage on the part of eighteenth-century women playwrights has a curiously modern feel that should resonate for today's audiences.

Elizabeth Griffith

Elizabeth Griffith was born in 1727. Her family was well connected, and Griffith received an education suitable for a fine lady in polite literature, French, poetry, and the social graces. But when her father died in 1744, Griffith was left without fortune, and in 1749 she had to attempt to make her own living on the stage. She made her acting début as Juliet at the Smock Alley Theatre and continued to perform in Dublin for two years.

Elizabeth met Richard Griffith (no relation, despite their shared name) in 1746. He was a libertine from a good but poor family from Kilkenny. They fell in love, but Richard's father wanted him to marry a woman with wealth, so for five years Richard tried, unsuccessfully, to convince Elizabeth to become his mistress. They kept up a voluminous correspondence during these years as Elizabeth steadfastly held out for marriage. The two were secretly married in 1751, and the marriage produced a son, Richard, and a daughter, Catherine.

Elizabeth found limited success in London as an actress at Covent Garden, performing minor roles from March 1753 to May 1755. After Richard suffered business reverses, the two decided to publish their correspondence. *A Series of Genuine Letters between Henry and Frances* was issued by subscription in 1757 and became a huge success. It is supposedly an unedited collection of the letters written during Elizabeth and Richard's five-year courtship, but most likely the correspondence was artfully revised for publication. The letters were greatly praised as models of politeness, for their wit, and for the candidness displayed by the authors regarding their conduct during their courtship. The volume made the Griffiths instant celebrities. 'Frances' was beloved by the public for her gentleness and virtue, and Elizabeth exploited her reputation, consistently presenting herself publicly as the meek, ladylike 'Frances', while behaving professionally with tenacity and determination.

Richard often returned to Ireland to campaign for political friends, and the separations these returns occasioned provided more opportunities for correspondence between husband and wife, which was published in four additional volumes. Despite the loving and polite tone of their letters, the Griffiths' marriage was rumoured to be troubled. Elizabeth was becoming a successful author on her own, and Richard appears to have been jealous of his wife's growing fame. Another celebrated eighteenth-century author and letter writer, Anna Seward, reported that about the time *The Times* was written, Richard briefly ran off with an heiress. The Griffiths' son became a wealthy man through business in India and bought an estate in Ireland, to which his parents seem to have independently retired. Richard died there in 1788 and Elizabeth in 1793.[42]

Elizabeth Griffith's other writings never eclipsed the collection of letters between Henry and Frances in the eyes of the public, but she produced a prodigious quantity of work, including many French translations, three epistolary novels, *The Morality of Shakespeare's Drama Illustrated* (1775), and a collection of *Essays Addressed to Young Married Women* (1782), as well as seven dramatic works. Of these, the most successful were: *The Double Mistake* (Covent Garden, 1766), an adaptation of George Digby, Lord Bristol's *Elvira* (1664), a Restoration Spanish-style comedy; *The School for Rakes* (Drury Lane, 1769), an adaptation of Pierre-Augustin Caron de Beaumarchais's *Eugénie* (1767) on which she collaborated with David Garrick;[43] and *The Times* (Drury Lane, 1779).

Griffith was already a celebrated letter writer and novelist before

---

[42] For biographical material on Elizabeth Griffith, I am indebted to Dorothy Hughes Eshleman, *Elizabeth Griffith: A Biography and Critical Study* (Philadelphia, 1949); Betty Rizzo, 'Elizabeth Griffith', in Janet Todd (ed.), *A Dictionary of British and American Women Writers* (Totowa, NJ, 1985), 141–2; and Elizabeth R. Napier, 'Elizabeth Griffith', in Martin C. Battestin (ed.), *Dictionary of Literary Biography*, 39, *British Novelists, 1660–1880*, pt. 1 (Detroit, 1985), 247–51.

[43] I explored this collaboration in depth in an unpublished dissertation, 'Power Plays: Women Playwrights of the Late Eighteenth Century and the Politics of Adaptation' (Princeton University, 2001), as well as more briefly in an unpublished paper presented at the Association of Theatre in Higher Education Conference in Chicago, 1987, 'Elizabeth Griffith and Uncle David: The Presence of Garrick in *The Times*'.

her first play, *The Platonic Wife* (1765), was produced at Drury Lane.[44] It was not well received, but she followed it the next year with a more successful comedy, *The Double Mistake*, at Covent Garden. Griffith greatly desired to work under the tutelage of the grand gentleman of the London theatre, David Garrick, the playwright, actor, and manager of Drury Lane. Despite Griffith's standing in London's literary circles, however, she did not approach Garrick until *The Double Mistake* had been successfully staged at Covent Garden. Garrick was well disposed to women playwrights. He frequently staged the works of Susanna Centlivre, and was a great admirer of Frances Sheridan (the mother of Richard Brinsley Sheridan) considering her *The Discovery* (1763) one of the best comedies he knew.[45] Garrick later helped launch the theatrical careers of Hannah More, Dorothea Celisia, and Hannah Cowley, whose *The Runaway* (1776) was the last new play he staged.

Garrick had not liked *The Double Mistake*, and his response to Griffith's overtures was not warm. However, Griffith persisted in writing to him, and eventually he suggested she try her hand at adapting Beaumarchais's *Eugénie*. The wished-for acceptance by Garrick proved stifling rather than inspirational for Griffith, and the two strong-willed artists wrangled over every detail of the writing and production of *The School for Rakes*. From Griffith and Garrick's correspondence, and from analysis of *The School for Rakes* itself, it is obvious that Garrick took a large part in the actual writing of the piece, which has more in common with Garrick and Colman's *The Clandestine Marriage* (1766) than it does with Griffith's other plays. The comedy was a great success, however, playing for thirteen nights in its first season and being revived for seven years.[46]

The School for Rakes had opened in February 1769, and by September of the same year Griffith was asking Garrick to accept another comedy from her. But the correspondence was characterized by mutual dissatisfaction. In 1773 Griffith apparently sent Garrick another proposal for a play which elicited a testy response. Garrick died shortly before *The Times* had its première. Despite Griffith's flattering eulogy to Garrick in the preface to *The Times*, and her lamentations over the loss of her friend, her final comedy would never have been produced at Drury Lane had Garrick still been its manager.

---

[44] But not by Garrick. Eshleman (*Elizabeth Griffith*, 60) seems to suggest he was out of the country when this play was produced.

[45] Mrs Clement Parsons, *Garrick and his Circle* (London, 1906), 198.

[46] Eshleman, *Elizabeth Griffith*, 69, and Dougald MacMillan (ed.), *Drury Lane Calendar* (Oxford, 1938).

Instead, Griffith was indebted to her friendship with Thomas Sheridan, which went back to her days at Smock Alley in Dublin, and his influence with his son Richard Brinsley Sheridan, Garrick's successor as manager of Drury Lane, for the production of *The Times* in 1779.

In the Advertisement at the beginning of *The Times*, Griffith claims to have found her source in Carlo Goldoni's *Le Bourru bienfaisant* (1771). Goldoni was an innovative playwright who was attempting to transform the old Italian *commedia dell'arte* form into a more modern comedy of manners. He used the stock characters of traditional Italian comedy, but cleaned up their characteristic ridiculous licentious behaviour in an attempt to introduce a higher moral tone. The merging of old traditions with new sensibilities was central to his writing.[47] Drawn by the reforms being made in Paris's *Théâtre Italien*, Goldoni had moved from Italy to Paris, where he was finding great success. The plays being written for the *Théâtre Italien* were concerned with eliminating the so-called *grossièretés* of Italian *commedia*, but kept the physical elements of comedy: gestural movements and acrobatics.[48]

The title character of Goldoni's *Le Bourru bienfaisant* is Geronte, a wealthy old man. He is a 'bear' because he is a gruff old curmudgeon, and 'beneficent' because his growl hides a soft heart. The plot centres on the love problems of Geronte's niece, Angelique. She is in love with Valère, but her financially ruined brother has spent her dowry and wants to put her in a convent. Geronte tries to help Angelique, but his gruffness frightens her out of admitting to him her love for Valère. Believing that Angelique is not in love with anyone but would rather marry than enter a convent, Geronte decides she should marry an old friend of his. Needless to say, all is straightened out and the lovers united.

Griffith appears to have had a serious interest in the developments in Continental drama, and to have been intrigued especially by the theoretical issues being raised by Goldoni. His concerns regarding moral correctness in the theatre would have appealed to her, and it seems likely she may have been attempting to rework his transformations to suit the sensibilities of an English audience. Griffith

---

[47] For my discussion of Goldoni's ideas for transforming Italian theatre, I am indebted to Elizabeth Blood, 'From *canevas* to *commedia*: Innovation in Goldoni's *Il servitore di due padroni*', in Franco Fido and Dino S. Cervigni (eds.), *Annali d'italianisitica*, 11 (1993), 111–19, and Ernest Hatch Wilkins, *History of Italian Literature* (Cambridge, Mass., 1978), ch. 39, 'Goldini and Carlo Gozzi'.

[48] Blood, 'From *canevas* to *commedia*', 112.

approaches her source play for *The Times* by keeping the original premiss of *Le Bourru bienfaisant*, and restructuring and recentring the piece to examine its dramatic questions in a new light. She retains the character of the well-intentioned but choleric old gentleman who connects the two plots concerning his nephew and his niece, and she even employs some of the dynamics of Goldini's comedy of humours, for example by setting the choleric old man against his phlegmatic friend, but she shifts her emphasis to contemporary English social concerns. Her title reflects the switch in her play's focus away from Goldoni's beneficent bear, the blustery Geronte (here, Sir William Woodley), to the corrupt times in which the characters are living. The comedy centres on the financially ruined brother, Mr Woodley, and his innocently extravagant wife, Lady Mary, rather than on the problems of the sister, Louisa, and her lover, Colonel Mountfort. The problems of the lovers are not even introduced until Act 3. Griffith further complicates the plot by the addition of two major characters, Mr and Mrs Bromley, a pair of con artists professing devoted friendship for Woodley and Lady Mary while draining them of the remains of their fortune.

Griffith's adaptation of Goldoni's work, however, is more complex than it first appears. *Le Bourru bienfaisant* is actually a revision of Goldoni's earlier comedy, *La casa nova* (1758), which he wrote for the company of the Venetian actor-manager, Medebac. There is no concrete evidence that Griffith ever saw this earlier source or could even read the Venetian dialect in which it was written, but, despite her lack of acknowledgement, her adaptation of *Le Bourru bienfaisant* bears some striking similarities to the Venetian original in particulars in which the French version differs. In *La casa nova*, the uncle is a relatively minor character and, as in Griffith's comedy, the story of the young married couple, Angiolino and Cecilia, takes precedence over the romantic difficulties of the husband's sister. The Venetian comedy also includes a pair of social parasites living off the prodigality of the extravagant young couple. The Count and Fabrizio may have provided the inspiration for Griffith's con artists.[49]

---

[49] There has been no previous scholarship on the possible relation of *La casa nova* to *The Times* or on Griffith's interest in contemporary Italian theatre. Much work remains to be done on the influence of *commedia dell'arte* on eighteenth-century English drama. For my discussion of *La casa nova*, I am indebted to Wilkins, *History of Italian Literature*, ch. 39, and to Renato Simoni's introduction to his edition of *La casa nova* (Turin, 1946).

Griffith's apparent familiarity with Goldoni's Venetian comedy suggests that she may have had more than a passing interest in Italian theatre. Although contemporary critics make no specific mention of physical comedy in *The Times*, if one keeps in mind the *commedia*-style acrobatics and gestures that would have been part of Goldoni's pieces, a new dimension is added to Griffith's play. For example, the character Forward retains elements of his origin in the *commedia*'s clown, Scapino, a greedy and ambitious servant, while Sir William is drawn from a stock *commedia* pattern that depends on bombastic gestures and slapstick humour.

However, the introduction of the Bromleys lends Griffith's comedy a more sinister undertone than either of her possible sources. Whereas the financial difficulties of the prodigal nephew and his wife in *Le Bourru bienfaisant* provide the motivation for the nephew to try to put his sister in a convent and for Geronte to come to Angelique's aid, the financial ruin of the Woodleys is a subject of its own and its connection to Louisa comparatively minor. In *La casa nova*, the Count and Fabrizio are happy to benefit from the extravagance of Angiolino and Cecilia, but they are comic opportunists mostly concerned with the source of their next meal; their actions do not approach the criminal. The Woodleys, on the other hand, are being deliberately led to their ruin by a pair of sharpers, who place Lady Mary in moral as well as financial danger. Although the Bromleys' motivation is never directly expressed, it appears that they continually try to lure Lady Mary into compromising situations in order to blackmail her. Griffith creates a dramatic tension between Lady Mary's trust of her friend Mrs Bromley and her sense of delicacy, as the innocent young woman warily evades the traps set for her by the jaded con artists.

In her first appearance, Mrs Bromley tries to encourage Lady Mary to attend a masquerade without her husband. Masquerades, extraordinarily popular entertainments in the eighteenth century, were morally suspect events. The anonymity created by disguise provided the opportunity for promiscuous mixing of classes and sexes, and the aura of sexual intrigue was pervasive. The literature of the day was full of accounts of heroines being abducted from masquerades to be seduced or raped by men posing as husbands or family members.[50] Richardson's Harriet Byron in *Sir Charles Grandison* (1753) barely escapes from such a fate, and Hannah Cowley makes use of this

---

[50] For more information on masquerades in eighteenth-century life and literature, see Terry Castle's intriguing and exhaustive study, *Masquerade and Civilization: The Carnivalesque in Eighteenth-Century English Culture and Fiction* (Stanford, 1986).

established plot in *The Belle's Stratagem* when Courtall plans to abduct Lady Frances. Mrs Bromley's suggestion that Lady Mary go escorted by Sir Harry Granger would raise the spectre of such a danger to Griffith's audience. Both Bromleys try to foist Sir Harry's attentions on Lady Mary, and, after one exchange, she reacts to Bromley's persistent harping on Sir Harry's virtues by snubbing him by refusing to take his arm in to dinner. Lady Mary's irritation with Bromley is part of the subtext of the comedy, and illustrates how Griffith's character dynamics are often manifest in what is not said rather than in what is said—in this respect, Griffith can be viewed as a rather modern playwright. When Bromley fawningly requests, 'Will your ladyship permit me the transcendent honour of your fair hand?', and Lady Mary declines with, 'I attend Mrs Bromley' (2.4.103), she conveys her distrust, suspicion, and repugnance for her friend's husband while maintaining the appearance of politeness.

Griffith also uses language in a subtle way to suggest physical comedy. For example, Sir William's hyperbolic language lends itself to hyperbolic gestures that contribute to the comic business of his scenes. Sir William's emphasis on haste and dislike of anything gentle suggest his style of movement. His gestures require large amounts of space and wreak havoc in the genteel drawing-rooms of London.

Both Lady Mary and Louisa keep their distance from him when called into his presence in 2.3 and 3.1. Sir William complains about this standoffishness (which causes him in one instance to mistake Lady Mary for Louisa), and the staging suggested by these complaints offers a clue to what Lady Mary and Louisa may have learned from experience: that Sir William requires a wide berth. By the time Sir William demands of Louisa, 'Why, my dear, it will neither be questions nor commands, but cross-purposes, if you keep at such a distance as will make it impossible we should hear one another. Come nearer, I say. What are you afraid of?' (3.1.130–3), previous stage business should have made it clear that Louisa fears being knocked over, hit by flying objects, or swept off her feet.

Griffith uses the character of Sir William to lampoon the notion of absolute patriarchal control. Sir William, who, like Geronte, loves his niece and wants the best for her, decides to marry Louisa to his friend Belford without consulting her. Unlike Geronte, however, Sir William does not assume he is anticipating his niece's wishes but acts in a peremptory manner because he thinks he knows what is best for his family. After he has decided the issue, Sir William informs Louisa that she is to be married, but he does not tell her to whom. When Belford tells Sir William that he does not think Louisa will wish to marry him, Sir William makes his point of view quite clear: 'Have I not told you, sir, that she had no consent, no choice, but what I please to give? And in twenty years acquaintance, have you ever known me say an untruth?' (4.2.126–8)

Whereas the comic confusion of Goldoni's *Le Bourru bienfaisant* is based on misunderstandings, Griffith draws her humour from the absurdity of the deliberate attempts to keep women in ignorance. She highlights the questions raised about women and knowledge by having Sir William and Woodley both attempt to keep Louisa and Lady Mary ignorant of their own circumstances. Louisa is one of the most rational characters in *The Times* and her scenes with Sir William are filled with comic chaos as they converse at cross-purposes with each other. And just as Louisa's good sense points out the absurdity of Sir William's attempts to keep her ignorant, so Lady Mary's resolve points out the fallacy of her irresponsible husband trying to protect her from the truth.

The Times reaches its dramatic climax in the scene of Lady Mary's card party (5.4). As with her use of subtext, Griffith is quite modern in her use of setting to shed light on the psychology of her characters. The entire comedy takes place indoors, in different drawing-, dressing-, and dining-rooms that reflect their inhabitants. Mr Woodley's dressing-room is described as having 'books, music, clothes scattered about'; it is a place of disorder. Lady Mary's dressing-room contains an 'elegant toilet', and is expensively furnished and well-ordered. Sir William's drawing-room contains a game table, and the chimney has a tendency to smoke—it is not a very comfortable room, and even Sir William likes to escape from it. His dining-room, however, is hospitable and contains wine bottles and glasses on the table; Mr Woodley's dining-table is used for gaming. After all these confined and defining spaces, the comedy suddenly opens up to a large room with blazing chandeliers and a crowd of people. The new scene also marks an explosion into a carnivalesque world in which the actions and language of the anonymous partygoers reflect the inner states and relational dynamics of the major characters.

The card party scene is a masterpiece of stage work. With stage shutters open to reveal a large drawing-room extending upstage, the partygoers are grouped around different card tables and involved in their card games. The major characters interact further downstage, perhaps even on the small forestage, with the party serving as a background to them. The audience hears the conversation of the card players during breaks in the dialogue of the major characters, and their conversation, made up of card game slang, comments upon the actions of the major characters in a bizarre, nightmarish way. The card players' chatter about 'monsters', 'beasts', and 'honours' is timed to highlight moments that reveal Mrs Bromley's duplicity and Colonel Mountfort's loyalty.[51]

As ruin closes in on the Woodleys, Mrs Bromley's immorality and deceit are unmasked, and she must flee in disgrace; Colonel Mountfort's strength of character passes the test and he heroically comes to the aid of his friends. The card party exposes the moral decay of fashionable life and teaches the Woodleys to value generosity and loyalty over the dazzling moral vacuum of the *ton*.

The critic who reported on *The Times* for the *Monthly Review* reflected the pressure on Griffith to conform to her public's expectations by praising her portrayal of 'touches of sentiment' while castigating the author for the coarse language of the card players at Lady Mary's rout.[52] Griffith's established reputation as an author of moral letters and essays prevented contemporary critics from seeing her in any other light, but she is an intriguing writer whose plays deserve reconsideration. The very qualities that contribute to her plays' insistence upon a reader or director's attention to detail are qualities that resonate for modern audiences, especially her dependence upon subtext and her use of settings and props to reveal the workings of her characters' inner life. Griffith's is a dramatic career of negotiation between her creative drives and established formulas, and while her previously established celebrity helped her become established as a playwright, it was also an obstacle to being taken seriously. Her dramatic adaptations specifically reveal the constraints under which eighteenth-century female dramatists worked, the tensions between what they may have wished to accomplish and what was deemed seemly for them to write.

Hannah Cowley

Hannah Cowley is one of the foremost playwrights of the late eighteenth century, and her skill in writing fluid, sparkling dialogue and creating sprightly, memorable comic characters compares favourably

[51] Griffith's card party scene may have been a precursor to Fanny Burney's masquerade scene in *Cecilia* (1782). The novelist was a great admirer of Griffith. See Napier, 'Elizabeth Griffith', 249.

[52] '*The Times*: A Comedy', *Monthly Review*, 62 (Mar. 1780), 246.

with her better-known contemporaries, Goldsmith and Sheridan, as well as with her Restoration and Augustan models, Behn, Congreve, Centlivre, and Farquhar. Cowley's comedies were some of the most frequently produced plays to the end of the century and continued to be popular on both sides of the Atlantic into the mid-nineteenth century.[53] Ambivalence about the legitimacy of female playwrights, their respectability, and their proper scope in the period after David Garrick's retirement contributed to Cowley's disappearance from dramatic histories, but the best of her comedies, *The Runaway*, *Who's the Dupe?*, *The Belle's Stratagem*, *A School for Greybeards*, and *Which is the Man?*, could be staged today with the same success revivals of Behn's works have found.

Hannah Parkhouse Cowley was born in Tiverton, Devonshire, in 1743, to Mr and Mrs Philip Parkhouse. Her father was a bookseller who had been educated for the clergy, and the playwright John Gay was a cousin of her paternal grandmother.[54] She married Thomas Cowley in 1772 and the couple then moved to London. Thomas Cowley was a newspaper writer as well as a clerk in the Stamp Office and seems to have been supportive of his wife's writing—at least to the extent of writing a favourable review of her play, *The Belle's Stratagem*, for the *Gazetteer*.[55] They had three or four children.[56] Cowley was fortunate to have had both a father and a husband who were supportive of her dramatic endeavours. Tiverton bordered the estate of Lord and Lady Harrowby, with whom Cowley's father had political connections. Ellen Donkin reports that Parkhouse appealed to Lord Harrowby to become a literary patron to his daughter. Harrowby came to think highly of Cowley's work and used his influence to gain promotion for her husband. She maintained a

---

[53] For a statistical examination of plays by women staged in London during this period, see Judith Phillips Stanton's '"This New-Found Path Attempting": Women Dramatists in England, 1660–1800', in Mary Anne Schofield and Cecilia Macheski (eds.), *Curtain Calls: British and American Women and the Theater, 1660–1800* (Athens, Ohio, 1991). Programmes for mid-nineteenth-century productions of *The Belle's Stratagem*, from the New Arch Street Theater in Philadelphia, and from the National Theatre in London are held at the Huntington Library in San Marino, California.

[54] 'Biographical Character of the Late Mrs. Cowley', *Gentleman's Magazine* (Apr. 1809), 377.

[55] Charles Harold Gray, *Theatrical Criticism in London to 1795* (New York, 1931), 209–10.

[56] Frederick M. Link claims that she had four, based on a comment in the 1813 edition of Cowley's *Works*. *Biographia Dramatica* (1812) mentions only three. See Link (ed.), *The Plays of Hannah Cowley*, 2 vols. (New York and London, 1979), vol. i, p. xlv n.

correspondence with Harrowby and his wife and dedicated her ill-fated tragedy *Albina* to him.[57] Perhaps because of Harrowby's preferment, and because he needed to secure the finances of the family, Thomas Cowley went abroad to join the East India Company in 1783 and died there in 1797, never having returned to England. Hannah Cowley mourned his departure in her preface to her comedy *More Ways than One* (1783), but she remained in London with their children. Between 1776 and 1794, Cowley produced ten comedies, two tragedies, a farce, and many poems. She retired to her native Tiverton in 1801 and lived in seclusion until her death in 1809.

Cowley was widely acclaimed by both the public and the critics of her day, but much of what has been handed down to us about her is inaccurate because all of her works and the stories about her life were heavily revised after her withdrawal from the theatre. In retirement in Tiverton, Cowley became more and more concerned about her own reputation for respectability, and she worked hard to make sure that no breath of scandal hung over her life. Contemporary writings about Cowley talk of a pious, saintly woman, who never went to the theatre if she could avoid it, who never engaged in any literary correspondence, whose writings flowed effortlessly from her pen, and who, like Shakespeare, never blotted a line. This is a flawed portrait. Cowley heavily revised her plays both in the course of production and after her retirement. Nor did she avoid either literary correspondence or controversy. She engaged in a 'paper war' with Hannah More in 1779 in the *Saint James's Chronicle* in which Cowley charged that much of More's tragedy, *The Fatal Falsehood* (1779) was taken from her own tragedy *Albina* (1779).[58] Cowley is also credited with playing 'Anna Matilda' to Robert Merry's 'Della Crusca' in a widely acclaimed

---

[57] For information on the Cowley/Harrowby connection, I am indebted to Ellen Donkin's *Getting into the Act: Women Playwrights in London 1776–1829* (London and New York, 1995), 59.

[58] Cowley was justified in recognizing plagiarism in More's play, but More was apparently innocent of intentional theft. Both David Garrick and Thomas Harris, the manager of Covent Garden, had been in possession of Cowley's manuscript before offering assistance to More. It appears likely that one of them inadvertently passed on suggestions to More from Cowley's play. The confrontation was played out and promoted in the newspaper more by outside parties than by its principals, and it captured the interest of the public more for, as Donkin phrases it, its aspects of 'meta-theatre, a mud hen wrestling match in which Cowley and More had been reluctantly pressed' than for the real issue that it raised regarding the role of the theatre manager in authorship. For more information on the controversy surrounding Cowley and More, see Donkin's thorough study, 'The Paper War of Hannah Cowley and Hannah More', in *Getting into the Act*.

poetical correspondence carried on in *The World*,[59] in 1787. Her risqué comedy *A School for Greybeards* (1786) became a *cause célèbre*, and although Cowley revised it to satisfy the offended sensibilities of her public and critics, she further fed the controversy by restoring much of the offending language to the first edition of the play and by prefacing that edition with an attack on her critics and a defence of her own creative judgement.

We do not really know how Cowley began her career as a dramatist. Her biographers claim that while attending a comedy with her husband, she exclaimed, 'and I too can write!' Thomas teased Hannah about her presumption, and to retaliate against his teasing she sat down the next day, and at dinner handed him the first act of *The Runaway* 'verbatim'.[60] In a prefatory letter to David Garrick in the first edition of *The Runaway*, Cowley herself states that no one interceded on her behalf with Garrick, that he merely responded to her unsolicited manuscript: 'Unpatronized by any *name*, I presented myself to you obscure and unknown.'[61] Cowley praises Garrick for his openness to dramatic newcomers, and his disinterested search for merit reflects back on herself: he produced her play because of its intrinsic quality, not because of her connections. Like Elizabeth Griffith before her, Cowley recognized the benefits of being linked to Garrick. He was the patriarch of the London theatre. As an actor, playwright, and manager, no other theatre professional wielded as much power as Garrick did, was as beloved by his public, or as encouraging to female playwriting talent. Cowley's prefatory letter to Garrick is not only gracious but good public relations. Whatever the myths surrounding its creation, *The Runaway* was Cowley's first produced comedy, the last new play Garrick produced as manager of Drury Lane, and an enormous success. *The Runaway* opened on 15 February 1776, played for seventeen nights (more performances than any other play that season[62]), its run only curtailed by the beginning of

---

[59] 'An Account of the Life and Writings of Mrs. H. Cowley', *The European Magazine and London Review* (June 1789), 427.

[60] 'Biographical Character of the Late Mrs. Cowley', 377. Also reported in *The Works of Mrs. Cowley*, vol. 1 (London, 1813), p. viii.

[61] Cowley, *The Runaway* (London, 1776), p. iii.

[62] *Drury Lane Playbills 1775–1776*, collection of bound playbills held at the Huntington Library, San Marino, California. A quote from a Mr Hopkins's diary written on the page facing 115 (the opening night playbill) records: 'This comedy is a first Production of Mrs. Cowley—It was received with very great Applause—Indeed the Performers played very well, and deserved it.—The Prologue was dull, but Mr. Garrick wrote an excellent Epilogue, which was received with the greatest Applause.'

the benefit season,[63] and became a staple of Drury Lane's repertory, being performed thirty-nine times before 1800. Cowley became instantly known for her skill at creating seemingly effortless dialogue and for her well-drawn high-spirited characters who test the boundaries of decorous behaviour.

The Runaway is a fresh, high-spirited comedy, but Garrick's hand is evident throughout. The Larpent manuscript[64] is covered with his corrections and deletions. Ellen Donkin has carefully examined Garrick's corrections and argues that he helped refine Cowley's natural talents without interfering with her originality. He taught her how, instead of writing speeches, to crystallize dramatic moments in dialogue that offered the actor more opportunity for characterization.[65] Cowley continued to hone her craft by learning from her adaptations of Aphra Behn and Susanna Centlivre, and in so doing she marks the beginning of a new stage in the history of women in the English theatre. Adaptation has been a common practice in the history of drama, but it was not until the late eighteenth century that the tradition of women writing for the stage had become well enough established for female playwrights to look to their female predecessors for inspiration. Cowley was the first professional female dramatist to draw directly from the works of other professional female playwrights. Her farce *Who's the Dupe?* (1779) is based on Susanna Centlivre's *The Stolen Heiress* (1702), and *A School for Greybeards, or, the Mourning Bride* (1786) is based on Aphra Behn's *The Lucky Chance* (1686). Cowley used Behn's and Centlivre's comedies as points of departure for her own imaginative flights.

The success of *The Runaway* brought Cowley to the forefront of contemporary playwrights and seemed to establish her position in London's theatrical scene well enough for her to survive Garrick's retirement at the end of the 1776 season. The advent of Sheridan as manager of Drury Lane caused setbacks for her, however, as well as for other playwrights who had flourished under Garrick's regime.

[63] Cowley, Preface to *Albina* (London, 1779), p. i.

[64] The Licensing Act of 21 June 1737 limited legitimate theatrical productions to theatres possessed of a royal patent or a licence from the Lord Chamberlain. It also required that a manuscript of any new production be submitted to the Lord Chamberlain for approval. John Larpent held the position of Examiner of Plays from 1778 to 1824, and a file of play manuscripts submitted for approval under the Licensing Act is preserved in a collection bearing his name at the Huntington Library in San Marino, California.

[65] Donkin, *Getting into the Act*, 62–3.

Sheridan was more interested in producing his own plays than in serving other dramatists, and less favourably disposed to producing the works of female playwrights, in particular,[66] than Garrick had been. Sheridan had also increased charges to authors for their benefit performances.[67] In his first season as manager he staged premières of his *The School for Scandal* and *A Trip to Scarborough*, as well as performances of *The Rivals*. Cowley blamed him for unjustly 'shelving' *The Runaway*, a comedy whose success should have augured well for more performances the following season. Sheridan staged it only four times: once in a drastically cut unsuccessful version and twice at actors' benefits. Only one production was a regular staging, and, as Frederick Link has noted, that production reaped a substantial profit for the theatre and supported Cowley's claim.[68]

Sheridan further grossly mismanaged the production of *Who's the Dupe?*, with the result that although the farce was very successful, Cowley's profits were small compared to those she enjoyed with *The Runaway*.[69] *Who's the Dupe?* became one of Cowley's most popular pieces and was performed 126 times before 1800.

The frustrations over the combined success and mismanagement of *Who's the Dupe?* were followed by Cowley's public altercation with Hannah More concerning *Albina*. She emerged from these difficulties with the huge success of *The Belle's Stratagem*. Cowley's most popular comedy was premièred on 22 February 1780 and ran for twenty-eight nights in its first season. It became part of Covent Garden's standard repertory and was acted 118 times in London before 1800.

In 1786 Cowley's name again became associated with a controversy that exposed the difficulties faced by a woman attempting to make a name for herself as a dramatist. The opening of her new comedy, *A School for Greybeards*, an adaptation of Behn's *The Lucky Chance* (1686), on 25 November 1786, caused a scandal of such magnitude that

---

[66] Sheridan even allowed his negative feelings towards women playwrights to be displayed in his epilogue to Hannah More's *The Fatal Falsehood* (1779), in which he satirized the female dramatist as a slovenly literary pretender so stringently that the audience was offended. For more information on this topic, see Donkin, *Getting into the Act*, 67.

[67] *Albina*, p. v.

[68] Link (ed.), *Plays*, vol. i, p. xi.

[69] Sheridan did not produce the farce until April 1779, in the middle of the benefit season. This prevented the play from having the long run it would have earned for itself, since many of the season's remaining nights were already booked. Despite this handicap, *Who's the Dupe?* was acted fifteen times before the end of the season. See Link (ed.), *Plays*, vol. i, p. xii.

Cowley was compelled to withdraw it from the stage and rewrite it, purifying both its language and plot before it could be staged again.

Cowley's frustration at having to revise her original version of *A School for Greybeards* was vented in the published edition, in which she restored most of the original language, but, interestingly, not the original plot. She prefaced this edition with an address to her readership in which she protests against the critical attacks that confuse a woman dramatist's personal reputation with the respectability of her characters. In contrast to the female novelist, who could safely write in the privacy of her own home for those who would read her works in the privacy of theirs, a female playwright wrote for a public venue. Questions about whether a woman's respectability could remain intact after she had put herself forward in such a public sphere were still being raised, and only such acknowledged exemplars of modesty and virtue as Hannah More and Elizabeth Griffith seemed safe from attack. Cowley, who had always been celebrated for her well-drawn characters and her skill with dialogue, complained that her writing was being judged on the basis of a gender-biased notion of propriety.

[Critics] will allow me, indeed, to draw strong character, but it must be without speaking its language. I may give vulgar or low bred persons, but they must converse in a stile of elegance. I may design the coarsest manners, or the most disgusting folly, but its expressions must not deviate from the line of politeness. . . .

It cannot be the *Poet's* mind, which the public desire to trace in dramatic representations; but the mind of their characters, and the truth of their colouring. Yet in my case it seems resolved that the point to be considered, is not whether that *dotard*, or that *pretender*, or that *coquet*, would so have given their feelings, but whether Mrs. *Cowley* ought so to have expressed herself.[70]

Cowley began to weary of the perpetual effort required to protect her name and works. The changing tastes of the audience for slapstick and farce, and the newly expanded stages that were inhospitable to drama based on wit and subtlety, made her decide it was time to retire. In the preface to the published edition of *The Town before You* (1795), Cowley bids farewell to the theatre. She laments that her comedy, as it now exists, reflects the changes the audience preferred rather than her original idea, and deplores that farcical stage business is more suited to the public taste than character development or 'the bewitching dialogue of CIBBER, and of FARQUHAR'.[71] Cowley concludes:

[70] *A School for Greybeards* (London, 1786), pp. v–vii.
[71] Cowley, Preface to *The Town Before You* (London, 1795), p. x.

Should the luckless Bard stumble on a reflection, or a sentiment, the audience yawn, and wait for the next tumble from a chair, or a tripping up of the heels, to put them into attention. Surely I shall be forgiven for satirising myself; I have *made* such things, and I blush to have made them.[72]

After Cowley retired from the stage, she dedicated herself to respectability and began revising, or rather expurgating, her plays. Her own revision of her career set the tone for her biographers. The most complete contemporary account of Cowley's life and career is the preface to the 1813 posthumous collection of her works, but in attempting to enshrine Cowley as a model of irreproachable virtue, this preface in effect whitewashes her out of existence. The anonymous editor of the posthumous collection emphasizes the purity of Cowley's mind and writing: 'Her mind is always perceived as paramount to the vulgarity or the folly she is describing . . . characters of coarse and peculiar outline she appears seldom to have attempted.'[73] What is so odd about this description of Cowley and her writing is that it is at odds with Cowley's complaints about the criticism she received for the vulgarity of her characters in *A School for Greybeards*. The characters 'she appears seldom to have attempted' are the very ones for which she earlier said critics were offended with her.

By the time of her death, Cowley had succeeded in purging her reputation. Her obituary in *The Gentleman's Magazine* records: 'The general tenor of her life was by no means theatrical. . . . Though public as a GENIUS, yet private as a WOMAN, she wore her laurels gracefully veiled.'[74] In trying to paint a demure portrait of Cowley, her biographer sets up a contradiction: to be crowned with laurel is to be publicly celebrated; to be veiled is to shun public recognition. Cowley's own writing suggests that the two aspects of this oxymoron were very troubling for her.

The Belle's Stratagem is a light-hearted comedy of manners set firmly in the fashionable society of late eighteenth-century London, but its style is reminiscent of Cowley's Restoration and Augustan predecessors. Even the title of Cowley's comedy pays homage to one of her favourite Augustan playwrights, George Farquhar (1677–1707), and his *The Beaux' Stratagem* (1707). Like many of these earlier comedies, *The Belle's Stratagem* juxtaposes two story lines: Letitia Hardy's

[72] Cowley, Preface to *The Town Before You*, pp. x–xi.
[73] *The Works of Mrs. Cowley*, pp. x–xi.
[74] 'Biographical Character of the Late Mrs. Cowley', 377.

ingenious plot to win the heart of her betrothed, Doricourt, and the marital problems of jealous Sir George Touchwood and his wife, the naïve Lady Frances. Both plots concern men learning the proper respect due to women and are further connected by questions about masquerade and true identity. Many critics have compared Letitia and Doricourt's sparring romance to that of witty Restoration couples such as Congreve's Millamant and Mirabell from *The Way of the World* (1700),[75] and even the more 'sentimental' plot line concerning the Touchwoods has its origins in Wycherley's renowned Restoration comedy, *The Country Wife*. Sir George and Lady Frances are modernized versions of Wycherley's Pinchwife and Margery, but whereas the rustic Margery learns the art of deception from the libertine Horner and cuckolds her jealous husband Pinchwife, Lady Frances is saved from Courtall's rakish plot, and Sir George learns to respect and value her.

In the title plot, Letitia Hardy, another young woman from the country, proves her mettle. Letitia sets herself up as playwright, director, and principal actor of her comedy and is one of the most engaging of Cowley's many high-spirited, intelligent, and witty heroines.[76] Some critics have noted that Cowley may have drawn her idea of Letitia posing as an ill-bred rustic from Oliver Goldsmith's *She Stoops to Conquer* (1773), but if she did, she gave the plot device a major twist. Whereas Goldsmith's Kate Hardcastle poses as a servant to attract her intended husband, Letitia demeans herself to repel her lover—a task she embraces with glee. Letitia's true precursor is more likely Cowley's own Bella from *The Runaway*, who delights in mischief and happily assists in schemes to deceive lovers for their own good. Bella, however, has no lover of her own, and Cowley felt compelled to rectify this situation by announcing at the play's conclusion that a never-before-mentioned fiancé has just landed at Dover and is coming to claim her, thereby allowing Bella to join the other soon-to-be-married couples. This unsatisfactory treatment of such a charming and vivacious character is redressed by reworking Bella as the mischief-minded Letitia and placing her at the centre of *The Belle's Stratagem*.

The ability to penetrate veils and masquerades lies at the heart of

---

[75] See Link (ed.), *Plays*, vol. i, p. xxi and Allardyce Nicoll, *A History of Late Eighteenth Century Drama 1750–1800* (Cambridge, 1937), 166.

[76] Letitia was a favourite role of many notable actresses, as late as Ellen Terry in the late nineteenth and early twentieth centuries.

the play. Doricourt's inability to see beyond Letitia's modest self-presentation when he first sees her at the lawyer's office is both the source and the symptom of his romantic problems. Because of his prejudice for Continental manners, Doricourt undervalues the charms of English women whose talents and accomplishments are veiled behind a socially approved mantle of reserve. He is too indolent to cultivate love and intimacy himself, but rather expects to be entertained and enthralled. In essence, Doricourt wants to play a passive, more traditionally female, role and be courted. Letitia is offended by his mistaking her discretion for lack of spirit or wit and makes him pay for his complacence. By exposing Doricourt's failure to understand her, Letitia unmasks the naïvety behind his façade of being a man of the world.

Given the questions regarding appearances and true identity that run through the comedy, it is not surprising that the dramatic centre of *The Belle's Stratagem* is Lady Brilliant's masquerade ball.[77] Cowley creates a magnificent spectacle, employing a large cast, and probably using the entire depth of Covent Garden's stage with all the shutters open. Dancers perform and various personages enact their masquerade roles before the major characters make their appearances. Lady Frances is enthralled by her surroundings and comments on the scene, 'Delightful! The days of enchantment are restored! The columns glow with sapphires and rubies. Emperors and fairies, beauties and dwarfs meet me at every stop' (4.1.65–7). Yet Cowley's tight construction of the scene ensures that the dramatic energies never flag. Every character is included in the intrigues of the masquerade, and as the characters of one story line exit in one direction, the players in another plot are already entering from another. As Courtall leads off the prostitute Kitty Willis, Doricourt enters with the masked Letitia. When Doricourt exits in pursuit of his fleeing incognita, Saville enters leading Lady Frances to safety. The stage is always full yet always in motion, each scenario reflecting on those that precede it or are to come.

The masquerade progresses as variations on a theme. The conventional story line of Courtall's attempt to abduct and seduce Lady Frances is introduced, defused by Saville's interference, and then inverted as Letitia plays out a scenario in which the innocent maiden

---

[77] Castle points out that Cowley's masquerade scene heavily influenced Elizabeth Inchbald's novel, *A Simple Story* (1791). Inchbald was a great admirer of Cowley and edited *The Belle's Stratagem* for her *British Theatre* series in 1808. For more information on Cowley's influence on Inchbald, see Castle, *Masquerade and Civilization*, 319.

becomes the deceiver and seducer of the man of the world. When Sir George, Lady Frances, Courtall, and Kitty Willis don neutral dominoes,[78] the different pairings that result in the course of the ball raise questions about the ease with which the rake can be interchanged with the devoted husband and the harlot with the virtuous wife. Courtall's inability to distinguish between the masked Kitty Willis and Lady Frances reflects on Doricourt's inability to distinguish the real Letitia behind her many masks.

The masks and disguises donned by nearly every character in *The Belle's Stratagem* create a dizzying parody of both the theatre itself and society. Mr Quick, the actor who originally played Hardy, Letitia's father, makes a joke of the confusion between actor and role. As Hardy, Quick tells the audience that he will borrow his old friend, the actor Quick's costume from his role in *The Duenna* to wear to the masquerade.[79] Thus Quick as Hardy plays Hardy playing Quick playing Isaac Mendoza! Carnivalesque conflations and inversions cannot be contained at the masked ball but spill over into the characters' lives. Sir George describes fashionable society as,

A mere chaos, in which all distinction of rank is lost in a ridiculous affectation of ease, and every different order of beings huddled together as they were before the creation. In the same select party, you will often find the wife of a bishop and a sharper, of an earl and a fiddler. In short, 'tis one universal masquerade, all disguised in the same habits and manners. (2.1.241–7)

His description proves an accurate prognostication of the confusions to come in and out of the upcoming masquerade. Neither clothing nor manner proves a true measure of identity. By adopting a conventional mask of reserve, Letitia makes herself indistinguishable from a sea of marriageable young ladies; it is only by literally masking herself that she unmasks her wit and talents. Hardy eagerly disguises his generosity behind the mask of a usurer at the masquerade, but he is more ambivalent about confusing masquerade and reality at home, superstitiously fearing that his masquerade may be an invitation to the angel of death:

I foresee some ill happening from this making believe to die before one's time. But hang it! A-hem! I am a stout man yet; only fifty-six. What's that? In the

[78] Masquerade cloaks that covered the wearer from head to toe.
[79] For a more complete discussion of Cowley's use of the actor to comment on himself, see the explanatory note to *The Belle's Stratagem*, 3.1.179.

last yearly bill there were three lived to above an hundred. Fifty-six! Fiddle-de-dee! I am not afraid, not I. (5.1.70–4)

There are clearly dangers to masquerade. When society is inverted and destabilized, one cannot be certain that order will be restored.[80]

While Cowley patriotically celebrates the virtues of the English court, English friendship, and English womanhood, she cannot refrain from satirizing English society's excesses and hypocrisies. Written between the American and the French Revolutions, *The Belle's Stratagem* reflects instabilities and uncertainties about English society and its future. The financial difficulties of both the lower and upper classes are brought together in the auction scene, where the auction-eer's employees complain about wages that can't feed them and pay for the clothes needed to disguise them as customers, and where society comes to prey upon the misfortunes of its own fallen members.[81]

Cowley does not attempt to lay to rest any of the social turbulence she notes in the play, and leaves a number of issues unresolved at the end of *The Belle's Stratagem*. As with many other eighteenth-century women playwrights, Cowley's discomfort with the constraints of the marriage plot are illustrated by the number of single characters remaining on stage at the play's conclusion. Mrs Racket and Villers seem well matched but do not pair off, and Sir George's last-minute attempt to offer the hand of his absent sister to the very eligible Saville is as unsatisfactory as Cowley's sudden introduction of Bella's previ-ously unmentioned fiancé in *The Runaway*. Sir George hopes to har-ness Saville's restrained but dangerous passion for Lady Frances by converting him from outsider to brother, but given the issues the comedy has raised about masks and identity, such an attempt to bind people together sight unseen seems a hazardous gamble.

The fop Flutter's mock advice to Courtall, 'And, Courtall, before you carry a lady into your bedchamber again, look under her mask, d'ye hear?' (4.2.70–1), resonates beyond Courtall's disgrace. In this carnivalesque world, it is not so easy to distinguish mask from identity. Is Letitia the modest English maiden or the passionate cosmopolitan from the masquerade? Or is she really comparable to Lord George Jennet's mistress? Who is the lady Doricourt will lead to the nuptial

---

[80] On masquerades in eighteenth-century life and literature, see p. xxxii and n. 50 above.

[81] This scene may have proved too uncomfortable for audiences because it was cut from the pirated Dublin editions of the play and condensed when Cowley edited the play after her retirement.

bedchamber? Cowley seems to be asking a very modern question, 'Is there true identity?' and perhaps even anticipates Henrik Ibsen's exploration of the issue in *Peer Gynt* (1867), in which Peer concludes that one's identity is like an onion, a multitude of layers with no core. In the cases of both Courtall and Doricourt, when the lady unmasks, it is not so much her identity that is revealed but the foolishness and vulnerability of the gentleman in question.

Once Doricourt, the only character unable to sustain a disguise, has been lifted from the depths of despair to the rapture of beholding Letitia's triumphant unmasking, he begins to understand his own folly. She tells him,

> You see I *can* be anything. Choose then my character; your taste shall fix it. Shall I be an *English* wife?—Or, breaking from the bonds of nature and education, step forth to the world in all the captivating glare of foreign manners?
> DORICOURT You shall be nothing but yourself—nothing can be captivating that you are not. I will not wrong your penetration by pretending that you won my heart at the first interview, but you have now my whole soul—your person, your face, your mind, I would not exchange for those of any other woman breathing.
>
> (5.5.237–45)

Letitia wins from Doricourt what she has most desired: his recognition of her multi-faceted character and his love of all that she is. She is therefore able to emerge from behind her masks and veils in a way never permitted to Cowley herself. Letitia's language in her explanation to Doricourt, 'The timidity of the English character threw a veil over me you could not penetrate. You have forced me to emerge in some measure from my natural reserve and to throw off the veil that hid me' (5.5.232–4), is oddly echoed by the writer of Cowley's obituary when he remarks on how 'she wore her laurels gracefully veiled'. That Cowley was swiftly censured for any attempts she made to emerge from her 'natural reserve' and succumbed to social pressures to retreat behind a veil of decorum is in large measure responsible for her too long disappearance from our dramatic history.

NOTE ON THE TEXTS

FOR the four plays in this volume, the first authorized published editions have been regarded as the most authoritative and have been used as the definitive texts. These editions are *The Innocent Mistress* (London: J. Orme for R. Basset, 1697); *The Busie Body* (London: Printed for Bernard Lintott, 1709); *The Times* (London: Printed for Fielding and Walker, J. Dodsley, T. Becket, and T. Davies, 1780), and *The Belle's Stratagem* (London: T. Cadell, 1782).

The only one of these choices that might be called into question is the edition of Hannah Cowley's *The Belle's Stratagem*, which had previously been published twice in Dublin in 1781. These two editions are piracies and are described as being versions of the play as it was performed in that city's Smock Alley Theatre. A number of liberties have been taken with Cowley's original script in these Dublin editions, including the deletion of the introduction to the auction scene. An argument might be made for using the version that appears in the posthumous collection of Cowley's *Works* in 1813, but this edition is the product of Cowley's drastic revisions to her plays after her retirement from the stage when she became almost obsessed with her reputation for respectability. I agree with Cowley's twentieth-century editor and critic, Frederick M. Link, preferring 'the Hannah Cowley actively engaged in the London theatre to the older one blue-penciling herself in retirement in Tiverton', whose revisions render her comedies 'bland, somewhat overwritten, and conventional—altogether less interesting than the early ones'.[1]

The first edition of Elizabeth Griffith's *The Times* used as a source for this volume is a copy autographed by Griffith in which she has made her own correction to the epilogue. In the line that reads, 'Were formed for chivalry, and love, and truth', Griffith has crossed out the word 'formed' and written above it 'famed'. I have transferred her correction to this edition, although it is not in agreement with other uncorrected copies of the first edition.

The Innocent Mistress has recently been reprinted in Fidelis Morgan's *The Female Wits* (London: Virago Press, 1981), a welcome

---

[1] Frederick M. Link (ed.), *The Plays of Hannah Cowley*, 2 vols. (New York and London, 1979), vol. i, pp. xlvii–xlviii.

edition of a play long out of print, but one that takes many liberties in modernizing Pix's language. *The Busybody* was reprinted frequently throughout the eighteenth and nineteenth centuries, but often with substantial revisions, such as reducing the play to three acts. *The Times* was only printed once. There have been two recent editions of *The Belle's Stratagem*: a facsimile edition in *The Plays of Hannah Cowley*, two volumes, edited and with an introduction by Frederick M. Link (New York and London, 1979), copied from the same 1782 first London edition used for this volume, and another edition contained in Robert W. Uphaus and Gretchen M. Foster (eds.), *The 'Other' Eighteenth Century: English Women of Letters 1660–1800* (East Lansing, Mich., 1991) that, without explanation, is based on an edition contained in *New English Drama*, edited by W. Oxberry (London, 1819). This version differs substantially from the 1782 first edition.

The texts have been modernized in spelling and in punctuation. Standard forms have been adopted for characters' names both in speech prefixes and entry/exit directions, and the necessary alterations to the first editions have been made without comment. Stage directions that use archaic or Latin phrases (with the exception of 'exit' and 'exeunt') have been silently modernized so that, for example, 'within' has been adjusted to 'offstage' and 'solus' has been translated as 'alone'. It is also series practice to use character names, not 'he', 'she', or 'they', in stage directions; these changes have also been made without each being separately recorded. Corrections have also been silently made when stage directions record 'exit' for a multiple departure from the stage or 'exeunt' for a single one. Finally, it is also series practice for the concluding stage direction of a scene to be either a simple 'exit' or 'exeunt' without listing the relevant characters' names, unless the direction requires the characters to depart separately. Such directions have also been silently standardized. It is fundamental to the principles of the series in which this edition appears that the reader should be offered all legitimate help possible to visualize the stage action the text demands. In the first editions of the four plays appearing in this volume, stage directions and scene descriptions are often confusing or lacking, and therefore editorial alterations have been made where necessary to clarify the staging and are marked by square brackets. In addition, since the language of drama is ideally meant to be heard rather than read, in modernizing punctuation, attention has been paid to how the words might be spoken by an actor, with the result that commas indicative of how a line might be emphasized or where an actor might take a significant breath have been retained even though they might seem superfluous to a strict grammarian.

Susanna Centlivre's use of Spanish in *The Busybody* presented particular difficulties. There were extensive flaws in the Spanish but distinctions needed to be made among printers' errors, eighteenth-century archaisms, and errors deliberately placed by Centlivre in the text to indicate the speaker's lack of skill with the language. Many approaches were possible, but each idiosyncratic. For this edition the assumption was made that although there were many corruptions in the Spanish, the flagrant errors in that spoken by Sir Jealous were intentional and so extreme that even a non-Spanish-speaking audience member would recognize them. This is supported by comments that Sir Jealous makes in 5.2 confessing his gratitude that a translator has been provided for him, 'for I find I have lost much of my Spanish' (5.2.12–13). It is further assumed that all other Spanish spoken is intended to be literate and has been corrected accordingly. 'Vind' is assumed to be, like 'Vd.' or 'Ud.', a form of 'usted' and has been so spelled out. The spelling of the address 'señor' appears in a variety of imaginative forms, and has been standardized to its modern form, except in the case of its usage by Sir Jealous, which, following the spelling most frequently used in his speeches in the 1709 edition, has been standardized to 'senior', a spelling that emphasizes his mis-pronunciation of the word. The translations provided in the notes to the play are my own.

All corrections and alterations have been made with an eye and ear to clarifying the text, but certainly differences of opinion are possible. Many choices were made after consultations with other scholars, for whose assistance I am profoundly grateful; however, in the event that more confusion has been created in any of the texts, or any errors made, I alone am responsible.

THE RESTORATION AND
EIGHTEENTH-CENTURY STAGES

THE comedies offered in this collection span nearly a century of English drama, a period of transition for London's playhouses, and since dramatists often write their plays to take advantage of the spaces in which they will be performed, these comedies reflect the physical changes that took place in the playhouses between 1695 and 1780. Restoration theatres, built in the late seventeenth century, were divided into three distinct spaces, delineated by Allardyce Nicoll as 'the house', the domain of the spectators; 'the platform', the area in front of the proscenium that served as the primary acting space; and 'the scene', the area of the stage behind the proscenium used to depict scenic backgrounds and effects. By the nineteenth century the theatres had been completely remodelled, eliminating the platform and leaving us with the bipartite theatre with which we are familiar today, where the audience and actors are divided by a massive, framing proscenium.

In the Restoration theatre, the proscenium was merely the frame that masked the stage curtain, separating the scene from the platform, or forestage. After the prologue, the curtain was drawn up in shallow festoons to reveal the scene and, although in rare cases it may have been lowered between acts to prepare for a particularly spectacular scenic effect, it generally remained open until the end of the play.[1] The scene and platform together provided an extremely versatile playing space capable of being used to create lavish scenic effects and spectacles, or to propel actors forward into a more intimate relationship with the audience.

Beyond the proscenium arch was the scenic stage, which featured three tiers of movable shutters and their corresponding tiers of masking wings. These shutters, large painted flats, could be manœuvred along grooves in the stage-floor to either open or closed positions. When closed, a pair of shutters would meet to form an alternative backdrop to the action. Each set of grooves was paired, allowing for two sets of shutters at each location. Thus, including the shutters at the rear of the stage, seven different scenes were easily available for

---

[1] Colin Visser, 'Scenery and Technical Design', in Robert D. Hume (ed.), *The London Theatre World 1660–1800* (Carbondale, Ill., 1980), 90.

quick changes during each performance.[2] Their corresponding painted side-wings could be angled to create the impression of one continuous set (somewhat like our notion of a box set). When opened, the shutters could create the illusion of perspective in relation to the backdrop or, since there was acting space available between the tiers of shutters, reveal a 'discovery scene', such as an inner room, a cavern, or characters in the midst of an action removed from the previous scene. In Restoration tragedy or heroic drama, much of the acting would take place in the scenic area of the stage, at a distance from the audience in the house both physically and psychologically. These dramas made regular use of sequential discovery scenes, each removing the action farther upstage from the audience, the highest drama or the most awful secrets being reserved for the last, most intimate discovery. Such staging lends itself to spectacle and a histrionic acting style, since, at such a remove, characters need to be larger than life in order to communicate with the audience.

Restoration comedy, however, emphasized the close connection between spectators and actors. In most comedies of manners the actors came forward to perform on the platform in front of the raised curtain, where the physical proximity of audience and spectator fostered an illusion of intimacy. This platform thrust out from the proscenium arch and was surrounded on three sides by spectators. The pit bordered the front of the platform. Along the sides, a line of box seats extended onto the platform itself. Originally, there were boxes on the platform even directly above the stage doors through which the actors made most of their entrances. The platform was thus, as Nicoll suggests, a location for the actors and spectators to meet. It provided an acting space where the actors could speak directly to the audience and a space where a segment of the house could mount the stage, erasing the clear distinction between spectator and performer. From the platform, actors could use naturalistic gestures and natural voices and still communicate the subtlest nuances to the audience. The characters were able to use that intimacy to comment on the spectators' morals as well as their own. Asides were spoken to the audience as if sharing a private moment or joke with a friend.

[2] Although it was possible to have as many as seven different scenes easily available by using the shutters, Peter Holland has his doubts that they were generally used in this way. Rather than have individual shutters painted for each scene of a play, use could be made of stock, or commonly used, sets, such as for house interiors, gardens, or streets. See Holland, *The Ornament of Action: Text and Performance in Restoration Comedy* (Cambridge, 1979), ch. 2, 'Performance: Theatres and Scenery', esp. pp. 35-6.

Centlivre's *The Busybody* provides an illustration of how the platform could be used to create a sense of intimacy between actors and audience. In 2.1, the so-called 'dumb scene', Sir George has paid Sir Francis for the privilege of an hour's conference with Sir Francis's ward and intended bride, Miranda. Sir Francis agrees, with the proviso that he be present. Miranda, wishing to encourage Sir George but incensed at the men trafficking in her favours, pays Sir George back by receiving his addresses in silence. When Sir Francis 'retires to the bottom of the stage' he himself becomes part of the audience to the scene being played by Sir George and Miranda further back on the platform. From that physical position, and through his chatty asides, Sir Francis makes the audience complicit in his voyeurism. As Miranda feeds the fires of comic jealousy and frustration, all three characters repeatedly turn to the audience to confide their thoughts, hopes, fears, and schemes. The audience becomes the only 'character' in the scene who shares the confidence of all the characters, and much of its enjoyment comes from being so intimately involved with the action.

The platform remained an important acting space until late in the eighteenth century, although the beginnings of its decline can be traced back as early as 1696, when Christopher Rich ordered alterations to increase audience capacity in the Theatre Royal, Drury Lane, by shortening the depth of the forestage by 4 feet to 17 feet and replacing the downstage proscenium doors with stage boxes. While the primary effect of this structural change was to create more seats in the pit, a secondary effect was to begin the process of reducing the intimacy between the actors and spectators fostered by the platform projecting into the house.[3] The formerly semicircular forestage that connected the audience to the actors became a straight and narrow apron that divided the two groups. The foreshortened platform encouraged the actors to move back toward the scenic area of the stage. In the early part of the eighteenth century, in order to create even greater seating capacity in the house, the last platform stage doors were removed completely, and replaced with more box seating on the platform. Thereafter, all entrances and exits had to be made from behind the proscenium arch, even though the audience surrounded the forestage.

Peter Holland observes that the fact that the forestage doors could

---

[3] These are the stages for which Mary Pix and Susanna Centlivre wrote. *The Innocent Mistress* was first produced in 1697 on Lincoln's Inn Fields' full platform; *The Busybody* was first performed in 1709 at Drury Lane on Rich's foreshortened platform.

be eliminated points to the fading significance of the platform as an acting space. The shift away from acting on the forestage was a gradual one; throughout the century some new comedies continued to look back toward Restoration sensibilities while others partook of the newer style. While playing on the forestage lends itself to comedy, moving action away from the audience behind a framing proscenium lends itself more to tragedy and spectacle. Holland asserts that moving the acting behind the proscenium contributed to more 'sentimental' comedy, perhaps a problematic term, but one which Holland defines as comedy based on romantic illusion and moral purity, or comedy bearing a closer resemblance to tragedy than its Restoration counterpart.[4]

Throughout the latter part of the eighteenth century, London's theatres were in a constant state of alteration and redecoration intended to increase the size of the scenic stage as well as the size of the house. The stage size needed to increase in order to accommodate the afterpieces, pantomimes, entr'acte songs and dances that had been added to the nightly bill to further attract larger audiences. Comedies written for these stages were shorter and less intimate than earlier plays and Restoration plays were cut and restaged to suit the new audience tastes and to allow time for these additional entertainments. For the most part, the playhouse alterations were limited by the basic shell of the existing theatre structure and its lot. Architects found ways of making more use of the width of the theatres by moving passages to the outside of the building and placing stairways within the thickness of the walls, thus leaving more internal space for seating. David Garrick, the great actor and manager of Drury Lane from 1747 to 1776, was fortunate enough to purchase the property directly behind Drury Lane with the result that, after Robert Adam's alterations in 1775, the depth of the stage was nearly doubled. Indeed, Adam's Drury Lane, which Edward Langhans believes may have been London's best theatre in the eighteenth century, can serve as a paradigm for the transitions that occurred in the London playhouses in the second half of the century.

Both Elizabeth Griffith's *The Times* and Hannah Cowley's *The Belle's Stratagem* show how dramatists made use of the depth of this new mid-century stage. Griffith's comedy was produced on Drury Lane's new stage and contains scenes depicting a card party in which the main actors speak from an anteroom in front of the room where the party takes place. A cast of at least twelve populates the party

---

[4] Holland, *Ornament of Action*, 29.

room, and their lively conversations and antics metaphorically comment upon the conversation and actions of the main characters (who are probably on the platform). The staging of the card party appears designed particularly to take advantage of the depth of the new stage. Whereas the rest of the comedy takes place in closed drawing-, dressing-, and dining-rooms, and uses a small cast, the party suddenly opens up spatially into the world of *ton* or fashion. Likewise, Cowley takes advantage of the depth of the Covent Garden stage[5] in *The Belle's Stratagem* by moving her comedy from intimate domestic scenes to large-scale public ones, first to a bustling auction house and later to a spectacular masquerade.

David Garrick dominated the theatrical scene of his day, and when he died in 1779 a theatrical era died with him. Garrick was renowned for his naturalistic acting style, the subtlety of his gestures, and the nuances of his voice; his technique was founded on the dynamic provided by a relatively small stage and an intimate connection with his audience, a dynamic that was becoming obsolete with the coming of the newer playhouses. Between 1775 and 1795, the old theatres were either drastically altered or destroyed and rebuilt on larger scale. Garrick retired in 1776, just a year after Robert Adam completed his renovation of Drury Lane. In 1794 Adam's Drury Lane was torn down and replaced by a new theatre designed by Henry Holland. This theatre, like other new theatres of the day, was geared to a new taste for spectacle and opera and was too cavernous for old styles and straight plays. Actors were dwarfed, and the writing and staging of intimate plays was ended for a time.

The sea change occurring in the plays and playhouses at the end of the eighteenth century was lamented by a contemporary spectator, John Byng, later Viscount Torrington, on 14 May 1794:

Restore me, ye overuling powers to the drama, to the warm close observant, seats of Old Drury where I may comfortably criticise and enjoy the delights of scenic fancy: These now are past! The nice discriminations, of the actors face, and of the actors feeling, are now all lost in the vast void of the new theatre of Drury Lane.

Garrick—thou didst retire at the proper time—for wer't thou restor'd to the stage,—in vain, would now thy finesse,—thy bye play, thy whisper,—thy aside,—and even thine eye, assist thee.—[6]

---

[5] For speculation about the dates at which Covent Garden extended its scenic stage, see Allardyce Nicoll, *The Garrick Stage: Theatres and Audience in the Eighteenth Century* (Athens, Ga., 1980), 51–5.

[6] C. Bruyn Andrews (ed.), *The Torrington Diaries* (London, 1938), iv. 18.

Interestingly, Frederick Link believes that Hannah Cowley gave up writing plays in 1792 partly because of the change in the theatres. Her style harked back to Restoration sensibilities and was dependent upon an intimate connection between actor and audience. She felt no affinity for the cavernous spaces of the new theatres.

The evolution of the tripartite Restoration theatre to the bipartite nineteenth-century playhouse was gradual and by no means strictly a linear progression. In this short essay, it has been necessary to condense and simplify the history. For more detailed accounts, the reader should turn to the following invaluable sources: Emmett L. Avery, *The London Stage 1700–1729: A Critical Introduction* (Carbondale, Ill., 1968); Peter Holland, *The Ornament of Action: Text and Performance in Restoration Comedy* (Cambridge, 1979); Robert D. Hume (ed.), *The London Theatre World 1660–1800* (Carbondale, Ill., 1980), especially chapters by Edward A. Langhans, Joseph Donohue, and Colin Visser; Allardyce Nicoll, *The Garrick Stage: Theatres and Audience in the Eighteenth Century* (Athens, Ga., 1980); and George Winchester Stone, *The London Stage 1747–1776: A Critical Introduction* (Carbondale, Ill., 1968).

SELECT BIBLIOGRAPHY

THE Restoration and eighteenth century marked a period of drastic change for English drama and the theatres for which it was produced. General introductions to the theatre of this long century include *The London Theatre World 1660–1800*, edited by Robert D. Hume (Carbondale, Ill., 1980), an extremely useful collection of writings on both technical and literary aspects of the theatre, including chapters by Edward A. Langhans on 'The Theatres', Colin Visser on 'Scenery and Technical Design', and Philip H. Highfill, Jr. on 'Performers and Performing'; and Hume's *The Rakish Stage: Studies in English Drama, 1660–1800* (Carbondale, Ill., 1983).

In looking back to the Restoration and Augustan periods, the following sources offer comprehensive introductory material to the drama of the age: Peter Holland's *The Ornament of Action: Text and Performance in Restoration Comedy* (Cambridge, 1979); and Hume's *The Development of English Drama in the Late Seventeenth Century* (Oxford, 1976).

For the latter part of the century, Allardyce Nicoll's *A History of Late Eighteenth Century Drama 1750–1800* (Cambridge, 1937) remains the most complete survey of the plays and playwrights of the era. Nicoll is notable for being a champion of the works of women playwrights, and calling for the return of their works to the stage. Nicoll's last work, the posthumously published *The Garrick Stage: Theatres and Audience in the Eighteenth Century* (Athens, Ga., 1980) is an invaluable resource on theatres, acting styles, and audiences, complete with a wealth of illustrations meticulously selected by Sybil Rosenfeld.

In the past, scholars have devoted comparatively little attention to the works of women dramatists writing in the eighteenth century. This situation has begun to change, but at present the scope of available material is limited. Nancy Cotton's *Women Playwrights in England, c.1361–1750* (Lewisburg, Pa., 1980) has become the classic text on the subject, and Jacqueline Pearson's *The Prostituted Muse: Images of Women and Women Dramatists 1642–1737* (New York, 1988) offers a broad survey of women dramatists writing before the Licensing Act of 1737. Ellen Donkin's *Getting into the Act: Women Playwrights in London 1776–1829* (London and New York, 1995) is a highly intelligent and insightful exploration of the work of seven late eighteenth-century women playwrights and how their careers were shaped by

David Garrick and his new style of theatre management. *Curtain Calls: British and American Women and the Theater, 1660–1820*, edited by Mary Anne Schofield and Cecilia Macheski (Athens, Ohio, 1991), is a very useful collection of essays on women dramatists and actresses, and especial attention should be drawn to William J. Burling's '"Their Empire Disjoyn'd": Serious Plays by Women on the London Stage 1660–1737', and Judith Phillips Stanton's '"This New-Found Path Attempting": Women Dramatists in England, 1660–1800' for their analyses of the scope and significance of the the the contributions of women playwrights.

Scholarship on Mary Pix has been limited, but good introductions to her work can be found in Constance Clark's *Three Augustan Women Playwrights* (New York, 1986) and Edna L. Steeves's Introduction to *The Plays of Mary Pix and Catharine Trotter* (New York, 1982). Paula Louise Barbour's Ph.D. dissertation, 'A Critical Edition of Mary Pix's *The Spanish Wives*' (Yale University, 1975) has been very influential for other Pix scholars. Linda Payne's entry, 'Mary Pix', in Paula R. Backscheider (ed.), *Dictionary of Literary Biography, 80, Restoration and Eighteenth-Century Dramatists*, 1st ser. (Detroit, 1989) draws largely on Clark, Steeves, and Barbour, but also provides very useful bibliographic information.

Critical interest in Susanna Centlivre has been growing in the latter half of the twentieth century. John Wilson Bowyer's full-length study, *The Celebrated Mrs Centlivre* (Durham, NC, 1952), helped rekindle interest in her, and F. Lock contributed a volume, *Susanna Centlivre*, to the Twayne series (Boston, 1979). Jean Gagen's entry, 'Susanna Centlivre', in Paula R. Backscheider (ed.), *Dictionary of Literary Biography, 84, Restoration and Eighteenth-Century Dramatists*, 2nd ser. (Detroit, 1989), provides a very helpful synopsis of Centlivre's life and works. Recent articles include Robert C. Frushell's 'Marriage and Marrying in Susanna Centlivre's Plays', *Papers on Language and Literature*, 22 (Winter 1986), 16–38; and Suz-Anne Kinney's intelligent essay linking Centlivre and Aphra Behn, 'Confinement Sharpens the Invention: Aphra Behn's *The Rover* and Susanna Centlivre's *The Busie Body*', in Gail Finney (ed.), *Look Who's Laughing: Gender and Comedy* (Amsterdam, 1994).

Most scholarship on Elizabeth Griffith focuses on her novels and collections of letters. Less work has been done on her comedies. J. M. S. Tompkins's *The Polite Marriage* (Cambridge, 1938) is an examination of the Griffith marriage. Dorothy Hughes Eshleman, *Elizabeth Griffith: A Biography and Critical Study* (Philadelphia, 1949) is an uneven work that offers a large amount of valuable information on finding reviews of Griffith's plays, but fills in scholarly gaps with novelistic suppositions. Elizabeth R. Napier's entry, 'Elizabeth Griffith', in Martin C. Battestin (ed.), *Dictionary of Literary Biography*, 29, *British Novelists, 1660–1800*, pt. 1 (Detroit, 1985) and Betty Rizzo's 'Elizabeth Griffith', in Janet Todd (ed.), *A Dictionary of Literary Biography* (Totowa, NJ, 1985) offer useful overviews of Griffith's life and works but scant attention is given to her dramatic works. Rizzo redresses this omission in what is probably the most sympathetic published scholarship on Griffith's playwriting in her article '"*Depressa Resurgam*": Elizabeth Griffith's Playwrighting Career', in Mary Anne Schofield and Cecilia Macheski (eds.), *Curtain Calls: British and American Women and the Theater, 1660–1820* (Athens, Ohio, 1991).

As with the work of Centlivre, there has been a recent resurgence of interest in the plays of Hannah Cowley. Jean Gagen's entry, 'Hannah Cowley', in Paula R. Backscheider (ed.), *Dictionary of Literary Biography, 89, Restoration and Eighteenth-Century Dramatists*, 3rd ser. (Detroit, 1989) offers a thorough synopsis of Cowley's life and works; and David W. Meredith's entry, 'Hannah Cowley', in Janet Todd (ed.), *A Dictionary of Literary Biography*, (Totowa, NJ, 1985), although brief, is a welcome encomium. Frederick M. Link has edited a two-volume facsimile edition of Cowley's works taken from first editions, *The Plays of Hannah Cowley* (New York and London, 1979), and his introduction to her works offers perceptive analyses of Cowley's *œuvre*. Erin Isikoff's article, 'Masquerade, Modesty, and Comedy in Hannah Cowley's *The Belle's Stratagem*', in Gail Finney (ed.), *Look Who's Laughing: Gender and Comedy* (Amsterdam, 1994), 99–117, is an uneven piece of scholarship that draws on an 1819 edition of *The Belle's Stratagem* for its source, without any explanation of this choice, and comments on a Prologue that does not appear in the comedy's first edition. Ellen Donkin's 'The Paper War of Hannah Cowley and Hannah More', first printed in Mary Anne Schofield and Cecilia Macheski (eds.), *Curtain Calls: British and American Women and the Theater, 1660–1820* (Athens, Ohio, 1991), was reprinted in her more thorough examination of late eighteenth-century women playwrights *Getting into the Act* (London and New York, 1995). Donkin's examination of Cowley's relationships with the theatre managers of her day and her role as a theatre professional represents the most intriguing Cowley scholarship in print, and includes new material drawn from Cowley's correspondence with her friends and patrons, Lord and Lady Harrowby.

A CHRONOLOGY OF RESTORATION AND EIGHTEENTH-CENTURY PLAYS BY WOMEN

The following is a sampling of plays by Restoration and eighteenth-century women dramatists. It should not be considered a complete listing. The accompanying dates are those of certain or likely first performance.

Aphra Behn, *The Forc'd Marriage* (1670)

Aphra Behn, *The Amorous Prince* (1671)

Aphra Behn, *The Rover* (1676/7)

Aphra Behn, *The Lucky Chance* (1686)

Aphra Behn, *The Emperor of the Moon* (1687)

Catharine Trotter, *Agnes de Castro* (1695)

Delarivière Manley, *The Lost Lover* (1696)

Delarivière Manley, *The Royal Mischief* (1696)

Mary Pix, *Ibrahim, the Thirteenth Emperour of the Turks* (1696)

Mary Pix, *The Spanish Wives* (1696)

Mary Pix, *The Innocent Mistress* (1697)

Catharine Trotter, *Fatal Friendship* (1698)

Susanna Centlivre, *The Perjur'd Husband* (1700)

Susanna Centlivre, *The Stolen Heiress* (1702)

Susanna Centlivre, *The Gamester* (1704/5)

Mary Pix, *The Conquest of Spain* (1705)

Susanna Centlivre, *The Basset Table* (1705)

Delarivière Manley, *Almyna* (1706)

Susanna Centlivre, *The Busybody* (1709)

Susanna Centlivre, *Mar-Plot: or, the Second Part of the Busybody* (1710)

Susanna Centlivre, *The Wonder* (1714)

Mary Davys, *The Northern Heiress* (1716)

Susanna Centlivre, *A Bold Stroke for a Wife* (1717/18)

Eliza Haywood, *The Fair Captive* (1720/1)

Penelope Aubin, *The Humours of the Masqueraders* (1730)

Eliza Haywood, *The Opera of Operas: or, Tom Thumb the Great* (1733)

Charlotte Charke, *The Art of Management* (1735)

Catharine Clive, *The Rehearsal* (1753)

Frances Brooke, *Virginia* (1756)

Frances Sheridan, *The Discovery* (1763)

Frances Sheridan, *The Dupe* (1763)

Elizabeth Griffith, *The Platonic Wife* (1765)

Elizabeth Griffith, *The Double Mistake* (1766)

Elizabeth Griffith, *The School for Rakes* (1769)

Charlotte Lennox, *The Sister* (1769)

Mrs Celisia, *Almida* (1771)

Charlotte Lennox, *Old City Manners* (1775)

Hannah Cowley, *The Runaway* (1776)

Hannah More, *Percy* (1777)

Hannah Cowley, *Who's the Dupe?* (1779)

Hannah Cowley, *Albina, Countess Raimond* (1779)

Hannah More, *The Fatal Falsehood* (1779)

Elizabeth Griffith, *The Times* (1779)

Hannah Cowley, *The Belle's Stratagem* (1780)

Frances Brooke, *The Siege of Sinope* (1781)

Frances Brooke, *Rosina* (1782)

Hannah Cowley, *Which is the Man?* (1782)

Hannah Cowley, *A Bold Stroke for a Husband* (1783)

Elizabeth Inchbald, *I'll Tell You What* (1785)

Hannah Cowley, *A School for Greybeards* (1786)

Elizabeth Inchbald, *Such Things Are* (1787)

Elizabeth Inchbald, *The Midnight Hour* (1787)

Hannah Cowley, *The Fate of Sparta* (1788)

Lady Eglantine Wallace, *The Ton* (1788)

Elizabeth Inchbald, *Next Door Neighbours* (1791)

Hannah Cowley, *The Town Before You* (1794)

Elizabeth Inchbald, *Lovers' Vows* (1798)

Charlotte Smith, *What is She?* (1799)

THE INNOCENT MISTRESS

MARY PIX

THE CHARACTERS OF THE PLAY

Sir Charles Beauclair,° *first a younger brother, married by his friends to a rich ill-favoured widow, afterward, master of a great estate, and in love with Bellinda*   Mr Betterton

Sir Francis Wildlove,° *his friend*   Mr Verbruggen

Searchwell, *his man*   Mr Knap

Beaumont,° *an honest country gentleman, friend to Sir Francis, and lover of Arabella*   Mr Hodgson

Spendall, *a sharper; and hanger on to Sir Charles*   Mr Bowman

Lywell,° *a rake, companion to Spendall*   Mr Freeman

Cheatall,° *a very foolish fellow; brother to the Lady Beauclair*   Mr Bowen

Gentil,° *his man; an ingenious fellow*   Mr Harris

Flywife,° *alias Allen, a merchant*   Mr Underhill

Bellinda,° *alias Mariamne, daughter to the Lord Belmour*   Mrs Barry

Mrs° Beauclair, *niece to Sir Charles*   Mrs Bracegirdle

Arabella,° *a young lady, left to the care of Cheatall's father*   Mrs Prince

Lady Beauclair, *an ill-bred woman*   Mrs Lee

Peggy,° *her daughter, of the same stamp*   Mrs Howard

Eugenia,° *Lady Beauclair's woman*   Mrs Lawson

Betty, *Bellinda's woman*

Dresswell,° *Mrs Beauclair's woman*   Mrs Du Qua

Mrs Flywife, *kept by Flywife, and going by his name*   Mrs Lassel

Jenny, *her maid*   Mrs Willis

Drawers° and servants

PROLOGUE

SPOKEN BY MR VERBRUGGEN
WRITTEN BY MR MOTTEUX°

This season with what arts both houses strive,°
By your kind presence, to be kept alive!
We've still new things, or old ones we revive;
We plot, and strive to bring them first o'th' stage,
Like wary pilot for his weather-gauge.° 5
We've every act, and every week a play;
Nay, we've had new ones studied for one day;
We've double duty, and we've but half pay.°
We've scaling monkeys; and we've dancing swans,°
To match our nimble cap'ring chairs and stands.° 10
There opera's with, and here without, machines;°
Here, scenes well-wrought, and there, well-painted scenes;
Castles and men i'th'air, *The World i'th'Moon,*°
Where you like swallows fly, but soon you're gone.°
We've something every different taste to hit, 15
Egad, I think, we've everything but wit;
For we've full scenes, and we've an empty pit.°
Faith, sirs, we scarce could hope you here would be
So numerous, though we have a new comedy.
For there's in plays, you know, a reformation° 20
(A thing to which y' have no great inclination),
I fear you'll seek some looser occupation.°
From those lewd poets all these mischiefs flow;
They, like Drawcansirs, mauled both friend and foe.°
Would they'd been served like their plays long ago! 25
All cautious dons and matrons hence they scared,
And all this did they do, because they dared.
Yet, that you're hardened sinners they may boast:
The more they lashed you, you seemed tickled most.°
But now no luscious scenes must lard their plays;° 30
No lady now will need to hide her face;
But I'll be hanged if one i'th'gallery stays.°
To hear ill-natured truths no more you'll sit,
But mortify an inoffensive wit;

Lord, how still we shall have you in the pit!   35
For I dare say, of what most pleased our guests,
Nine parts in ten were still sheer bawdy jests.
Methinks I see some here who seem to say,
'Gad, ere the curtain's drawn, I'll slip away;
No bawdy, this can't be a woman's play.'°   40
Nay, I confess there's cause enough to doubt;°
But, faith, they say there was a deal cut out.°
Then stay and use it gently, some of you,
Since to be maimed° y'are somewhat subject to.
Spare it, you who for harmless sports declare,   45
Show that this age a modest play can bear.
Twice has our poetess kind usage found;°
Change not her fortune, though she changed her ground.°

1.1

Sir Francis Wildlove's chamber
Sir Francis Wildlove, dressing

SIR FRANCIS Searchwell!

[*Enter Searchwell*]

SEARCHWELL Sir!

SIR FRANCIS Get me some small beer, and dash a little Langoon° in it; else 'twill go down my burning stomach ten degrees colder than ice. I should have met my old friend and collegian,° Beaumont, who came to town last night, but wine and women drove it clear out of my head.

SEARCHWELL Sir, he's here.

Enter Beaumont. [*Exit Searchwell*]

SIR FRANCIS Welcome, dear friend, I prithee pardon my omission. Faith, 'twas business that could not be left to other hands.

BEAUMONT Women, I suppose, and that excuse I know a man of your kidney° thinks almighty.

SIR FRANCIS Even so. Well, by my life, I am heartily glad to see you. Why, thou hast been an age confined to barren fields and senseless groves, or conversation stupid and dull as they. How canst thou waste thy youth, happy youth, the very quintessence of life, from° London, this dear epitome of pleasure?

BEAUMONT Because excess of drinking cloys my stomach, and impudence in women absolutely turns it. Then,° I hate the vanity of dress and fluttering, where eternal noise and nonsense reigns. This considered, what should I do here?

SIR FRANCIS Not much, in troth.°

BEAUMONT But you, my friend, run the career° your appetite directs, taste all those pleasures I despise. You can inform me what humour's° most in fashion, what ruling whim, and how the ladies are.

SIR FRANCIS Why, faith, there's no great alteration. The money is indeed very much scarcer; yet what perhaps you'll think a wonder, dressing and debauchery increases. As for the damsels, three sorts make a bushel, and will be uppermost.° First, there's your common jilts will° oblige everybody.

BEAUMONT These are monsters sure.

SIR FRANCIS You may call 'em what you please, but they are very

5

plentiful, I promise you. The next is your kept mistress. She's a degree modester, if not kind to each,° appears in her dress like quality,° whilst her ogling eyes, and too frequent debauches, discover her the younger sister only to the first.   35

BEAUMONT This I should hate for ingratitude.

SIR FRANCIS The third is not a whore, but a brisk, airy, noisy coquette,° that lives upon treating.° One spark has her to the play, another to the park,° a third to Windsor,° a fourth to some other place of diversion. She has not the heart to grant 'em all favours, for that's their design at the bottom of the treats, and they have not the heart to marry her, for that's her design, too, poor creature. So perhaps a year, or it may be two, the gaudy butterfly flutters round the kingdom; then if a foolish cit° does not take compassion,° sneaks into a corner, dies an old maid, despised and forgotten. The men that fit those ladies are your rake, your cully, and your beau.°   40   45

BEAUMONT I hope Sir Francis Wildlove has more honour than to find a mistress amongst such creatures.   50

SIR FRANCIS Gad, honest, honourable Ned, I must own I have a fling at all. Sometimes I think it worth my while to make a keeper° jealous, frequently treat the coquette, till either she grows upon me, or I grow weary of her. Then 'tis but saying a rude thing, she quarrels, I fly to the next bottle, and there forever drown her remembrance.°   55

BEAUMONT 'Tis pity that the most noblest seeds of nature are most prone to vice.

SIR FRANCIS Such another grave speech would give me a fit of the colic.°   60

BEAUMONT Well, I find 'tis in vain to tell you my story, without I have a desire to be swingeingly laughed at.

SIR FRANCIS Nay, nay, why so? I'd sacrifice my life to serve my friend.

BEAUMONT To confess the truth, I'm in love.   65

SIR FRANCIS Is that such a wonder? Why, I have been so a thousand times, old boy!

BEAUMONT Ay, but desperately, virtuously!

SIR FRANCIS There the case differs. I doubt,° friend, you have applied yourself to a wrong man.   70

BEAUMONT Are not you acquainted with Sir Charles Beauclair?

SIR FRANCIS Yes, intimately.

BEAUMONT Then, in short, his lady and a booby brother of hers have got my mistress in their power. She was the daughter of an eminent

merchant, one Sir George Venturewell,° who, dying, left her to the   75
care of my Lady Beauclair's father. He proved, like most guardians,
a great knave, forged a will, which gave my Arabella nothing, unless
she married this two-legged thing, his son.° Some of her friends
contested with 'em,° but the lawyers' roguery, through the guardian's wealth, prevailed, and she is again in their possession. The old   80
fellow is dead, but the sister and brother pretend to manage her.

SIR FRANCIS Your case is desperate, and I fear Sir Charles can do you
but little service in't.

BEAUMONT Why, he lives with his wife.

SIR FRANCIS Yes, modestly.° He knows nothing of her concerns, and   85
desires she should know nothing of his. Did you never hear of her
character?

BEAUMONT No.

SIR FRANCIS She is certainly the most disagreeable of the whole sex,
has neither sense, beauty or good manners. Then, her humour is so   90
implacable; she hunted her first husband into the Indies,° where he
died, heaven knows when or how.

BEAUMONT What the devil made Sir Charles marry her?

SIR FRANCIS Even° that tempting devil interest.° She was vastly rich,
he a younger brother.° Since,° the estate and title of his family is   95
fallen to him, and I dare swear he'd willingly give a leg or an arm to
be freed from the intolerable plague of a wife, whom no mortal can
please.

Enter Searchwell

SEARCHWELL Sir Charles Beauclair is coming to wait upon your
honour.   100

SIR FRANCIS I am glad on't. I fancy there's a sympathy in your
humours that will soon excite a friendship, for he, notwithstanding
the provocation of an ugly scolding wife at home, and the temptation of a good estate, and a handsome fellow° into the bargain,
instead of making his life easy with jolly *bona robas*, dotes on a   105
platonic mistress,° who never allows him greater favours than to
read plays to her, kiss her hand, and fetch heart-breaking sighs at
her feet. With her he has obliged his charming niece to be almost
always. Faith, nothing but the horrible fear of matrimony before my
eyes keeps me from loving Mrs Beauclair.° She is pretty without   110
affectation, has but just pride enough to become her, and gravity
enough to secure her from scandal. To all this add twelve thousand
pounds in ready money.

Enter Sir Charles Beauclair and Spendall

SIR CHARLES And is not that last the most prevailing argument, ha, Frank?   115

SIR FRANCIS No, Sir Charles, chains of gold won't tempt my freedom from me. But here's a gentleman, fixed in the dull matrimonial road, uneasy if he meets with interruption, though it throws him on the flowery fields of liberty. He's my particular friend and labours under the pangs of disappointed love. 'Tis in your power to   120 assist him in his delivery. I know you are compassionate in these cases.

SIR CHARLES You may promise for me to the utmost; I am ready.

BEAUMONT Fame reports you a true English gentleman.

SIR CHARLES You may command me, sir.   125

SPENDALL (*aside to Sir Charles*) Dear Sir Charles, lend me one guinea more; the estate's entailed,° my father will die, and I shall get an heiress.

SIR CHARLES Here, take it, and leave° lying.

SPENDALL I'll be with you again at dinner.   130

SIR CHARLES I don't question it.

    Exit Spendall

SIR FRANCIS Searchwell, has there been no letters for me this morning?

SEARCHWELL No, sir.

SIR FRANCIS Stay you at home, and if there come one, find me out   135 with it.

SEARCHWELL I will, sir.

    [*Exit Searchwell*]

SIR FRANCIS Come, Sir Charles, shall we to the chocolate-house?° There you shall hear Mr Beaumont's story.

SIR CHARLES With all my heart. Hark you, Sir Francis, I have an   140 entertainment of excellent music promised me this afternoon. You know I cannot have it at home, so I have borrowed some apartments of obliging Mrs Bantum, the Indian woman,° and will try to prevail with the ladies to come.

SIR FRANCIS Dear Sir Charles, introduce me.   145

SIR CHARLES You'll think your hours thrown away in the company of civil° women.

SIR FRANCIS Faith, I scarce dare trust your niece's eyes, they gain too much upon my heart. I am always forced, after I have seen her, to have recourse to the glass, to secure myself from romantic   150 constancy.

BEAUMONT Now you talk of romances, in troth, I think I'm a perfect

8

knight errant,° for, besides my own lady, I'm in quest of another fair fugitive, by the desire of her father. Have you not heard of the death of my Lord Belmour's heir, and absence of his only daughter,   155
Mariamne?

SIR FRANCIS Yes, yes.

BEAUMONT The old lord has given me her picture, with an earnest petition that I would endeavour to find her. He pressed me so, I could not refuse it, though I have small probability of my side.°   160

SIR FRANCIS She's now a prodigious heiress. What could be the meaning of running from all her friends?

BEAUMONT Too studious for her sex, and fell upon° the seducers of the women: plays, and romances. From thence she formed herself a hero, a cavalier, that could love and talk like them; whilst her father,   165
without consulting her, provided a husband, rich, but wanting all Scudéry's° accomplishments. This man she called monster, and finding the marriage unavoidable, took her jewels and what money was in her power, and in the stage-coach fled to this populous wilderness,° if that can be proper, for here we are, in crowds,   170
concealed as well as in a desert.

SIR FRANCIS 'Twas strange.

SIR CHARLES I pity her, for I hate an innocent inclination crossed.
        Enter Searchwell

SEARCHWELL Sir, your coach is ready.

SIR FRANCIS *Allons,*° gentlemen.   175
        Exeunt

1.2

Bellinda's apartment
Bellinda appears with a book

BELLINDA In vain I fly to books; the tuneful numbers° give me not a moment's ease. In vain I've strove to walk in virtue's high, unerring paths; blind, rash, inconsiderate love has pushed me from the blissful state, and fixed me struggling midst ten thousand dangers.
        Enter Mrs Beauclair [and Betty]°
Here, sweet bard, thou suits me well. (*Opening the book*)   5

        'My anxious hours roll heavily away,
        Deprived of sleep by night or peace by day.'°

MRS BEAUCLAIR Poor disconsolate damsel, come leave this soft melancholy poetry; it nurses your disease.

BELLINDA You indeed, like a bright ray of comfort, shoot through my 10 endless night. Where's my dear destruction?

MRS BEAUCLAIR Mr Spendall said he would be here at noon.

BELLINDA He's ever here; I feel him busy at my heart, and when the wished minute of his approach comes on, every artery catches the convulsive joy. Do not you think me mad? 15

MRS BEAUCLAIR A little crazed or so, my dear.

BELLINDA Bedlam,° ere this,° had been my proper mansion if your sweet company had not composed my jarring thoughts, and given the warring torments intervals of rest.

MRS BEAUCLAIR I must confess, though I am wild to the very verge 20 that innocence allows, yet when my uncle, that dear good man, told me if ever I meant to oblige him I must be a companion, friend, and lover of his mistress, the proposition startled me. But then I did not think there had been such a mistress as my Bellinda, nor platonic love in real practice. 25

BELLINDA True, my dear friend, our love is to the modern age unpracticed and unknown; yet so strict and so severe are rigid honour's laws that, though not grossly, yet we still offend. Had not fate fixed a bar unpassable between us, how should I have blessed the accident that brought us first acquainted. 30

MRS BEAUCLAIR You never told me the story.

BELLINDA In short, 'twas thus: coming from the play, masked,° with a young lady, a fluttering fellow seized me, and spite of my entreaties, grew rudely troublesome. I was never used to such behaviour, and it throughly frighted me. Sir Charles, being near, saw my unfeigned 35 concern, and generously° made the brute desist, then led me safely to a coach. Observing where I bid the coachman drive, he came to wait upon me.° My fair friend again was with me and 'twas by her persuasions that I saw him. We found his conversation nicely° civil and full of innocent delight. I blushed and fondly thought this man 40 my amorous stars, in kindness, destined for my happiness. But oh!—

MRS BEAUCLAIR But oh, he was married, and that spoiled all.

BELLINDA Therein I only can accuse him of deceit. He kept his marriage a fatal secret till I had lost the power to banish him. 45

MRS BEAUCLAIR I prithee, dear Bellinda, where wert thou bred? I'm sure this lewd town never gave you such nice notions of honour.

BELLINDA My friendship bars you of nothing but enquiring who I am.

MRS BEAUCLAIR 'Tis true. I beg your pardon and am silent.

BELLINDA Only this I'll tell you, madam, and as a warning; never   50
resolve, although you think it fully in your power to keep your
resolution. Mark it in me, I that thought to have stood the fairest
pattern of my sex° and would have blotted° all the annals of guilty
love, yet now am lost, fonder of my Beauclair than of family or
fame, yet know him married, and divine and human laws against   55
me.

MRS BEAUCLAIR For human laws, I know not what to say, but sure
heaven had no concern; 'twas a detested match. Ruling friends and
cursed avarice joined this unthinking youth to the worst of women.
But no more of this. How d'ye like your new lodgings? The house is   60
very large. Have you no good neighbours?

BELLINDA You know 'tis not my way to be acquainted. My impertinent maid sometimes teases me with a relation° of a merchant and
pretty lady who came from the Indies and lodge here.

MRS BEAUCLAIR What are they, Mrs Betty?   65

BETTY Nay, my lady will ne'er hear me out, but I'm sure they are
worth anybody's observation. He looks like a surly, old, rich cuff,
and she like an intriguing beautiful jilt, as fine as a queen covered
with jewels.

BELLINDA Ha' done with your description; I'm sick of 'em both.   70

MRS BEAUCLAIR Lord, you are so peevish. Pray give me leave to
ask Mrs Betty little more° questions about 'em. What's his
name?

BETTY An odd one, madam. They call him Mr Flywife.°

MRS BEAUCLAIR An odd one indeed, and contradicting his actions   75
when such a fine dame belongs to him.

BELLINDA Thou art a little gossip to trouble thy head with other
people's affairs. I heard news of you, madam, the other day. They
say you are in love, for all your seeming indifference.

MRS BEAUCLAIR Yes, in troth, I am a little that way inclined, but my   80
spark is indeed too far from your Cassandra rules;° his mistresses
are neither angels nor goddesses. Truly, Sir Francis Wildlove is too
mad even for me; though the devil's in it, I can't forbear thinking of
the rambler.°

BELLINDA Your virtue and beauty may reclaim him.   85

MRS BEAUCLAIR It may be so, but I doubt he don't like reforming so
well as to try it.

        Enter Sir Charles Beauclair

Ha!

> See who appears, comely as rising day,
> Amidst ten thousand eminently known.°   90

Bellinda, this heroic° is designed for you, though, somewhat barren of invention, I was forced to borrow it.

BELLINDA Cheerful, and thy mind at ease, happy girl.

SIR CHARLES (*taking Bellinda's hand*) My blessing.

BELLINDA My fate, which I should, but cannot curse.   95

SIR CHARLES Cousin,° I'm glad to find you here. You shall help persuade Bellinda to go abroad.° I have promised to bring you both to Mrs Bantum's. I have provided a trifle of a dinner, and excellent music for digestion. There's only a country gentleman and Sir Francis. I know you love Sir Francis, niece.   100

MRS BEAUCLAIR° You may be mistaken, sir. Grant I did, would you have me meet him? Dear uncle, don't make me so ridiculous.

SIR CHARLES I thought, niece, you durst have trusted me with your conduct.° My friends are no brainless beaux, no lady libellers, that extend innocent favours,° and bespatter the reputations they 105
cannot ruin.

MRS BEAUCLAIR Then you think your friend Sir Francis a very modest man.

SIR CHARLES No, my dear, but your wildest° men, if they have sense, as I am sure he has, know how to treat women of honour.   110

MRS BEAUCLAIR Nay, I'm soon convinced. What say you, madam?

BELLINDA I will go; for perhaps, Sir Charles, you think I've only invented fears of being known, but you'll surely find if any accident discovers me, I shall be seen by you no more.

SIR CHARLES See thee no more! Yes, I would see thee, though barred 115
by foreign or domestic foes. Set on thy side father or husband, on mine wife and children, I'd rush through all nature's ties to gaze on thee, to satisfy the longings of my soul, and please my fond desiring eyes.

BELLINDA Chide him, Beauclair; let him not talk thus.   120

MRS BEAUCLAIR Before he came, you were at it. What can I say to two mad folks?
        Enter Spendall

SPENDALL Your servant, ladies. Sir Charles, is it not dinner-time? I am as hungry as a ——

MRS BEAUCLAIR Horse. I know the old expression. Were I my uncle, 125
I'd as soon build a hospital° for the lazy as undertake to satisfy thy voracious appetite.

SIR CHARLES How hast thou of late disobliged my niece that she is so severe upon thee?

SPENDALL Only told her ladyship a truth she could not bear.

MRS BEAUCLAIR A truth from thee? I rather think I could not hear it.

SPENDALL I said a she-wit° was as great a wonder as a blazing star,° and as certainly foretold the world's turning upside down. Yet, spite of that, the lady will write.

MRS BEAUCLAIR Brute! What did I ever write, unless it was thy character, and that was so adroit,° you had like to° have hanged yourself?°

SIR CHARLES For my sake, cousin, forbear.

MRS BEAUCLAIR Let him take pet° and not come to dinner today, if he thinks fit; 'tis not I that care.

SPENDALL No, I will come.

MRS BEAUCLAIR That I would have sworn.

SPENDALL To give occasion that you may draw this shining weapon wit. It will dazzle the assembly;° if it pierces only me, no matter.

MRS BEAUCLAIR Stuff,° pshaw! Will you come, madam, and put on your things?

Exeunt Bellinda, Mrs Beauclair and Betty

SIR CHARLES Dear Spendall, I must beg of you to step to our house. I made my wife a kind of promise to dine with her today.

SPENDALL What shall I say?

SIR CHARLES Say I am gone to Court.° She loves the thoughts of being great, though most unfit for it.

SPENDALL But you know you promised to carry her daughter, Miss Peggy, with you next time you went thither.

SIR CHARLES True. Say I'm gone to the Tower.°

BELLINDA (*offstage*) Are you ready?

SIR CHARLES I'm called. Say anything the devil puts into your head.

Exit Sir Charles Beauclair

SPENDALL Yes, I shall say what the devil puts into my head, but not what you expect. Am I not then ungrateful? Has he not for several months fed, clothed, and supported me? But what for? To be a mere letter-carrier, an honourable pimp for platonic love? He shall find I can employ my parts better. He trusts me for his pleasure, and I'll betray him for mine.

Enter Lywell°

Ha, Lywell! Why come you hither?

LYWELL Foh, I saw Sir Charles and the ladies go out. Besides, I want

money. I did not serve you so, when I was in my Lord Worthy's
family.°

SPENDALL Prithee don't be so surly. Here's a crown° for thee, but I
expect some service for it. Is there ever a strumpet in your
catalogue so well bred as to write?   170

LYWELL All the whores in town can scrawl if that will do.

SPENDALL Let one of 'em send immediately a nameless letter to my
Lady Beauclair, and inform her that Sir Charles will be today at
Mrs Bantum's with a whore between three and four—by that hour,
lest she come too soon and disturb our dinner. Well, the heiress is   175
coming. I shall make thee amends.

LYWELL Ay, when you marry Mrs Beauclair.

SPENDALL Hang her. I hinted love but once, and she has abused me
ever since. I have no luck with the wits. Now I have better chase in
view, a wealthy fool, a fool, the perquisite° of a sharper. Come with 180
me, and I'll instruct you further.

Exeunt

1.3

[*Flywife's apartment*]°
Enter Mrs Flywife and Jenny

MRS FLYWIFE O how happy am I, to breathe again my native London
air! I vow the smoke of this dear town delights me more than all the
Indian groves. Happy, too, in meeting with one like thee; thou
understand'st intrigues, art cunning, subtle, as all our sex ought to
be who deal with those deluders, men.   5

JENNY Then your ladyship liked not the Indies.

MRS FLYWIFE How was't possible I should? Our beaux was the refuse
of Newgate,° and our merchants the offspring of foolish plodding
cits.

JENNY Why went you, madam?   10

MRS FLYWIFE So great is my opinion of your faith,° I dare trust you
with all my past life. My friends bred me at a boarding-school, and
died when I was but fourteen, leaving me nothing for my portion°
but pride and a few tawdry clothes. I was a forward° girl, and,
bartering what I had not the wit to prize, a never-to-be-recovered   15
fame, was soon maintained in finery, idleness, and darling pleasure.° But the deceitful town grew weary of me sooner than I

expected, and I, sick of that, seeing other new faces preferred before me. So, picking up some moneys, and a handsome garb, I ventured to Jamaica.   20

JENNY Madam, I hear my master unlock his study.

MRS FLYWIFE Oh heavens! And this foolish story put Sir Francis Wildlove's letter quite out of my mind. Have you writ as I directed?

JENNY Yes, madam.

MRS FLYWIFE Give me the letter and be gone. I would not have him   25
think us great.°

> *Exit Jenny. Enter Flywife. As Mrs Flywife goes to put up the*
> *letter hastily, she drops it*

Come, Fubby,° will you go into the dining room? The chocolate is ready.

FLYWIFE And you, methinks, are ready, too, madam. Beyond sea 'twas a courted favour,° dressed seldom, and careless; but, since arrived   30
at this damned town, no cost nor pains is spared. Curse upon my doting folly that listened to your prayers and, spite of my oath and strong aversion,° brought you back to the high road of hell.°

MRS FLYWIFE Is then my tried constancy suspected? Did I for this deny the richest planters of the place, who courted me in an honest,   35
lawful way,° and would have parted with their wealth, dearer than their souls, to have called me wife, whilst I, slighting all their offers, gave up my unsullied bloom to you, only on your protested love,° leaving Jamaica, fled with you to a remoter world, because you said your circumstance was such that, if you lived with me, your English   40
friends must believe you dead?°

FLYWIFE Well, and what was my return to all this boasted kindness? You may remember, madam, your cargo was sunk so low,° 'twould scarce afford at the next ship's approach another London topping;° when I, without a hated lock for life,° poured on ye more riches   45
than all your husband-pretenders joined together could aim at, gave you such a separate fortune° that, indeed, I was forced to obey your desires in coming into England, lest you should do't without my leave.

MRS FLYWIFE Well, well, thou art a good boy; prithee no more wran-   50
gling, Fubby. I vow and swear, tomorrow I'll be as great a slattern as ever was, if that will please you, so I will.°

FLYWIFE Ay, and want to go out today, for all the gazing fops to admire, though I have told you I can't appear till I have enquired into my affairs. Then tomorrow, if you stay at home with me,   55
sackcloth° will serve turn.

MRS FLYWIFE Lord, you are so froppish. If I was your wife, sure, Fubby, you would not be so jealous.

FLYWIFE My wife, quotha! No, no, I was once bewitched, but I found such a plague that—No more wives, I say.   60

MRS FLYWIFE Well, I'll be anything to please Fubby. Will you go in? Our breakfast will be cold.

FLYWIFE I'll follow you.

    Exit Mrs Flywife

Ha! What's here? (*Takes up the letter*) A sonnet,° I'll warrant. Her gaping abroad has brought this. A letter of her own; only the hand°   65
is scrawled to disguise it. (*Reads*) 'If I were convinced your passion was real, perhaps you might have no cause to complain.'—Fine advancing devil!—'Be constant and discreet; you'll find none of our sex ungrateful.' By thy burning lust, that's a damned lie, for thou art thyself a most ungrateful jilt. I'll catch her now, ere the devil can   70
be at her elbow to invent a lie, and if one wheedling tongue does not destroy all my senses, she shall feel my rage.

    Enter Servant

SERVANT Sir, the captain comes to bring you news your ship is safe in the river.

FLYWIFE Be damned, there let it sink.   75

SERVANT Shall I tell him so, sir?

FLYWIFE Jackanapes, I'll come to him.

    Exit Servant

Is it possible in nature to be happy with or without a woman? If they are virtuous, they are peevish, ill-natured, proud and coy;

       If fair and complaisant, they please as well,   80
       For then, by heaven, they are false as hell.

    [*Exit*]

2.1

[*Flywife's apartment*]
Enter Mrs Flywife and Jenny

MRS FLYWIFE Ha, ha, ha! I can't forebear laughing at your great concern.

JENNY O madam, if you did but see what a passion my master was in, you would not be so merry. He was like to beat the sea-captain, though he brought him the good news of his ship's arrival.   5

MRS FLYWIFE Foh! Mind what I say, and fear not. I warrant you shall have the letter again, and liberty to find Sir Francis Wildlove with it.

JENNY Madam, he comes.

MRS FLYWIFE Well, well, be sure you do it handsomely. (*Sings*)

> *Never, never let her be your wife.*°   10

That was loud that he might think me merry. Speak, hussy.
Enter Flywife

JENNY (*crying*) Pray, madam, search again. I have been a month of writing on't, and took it out of a book, too. The man has sent me forty, before I could make shift° to answer one till now. Oh! Oh!

MRS FLYWIFE Prithee don't tease° me. I dropped it. 'Tis gone. I'll   15
write another for you, since you say the man is for a husband and can so well maintain you. Be quiet.

FLYWIFE (*aside*) What's this? Faith, not improbable. 'Tis not my damsel's hand, now I have considered on't again.

JENNY I had rather have lost my best petticoat by half.   20

MRS FLYWIFE Cease your noise, or leave the room.

FLYWIFE What's the matter? (*Aside*) Having no occasion for a quarrel will be money in my pocket,° I am sure.

MRS FLYWIFE Why, Fubby, this foolish wench, it seems, has a country lover, and begged of me to direct a letter to him, which in troth I   25
have lost, so she howls. That's all, Fubby.

FLYWIFE And I have found it. Come, Jenny, to make amends for your sorrow, I'll write the superscription. Whither is it to go?

JENNY (*aside to Mrs Flywife*) Madam, madam.

MRS FLYWIFE Oh, I think I remember. To Geoffrey Scatterlove, at the   30
Bull-Inn in Cambridge. So seal it and carry it,° for these silly girls never think it safe, unless they give it into the post-house° themselves, but make haste.

JENNY Have I got thee again, my dear sweet letter? (*Kissing it*)
　　　[*Exit Jenny*]
MRS FLYWIFE A very raw foolish girl this, my dear.　　　　　　　　　35
FLYWIFE Faith, Puggy,° there had like to have been a quarrel; I was
　　almost afraid that letter was a piece of gallantry of yours.
MRS FLYWIFE Ay, ay, you are always suspecting me, when heaven
　　knows I am such a poor constant fool, I never so much as dream of
　　any man but my own dear Fubby. [*Flywife tries to steal an embrace*]　40
　　Fubby, let I go.
FLYWIFE No, no, I'll run away. I won't hear you, I won't hear you!
　　　Exit [*Flywife*]
MRS FLYWIFE Then I'll follow, and I am sure prevail. Oh, had my sex
　　but half my cunning, the deceivers would find themselves deceived;
　　from my gallants I never found, but gave 'em, killing charms.　　　45
　　　　Fools! when we love, our liberties we lose;
　　　　But when beloved, with ease we pick and choose.

　　　Exit

2.2

[*Sir Charles Beauclair's house*]°
Enter Lady Beauclair and Cheatall
LADY BEAUCLAIR Brother, I say you're a fool.
CHEATALL Fool in your face! I'm no more a fool than yourself. What
　　would you have a man do? Must I ravish her? Don't I know acces-
　　sories have been hanged; and here you'd have me principal!°
　　What,° I understand law; I won't hang for your pleasure.　　　　　5
LADY BEAUCLAIR Yes, you understand law. D'ye understand parting
　　with a good estate, which you must do if you han't this Arabella?
　　Don't tell me of ne—ne—necessaries,° I say you shall marry her.
CHEATALL Ay, but the craft will be in catching, as the saying is.° Why,
　　I went but e'en now to take her by the lily-white hand, as the poet　　10
　　has it,° and she threw a whole dish of scalding hot tea full in my
　　face, dish and all. Cousin Peggy saw her. She called her all the
　　names in Christendom; she'll tell ye the same.
LADY BEAUCLAIR Ah poor Peggy! Ay, she don't love to see you
　　abused. Were that minx like Peggy, you were but too happy. Well,　15
　　when will you give Peggy that diamond necklace? The sparks are

almost mad for her; she has the lord knows how many sweethearts.
There's Squire—what d'ye call him?

CHEATALL (*aside*) So, now she's got upon her daughter's sweethearts.
She'll ne'er have done!   20

LADY BEAUCLAIR There's Sir John Empty, and Mr Flutter, and Captain Noisy,° say the finest things to her, but the wench is so coy, and
my rogue of a husband will let none of 'em come home to her, but
calls 'em fops, and boars; and the lord knows what.

CHEATALL O lord, 'boars!' Beaux, you mean. O lord, 'boars!'   25

LADY BEAUCLAIR Well, she has of all sorts; and if there be twenty
women in company, all the rout° is made about her. And the girl
doth so blush; I vow and swear it makes her look woundy
handsome.

CHEATALL Ay, you called me fool, but I'll be hanged if ye don't make   30
a fool of her. Mark the end on't.° Marry her to some honest
tradesman, that's fittest for her.

LADY BEAUCLAIR Pray don't you trouble your musty pate about her.
No, she scorns a citizen.° She would not have my Lord Mayor's
son.° She's a girl of discretion. I was married young, too, and I   35
looked after all my first husband's affairs.

CHEATALL (*aside*) True, till he went the lord knows whither to be
quiet.

LADY BEAUCLAIR Indeed this young fellow° is not worthy the name
of a husband. I have a good mind to let the world know what a   40
deceitful piece 'tis.

Enter Peggy, eating plum-cake

PEGGY Mother! Mother!

LADY BEAUCLAIR What's the matter, child?

PEGGY Here's Mrs Arabella does nothing but jeer and abuse me. She
says eating between meals will spoil my shape, and I snatched a   45
book out of her hand, and she said a primer° was fitter for me.

LADY BEAUCLAIR I'll never endure this. How dare she affront my
daughter?

CHEATALL So, I'm like to have a fine life, nothing but scolding and
noise. For my part, I'd rather not marry at all. If she is thus randy   50
beforehand, what will she be afterwards? In a short time I shall
be made ballads on, and my picture set before 'em just like the
summons to horn-fair.°

LADY BEAUCLAIR Yes, yes, you shall marry her, and we'll tame her,
too, I'll warrant you.   55

PEGGY Here she comes, here she comes, as mad as a turkey-cock.

Enter Arabella

ARABELLA Why am I used thus? Your servants are forbid to call me either coach or chair.° Are you my jailer? You, oaf, I speak to.

CHEATALL Mistress, 'twould be better for you if you had other words in your mouth, I'll tell you that.   60

PEGGY You shan't gallop your—

LADY BEAUCLAIR Hold, Peggy, let me speak.—What's the reason, Mrs Arabella, you take this privilege here? You know your fortune is at our dispose.° So shall your person be, else you must expect nothing.   65

ARABELLA Had I but heard your characters, I'd sooner have been exposed a beggar in this inhospitable world, than e'er set my feet within your doors.

LADY BEAUCLAIR I'd have you to know our corectors° are honest corectors; I wish yours prove so.   70

CHEATALL Don't provoke me, I say, don't.

ARABELLA Why? You won't beat me.—I hear there is a sensible man amongst ye; I'll appeal to him, if you'd let me see him.

LADY BEAUCLAIR That's my husband you mean. No, you shan't see him, nor such as you are,° if I can help it.   75

PEGGY What, would you see my vather-in-law,° to tell lies and stories to him? No, no, don't mistake yourself.

ARABELLA Away, you smell of *aqua mirabilis.*

LADY BEAUCLAIR Oh impudence! She smell of strong waters! She hates it.—Come hither, Peggy, let me smell. Thy breath used to be   80
as sweet as any cow's.

PEGGY (*aside*) What shall I do? I've been at my mother's bottle. [*To Lady Beauclair*] I won't come to satisfy her, nor you neither. [*To Arabella*] What ails ye, d'ye know?

ARABELLA No, don't, miss.—Well, since I must have neither attend-   85
ance nor conveniency,° I'll go a-foot. (*Arabella is going*)

CHEATALL (*takes Arabella by the arm*) Hold ye, hold ye, you are not gone yet, as the saying is.

ARABELLA Was ever usage like this?

LADY BEAUCLAIR Your usage has been but too good, let me tell you   90
that; I'll show you such usage as you deserve. [*Calling offstage*] Hug—Uggun—° What a devil is your name? I hate a wench with a hard name.

Enter Eugenia

Here, lock up Mrs Flippant° in the dark room.

PEGGY (*jumping about*) Ay, lock her up, lock her up, I say.   95

CHEATALL (*grinning in Arabella's face*) Yet, Mrs Bella, be ruled by me. Give me one sweet look, and let me take a honey kiss, and you shan't be locked up. No, you shan't be locked up, but go abroad with me, and have your bellyful of cakes and custards. Shall I? Shall I?

ARABELLA There's the kiss. (*Strikes Cheatall*) And for a look, I wish   100
my eyes were basilisks.

PEGGY O lord, mother, how she swears!

CHEATALL Oh, my chops, my chops! Lock her up; hang her! She's a Fury.

LADY BEAUCLAIR Abominable! Come hither, hath she hurt ye?   105

ARABELLA [*aside to Eugenia*] Oh Eugenia! Last night, when you heard my story, you, in gentle pity, wept. Assist me now, or I'm lost.

EUGENIA [*aside to Arabella*] Have patience, madam, and believe me yours.

LADY BEAUCLAIR (*aside to Cheatall*) I say, keep the key yourself, I   110
don't like her greatness with the maid.

CHEATALL 'Tis locking up. I fear 'tis against law, sister.

LADY BEAUCLAIR Foh, I fear nothing. Are not you a squire, and rich? You're above the leaw.°

CHEATALL Ay, but knights have been hanged. I dread hanging; I   115
tremble always when I think on't.

LADY BEAUCLAIR Hanged! There's no danger of being hanged. What, ha' ye no courage?

CHEATALL Yes, I have courage, and that she shall find. My injuries, as I have read it, steel my eyes.°—Mrs Arabella, I could swear the   120
peace against you, and have you before a justice, but I will spare you the shame and punish you myself. Come along.

ARABELLA Resistance is in vain; but I will be revenged, or kill myself.

CHEATALL Ay, ay, kill yourself, and then I shall have your estate, without being troubled with your person. I'll humble you.   125

ARABELLA And heaven punish thee.

CHEATALL Don't trouble your musty pate about heaven (as my sister says), but come along.

PEGGY Away with her, away with her.

ARABELLA I take heaven and earth to witness, I believe you design to   130
murder me.

CHEATALL There's no such design. Besides, your witnesses are not valid; I never heard their evidence go in any trial in all my life.

LADY BEAUCLAIR No, it is not to murder ye, but make ye better. No more words, but let it be done.   135

Exeunt Cheatall, Arabella and Eugenia

PEGGY I'm glad she's to be locked up; for, had any gentlemen come to see me, she's so pert, her tongue would ha' been running.

Enter Cheatall with a key, Gentil and Eugenia

CHEATALL Here I have her double locked, i'faith neither window nor mousehole in the room. Gentil, fetch my cloak. I'll to my lawyer Mr Cobblecase,° for my mind misgives me plaguily.   140

GENTIL Shall I wait on you, sir?

CHEATALL No, no, stay at home, and if anyone asks for Mrs Arabella, say she does not lodge here.

GENTIL Yes.

CHEATALL B'w'y, sister.   145

LADY BEAUCLAIR Your journey is needless; but you may go if you will. And, d'ye hear, ask Mr Cobblecase to come and dine here. He's a bachelor. You should always be thinking of Peggy.

CHEATALL Well, well.

Exit [Cheatall]

PEGGY O mother, yonder's Mr Spendall a-coming. He's grown very   150
fine of late.

LADY BEAUCLAIR Ay, if he would leave your vather's company, and make out° what he says about his entailed estate, the man is not to be despised.

Enter Spendall

SPENDALL My Lady Beauclair, your most humble. Dear pretty crea-   155
ture, yours. [*Spendall kisses Peggy*]

LADY BEAUCLAIR Lord, Mr Spendall, what d'ye do? Well, I wonder Peg endures it. I'll vow and swear, Mr Spendall, knights presume no farther than to kiss the tip of my daughter's little finger, and you make nothing of her lips.   160

SPENDALL How! Make nothing of 'em! Pardon me, madam, I put 'em to the use nature designed. They are as sweet as—and as soft as— gad, I must taste 'em again to raise my fancy.

PEGGY Be quiet, let me alone, Mr Spendall.

SPENDALL (*singing*)

> Oh, give your sweet temptations o'er,   165
> I'll taste those dangerous lips no more.°

LADY BEAUCLAIR You're a strange man. But come, sing us a song of your own. Husband says you can make varses.°

PEGGY But let it be as like that as you can, for methinks that is very
pretty.   170

SPENDALL (*aside*) Does the fool think I shall make it extempore?

However, I have one pretty near it, as it happens. [*To Lady Beauclair and Peggy*] I'll rather expose myself° than not endeavour to divert you, madam.° (*Sings, whilst Lady Beauclair and Peggy imitate his gestures*) 175

> At dead of night, when wrapped in sleep
>   The peaceful cottage lay,
> Pastora° left her folded° sheep,
> Her garland, crook, and needless scrip.°
>   Love led the nymph astray. 180
>
> Loose° and undressed° she takes her flight
>   To a near myrtle-shade:°
> The conscious° moon gave splendid light,
> To bless the ravished lover's sight
>   And gain the loving maid. 185
>
> His eager arms the nymph embrace,
>   And, to assuage the pain,
> His restless passion he obeys;
> At such an hour, in such a place,
>   – What lover could contain?° 190
>
> In vain she called the conscious moon,
>   The moon no succour gave;
> The cruel stars, unmoved, looked on,
> And seemed to wink at what was done,
>   Nor would her humour° save. 195
>
> Vanquished at last by powerful love,
>   The nymph expiring° lay.
> No more she sighed, no more she strove,
> Since no kind stars were found above.
>   She blushed and died away.° 200
>
> Yet blessed° the grove, her happy flight,
>   And youth that did betray.
> And, panting, dying with delight,
> She blessed the kind transporting night
>   And cursed approaching day. 205

LADY BEAUCLAIR Thank ye; 'tis very fine, I'll vow and swear.
PEGGY So 'tis indeed, mother.
LADY BEAUCLAIR Now, to leave fooling, where's my husband?
SPENDALL I know not. I han't seen him these two days.° [*Producing a letter*] Here my father writes to me, if I will take up°—that's the old 210

23

man's expression—and find a virtuous woman with a fortune, he will give me three thousand pounds down, and settle eight hundred a year. And, faith, I am trying to obey the rich cuff, and wean myself from my old friends and the dear bottle.

LADY BEAUCLAIR Ay, you do very well, Mr Spendall; I should be   215
overjoyed to see you take up, and perhaps a fortune may be found. I'll say no more. But a thorough reformation will produce strange matters, matters I little thought of. But I'll say no more.

SPENDALL Your ladyship must not say a word of this to Sir Charles, for then he'll forbid me the sight of this dear creature, whose   220
charms alone have power to work the mentioned reformation.

LADY BEAUCLAIR No, no, fear not that; I han't so many friends to go the ready way to lose 'em.°

PEGGY For my part, I don't love vather so well to tell him anything of us.   225

Enter Boy with a letter

BOY Madam, here's a penny-post letter to your ladyship.

LADY BEAUCLAIR To me!

PEGGY I warrant 'tis to me, from some spark.

LADY BEAUCLAIR Stand away, hussy. 'Tis durrected to my—my Lady Beauclair.°   230

[*Exit Boy*]

What's this? [*Reading with difficulty*] Mrs Banter's, the Indian house?°—Read it, Mr Spendall. Some mischief, I believe.

SPENDALL (*reads*) 'Though unknown, I cannot forbear, in justice to your ladyship's merit, informing you that Sir Charles, at four o'clock, will be with a mistress, at Mrs Bantum's. Use your   235
discretion, but assure yourself it is a truth.'

LADY BEAUCLAIR O the villain, the rogue! The confounded whore! I'll tear his and her eyes out. Always at home he's sick, his head aches, and he must lie alone. Ah, Mr Spendall, if I should tell you the naked truth, you'd say he was a villain, too. I've often told him his   240
own with tears,° and the brazen-faced villain has forsworn° it. My husband with a whore! I have no patience; I'll go there immediately and stay till he comes.

PEGGY Ay, do, mother, and I'll go with you, and help to pull their eyes out.   245

SPENDALL Are you both mad? Why, all there love Sir Charles to that degree they'd watch and turn him back;° you'd never conceal your passion. Your only way is to come after the hour, and then you'll certainly surprise 'em.

LADY BEAUCLAIR That's true; well, good Mr Spendall, stay and com-   250
fort me. I fear I shall have my fits, and then no two men can hold
me.

SPENDALL I would with all my heart, and esteem myself happy to
serve you. But my father has sent me twenty guineas for a token;
and if I don't go this minute, the man will be gone out of town, and   255
carry 'em back with him.

LADY BEAUCLAIR Nay, that is not to be neglected.—Come, child, we'll
go to my cousin Prattle's and tell her this news. My husband with a
whore! I cannot bear it.

SPENDALL I must seize a kiss, else I shall faint before I see you again.   260

PEGGY Pish, pish, I think the man's distracted.

LADY BEAUCLAIR Is this a time, and my husband with a whore! I wish
my nails were twice as long for her sake.—Ah child, thy vather was
anotherguess man than this, though he had faults, too. Come away.
Your servant, Mr Spendall.   265

PEGGY Your servant, sir.

LADY BEAUCLAIR My husband with a whore!

SPENDALL Ladies, your most obedient slave.

   Exeunt Lady Beauclair and Peggy

Thus far affairs go on as I could wish. Now if my lady does but
abuse Bellinda till it come to parting between Sir Charles and she,   270
then, my miss being out of his tuition,° I fear not her falling into
mine. She's damned silly; I am forced to let all courtship lie in
kissing, for she understands a compliment no more than algebra.
Well, her wealth makes it up. Now for dinner.

   Exit

2.3

St James's Park°
Enter Sir Charles Beauclair, Bellinda and Mrs Beauclair

MRS BEAUCLAIR This walk i'the park has done me good.

BELLINDA 'Twas very refreshing.

MRS BEAUCLAIR Is not this better now, dear Bellinda, than reading
and sighing away every beauteous morning?

BELLINDA Yes, if at each gazer the conscious blushes would forbear to   5
rise. If I could look upon this object of my love and virtue, [and] not
shrink back, it were true happiness.

SIR CHARLES My lovely charmer, let me call this day mine, and oblige you to be cheerful.

MRS BEAUCLAIR I warrant ye, by and by we'll be as merry as the—you know the title° that sticks ahand,° uncle—ha, yonder's Sir Francis Wildlove, for heaven's sake step behind the trees, whilst I clap on my mask, and prowl towards Rosamond's Pond,° and he, no doubt, pursues.

BELLINDA You will not, sure.

MRS BEAUCLAIR Indeed, my dear gravity, I will. That is, with your leave, sir.

SIR CHARLES Well, thou art a mad girl, but I dare trust thee. Come this way, madam.

Exeunt [Sir Charles Beauclair and Bellinda.] Mrs Beauclair [puts on her mask and] crosses the stage, Sir Francis Wildlove following at a distance

SIR FRANCIS What's there? A woman well-shaped, well-dressed, masked and alone! How many temptations has the devil tacked together for a poor frail mortal that scarce needed half a one! [*Mrs Beauclair drops her handkerchief*] The handkerchief dropped, a fair invitation. [*Mrs Beauclair retrieves her handkerchief*] A deuce take her agility, she has been too nimble for me. However, I'll venture. [*To Mrs Beauclair*] Madam, by your remaining, when the whole army of beauties are retired, I should guess you pickeer for a particular prize.°

MRS BEAUCLAIR Then I suppose you have vanity enough to think your well-rigged pinnace° worth securing.

SIR FRANCIS Faith, child, I hope you would not find the freight° disagreeable.

MRS BEAUCLAIR Now I could not have thought such a hopeful, proper gentleman would have been straggling in the park this hour.° What, no lady of quality,° nor miss° that appears like one, to lead out today? No assignation? Or is the plague upon your fine clothes, credit out,° and pocket empty?

SIR FRANCIS° Shall I tell you the truth?

MRS BEAUCLAIR Yes, if you can find in your heart.

SIR FRANCIS Why then, faith, I have an appointment, and that with ladies, nay, and music. Yet if you'll be kind, my dear chicken, they shall wait for me in vain. (*Coming nearer her*) By heaven, a charming side face.°

MRS BEAUCLAIR Stand off, or I vanish. But tell me what makes you so indifferent to your first engagement? The women are old, I suppose.

26

SIR FRANCIS Alas, very buds,° my dear.

MRS BEAUCLAIR Ugly, then.

SIR FRANCIS Beautiful as angels.

MRS BEAUCLAIR What can be the matter?

SIR FRANCIS Don't you guess? Why, they are virtuous. I have a mis- 50
tress there, confound me if I am not damnably in love with her, and
yet could never get myself in a vein serious enough to say one dull,
foolish, modest thing to her.

MRS BEAUCLAIR Poor gentleman, suppose you practiced before you
went, and fancied me the lady. 55

SIR FRANCIS A match.°

MRS BEAUCLAIR With arms across.°

SIR FRANCIS And the looks of an ass, I begin. 'Ah madam!' How was
that sigh?

MRS BEAUCLAIR Pretty well. 60

SIR FRANCIS 'Behold the humblest of your slaves; see the martyr of
your frowns. Those arms must heal the wounds your eyes have
made, or else I die. They must, they must.' (*Rushing upon her*)

MRS BEAUCLAIR Hold, hold! (*Unmasking*) Sir Charles, Sir Charles!
Here I shall be ravished in the open park! 65

SIR FRANCIS O heavens! Mrs Beauclair!

Enter Sir Charles Beauclair and Bellinda

SIR CHARLES Why, how now, Frank! In raptures before the face of the
world and the sun?

SIR FRANCIS Pshaw, I do confess I am caught.

BELLINDA If you had come to any harm, madam, you might have 70
thanked yourself.

MRS BEAUCLAIR (*aside*) No great harm neither, to have a hearty hug
from the man one loves.

SIR FRANCIS Madam, I humbly ask your pardon.

MRS BEAUCLAIR It is easily granted; 'twas a frolic of my own 75
beginning.

SIR FRANCIS This generosity wholly subdues my wandering heart.

MRS BEAUCLAIR Have a care of getting into the dull, foolish, modest
road, Sir Francis.

[*Mrs Beauclair and Bellinda put on their masks*]

SIR FRANCIS No more of that, dear madam. 80

SIR CHARLES Come, I believe dinner stays.° Where's your friend Mr
Beaumont?

SIR FRANCIS He'll be there before us.

SIR CHARLES Let's to our chairs; I dare say the ladies are tired.

27

BELLINDA Truly I am.   8

    Enter Jenny, and pulls Sir Francis by the sleeve; he steps aside
    with her

JENNY Sir, the lady that came lately from the Indies, whom you have
seen at the play, sends you this. [*Giving him a letter*] The oddness of
the superscription she'll explain to you.

SIR FRANCIS O the charming angel! Dear girl, accept my acknowledgement,° and step behind those trees whilst I lead my mother and   90
aunt into their chairs. I'll be with you in a moment.

    [*Jenny withdraws*]

MRS BEAUCLAIR [*aside, having watched Sir Francis and Jenny together*]
O the wretched libertine! But to take notice on't would show too
much concern.

SIR CHARLES Sir Francis, where are you?   95

SIR FRANCIS Here, at your elbow, Sir Charles. Madam, may I presume
to lead you to your chair?

MRS BEAUCLAIR Yes, sir, though I believe, as your affairs stand, you
could 'bate the ceremony.°

SIR FRANCIS The greatest affairs in Christendom should not hinder   100
me from waiting on your ladyship.

    Exeunt Sir Charles Beauclair, Sir Francis Wildlove, Mrs
    Beauclair and Bellinda. Enter Jenny

JENNY No, faith, they are not of the shape of motherly and elderly
aunts. I'll not stay here, but watch where they go, and tell my lady
what a rambler she has chose.

    Exit

2.4

    A house°
    Enter Mrs Flywife

MRS FLYWIFE So, with much coaxing, I have got my jealous fellow to
let me go out this afternoon, on the pretence of buying things, and
seeing an old aunt. If this wench would come and tell me where the
mad spark will be, I'll venture to give him the meeting.

    Enter Jenny

Have you found him?   5

JENNY Yes, madam, but I perceive he's a sad wild man. He was
engaged with two masks,° and would fain have flammed me off

'twas his mother, but I saw by their mien and dress they were
young.

MRS FLYWIFE What said he to you? 10

JENNY Seemed much pleased, but shy.° Bid me stay, and promised to
return presently. I thought I should do your ladyship more service
in seeing where they went; so I dogged 'em to Mrs Bantum's, our
neighbour, and housed 'em° all there.

MRS FLYWIFE Very good; and, by and by, I'll to Locket's,° and send 15
for him. I fancy I know the gentleman's humours so well, that he'll
certainly forsake old acquaintance for those of a newer date, though
he ventures changing for the worse. He seemed eager and pleased,
fierce and fond, and swore my charms were unequalled. His
swearing indeed signifies but little, the banquet o'er.° 20

      Yet sure he'll meet when Love and I invite,
      For Love's his god, and leads him to delight.

   [*Exeunt*]

3.1

[*Sir Charles Beauclair's lodgings*]
Enter Eugenia, followed by Gentil

GENTIL Whither so fast, Mrs Eugenia?

EUGENIA Stop me not. I am upon an act of charity, trying to free the immured lady. I have been picking up all the rusty keys in the house in hopes to accomplish it.

GENTIL Why, you'll lose your place. 5

EUGENIA Hang my place. There's not one in the family understands a grain of civility, except Sir Charles; and if he speaks to me, my lady pulls my headclothes° off.—Come, I know you don't love that lubberly coxcomb, your master. E'en join with me, assist in Arabella's liberty, and recover her fortune, and I dare engage she'll make ours. 10 Besides, to tell you the truth, I have received ten guineas today, from one Mr Beaumont, to endeavour her freedom.

GENTIL That's a most prevailing argument, I confess. What I do is for your sake, Mrs Eugenia.

EUGENIA In hopes to go snacks with° the gold. Ha, Gentil! Well, well, 15 stay here; I'll return immediately.

Exit Eugenia. Enter Eugenia with Arabella

'Tis done, 'tis done. Is this a bird to be concealed in such a dark and dismal cage?

ARABELLA Well, thou art a rare girl. O if thou couldst but conjure now, and get the writings of my estate° for me, five hundred pound 20 should be thy own next moment, wench.

GENTIL Say you so, madam? Gad, I'll turn devil, but it shall be done.

EUGENIA Why, what would that signify to you, fool?

GENTIL Well, mind the lady's business, and let me alone° to take care 25 of yours.

EUGENIA First let us take care of the squire. Gad, if I don't manage that booby, I'll give you leave to cut my apron, and make a slobbering bib on't.°

ARABELLA° Well, what's your contrivance? 30

EUGENIA Why, I'll go in again, pour down a bottle of red ink I know of, make all fast,° and swear he has murdered ye. A cross old woman lately, to whom he would give nothing, told him she read it in his phiz that he would come to be hanged, which the superstitious fool

has ever since been afraid of. Very indifferent° circumstances will   35
confirm that fear, and bring him to a compliance.

ARABELLA My better angel! It has a lucky face. It looks like thee. But
how must I be disposed of?

EUGENIA If you please to go to Mrs Beauclair's, Sir Charles's niece,
she's a woman cheerful, witty, and good, and will assist you in   40
everything.

ARABELLA I've heard so well of her, I dare venture to be obliged to her.
Come, let's make haste.

EUGENIA Gentil, get the back door open, and let none of the servants
see us go out. I'm sure we shall be lucky, because my termagant   45
lady won't be at home today to disturb us.

ARABELLA Come then. I long to quit the house I have been so ill used in.
Exeunt

3.2

The India House
Enter Sir Francis Wildlove

SIR FRANCIS A deuce of all ill luck! I have lost my little ambassadress
from my dear Indian queen;° 'twas a charmer. How can an old
curmudgeon have the impudence to hope he should keep such a
lovely creature to himself? For a husband or cully, I find by her
discourse, she has; and by the description, she hates him, which is a   5
good step for me.

Enter Searchwell

SEARCHWELL Sir, all the company is coming into this room to hear the
music.

SIR FRANCIS Gadso, are they? Then I must wait upon Mrs Beauclair
down. Sirrah, you are a purblind dog not to find the pretty letter-   10
carrier.

SEARCHWELL I think I see a woman as soon as another; else I'm sure
I were not fit for your honour's service. I'll swear she was not
in the park; I searched it three times over as carefully as° I had
been to look a needle in a bottle of hay,° and hanged if I did not   15
find it.

SIR FRANCIS What a comparison the puppy has! D'ye hear, if you do
not find her out, I shall discard you for° an insignificant blockhead,
for I am damnably and desperately in love with her mistress.

Exit Sir Francis Wildlove

SEARCHWELL Ah lard,° ah lard, desperately and damnably in love   2
with her, and never saw her but twice at a play, and then she was in
a mask. Well, my master would be the best of men if 'twere not for
these whores. I am harassed off my legs after 'em; the pox, the
plague that belongs to 'em, consume 'em all I say.

*Exit [Searchwell]. Enter Sir Charles Beauclair, Sir Francis
Wildlove, Beaumont, Spendall, Bellinda and Mrs Beauclair°*

SIR CHARLES Ladies, how d'ye like your small regalo?°   2

MRS BEAUCLAIR Extremely; for aught I know, Sir Charles,° you may
repent showing me the way to gad abroad.

BELLINDA What opinion, madam, do you think this gentleman will
have of us, for I presume the young ladies in the country are not so
free of their company?°   3

MRS BEAUCLAIR No, poor gentlewomen. They are condemned to the
government of some toothless aunt or grannum, visit but once a
year, and that in the summer season,° when the heat covers the
ruddy lasses with sweat and dust. The winter they divert themselves with blindman's buff among the servingmen; where, too   3
often, one sprucer than the rest whispers love to Miss Jenny, and
seduces even the eldest daughter.

BEAUMONT Though some have been guilty of those weaknesses, you
must not accuse all.

MRS BEAUCLAIR All who are confined there, never suffered to see the   4
world. For, granting one more thinking than the rest,° who has
power° and obeys her father in suffering the addresses of the next
adjacent squire, she either dies of a consumption,° pining after
pleasures more refined, or else, o'ercome with vapors, runs melancholy mad.   4

BEAUMONT (*to Bellinda*) Madam, you sighed at this pretty
description.

BELLINDA Did I?

BEAUMONT (*aside*) Both her deportment and face confirm my
suspicions.   5

SIR CHARLES You are thoughtful,° Frank.

MRS BEAUCLAIR Would you have him brisker,° uncle? 'Tis but my
clapping on a mask, and 'tis done. Sir Francis, do I wrong you?
Have I not seen you at a play slighting all the bare-faced beauties,
hunting a trollop in a mask with pains and pleasure? Nay, more: for   5
her gaping nonsensical banters neglecting immortal Dryden's°
eloquence, or Congreve's° unequalled wit.

SIR FRANCIS I own sometimes I divert myself with the little gypsies.

MRS BEAUCLAIR Ay, and disturb the audience.

SIR FRANCIS Faith, madam, I must speak freely. Though you are a   60
woman of quality and my friend's niece, you talk so prettily, 'tis
pity you should not do it often in a mask. But then again, you are so
pretty, 'tis pity you should ever wear one.

MRS BEAUCLAIR I did not design by railing° to beg a compliment. Sir
Charles, where's the music?   65

> [*Sir Charles signals for Musicians and Singers. Enter Musicians
> and Singers*]°

[SINGERS] [*perform*]

> *When I languished, and wished you would something bestow,*
> *   You bade me to give it a name;*
> *But, by heaven, I know it as little as you,*
> *   Though my ignorance passes for shame.*
> *You take for devotion each passionate glance,*   70
> *   And think the dull fool is sincere,*
> *But never believe that I speak in romance*
> *   On purpose to tickle your ear.*
> *To please me then more, think still I am true,*
> *   And hug each apocryphal text:*°   75
> *Though I practice a thousand false doctrines on you,*
> *   I shall still have enough for the next.*
>
> *   A dance*°

HE° *How long must I the hours employ*
> *   To see, be loved, yet ne'er enjoy?*
> *Though to curb loose desires I try,*   80
> *   Sure I may wish at least to die?*
> *Die then, poor Strephon,*° *wretched swain;*
> *   Nor only live to love in vain.*

SHE *Live, hopeless lover, while I grieve*
> *   Much for thy fate, but more for mine—*   85
> *For mine, my dear, condemned to live,*
> *   To love, be loved, yet ne'er be thine.*

HE *Oh, see me, love me, grieve me still,*
> *   Till love's excess, or sorrow's, kill.*
> *'Tis not myself I love, but thee;*   90
> *   Then I must die to set thee free.*

SHE *No, live and love, though hope is dead;*
> *   For 'tis a virtue so to love.*

>   *The gold's refined, the dross is fled.*
>   *The martyrs thus in flames improve.°*   95
> BOTH   *Then let us love on, and never complain,*
>   *But fan the kind fire, and bless the dear pain.*
>   *For why to despair should true lovers be driven?*
>   *Since Love has his martyrs, he must have his heaven.*

>   [*Exit Musicians and Singers*]

SPENDALL My Lady Beauclair will be here straight, I'll e'en march   100
off. (*Going*)

SIR CHARLES What, desert us, Jack! Though the ladies won't drink,
you may.

SPENDALL I beg your pardon, Sir Charles. I have made an assignation
with some women of quality of my acquaintance.   105

MRS BEAUCLAIR Women of quality! What, your laundress's daughter,
or some pert, fleering, tawdry thing of a shop, vain, and proud to
lose what she understands not, her reputation? She also brags she's
coming to quality when she meets you.

SPENDALL I shall not expose their names to convince your ladyship of 110
their rank.

BELLINDA Oh, by no means debar the gentleman of his quality.

SIR FRANCIS You see the ladies are willing to dismiss you, Jack.

SPENDALL I'm their very humble servant.

>   *Exit* [*Spendall.*] *Immediately after, enter Lady Beauclair,*
>   *pushing away a Servant-maid, and Peggy*

LADY BEAUCLAIR [*to Servant-maid*] Ye lie, ye damned quean; he is   115
here. Ha, and his minion with him! Let me come at her!

>   *Lady Beauclair leaps and catches hold of Bellinda*

SIR CHARLES Hell and furies! My wife!—Madam, why all this rage?
Don't you see my niece? The other is a friend of hers, a woman of
honour.

LADY BEAUCLAIR Your niece is a pimp, and she's a whore! I'll mark   120
her, sirrah. Villain! Oh, oh my fits! My fits!

>   *Lady Beauclair falls in a chair*

SIR CHARLES Fly, my Bellinda, from her brutal rage, whilst I,
wedlock's slave, stay and appease this hateful storm.

BELLINDA 'Tis but what I ought to have expected; 'tis just I should be
punished to prevent my being guilty.   125

SIR FRANCIS Dear Beaumont, carry this injured lady off, whilst we
bear the brunt.

MRS BEAUCLAIR Go to my lodgings, child.

BELLINDA Anywhere, to death or hell, if there can be a greater hell
than what this bosom feels.   130
    Exeunt Beaumont and Bellinda

PEGGY O lo! O lo! I believe my mother's dead.

SIR CHARLES You know the contrary; these fits are a new trick nature
has furnished the sex with. Heretofore tears and smiles were the
highest part their dissimulation could attain.
    *All this while Lady Beauclair has been faintly striving, as in a fit,
    and now shrieks out*

LADY BEAUCLAIR Oh! Oh!   135

MRS BEAUCLAIR Give her some water.

SIR CHARLES Give her some wine, else you'll disoblige her more, to
my knowledge, than the fits.

PEGGY (*aside*) And well thought on. I'll steal behind and drink a glass
of wine; my stomach's a-cold.   140
    *Peggy goes to the side-table, whilst Sir Charles, Sir Francis, and
    Mrs Beauclair are about Lady Beauclair's chair, and drinks two
    or three glasses of wine*

LADY BEAUCLAIR (*starting up*) No, villain, devil! I'll drink none of
your wine; it may be poisoned.

SIR CHARLES Oh, you had not lost all your senses; you could hear, I
find.

LADY BEAUCLAIR Rogue, and I'll make thee feel. I'll tear thy linen,°   145
hair, thy cursed eyes.

SIR CHARLES Hold, madam. As I'm a gentleman, use me like
one.

MRS BEAUCLAIR Sir Francis, here's an excellent argument on your
side. Here's matrimony in its true colours.   150

SIR FRANCIS No, madam, her carriage° is not a satire on the whole sex;
it but sets off better wives.

LADY BEAUCLAIR Yes, you were a gentleman, and that was all, when I
married ye, the poor third brother of a knight. 'Twas I brought
your estate.° If, since, by your friend's death one has fell,° must I be   155
abused, sirrah?

SIR CHARLES Madam, you have not been abused; you know that I was
in my nonage married, saw not with my own eyes, nor chose for my
unhappy self. Ere I lived with ye, I possessed an estate nobler, a
larger far than yours, which you have still commanded.° Nay, I have   160
often urged ye to diversions, in hopes it would have altered that
unquiet mind; but all in vain.

LADY BEAUCLAIR Divertions! What divartions? Yes, you had me to

the playhouse, and the first thing I saw was an ugly black devil kill
his wife, for nothing;° then your Metridate, King o' the Potecaries,°   165
your Timon the Atheist,° the Man in the Moon,° and all the rest.
Nonsense, stuff; I hate 'em.

SIR CHARLES I need say no more. Now, madam, you have shown
yourself.°

LADY BEAUCLAIR Shown? What have I shown? Send for your gillflirt   170
to show: I have shown nothing but a vartuous face.

MRS BEAUCLAIR All virtue does not lie in chastity, though that's a
great one.

LADY BEAUCLAIR Well cousin, I'm sorry to see you take such
courses;° I would not have my Peg like you for the varsal° world.   175
Peg! What a colour this child has got! Fretting for me, I'm afraid,
has put her into a fever.

SIR FRANCIS Come, madam, let's compose these differences; your
anger is groundless, upon my word.—Not well, pretty miss? Will
you drink a glass of wine?   180

   Peggy hiccups

PEGGY No, I thank you. I cannot abide it.

LADY BEAUCLAIR Poor girl, she never drinks anything strong, except
she's very sick indeed.

SIR CHARLES And she's very often sick, poor creature! About some
five or six times a day.—Madam, shall I wait on you home? I think   185
we may quit this place with shame enough.

PEGGY (*aside to Lady Beauclair*) Don't be friends, for Mr Spendall
sent me word he'd meet us in the park; and if vather goes with us,
how shall that be?

LADY BEAUCLAIR [*aside to Peggy*] I dan't intend it. [*To Sir Charles*]   190
No, hypocrite, you shan't stir a step with me. If thou dost, I'll make
a bigger noise below, and raise the house about thy ears. Come, Peg.

   Exeunt Lady Beauclair and Peggy

MRS BEAUCLAIR My aunt's noise is her guard; none dare approach
her.

SIR CHARLES Her going out can't be more ridiculous than her coming   195
in.

MRS BEAUCLAIR Sir Charles, let not your noble courage be cast down.

SIR CHARLES Outrageous clamours are no news to me, but I dread
how my Bellinda may resent it.

SIR FRANCIS I wonder, Sir Charles, you have patience to live with this   200
violent woman.

SIR CHARLES 'Tis for my fair one's sake, who, nicely jealous° the world would say she had occasioned our parting, has sworn never to see me more if I attempt it.

    Enter Searchwell

SEARCHWELL (*aside to Sir Francis*) Sir, sir, the lady you are so dam-   205
nably in love with sends word, if you disengage yourself from your company, she'll be at Locket's in half an hour.

MRS BEAUCLAIR Is it so, i'faith?

SIR FRANCIS (*to Searchwell*) Coxcomb, what need you ha' spoke so loud? [*Aloud*] Tell him I'll not fail to wait on him.   210

    [*Exit Searchwell*]

– Well, Sir Charles, you'll to Bellinda.

SIR CHARLES No, I'll first go home, and try to stop the farther fury of my wife.

SIR FRANCIS [*To Mrs Beauclair*] Madam, I had hopes you would have done me the honour to let me wait on you this afternoon. But it has   215
happened so unluckily that an old uncle of mine, to whom I am much obliged—

MRS BEAUCLAIR (*aside to Sir Francis*) Oh, I'm your uncle's servant. Sir, there needs no excuse, your company being at this time a favour I neither expect nor desire.   220

SIR CHARLES Will you go in a chair, niece, or in my coach?

MRS BEAUCLAIR A chair if you please, sir.

SIR FRANCIS To that give us both leave to wait on you.

MRS BEAUCLAIR Pray give me leave to speak a word to my boy first.
    [*Calling offstage*] Will.   225

    [*Enter Will*]

WILL Madam.

MRS BEAUCLAIR [*aside to Will*] Run to my woman, and bid her come to her aunt's immediately, and bring me the suit Sir Charles made for the last ball, and left at my lodgings. Make haste; fly.

WILL I will, madam.   230

    [*Exit Will*]

MRS BEAUCLAIR [*aside*] Hang it, 'tis but one ridiculous thing, I'm resolved to do it. I'll find these pleasures out that charm this reprobate. Money will make all the drawers mine.

SIR CHARLES I'm ready to go.

SIR FRANCIS Madam, be pleased to accept my hand.   235

    Exeunt

3.3

Mrs Beauclair's lodgings
Enter Beaumont, leading Bellinda

BEAUMONT Now, madam, you're safe in the lodgings of your friend, forget the rudeness past.

BELLINDA Forget it! Impossible. Her words, like poisonous shafts, have pierced my soul, and will forever dwell upon my memory with endless painful racks.° Yet look not on me as that vile creature she 5 has represented, but believe me, sir, I engaged my heart too far before I knew Sir Charles was married. When I found my love unjust, how exquisite the torment proved, chilled with watchings, sighs, and tears. Yet, spite of my distractions, spite of the rising damps and falling dews,° 'twas grown too great to be extinguished, 10 till this last storm has torn it by the roots to spring no more.

BEAUMONT [*aside*] Her every word and looks confirms my thoughts. [*To Bellinda*] Madam, this I dare presume to say, both from his character and my small acquaintance: Sir Charles Beauclair has moral virtues to our late English heroes unpracticed and unknown. 15 Yet if I might advise, you should never see him more, or only to take an everlasting leave.

BELLINDA Your freedom, I confess, is strange, and your advice is what I had resolved on before.

BEAUMONT None but the lovely Mariamne could with such becom- 20 ing majesty have checked a stranger's boldness.° (*Beaumont gives Bellinda a picture*) View well these lines, and then confess if they do not the resemblance bear of a soft, charming face you have often by reflection seen.

BELLINDA [*aside*] Ha! My own picture, one of the effects of my dear 25 mother's fondness, which she, dying, left in my father's hands. He named me, too. Then let everlasting darkness shroud me; let me no more behold the sun or humankind, forget the world, as I would be of that forgotten.

BEAUMONT Turn, madam, and look upon me as your friend. If you 30 would still remain unknown, my breast shall keep this discovery silent and safe as secrets buried with the dead. Your father gave me that picture, with desires so tender for your return that, I confess, they moved me. I undertook the inquiry, though scarce could hope to have succeeded. Since your absence, your brother's dead; so that 35 your father, hopeless and childless, mourns, and says your sight would revive him more than when he first blessed heaven for your happy birth and mother's safety.

BELLINDA My brother dead! Loved youth, I grieve thy untimely fate, but thou art gone to rest and peace, whilst I am left upon the rack.° 40
Sir, I read in all your words a piercing truth and an unbiased honour. They have set my errors full before me; my fled duty returns as swift as I will do to this wronged parent, hang on his aged knees, nor rise till I have found forgiveness and my blessing there.

BEAUMONT Though much I wish your honour and your fame secure, 45
yet to part such lovers, whom this lewd age will scarce believe there ever were, grates my very nature.

BELLINDA Oh, let me not look back that way, but generously assist me on. Tell° that dear man, who, witness my disgraces, I value more than all earth's richest treasures—tell him, lest he should take it ill 50
of you, that I have confessed my birth, and have resolved to fly from him and all the world, and in my father's house remain as in a cloister.

BEAUMONT How will he brook the message?

BELLINDA Oh, tell him, sir, that the pangs of parting will scarce excel 55
those my struggling virtue gave at every guilty meeting, for there was guilt. Tell him I have sworn to die if he pursues. I blush to impose all this on you; but, if a lover, sure you'll forgive my follies.

BEAUMONT I'll tell him all; but I must send him too a parting kiss, at least, which must be allowed to such unequalled love. 60

BELLINDA Not till all is fixed for my remove. Then I once more will see him, though my heart-strings crack. I'll conquer all these criminal fires; I have the goal in view; bright honour leads me on. The part is glorious; but, oh, 'tis painful, too. Let me retire, and tear him from my doting thoughts; or in the bitter conflict, lose the use 65
of thought.
  Exit [*Bellinda*]

BEAUMONT How strong are the efforts of honour where a good education grounds the mind in virtue! This unexpected hurry has for some moments banished my dear Arabella from my thoughts.
  Enter Gentil°
O, here comes my implement!—Well, how goes affairs? 70

GENTIL Rarely,° sir. The chambermaid swallowed the guineas as glibly as a lawyer a double fee from his client's antagonist. She's bringing the young lady hither. Eugenia talks of a contrivance that you should instantly appear like a tarpaulin, pretend to be related to the lady, and fright the squire into a compliance. 75

BEAUMONT Anything to serve my Arabella. We'll meet 'em, and receive their instructions.

    Exeunt

3.4°

    Sir Charles Beauclair's house
    Enter Sir Charles Beauclair

SIR CHARLES Sure the world's all running mad, or else resolved to make me so. At home I cannot meet with a sensible answer; but, oh, what touches nearest, the dear, the cruel, the charming maid, Bellinda, will not see me. How shall I appease the offended fair? My wife, too, not returned. Where will this end? [*Calling offstage*]—Gentil! Eugenia! James!   5

[SERVANTS] [*offstage*] Sir.

SIR CHARLES Sir! Where, ye everlasting dormice? Will none come near me?

    Exit [Sir Charles Beauclair] Enter Cheatall and Gentil

CHEATALL Gadzooks! This Counsellor Cobblecase has talked law and drank claret with me till my brains are turned topsy-turvy. Gad, I would not have my lady-sister see me now for a king's ransom. Though, udsbores, I know not why she should, because she's a little older, set her eternal clack a-running upon all my actions.   10

GENTIL Sir, my lady and miss are both abroad.   15

CHEATALL That's well! Why, Gentil, here Cobblecase advises me not to lock up the young woman, but to use her kindly, and, gadzooks, I'm in a plaguy loving humour. I'll try her good nature once again. Hold. Yonder comes Sir Charles. My sister will never forgive me if I let him see her. He's a well spoken man. If I durst trust him, he should solicit for me; but then he's so woundy handsome, and so amorous, I doubt° he'd speak one word for me, and two for himself, as the saying is.°   20

    Enter Sir Charles Beauclair, talking to Eugenia

SIR CHARLES You say you will not injure the squire.

EUGENIA No, not in the least. She has sworn never to marry him, and the law will in time recover her right. Only this way is sooner and cheaper.   25

SIR CHARLES The lady's free, and I'll neither oppose [n]or assist it further. Ha, there he stands. [*To Cheatall*] How is't brother?

    40

CHEATALL Very well, I thank you, Sir Charles.   30

SIR CHARLES (*Going*) Your servant.

CHEATALL Brother, you never care for my company! You take me for a
     numbskull, a half-witted fellow, and, udsbores, would you but ha'
     me to the tavern, you should find I could drink my glass, break my
     jest, kiss my mistress with the best of ye. Flesh! Try old Barnaby   35
     Cheatall at your next jovial meeting.

SIR CHARLES You're merry,° sir, but I'm in haste.

          Exit [*Sir Charles Beauclair*]

CHEATALL Udsbores! Women and wine, both unwholesome, punish
     ye. There's taste of my wit in my cursing, as the whole cargo° o' the
     bullies lies in swearing. There 'tis again, i'faith! Am not I damnable   40
     ingenious,° Gentil? Live and learn, sirrah, and be hanged, and
     forget all, as the saying is.° What a dickens ails me! Hanging never
     comes in my mouth, but a qualm° comes o'er my stomach. That
     cursed old woman! Didst observe how she looked like the witch
     before the last new ballad?°   45

GENTIL She had, indeed, a very prophetic face.

          *One knocks. Gentil opens the door. Beaumont enters, dressed like
          a seaman*

GENTIL Who would you speak with, sir?

BEAUMONT With Mrs Arabella Venturewell.

GENTIL She's not here.

BEAUMONT Now, by the cannon's fire, 'tis false. I have come ten   50
     thousand leagues to see her, and will not be so answered.

CHEATALL A terrible fellow! Gadzooks!—Pray, sir, what's your
     business with her?

BEAUMONT She's my sister; that's sufficient for your impertinence.

CHEATALL You, the lawful begotten son of Sir George Venturewell?   55
     Begging your pardon, I believe you are mistaken, friend, in your
     father, as many a man may be, for Sir George had never any but this
     daughter.

BEAUMONT No, I'm not his lawful begotten son, not the weak off-
     spring of—   60

CHEATALL [*aside*] O lard! What pains he takes to tell me he's the son of
     a whore!

BEAUMONT Born in India, bred a buccaneer, sword and fire have been
     my playfellows, and ravishing my pleasure. In far distant worlds I
     have scattered my rough image;° and as my sword has cut off their   65
     dull breed, so my vigorous youth has left a race of future heroes.

CHEATALL [*aside*] A very terrible fellow, as I hope for mercy.

BEAUMONT Rich with the spoils of long successful war, I have visited
   this climate in search of Arabella, whom I have often heard my
   father mention with much tenderness. I am directed hither, there- 70
   fore do not raise my fury with delays. For, cause or not cause, if I
   am angry, blood must appease it.

CHEATALL [*aside*] O lard! O lard! What shall I do? He'll fright me into
   a Kentish ague.° I must speak him fair. [*To Beaumont*] Good sir, all
   your desires shall be fulfilled; have but a minute's patience. [*Aside,* 75
   to Gentil] Come along, Gentil, come along, and help me. Entreat
   her to speak him fair, or I'm a lost man! [*To Beaumont*] I'll wait
   upon ye in a twinkling, sir.
        Exit [*Cheatall*] *with Gentil*

BEAUMONT It works as I could wish. It goes against me to terrify this
   fool so much, but he deserves it. 80
        Enter Cheatall and Gentil

CHEATALL [*aside to Gentil*] Oh, Gentil, what shall I say?

GENTIL [*aside to Cheatall*] The lord knows; I don't.

BEAUMONT Well, sir, where's my sister?

CHEATALL Alas, I think she's vanished.

BEAUMONT How! D'ye trifle with my anger, bring me stories fit for 85
   a baby? Blood and thunder! If I unsheath my sword, it finds a
   scabbard in your guts! Confess, or by the cannon's fire—

CHEATALL I do confess that, thinking of your coming, and knowing
   her to be a little wild, lest she should have been out of the way, I
   locked her up. But what is now become of her, by the cannon's fire, 90
   the dreadfullest oath I ever heard, I cannot tell.

BEAUMONT (*aside*) I shall never hold laughing.°
        Enter Eugenia

EUGENIA Oh, my conscience! My tortured conscience! I cannot keep
   it!°

BEAUMONT What's the matter? 95

EUGENIA Oh! I went into the room where the lady was locked up, and
   there's at least a pail full of blood. All the water in the sea will never
   wash the stains out!° I believe Squire Barnaby and Gentil have
   killed her, cut her to pieces, and carried her away under their
   cloaks. 100

CHEATALL Oh, impudence! O lard! O lard! Sir, I han't the heart to kill
   a chicken! I always swoon at the sight of my own blood.—Speak
   Gentil, why, thou hast never a cloak.—[*To Beaumont*] That's a
   strong proof, sir. Gentil has ne'er a cloak.

EUGENIA Why, then it went all under yours. Besides, Gentil has a large 105

pair of trousers; that I'll swear, for you made him bring my lady
home half a venison pasty in 'em. (*Shrieks out*) Ah! Look o' their
shoes; they have paddled in it.

BEAUMONT Ay, 'tis so, and so I'll be revenged, [*draws his sword*] cut
thee small as the first atoms that huddled up° thy senseless carcass.   110
Nor will I be troubled to bear thee hence, but stamp thy vile clay to
its kindred dust, and leave thee here for rubbish!

CHEATALL [*kneeling*] O sir, upon my knees I beg you'd hear me.

EUGENIA (*interposing*) Hold, sir, don't kill the miscreant. That will
bring yourself into trouble. Our law will hang him, I warrant ye.   115
What made him order her, being here, to be denied?°

CHEATALL Ay, good sir, let me be hanged! That's my destiny! I see
there's no avoiding it. Gentil, beg I may be hanged.

GENTIL Pray, sir, let my master be hanged.

BEAUMONT Well, I'll try your law. If that fails, this, I'm sure, never   120
will. (*Puts up his sword*) How must we proceed, madam?

EUGENIA I'll go with ye for a man with the staff of authority. He shall
order him. The very stones in the street would turn constables to
seize such a monster. Kill a pretty lady and cut her to pieces? Oh,
horrid!   125

CHEATALL (*aside*) You are a lying whore, if I durst tell you so!

BEAUMONT You, fellow! Come hither.

CHEATALL Run, Gentil, run. Proffer him all I'm worth.

BEAUMONT (*aside to Gentil*) When we are gone, carry him to my
lodgings. I have told my landlady the story, and she's provided for   130
him.

GENTIL [*aside to Beaumont*] It shall be done. [*Aloud to Beaumont*] Is
there no mercy?

CHEATALL Ah lord, no mercy.

BEAUMONT Well, we'll be with you immediately. Come, madam.   135

EUGENIA Ay, ay, repent and pray; do, squire, do.
    Exit Beaumont and Eugenia

CHEATALL Oh, Gentil, that ever I was born! That ever I was born!
What did he say to thee, Gentil?

GENTIL He would have had me turned evidence against your worship
and confess. But I'll be hanged first!   140

CHEATALL I'd confess, if I thought 'twould do me any good!

GENTIL What! Confess you murdered her?

CHEATALL Ay, anything! Anything! Anything! Oh, Gentil, it must be
this witch! She has carried her away and spilt the blood that her
prophecy might come to pass.   145

GENTIL Not unlikely. Sir, sir, I have thought of a thing.

CHEATALL What is't, dear Gentil?

GENTIL Suppose you and I run away before the constable come. I
know a friend will conceal you, and then we may hope to make it
up,° or hear of her. I can't think she's murdered.   150

CHEATALL Nor I neither, except the devil has done't. But let's away,
good Gentil. Methinks I hear this magistrate's paw, this constable,
just behind me, his voice hoarse with watching and swallowing
claret bribes. Oh, Gentil, if I should fall into his grip!

GENTIL Therefore let's hasten to avoid it. Ah, sir, this is no time for   155
jesting.

CHEATALL Too true, Gentil, but wit will o'erflow! I fear I shall quib-
ble° in my prayers, and die with a jest in my mouth. Come, come!
Hanged! O lard, any of the family of the Cheatalls hanged! O lard,
and I the only branch on't? Oh, Gentil, 'tis unsupportable.   160

GENTIL Away, away, sir.

CHEATALL Oh that ever I should live to see myself hanged.

    Exeunt

4.1

A room in Locket's
A table with a flask upon it
Enter Sir Francis Wildlove and Mrs Flywife

MRS FLYWIFE Well, this is a strange mad thing, but my old cross°
fellow will never let me take a mouthful of air. I am sure you will
have an ill opinion of me.

SIR FRANCIS A kind one, you mean, madam; I think you generous,
lovely, and all my heart desires.   5

MRS FLYWIFE My maid is gone the lord knows where for fruit. I swear
I tremble, coming into a tavern alone.

SIR FRANCIS A glass of wine will recall the fled roses, but here's the
nectar thirsty love requires.

    Sir Francis kisses Mrs Flywife. Mrs Beauclair bounces in, in
    men's clothes

MRS BEAUCLAIR O pardon and protect me. I'm pursued by   10
hell-hounds, bailiffs, and, if taken, inevitably ruined.

SIR FRANCIS The devil take thee and the bailiffs together for an inter-
rupting young dog.

MRS BEAUCLAIR You look with a face cruel as they, but sure, [*turning
to Mrs Flywife*] in those fair eyes, I read some pity.   15

MRS FLYWIFE (*aside*) A very handsome fellow. [*To Mrs Beauclair*] How
came you in trouble, sir?

MRS BEAUCLAIR Alas, madam, I was put to an attorney,° but, longing
to turn beau,° have half-ruined my master, wholly lost my friends,
and now am followed by the several actions° of my tailor, semp-   20
stress,° peruke-maker,° hosier,° and a long *et cetera*; besides the
swingeingest debt, my perfumer; essence and sweet powder has
completed my ruin.

SIR FRANCIS 'Tis monstrous to cheat honest tradesmen in dressing up
a fop;° therefore, unwelcome° intruder, I desire you would seek   25
your protection elsewhere.

MRS FLYWIFE Nay, now you are too severe. The young gentleman in
liberty may mend his fortunes and live to pay his debts. He has a
promising face.

SIR FRANCIS Your pity, madam, but hastens absence.   30

MRS BEAUCLAIR (*aside*) Will this fellow I thought I had so well
instructed never come?

45

Enter Drawer

DRAWER Sir Francis, a man out of breath says he must speak with you on what concerns your friend's life.

SIR FRANCIS The devil's in the dice today.° Where is he? What's the matter?   35

Exeunt [Sir Francis and the Drawer]

MRS BEAUCLAIR (*aside*) Now impudence and eloquence assist me. [*To Mrs Flywife*] What have I done? In seeking to preserve my liberty, I have forever lost it. My inexperienced youth ne'er viewed such charms before, and, without compassion, this bondage may be   40
worse than what I avoided.

MRS FLYWIFE (*laughing*) Meaning me, sir?

MRS BEAUCLAIR Nay, I'm a fool, for, bankrupt in wealth, how can I hope to thrive in love, since scarce any of your fair sex, though merit was thrown into the scales, value a man on whom fortune   45
frowns.

MRS FLYWIFE (*aside*) I think it is the prettiest youth I ever saw. I have wealth enough to supply his wants; what should then debar me?

MRS BEAUCLAIR [*aside*] So, she eyes me kindly, I'm sure.   50

MRS FLYWIFE Your looks, sweet youth, plead powerful as your language; and to let you see I value not riches, the want of which makes you miserable, accept this ring. 'Twill stop a creditor's mouth, and pay two or three ordinaries° at the Blue Posts.°

MRS BEAUCLAIR O wondrous bounty! Thus encouraged, shall I beg   55
another favour, that you would fly from hence before that angry man returns, lest I fall a sacrifice to his jealousy, and see those charming eyes no more.

MRS FLYWIFE If my maid would come.

Enter Jenny

Ha, here she is. [*To Jenny*] Sure you have flown.   60

JENNY I beg your pardon, madam, I ne'er went. Sir Francis's gentleman and I were solacing° ourselves below and sent a porter for the fruit, till, hearing Sir Francis was gone in a great hurry, he ran after his master, and I came up to see what was the matter.

MRS BEAUCLAIR (*aside*) A hopeful mistress and maid! Deliver me from   65
these town-ladies.

MRS FLYWIFE Ungrateful man, on any pretence to leave me!

MRS BEAUCLAIR Ungrateful! Monstrous! Had a thousand friends been dying, they ought all to have expired ere you have° suffered a moment's neglect.   70

MRS FLYWIFE This flattery's too gross, young courtier; you must treat
me with truth.

MRS BEAUCLAIR All is truth; my heart, my life is yours.

JENNY (*aside*) Another spark! Sure the devil's in my mistress.

MRS FLYWIFE Well sir, I'll consent to your desires, and we'll go from   75
hence at the door towards the park;° there's no danger.

MRS BEAUCLAIR If you are kind, I fear none, madam.

MRS FLYWIFE Let me find you what you seem and you shall brave the
world and scorn your debts. Jenny, get me a chair and show this
gentleman the house where we lodge. Then come in; let him ask for   80
you. If you can prevent your master's seeing him, do. If not, say it is
one you waited upon in his infancy. The disparity of years between
you considered, that may pass.

JENNY (*aside*) Humph, I shall never like him for this affront. [*To Mrs
Flywife*] Yes, madam, it shall be done.   85

MRS BEAUCLAIR Your hand, dear obliging creature, I hear a
noise.

MRS FLYWIFE Quick, this way. [*To Jenny*] Run you before, and pay
one of the drawers for this flask of champagne.

> *Exeunt Mrs Beauclair, Mrs Flywife and Jenny. Enter Sir*
> *Francis Wildlove, Searchwell, and a Drawer*

SIR FRANCIS Ha, gone! So I thought. [*To Drawer*] Eternal dog, you   90
have been helping in this contrivance. Did you take me for a cully,
spawn of hell? Have I known this damned town so long at last to be
catched with such a gross banter? Speak, sirrah! Who was that
imposter that told me my friend Mr Beaumont was taken up for a
Jacobite,° and the mob was pulling him to pieces?   95

DRAWER As I ever hope to outlive your anger and taste again your
noble bounty, I knew nothing of him.

SIR FRANCIS [*to Searchwell*] Shut the door, you careless blockhead,
whom I charged to watch and let nobody come up to me. [*Sir
Francis Wildlove draws his sword*] [*To Drawer*] Now, sirrah, confess,   100
or I'll make that rogue help me kick thee into mummy, for though
my sword's drawn, I scorn to hurt thee that way.

DRAWER If I should confess, you'll kill me, sir.

SIR FRANCIS No.

DRAWER Truly then, sir, the young spark gave me a guinea to show   105
him the room where your honour was; but, for the fellow that
seemed so much concerned, I wish I may be hanged if I knew of
him anything at all, sir, anything at all, sir. Good your honour,
break my head, and forgive me.

SIR FRANCIS I will not touch thee. Could I expect more from thy   110
sordid soul? Gold corrupts mankind. Be gone.

    Exit Drawer

This unaccountable jilt has so abused me, I could find in my heart
to forsake the gang° and lay a penitential dunce at the feet of virtue,
fair Mrs Beauclair.

SEARCHWELL I pray heaven keep you in that good mind.   115

SIR FRANCIS Good lack,° canting sot,° I suppose you was shut up with
a whore, rascal, whilst you ought to have been pimping for me.

SEARCHWELL Trim tram, sir.

SIR FRANCIS How, impudence!

SEARCHWELL I meant the rhyme should be, 'Like mistress, like   120
maid',° for indeed I was employed with my lady's waiting
gentlewoman.

SIR FRANCIS Was ye so, rascal? Could I but find the young stripling,
'twould be some satisfaction. Hang't, if I am balked both in love
and revenge, the cross adventures shall be drowned in brisk   125
champagne.

       'Tis the dear glass which eases every smart,
       And presently does cure the aching heart.

    [*Exeunt*]

4.2

    [*Outside Mrs Beauclair's lodging*]°
    Enter Mrs Beauclair,° meeting Dresswell

MRS BEAUCLAIR Oh, Dresswell! I'm glad I've met with thee.

DRESSWELL Lord, madam, I have been in a sad fright for ye, and
hunted up and down this hour.

MRS BEAUCLAIR All's well. Let's in there: I'll tell you my adventures.

DRESSWELL Then I hope your frolic has been to your ladyship's   5
satisfaction.

MRS BEAUCLAIR Yes, yes. I got Sir Francis's mistress from him, and
faith, I was pursuing my conquest and venturing to her lodging,
when coming to the house, it proved that where Bellinda lodged,
and the lady, I suppose, the merchant's wife. I feared I should meet   10
with my uncle there, and fairly gave the maid the drop.° Come, I
long to change my clothes; I'm quite tired with wearing the
breeches. This way.

Exeunt [Mrs Beauclair and Dresswell.] Enter Sir Francis
Wildlove and Searchwell

SIR FRANCIS Ha, is not that the young devil that abused me? He has
entered the house, and I'll be with him presently. Walk hereabouts   15
till I come out.

SEARCHWELL Yes, sir.

[*Exit Sir Francis Wildlove to the house. Exit Searchwell*]

4.3

Inside [Mrs Beauclair's lodging]
Enter Mrs Beauclair and Dresswell

MRS BEAUCLAIR Are my things ready and a good fire in the room?

DRESSWELL Madam, they are.

One knocks

MRS BEAUCLAIR Peep out and see who knocks.

DRESSWELL [*peeping*] Madam, 'tis Sir Francis Wildlove, and he seems
in a fury.   5

MRS BEAUCLAIR Let him in; I'll do well enough with him. Now get
you gone and fear nothing.

[*Exit Dresswell.*] *Enter Sir Francis Wildlove*

SIR FRANCIS So, sir, I suppose you think matters have gone swingeingly on your side, and have laughed immoderately at the reflection
how those green years° have made a fool of me. But chance has   10
thrown me on thee once again, and now for those feasts of joy, an
after reckoning must be paid, young gentleman. [*Sir Francis draws
his sword*] You understand my meaning.

MRS BEAUCLAIR Yes, and will answer it, but hear me first. 'Tis to provoke you I speak. Know then, your mistress was my easy conquest. I   15
scarce had time to say one soft thing before she cried, 'Let's fly, sweet
youth, ere that rough man returns, and in thy arms forget him.'

SIR FRANCIS She's a jilt, and for a well-dressed fop would quit a man
that saved her life.

MRS BEAUCLAIR Then this ring was presented. I suppose you may ha'   20
seen it. 'Adorn thy fair hand, and', with ten thousand kisses 'twas
whispered, 'you shall not want for gold.'

SIR FRANCIS Though I value her no more than I do thee, yet I will
have thy life for harbouring so damned a thought, that I was fitter
for your sport. Come on.   25

MRS BEAUCLAIR Hold, hold, Sir Francis, I'll not pretend to take your
    sword, though I could your mistress from ye. See my credentials for
    my cowardice. (*Mrs Beauclair puts up her ring*)°

SIR FRANCIS Mrs Beauclair! What a blind puppy am I! Twice in one
    day, that's hard, i'faith.   30

MRS BEAUCLAIR Pray return your lady back her favour.

    [*Mrs Beauclair gives Sir Francis Mrs Flywife's ring*]

SIR FRANCIS Madam—

MRS BEAUCLAIR Nay, look not concerned. Upon my word, I'll never
    interrupt you more. Hug in your bosom the plastered° mischiefs,
    their blotted souls and spotted reputations no varnish can cover   35
    o'er. Pursue, o'ertake, possess the unenvied 'mongst the painted
    tribe.° Most worthily bestow your heart.

SIR FRANCIS Think ye so meanly of me? My heart bestowed amongst
    your sex's shame! No, madam, glorious virtue alone can reach at
    that. My loving° is a diversion I can soon shake off.   40

MRS BEAUCLAIR That's hard to believe, but I must beg your pardon;
    I'm in haste to unrig.°

SIR FRANCIS Hear me a moment. You have seen my frailties. If, like
    heaven, you can forgive, a truer penitent or a more constant votary
    no cruel virgin ever found.   45

MRS BEAUCLAIR Have a care of the dull road. Sir Francis, farewell.

    Exit [*Mrs Beauclair*]

SIR FRANCIS Go thy ways for a pretty witty agreeable creature. But if I
    should seduce her into matrimony, I fear the common fate will
    attend her: beauty quickly tarnish and good humour vanish.

    Exit

4.4

    [*Outside Mrs Beauclair's lodgings*]°
    Enter Spendall and Lywell

SPENDALL Ha, Lywell! I am the happiest man alive, almost out of
    Fortune's power!

LYWELL What is't transports you so? Some whim, some chymical°
    delusion, that will fail in the projection° and vanish into air.

SPENDALL Hear me, and then with admiration be dumb; nor dare to   5
    contradict my wit or plots again. In short, my Lady Beauclair and
    Miss are in open rebellion, by my persuasion, and to complete my

good fortune, I have borrowed ten guineas of Sir Charles, with the
help of which I'll be married to his daughter-in-law° within these
two hours.   10

LYWELL Ha, I begin to think the devil has left playing at legerdemain
with thee, and, having secured thee, resolves to bestow some of this
world's wealth upon thee.

SPENDALL Canst not thou procure a Templar's chamber° for an hour
or two, and appear with the gravity of a long robe?°   15

LYWELL With ease. I know a young spark that has fine lodgings there,
but by his old father is kept at short allowance. A treat, or a very
small sum, will engage that and all his habiliments.

SPENDALL Canst thou not put on the grave look of a starched
counsellor?   20

LYWELL 'Hum! Hum! I'll speak with you immediately.—You see,
friend, I'm busy.'—How was that?

SPENDALL Pretty well. Come, about it presently, and I'll bring the
ladies to you, as my father's chief lawyer. Be sure you tell 'em you
have the settlement of his estate upon me in your hands, and seem   25
very desirous I should do well.

LYWELL I warrant ye, and shan't we have lusty° treats, old boy?

SPENDALL I thought your conscience had scrupled the proceedings.

LYWELL O pox, my conscience never troubles me but when affairs go
ill.   30

SPENDALL Well, make haste, and doubt not feasting. I must to my
charge, lest they cool. Fools are seldom long resolved, and I know a
finer fellow would get both mother and daughter's heart. They're
now in a kindly growing warmth, and the old one's imagination
tickled as much with thoughts of darling Peggy's marriage as   35
ever 'twas with her own. Farewell! Be sure you observe your
directions.

LYWELL It shall be done, dear lucky devil. (*Coughs*) Hum, hum! I shall
be perfect in a grave cough, and a 'hum', of business by that time
you come to my chamber.   40

SPENDALL Hold! For I had forgot—whereabouts is this chamber? For
I guess your worship's name is not so famous to direct.°

LYWELL Come, as we go along I'll tell you.

　　　Exeunt [*Spendall and Lywell.*] *Enter Arabella, meeting Eugenia*

ARABELLA So, my dear deliverer, how have you succeeded?

EUGENIA Oh, madam, the poor squire's frighted out of the little wit he   45
had. One scene more and the day's our own.

ARABELLA What's become of Mr Beaumont?

EUGENIA He's about some earnest business of Sir Charles Beauclair's. I know not what 'tis, but there's a heavy clutter° amongst 'em.

ARABELLA Well, you brought me to the lady's lodging, but I believe   50
that's the only place she is not to be found at, for I have waited in vain with much impatience to see her.

EUGENIA Her footman's below, and says she'll be here immediately.

ARABELLA Prithee, let's into the chamber first, and you shall give an account of the squire's fright.   55

EUGENIA I follow you, madam.

    Exeunt

4.5

    A chamber in the Temple°
    Enter Lywell in a gown

LYWELL So! I'm equipped. The young lawyer snapped at the guineas and has furnished me throughout; nay, left his boy to boot.° Gad, I believe he'll be famous in his generation, he encourages mischief so readily. Pox, would they would come. I'm weary of Coke upon Littleton.°   5

    Enter Boy

BOY Sir, sir, a gentleman and two ladies are coming up.

LYWELL 'Tis they. You know your cue.

    [*Exit Lywell.*] *Enter Spendall, Lady Beauclair and Peggy*

SPENDALL Young man, is Counsellor Smart within?

BOY Sir, he's dispatching some half a score clients, but he'll do that with a wet finger° and wait on you immediately.   10

SPENDALL A witty whoreson. What, a wet finger to lick up the gold, ha! Well, tell him I'm here.

BOY Yes, sir.

    Exit [Boy]

PEGGY Fine chambers, mother! And a fine place, I'll swear! Vather would ne'er let me walk here. Zed° 'twa'n't fit for young ladies. I'll   15
vaw,° I like it waundily.°

LADY BEAUCLAIR Here were counsellors not unfit for you,° but husband was never free you should be seen.°

SPENDALL Now I'm, by promise, the happy man, my charming dear, let me beg you'd entertain no other thoughts. Where's this lawyer?   20
A moment's delay seems an age.

Exit Spendall

LADY BEAUCLAIR Well, daughter, feel how my heart beats. I'm almost afraid to venture on him for thee.

PEGGY Don't tell me of your fears! Now you've put a husband in my head, I will be married, so I will.   25

LADY BEAUCLAIR Ah, send thee good luck! I shall fall in a fit, I believe, whilst thou art marrying.

PEGGY I fear not marrying, not I.

Enter Spendall and Lywell

LYWELL Well, sir, I understand the business. Your father, considering your extravagance, has done more than I thought fit to tell ye; but   30
after such a proposal, you may hear it all. What, this is the pretty creature, I suppose, you are about marrying?

PEGGY Yes, sir.

LADY BEAUCLAIR Lord, Peggy, you're too forward! I wonder on ye now. [*To Lywell*] Sir, she is my daughter, and she'll be worth eight   35
thousand pounds and a better penny. I would not have her cast away, sir.

LYWELL To be thrown into a young gentleman's arms with a great estate will be a good cast, I take it, madam.

LADY BEAUCLAIR If I were satisfied in that!   40

LYWELL Look ye, madam, I am a man of business, and many words are but superfluous. Hum! Hogh! D'ye see, here's the settlement of his father's estate. Eight hundred pounds a year, and some thousands in money, a well-made fellow into the bargain. Let me tell ye, madam, such offers don't stick o' hand now-a-days.° You may read   45
the writings if you please. If you dislike 'em, look ye, I have a match in my eye for the gentleman beyond your daughter's; though I must own this young lady is much handsomer.

PEGGY (*aside to her mother*) D'ye hear what he says now! You'll never leave your impartinence, as vather calls it. Pray be quiet. I'm   50
satisfied, so I am.

LYWELL Will you read 'em, madam?

LADY BEAUCLAIR (*reads*) *Noverint, etc.*°—Nay, sir, I don't understand lay,° but you look like a good honest man, sir, and I dare take your word. I wish you had seen my daughter sooner.   55

SPENDALL (*aside*) Well said, mother-in-law that is to be, in love with every new face. I must secure the young one, lest she's of the same mind.

Spendall goes to Peggy

LADY BEAUCLAIR I'd willingly have him keep his coach and six. I

think the young woman's face will bear it,° and their estates, I   60
hope.

LYWELL No doubt on't, madam. A handsome wife and a coach and
six, how it attracts all eyes, the envy and wonder of the park.

SPENDALL Well, you may do what you please, but the dear one and
I are agreed. We'll to church without ye if ye dispute it any   65
longer.

PEGGY Ay, and so we will, I vow and swear, Mr Spendall.

LADY BEAUCLAIR For shame, what d'ye talk on! Why, 'tis past the
cannick hour.°

SPENDALL Madam, all people of quality marry at night.   70

LYWELL That they may be sure to go to bed before they repent; a day's
consideration might take off their appetite.

LADY BEAUCLAIR Nay, if people of quality do it, I'm for ye.

PEGGY And so I am, I vow and swear.

LYWELL First, ladies, be pleased to visit my withdrawing room. I have   75
sweetmeats and trinkets° there fit for the fair sex, which secures me
female visitants.

SPENDALL Agreed, we'll plunder him.

LYWELL   Then we will seek to join this amorous pair,
            And drown in pleasure thoughts of future care.   80
        Exeunt

4.6

[*Flywife's lodgings*]
Enter Flywife, pulling in Mrs Flywife

FLYWIFE Come, prithee, Puggy, do.

MRS FLYWIFE I'm not in humour.

FLYWIFE What, don't you love none° Fubby?

MRS FLYWIFE I hate mankind! Would they were in one consuming
blaze, though I were in the midst of 'em.   5
        Flying from Flywife, exit [Mrs Flywife]

FLYWIFE Hum, a consuming blaze. What's the matter, now? This is
some damned intrigue has gone cross. I heard her bid Jenny come
into this room, and she'd be with her. That's a quean, I dare swear,
at the bottom. I'll creep behind the hangings and hear their
discourse.   10
        Exit [Flywife]. Enter Mrs Flywife and Jenny

MRS FLYWIFE To be tricked thus by a boy, a booby. Sure this will humble the damned opinion I have of my own wit, and make me confess to myself, at least, I am a fool.

JENNY Ay, your ladyship was pleased to say I might pass for his nurse. Indeed I believe he has had as good instructors, for I find he's old enough to be too cunning for his benefactress.

MRS FLYWIFE What did he say when you parted?

JENNY Madam, I have told you several times. I no sooner showed him the house, but he leaped back and seemed surprised. Then, recovering himself, he said he would follow me in. I, according to your directions, watched carefully, but no pretty master came. Nothing vexes me so much as that the little dissembling sharper should get the ring.

MRS FLYWIFE Pish, I don't value the trifle three farthings. What's my doting keeper good for unless it be to give me more? But to lose the tempting youth!

JENNY Pray add Sir Francis Wildlove's loss to't.

MRS FLYWIFE Peace, fool. I'm thinking why the house should startle him. Ha, is not here a fine woman lodges, much retired, that seems of quality?

JENNY Yes, madam. I never saw her but once. She's a perfect charmer.

MRS FLYWIFE It must be so. This is some perdu devil of hers,° that durst not venture in for fear his constancy should be suspected. Pray watch who comes to her, dog 'em; do something for my ease.

JENNY Madam, I will.

MRS FLYWIFE Get me a hackney-coach. I'll range the town over, but I'll find Sir Francis Wildlove.

JENNY My master will be mad.

MRS FLYWIFE Then he may be sober again. Better he mad than I. If he be angry, 'tis but dissembling a little nauseous fondness and all's well again.

Exeunt [Mrs Flywife and Jenny.] Enter Flywife

FLYWIFE Is it so, thou worst offspring of thy grannam Eve? But I'll stifle my rage—lest without further proof she wheedles me into a reconciliation—take another coach and follow her, catch her amongst her comrades, without the possibility of an excuse, cut her windpipe and send her to hell without the possibility of a reprieve. Damn her, damn her.

Exit

4.7

Bellinda's apartment
Enter Bellinda

BELLINDA The little hurry of my quick remove has took up all my thoughts, and I have not considered what I am about. See him no more, him, whom I could not live a day, an hour, without! No more behold his eyeballs tremble with respectful passion! Hear no more the soft falling accents of his charming tongue! View him dying at 5 my feet no more! O Virtue, take me to thee; chase from my struggling soul all this fond tenderness. Secure me now, and I'm thy votary forever.

Enter Beaumont

BEAUMONT Madam, neglecting even my love, I come to wait on your commands. 10

BELLINDA Such thanks as an indiscreet and wretched woman can return are yours. What said Sir Charles?

BEAUMONT He received the message as wretches that are afraid to die hear the condemning voice, or as the brave the loss of victory, or the ambitious that of crowns. He begs that he may haste to plead 15 his cause, and seems to live alone upon the hopes his love and innocence may alter your resolves.

BELLINDA O stop him, sir, some moments longer, till I am just ready to be gone. He has a friend too powerful within,° and I must fly, or I shall never overcome. 20

BEAUMONT I'll prevent his coming till you send. Your servant, madam.

Exit [Beaumont]

BELLINDA Honour and love, oh the torture to think they are domestic foes that must destroy the heart that harbours 'em! Had my glass but been my idol, my mind loose, unconstant, wavering, like my sex, then I might have 'scaped these pangs. Love, as passing 25 meteors with several fires, just warms their breasts and vanishes, leaving no killing pain behind. 'Tis only foolish. I have made a god of my desire, greater than ever the poets feigned. My eyes received no pleasure but what his sight gave me. No music charmed my ears, but his dear voice. Racks, gibbets, and dungeons, can they equal 30 losing all my soul admires? Why named I them? Can there be greater racks

Than what despairing parting lovers find,
To part when both are true, both would be kind?

[Exit]

5.1

Bellinda's apartment
Enter Bellinda

BELLINDA He comes. Keep back, full eyes, the springing tears! And thou, poor trembling heart, now be manned with all thy strongest, stoutest resolutions! There will be need.

Enter Sir Charles Beauclair

SIR CHARLES Ah! Whither shall I throw me? What shall I say? 'Mariamne' hangs like icicles upon my tongue, but 'Bellinda' flows.   5
O Bellinda, I charge thee by that dear name, hear and pity me.

BELLINDA (*coldly*) What would you say?

SIR CHARLES Why, nothing; I do not know that voice. It has stopped the rising words, and I must only answer with my sighs.

BELLINDA Sir Charles, we have both been punished with unwarrant-   10
able love.

SIR CHARLES Punished! Have we been punished? Now, by all my woes to come, by all my transports past, all thought of my Bellinda, there's not a pang, a groan, but brought its pleasure with it. Oh, 'tis happier far to sigh for thee than to have enjoyed another.   15

BELLINDA You interrupt me when I just begin. Grant it true: we might have lived till weary grown of one another, till you, perhaps, might coldly say, 'I had a mistress.' Now to part, when at the mention of each other's name our hearts will rise, our eyes run o'er, 'tis better much than living to indifferency, which time and age   20
would certainly have brought.

SIR CHARLES Oh, never, never. Though the bauble, gaudy beauty, die, yet sense and humour still remain; on that I should have doted.

BELLINDA You cannot guess your future by your present thoughts; or, if you could, I am not to be moved forsaking thee, and when I have   25
said that, I need not add all pleasures.° In remote and unfrequented shades I'll pass my solitary hours, and, like a recluse, waste the remainder of my wretched days.

SIR CHARLES And am *I* the cause of this melancholy penance? Must my unhappy love rob the world of its fairest ornament?   30
No, madam, stay and enjoin me what you please; condemn my tongue to everlasting silence; let me now and then but gaze and tell you with my eyes what's acting in my heart. Or, if you will retire, permit me to follow, under the pretence of hunting, the

air°—a thousand things I can invent—create new friendship,   35
caress the whole country o'er,° to have an opportunity of seeing
you, though at a hateful distance and surrounded by severest
friends.

BELLINDA Ha, is this the awful love I thought possessed ye? How
fatally I was mistaken! What, pursue me to my father's house? Fix   40
on my name a lasting blot, a deathless infamy? Pollute my native air
with unhallowed love, where all my ancestors have for ages flourished and left an honest fragrancy° behind? Mark me, sir, you know
I do not use° to break my word. If, by letters, messages, or the least
appearance (though cautiously, as treasons plotted against the   45
state), you approach me, I'll fly the kingdom, or, if that's too little,
the world.

SIR CHARLES No, 'tis I have been mistaken. Now, by all the racks I
feel, not worth° a sigh, a parting drop, no regard of tenderness,° no
beam of pity from those dear eyes, nor sidelong glance to view my   50
sad distraction! Methinks you have already left me, and I am got
amongst my fellow madmen, tearing my hair, chained to the
ground, foaming and digging up the earth, yet in every smallest
interval of sense calling on Bellinda.

BELLINDA A noble birth, a censorious world, a mourning father, all   55
plead against thee. Oh, talk no more, lest you force my hand to
some desperate act; and yet your words pierce my bosom with
greater pain than pointed steel.

SIR CHARLES I see you are resolved on my undoing, fixed like my
relentless fate; therefore I'll not urge another syllable, but quietly,   60
as dying men, when hope's all past, quit life and their dearest
friends, for ever, ever leave thee.

BELLINDA That sad, silent look discovers such inward worlds of woe,
it strikes me through, staggers my best resolves, removes the props
I have been raising for my sinking fame, and, blind with passion, I   65
could reel into thy arms. Tell me, on what are thy thoughts
employed?

SIR CHARLES On the curse of life, imposed on us without our choice,
and almost always attended with tormenting plagues.

BELLINDA Yet we may meet again, in peace and joy, when this gigantic   70
honour appears no bugbear, and our desires lawfully be crowned.
It is a guilty thought;° nor shall I ever dare to form it to a
wish.

SIR CHARLES But dost thou think we may? What, uncontrolled clasp
thee thus? (*Embracing her*) Oh, ecstasy! With wild fury run o'er   75

each trembling beauteous limb, and grasp thee as drowning men
the dear bark from whence they were thrown.

BELLINDA Away, away! What are we doing? Divide him, heaven, from
my fond guilty eyes. Set seas and earth and worlds of fire between
us, for virtue, fate, and honour, with an united cry, have doomed   80
that we must meet no more.

Exit Bellinda

SIR CHARLES To raging seas, sieges, and fields of battle will I fly,
pleasures and pastimes to the woes I feel. O Bellinda!

Exit

5.2

[*Sir Charles Beauclair's house*]
Enter Gentil

GENTIL I could laugh my heart sore to see what a condition the fool
my master's in. Every knocking at the door is as good as a dose of
rhubarb,° and every noise makes him leap like a vaulter.° Ha, he's
coming! The poor baby dares not be alone.

[*Enter*] *Cheatall, peeping*

CHEATALL Gentil! Is the coast clear?   5

GENTIL Yes, sir.

CHEATALL Oh, Gentil!

GENTIL What's the matter? You look worse frighted than you were.

CHEATALL Ay, and well I may! You leave me alone and° I shall grow
distracted. I have . . . I have seen a ghost.   10

GENTIL A ghost! What, Mrs Arabella's ghost?

CHEATALL Nay, I did not stay to examine that, for, as soon as ever I
perceived the glimpse on't,° I shut up my eyes and felt my way out
of the chamber.

GENTIL Where was this ghost, sir?   15

CHEATALL Oh, behind the bed, behind the bed, Gentil!

GENTIL Lord, sir, 'twas nothing but the cloak; I hung it there.

CHEATALL Was it not? O' my conscience, I thought it had been a giant
of a ghost.

A cry offstage, seeming at a distance. Cheatall starts

Hark, hark! What's that?   20

BOY (*offstage*) A full and true relation° of a horrid and bloody murder
committed on the body of Mrs Arabella Venturewell, a young lady,

by one Squire Barnaby Cheatall and his man Gentil; showing how
they locked her up in the dark, then cut her to pieces and carried
the pieces away under their cloaks and threw 'em into Chelsea   25
Reach,° where, at low water, they were found.

CHEATALL O lard! O lard! The pieces found, Gentil!

GENTIL So it seems, sir.

BOY (*seeming farther off*) A full and true relation of a . . . *etc.*

CHEATALL Nay, now we shall be hanged for certain. Not the least   30
hopes. (*Crying*) Oh! Oh! Oh!

GENTIL Come, sir, have a little courage.

CHEATALL To confess the truth to thee, I never had any courage in my
life; and this would make the stoutest man tremble. Oh!

GENTIL I am thinking, sir—why—we was not at Chelsea Reach that   35
day.

CHEATALL No, no. But, maybe they'll swear we was.

GENTIL My lady and Miss hated her. Sure they han't been so
barbarous.

CHEATALL Like enough. Pin-up petticoats° are as convenient as   40
cloaks. Besides, my sister is a Fury. I've heard her threaten pulling
folks a-pieces a hundred times, and now she has done't. We'll e'en
peach.°

GENTIL What, your own sister!

CHEATALL Ay, my own mother to save myself. I say, we'll peach.   45

GENTIL That's not so good; for if they prove themselves innocent,
'twill fall upon us again. Hark ye, sir. There's only Eugenia can
witness against us. Suppose we tried to stifle her evidence with a
swingeing bribe? I never knew a chambermaid refuse greasing in
the fist° upon any account.   50

CHEATALL My dear Gentil, if she inclines, my offers shall be so large
that for the rest of her life she shall have nothing to do but study to
make her hands white;° that she may burn all her frippery and be
able to spark it with quality.°

GENTIL Sir, I'll send her propositions.   55

CHEATALL Do. But if the stubborn jade won't comply, appoint a private meeting and stop her mouth with this: (*Cheatall half draws his
sword [and pretends to stab with this]*) Ugh! You understand me.
[*Cheatall sheathes his sword*]

GENTIL Yes, sir. (*Aside*) I find his conscience would swallow a real   60
murder. [*To Cheatall*] Sir, if you please, we'll go in and write what
you design to offer her.

CHEATALL Let us. If you meet her, Gentil, and she's surly, remember:

(*Cheatall half draws his sword* [*and pretends to stab with this again*])
Ugh! Ugh!   65
    Exeunt

5.3

    [*Sir Francis Wildlove's lodgings*]
    Enter Sir Francis Wildlove, and to him, Searchwell

SEARCHWELL Sir Charles sends you word he is busy ordering his
    affairs, designing with all speed to travel, and says he shall never see
    you more, only to take his leave.

SIR FRANCIS Heyday! O' my conscience, this charming little Beauclair
    has me under a spell, and I shall meet with nothing but disap-   5
    pointments till I submit to her.

SEARCHWELL Ay, sir, you would soon find the true pleasures of
    virtuous love, and a satisfaction in denying your appetite.

SIR FRANCIS Preaching fool, hold you your peace.
    Enter Servant

SERVANT Sir, a gentlewoman below desires to speak with you.   10

SEARCHWELL (*aside*) So, there's no great danger my master should
    reform when the devil is always at hand with a temptation in
    petticoats.

SIR FRANCIS Searchwell, wait on the lady up.

SEARCHWELL Ah lord!   15

SIR FRANCIS Sirrah, I shall break your head if you don't leave this
    canting trade.°

SEARCHWELL I am gone, sir.
    [*Exeunt Searchwell and Servant.*] [*Searchwell*] *enters with*
    Dresswell

DRESSWELL (*aside*) This is a mad message my lady has sent me with to
    her lover. I'm afraid he'll kick me for my news. Hang't, he's a   20
    gentleman and I'll venture.

SIR FRANCIS Ha, pretty Mrs Dresswell! This is a favour I never
    received from you before. Must I own the blessing only to your
    goodwill, or is my happiness greater? Did your lady send?

DRESSWELL I came from my lady, sir, but what happiness you'll find I   25
    know not. Methinks she has done a strange mad thing.

SIR FRANCIS What's the matter?

DRESSWELL She's married, sir.

SIR FRANCIS The devil she is.

DRESSWELL Even so. She said those that she fancied cared not for   30
her; therefore, she resolved to bestow herself and fortunes on a
secret lover, whom indeed her ladyship owns she never valued, a
gentleman you know, sir, the worthy Mr Spendall.

SIR FRANCIS (*walks about enraged*) Damnation! That rake, bully,
sharper! Damn it, damn it!   35

DRESSWELL Here's a note where they are. She desires to see you.

SIR FRANCIS Tell her I esteem her so much, I'll cut the rascal's throat
she has thought fit to call husband. I'll do it, madam, though I'm
hanged at the door. 'Tis the only way I can express my love to her
now.   40

DRESSWELL [*aside*] Would I were well gone. [*To Sir Francis*] I'll tell
her, sir.

   Exit [*Dresswell*]

SIR FRANCIS Married! And to Spendall! Oh, that I could despise her.
Ha, I find 'tis worse with me than I thought! What makes this gnaw
my heart so else? My fellow libertines will laugh to see me play the   45
fool and kill myself. Oh, I could tear in piecemeal the villain that
betrayed her to endless ruin.

   Enter Servant

SERVANT Sir, there's another lady, out of a coach, coming upstairs.

SIR FRANCIS Blockhead, tell her I desire she would break her neck
down° again and oblige me in riding post° to the devil. My coach,   50
there!

   (*Sir Francis throws Servant down.*) *Exit* [*Sir Francis
   Wildlove*]

SERVANT Oh, my nose, my nose! Why, what's the matter now? I
thought I should have had a reward for my news; and so I have, I
think. Oh, my nose!

   Enter Mrs Flywife

MRS FLYWIFE Where's Sir Francis? Did you tell him I was coming up?   55

SERVANT Yes, and he says you may go to the devil. He has spoiled the
ornament of my face, and flung into his coach stark mad.

MRS FLYWIFE Much of passion shows much of love.° My coach shall
follow his. I'll not leave him so.

   Exeunt

5.4

[*Sir Charles Beauclair's house*]
Enter Mrs Beauclair [*and*] *Dresswell*°

MRS BEAUCLAIR I must confess I am fool enough to be pleased
with Sir Francis's concern. But, oh, my uncle's troubles draw
a veil upon my rising joys and damp all mirth. Poor Bellinda!
She sent a note to tell me her disorder was such she could not
see me. With much ado I have persuaded Sir Charles to come   5
hither for half an hour and look into this unlucky piece of matrimony.

DRESSWELL Madam, they are coming.

MRS BEAUCLAIR In, in, then!
Exeunt [*Mrs Beauclair and Dresswell.*] *Enter Lady Beauclair,*
Spendall, Peggy and Lywell

LYWELL Here, give me a glass of wine. Mrs Bride's long life and   10
lasting happiness.

PEGGY Thank ye, sir. Give me a glass, you.°

SPENDALL To me, my love?

PEGGY Yes.

SPENDALL Yours, forever.   15
[*Peggy*] *drinks it off*

LADY BEAUCLAIR Lard, child, you'll drink too much wine.

PEGGY Pray be quiet. I'll drink what I please. I am married now. Why
sure, I'll ha' none of your tutoring. Ecod, I'll long for everything I
see, shan't I, you?

SPENDALL Ay, and have it too, my dear.   20

PEGGY Ecod, I'll long for green pease at Christmas,° so I will.

LADY BEAUCLAIR My heart aches. This great concern has made me
sick. Give me a glass.

PEGGY I am mother's own daughter. Feth, I dare confess it now. I
always used to be sick for a glass of wine. Ho, ho!   25

LADY BEAUCLAIR Sure the wench is mad.
One knocks [*off-stage*]

SPENDALL Ha, dear ladies, go in. 'Tis somebody from Sir Charles, I
believe. I would willingly speak with 'em first.

PEGGY Ay, ay, let's go in. There's more wine within.

LADY BEAUCLAIR Be sure you make your estate out plain.   30

SPENDALL Yes, yes. [*Aside to Lywell*] Hark ye, Lywell, carry 'em out of
earshot lest it should prove a dunner.

LYWELL [*aside to Spendall*] I warrant. [*To Ladies*] Come, ladies, we'll in and take a bumper.

PEGGY O la, you make me so blush—

35

[*One*] *knocks again* [*off-stage.*] [*Exeunt Lady Beauclair, Peggy and Lywell*]

SPENDALL [*calls off-stage*] Boy, open the door!
Enter Sir Francis Wildlove

SIR FRANCIS What, grown so great already that I must wait half an hour for admittance?

SPENDALL (*aside*) He is come from Sir Charles. I'll speak him fair. [*To Sir Francis Wildlove*] Sir Francis Wildlove, your very humble servant, I beg ten thousand pardons.

40

SIR FRANCIS Keep your fawning and bestow it on fools; 'tis lost on me and will be grossly answered. I tell ye, you are a rascal.

SPENDALL Poverty makes many a man so, sir.

SIR FRANCIS A presuming rascal! Do I not know thee for the dreg of humankind, and shall thy detested arms receive her virgin beauties, life of goodness, soul of honour, wit, and sweetness, the only woman upon earth I could have loved?

45

SPENDALL Sure you design to banter me: soul of wit and sweetness? The devil might had her sweetness for me. 'Twas her money I married, faith, Sir Francis. I always took her for a fool!

50

SIR FRANCIS Profaner! This last action only calls her judgement in question. Thy death is justice! First to deceive, and then abuse her! Draw! [*Sir Francis draws his sword*]

SPENDALL I will draw, though, gad, I would have sworn never to have fought on this occasion.

55

Enter Mrs Beauclair and Dresswell, laughing

MRS BEAUCLAIR Ha, ha, ha!

DRESSWELL Ha, ha, ha!

SIR FRANCIS Nay, madam, I'll not disturb your mirth, but be so calm to wish it may continue. (*Sir Francis puts up his sword*)

60

SPENDALL What's the meaning of all this? How came Mrs Beauclair here?

SIR FRANCIS Are you not married to this lady?

SPENDALL No such honour was ever designed for me. Lard, sir, I am married to Miss Peggy, Lady Beauclair's daughter. My fool's within. Now I hope I may call her so.

65

MRS BEAUCLAIR I doubt, Sir Francis, you counterplotted me, knew the truth, and only acted this concern.

SIR FRANCIS No, by heaven; nor, perfectly, my own heart till this

severe trial searched it. Did I dissemble, madam, your sense would 70
soon discover it. But by my soul, I love you truly, and if you
dare venture on me, my future life shall show how much I honour
you.

MRS BEAUCLAIR Can you then leave all the pretty city wives, which a
man of your parts and quality, in a quarter of an hour's siege, could 75
overcome? In fine, all the charming variety of what was pretty or
agreeable in the whole sex, and be confined? Oh, that's a hard word
to me.

SIR FRANCIS With more delight than those surfeiting joys, that always
left a sting behind 'em, afforded. 80

MRS BEAUCLAIR Well, sir, if you can give me your heart, I can allow
you great liberties. But when we have played the fool and married,
don't you, when you have been pleased abroad,° come home surly.
Let your looks be kind, your conversation easy, and though I should
know you have been with a mistress, I'd meet you with a smile. 85

SIR FRANCIS When I forsake such charms for senseless mercenary
creatures, you shall correct me with the greatest punishment upon
earth, a frown.

MRS BEAUCLAIR You'll fall into the romantic style,° Sir Francis.—Mr
Spendall, shan't we see your bride? 90

SPENDALL Yes, madam, and I hope your ladyship will prove my friend
to Sir Charles.

MRS BEAUCLAIR Ay, ay, we'll all speak for ye. Had she missed ye, there
was no great likelihood, as the case was, she would have done better.

SIR FRANCIS Where is the pretty miss? Pray conduct us to her. 95

MRS BEAUCLAIR Sir Charles will be here presently. I long to hear my
aunt set out the greatness of the match.

SPENDALL This way, sir.
    Exeunt [Sir Francis Wildlove, Spendall, Mrs Beauclair and
    Dresswell.] Enter Mr Beaumont, Arabella and Eugenia

ARABELLA Is this the house, Eugenia?

EUGENIA Yes, madam. 100

ARABELLA Well, thou art a lucky girl to recover my writings with such
speed.

EUGENIA Madam, the squire would have parted with a limb if I had
required it.

BEAUMONT Madam, it was your promise, whenever you possessed 105
your fortune (though I'm sure I never insisted on't), you would be
mine.

ARABELLA I have no occasion to break my word, Mr Beaumont.

BEAUMONT Then I am happy.

ARABELLA Mrs Eugenia, will you enquire where these bride-folk° are?   110

EUGENIA See, madam, they are coming.

    Enter Lady Beauclair, Mrs Beauclair, Peggy, Sir Francis
    Wildlove, Spendall and Lywell

ARABELLA Will the squire be here?

EUGENIA Yes, madam. I told him of his cousin's marriage, and he seems pleased his sister has been tricked.

PEGGY Lard, you, what° d'ye bring one to these folks? They'll do   115
nothing but jeer us.

SPENDALL Oh, my dear, carry yourself civilly, and everybody will love ye.

MRS BEAUCLAIR Sir Charles will be here presently to wish you joy, madam.   120

LADY BEAUCLAIR So, then we shall have noise enough; but I'll be as loud as he, I'll warrant him.

MRS BEAUCLAIR And louder too, or I'm mistaken.

    Enter Sir Charles Beauclair

SIR CHARLES Niece, why have you dragged me to this unwilling penance? If the girl is ruined, what is't to me? My thoughts are full   125
of something else.

MRS BEAUCLAIR My uncle, my father, and my friend, yet the names do not express half my tenderness. The best of guardians and of men, pray change your thoughts of travel. I'll study ten thousand things for your diversion.   130

SIR CHARLES Not angel's eloquence should alter me; I'll act the uneasy part no longer. That woman, the bar to all my happiness, by heaven, she's not my wife. 'Tis true, the ceremony of the church has passed between us, but she knows I went no further.°

MRS BEAUCLAIR Stay then, and live asunder.   135

SIR CHARLES No. [*To Lady Beauclair*] So, madam, you've married your daughter.

LADY BEAUCLAIR Yes, what then? He has a good estate, when his father dies, beside° the present settlement, and ready money.

SIR CHARLES Poor deluded women! He has no estate, nor relation   140
worth owning. Mr Spendall, generous charity induced me to relieve your wants. You have betrayed this young woman, but use her well. I have not much to say; I suppose they were both so willing, a very little pains effected the matter.

LADY BEAUCLAIR How, rascal! Devil! Have ye married my daughter,   145
and have ye nothing, sirrah?

66

SPENDALL Ask Mrs Peggy that.°

PEGGY You make one laugh, I vow and swear.

LADY BEAUCLAIR Beast! I don't mean so! But have ye no estate, sirrah? 150

SPENDALL No, faith, madam, not I. My wife has enough for us both, and what's matter.°

LADY BEAUCLAIR Oh, dog! Come away, Peggy, we'll go to Doctor's Commons,° and thou shalt be divorced.

PEGGY I won't be divorced! I've got a husband, and I don't care, I'll 155 stay with him.

SPENDALL That's kindly said, and I engage you shan't repent it.

LADY BEAUCLAIR Why, Counsellor Smart, why, Counsellor Smart, did not ye tell me—

SIR FRANCIS Hey day, Counsellor Smart! Why this is a fellow many 160 degrees worse than your new son-in-law. Hark ye, friend, leave this counterfeiting trade or you'll lose your ears.° Reform, as your friend has done, and marry.

LYWELL Hang him, rogue. He's a smock-faced° fellow and handsome; I shall do no good with the women. 165

SPENDALL (aside [to Lywell]) Go, be gone, devil, don't disgrace me. I'll meet you at the old place.
  Exit Lywell

MRS BEAUCLAIR Look what a puff the old lady's in.° [To Lady Beauclair] Aunt, you always said you'd match your daughter yourself; you did not desire a cunninger head than your own. 170

LADY BEAUCLAIR Well, Mrs Flippant! I hope your mad tricks will bring you a bastard home at last, and that will be worse.

SIR CHARLES Nay, madam, spare my niece. She ever was most respectful to you, till you abused her beyond all bearing.

SIR FRANCIS Mind not a madwoman. 175
  Enter Cheatall

CHEATALL Your servant, gentiles!° [To Lady Beauclair] O la, sister! I hear strange news: cousin Peggy's married to a sharper, a rake, a bully, they say! I told you so! I told you so! Gadzooks! You would not be warned.

LADY BEAUCLAIR Well, booby, what's that to you, underhead?° 180
  Lady Beauclair strikes Cheatall

CHEATALL Pox take your nasty fist! You love fighting plaguily.

LADY BEAUCLAIR Well, 'twas passion. You may excuse it when you consider my afflictions. To make ye amends, I'll come live with you and take care of your estate and Mrs Arabella's.

CHEATALL No, no, don't mistake yourself. I'll be a stingy cur no 185
longer, but drink my bottle freely; nor sneak out o' the company
without paying my club° for fear of having my pocket examined by
you.

Seeing Arabella, Cheatall runs behind Spendall

O lard! The ghost! The ghost!

SPENDALL What, is the man mad? 190

MRS BEAUCLAIR You don't understand the whim.

ARABELLA Come, gi' me thy hand, old boy, and we'll be friends. I am
no ghost, I assure ye.

CHEATALL And, is not that the hectoring spark your brother, with his
monstrous whiskers pared?° 195

BEAUMONT Not her brother, sir, but one who hopes to pretend to the
lady by another title.

CHEATALL Oh, I find how matters ha' been carried! Much good may
d'ye° with her. Gadzooks, she wa'n't fit for me. I'm a fool, you
know, sister. 200

ARABELLA You must grant me one request.

CHEATALL What's that?

ARABELLA To forgive Gentil. He's going to be married to Eugenia,
but shall have no joys without your pardon.

CHEATALL Ay, ay. I forgive him and leave his wife to punish him. She 205
has a fruitful invention; let him take care it does not one day fall
upon his own head.° Gentil, I am friends,° and will give thee
something towards housekeeping.°

GENTIL I thank you, sir.

EUGENIA I'm sure it went to my very heart to fright your worship so. 210

CHEATALL You are a wheedling baggage, but 'tis all well. I'm
contented.

Enter Mrs Flywife in a fright

MRS FLYWIFE O save me! Save me! I am pursued by a bloody-minded
monster.

SIR FRANCIS What's the matter? Is it your husband, madam? 215

MRS FLYWIFE 'Tis my tyrant, the devil 'tis.

*Enter Flywife, his hanger drawn. [Mrs Flywife hides behind
Cheatall]*

CHEATALL Nay, hold ye, mistress! Don't ye run behind me, udsbores,
so I may have the sword in my guts by mistake.

BEAUMONT We'll all protect the lady.

FLYWIFE Protect! Damnation! Do but hear how vile a thing it is. 220

CHEATALL Hear! What do I hear and see! Why, sure this is our brother Allen, my sister's first husband, we thought dead in the Indies.

SIR CHARLES What's that? Speak again, but speak aloud lest I should only catch the sound of happiness and be deceived.   225

LYWIFE [*aside*] Has my damned jilt brought me to a greater plague, my wife? But I'll own it to punish her, though I suffer an abominable torment till next fair wind.° The sea's my element, once there, I'm free. [*To the others*] Well I confess I have found a wife here. Why stare you so? I am not the first has thought the sight   230 unpleasing.

SIR CHARLES No, no, talk on; all are hushed, as if a midnight silence reigned.

LADY BEAUCLAIR Who's this? Are you my first husband, Allen? And did you pretend you was dead rather than come home to me,   235 sirrah?

LYWIFE Here's a fine greeting.

MRS FLYWIFE How! Your husband! He's mine before heaven. Mr Flywife, won't you own me, Fubby?

LYWIFE In troth, I think there's scarce a pin to choose.° [*To Mrs*   240 *Flywife*] But you have disobliged me last; therefore, avaunt, strumpet. [*To Lady Beauclair*] Come hither, thou natural° noisy spouse.

MRS FLYWIFE That shape and face preferred to me?

LADY BEAUCLAIR I'll be revenged of her, I'm resolved. (*Flies on her*)   245

MRS BEAUCLAIR I'm all amazement. Sir Francis, save the lady, because she was my friend.° Return her ring; that may help console her.

SIR FRANCIS (*parting Lady Beauclair and Mrs Flywife*) Hold, ladies! Ladies! [*To Mrs Flywife*] March off, here's the bountiful present. Come, come, I doubt not but you've a private pocket.°   250

MRS FLYWIFE The devil take you all.
          Exit [*Mrs Flywife*]

MRS BEAUCLAIR° What miracle is this? Madam, leave your passion and explain it.

PEGGY Is my own vather come again? O la!

PENDALL Your own vather come again! O la! Then, I fear, your   255
portion is not at your own dispose, Miss.

PEGGY Good lord! Does that disturb ye?

LYWIFE Gentlemen, now your wonder is a little over, pray let me ask why all this company, and why that gentleman, who I know not, appears transported.   260

SIR CHARLES° I'll tell you, sir; 'twas my hard fate to marry your lady before your death was well confirmed. That kept it some time private,° when, before we came together,° a quarrel, from her uneasy temper, arose, and I swore never to bed her. Yet, for our friends' and conveniency's° sake, we seemed to live like man and wife. Speak, madam. Is not this true?   26

LADY BEAUCLAIR Yes, yes, 'tis true; the more shame for ye.

SIR CHARLES Here, sir, receive her, and with her a new date of° happiness.

FLYWIFE I guess my future happiness by the past; but since it must be so . . .   27

SIR CHARLES Dear niece, go to my house,° and deliver up whatever is that lady's.

MRS BEAUCLAIR You'll send to Bellinda?

SIR CHARLES Myself, myself shall be the messenger;   27
    In my eager mind I'm already there:
    Methinks the earth's enchanted and I tread on air.
            Exit [Sir Charles Beauclair]

MRS BEAUCLAIR So, there's one pleased, I'm sure.

CHEATALL Well, brother, you're welcome home, as I may say. Why, here's Cousin Peggy grown up and married since you went.   28

FLYWIFE What! Is that bud come to the blossom of matrimony? All by the mother's contrivance; a wise business, I believe. [*To Spendall*] Sir, I shall make bold to examine into your estate before I give my daughter any.   28

SPENDALL Say ye so? And if you give your daughter none, I shall prove a second Mr Flywife.

PEGGY What's that, bold-face?

SPENDALL Nothing, child.

LADY BEAUCLAIR Ay, that's a hopeful° match. I could find in my heart to lock myself up and never see your ugly faces again.   29
            Exit [Lady Beauclair]

MRS BEAUCLAIR Let's follow and appease her.

ARABELLA And as we go, you shall tell me what makes Sir Charles thus overjoyed.

MRS BEAUCLAIR I will. And when we have done what he desired, we'll go all to Bellinda's. There we shall find my uncle.   29
            [*Exeunt Mrs Beauclair and Arabella*]

SIR FRANCIS Come, Beaumont, let's see the end of this surprising accident.

[*Exeunt Sir Francis and Mr Beaumont*]

FLYWIFE   How like a dog a man looks once escaped!°
　　　　　　Forced back into the matrimonial noose,　　　　　300
　　　　　　'Tis a damned joy to find the wife I'd loose.°
Exeunt

5.5

Bellinda's apartment
On a table lies Bellinda's hood and scarf
[*Enter Bellinda*]

[BELLINDA] Sure some unseen power holds me a moment longer. Ah,
'tis no power but foolish love that shows the path which carries me
from Beauclair, leading to death or, what's worse, despair.
　　　Enter Betty

BETTY Madam, the coach is ready.

BELLINDA I'm coming.　　　　　　　　　　　　　　　　　　　5
　　　Bellinda goes towards the table
Be sure you let none have admittance.

BETTY I will not, madam.
　　　Enter Sir Charles Beauclair

BETTY Oh, sir! My lady charged you should not enter.

SIR CHARLES Away, you trifler.
　　　[*Exit Betty*]
Where's my Bellinda?　　　　　　　　　　　　　　　　　　10

BELLINDA This is unmanly; not conquer your desires, nor obey my
positive commands.

SIR CHARLES Oh, stay and hear me. Let me hang upon your knees, for
I am out of breath, clasp and prattle o'er thee like a glad mother
when she hugs her first-born blessing after the pangs of death.°　　15
Mine,° like hers, is folly all, but full of fondness.

BELLINDA Oh!

SIR CHARLES Sigh not, my fair. By heaven, I am free from any chains
but thine; free as thy own clear soul's from vice.

BELLINDA How! What mean ye? Oh, rise, and stop my growing fears.　　20
Where's your wife? Is she well?

SIR CHARLES Think not so basely of me. She's well, and in her husband's arms. Oh, my Bellinda! In her husband's arms; her first and
only husband, Allen, is returned.

BELLINDA Forgetting all colder, nicer forms, in thy faithful bosom let   25
me receive such news.

    Sir Charles and Bellinda embrace

SIR CHARLES My life.

BELLINDA My soul.

SIR CHARLES Ha! The transporting joy has caught her rosy breath,
and those bright eyes are in their snowy lids retired. Oh, this is   30
more, much more than ten thousand words could have expressed.
Wake, my Bellinda, 'tis thy Beauclair calls.

BELLINDA Do not view my blushing face. I fear I have offended that
virgin modesty by me still practised and adored. Now we must
stand on forms till time and decency shall crown our wishes.   35

SIR CHARLES My goddess, conqueress, by thee forever I am directed.

BELLINDA I know thy honest heart so well, I do not scruple the truth
of what you have said.

SIR CHARLES You need not, dearest. See, all our friends come to
confirm it.   40

    Enter Sir Francis Wildlove, Beaumont, Cheatall, Mrs Beauclair
    and Arabella

MRS BEAUCLAIR Joy to my dear Bellinda.

ARABELLA Permit a stranger to rejoice at the reward of virtue and
constant love.

BELLINDA Pardon my answers, ladies, when I confess I scarce know
where I am.   45

SIR CHARLES Now I can mind the affairs of my friend. Sir Francis, I
observe you very assiduous to my niece. Has she received you for
her servant? And are you resolved on the truest happiness,
constancy?

SIR FRANCIS Yes, faith, Sir Charles, I am the lady's dog on a string,   50
and have violent pantings towards the delicious charmer. I hope she
won't long defer my desires—but let that black gentleman° I've so
long dreaded do his worst, he shan't spoil my stomach.

MRS BEAUCLAIR Ah, those pantings, Sir Francis, I doubt they have
moved your stomach so often till° they've quite took it away.   55

SIR FRANCIS A little forbearance, and such a tempting meal——

SIR CHARLES (*to Mr Beaumont*) You, sir, too are blessed. I read it in
your eyes and see the lady with ye.

BEAUMONT I fear no danger now, but dying of that pleasing fever
called rapture.   60

CHEATALL To any man's thinking, these° now are going to heaven,
ding-dong.° But hear me, ladies: faith, all young handsome fellows

talk just so before matrimony. Seven years hence, let me hear of
pantings, heavings, and raptures. No, gadzooks, scarce risings°
then. I shall live a jolly bachelor and laugh at your indifference,   65
gadzooks, I shall!

MRS BEAUCLAIR Well said, squire. We would° bring him along, Sir
Charles. I think him very good-humoured to this lady,° and believe
his sister only made him otherwise.

SIR CHARLES I read in every face a pleasing joy, but you must give me   70
leave to think that mine exceeds, raised to unexpected worlds of
bliss when sunk in sorrows and despair.

> Kind fate, beyond my hope, the weight removed,
> And gave me all, in giving her I loved.

Exeunt

EPILOGUE

SPOKEN BY MR SCUDAMORE°
WRITTEN BY MR MOTTEUX°

Scribblers, like bullies, sometimes huff the pit,°
Though their feigned courage has an ague fit;°
But oftener, from a sense of their condition,°
An epilogue resembles a petition.
Thus they make Mr Bayes his notion just:°   5
If thunder cannot save them, halters must.°
Which way to use, I swear I do not know:
Huffing's too haughty; cringing is too low.
I'll use the middle way; perhaps 'twill do;°
At least, I fancy, 'tis most liked by you.   10
Thus then, to every judge of wit I bow.
I hope all the audience think I mean them now.
If so, you'll scorn to judge of woman's wit.°
Though in wit's court the worst of judges sit,
Sure none dare try such puny causes yet.   15
Faith, if you're strict, now there's a reformation,°
We've sworn t'invite the grave part of the nation:
Rich sparks with broad-brim hats and little bands,°
Who'll clap dry morals till they hurt their hands;
Nice dames, who'll have their box as they've their pew,   20
And come each day, but not to ogle you.°
No, each sidebox shall shine with sweeter faces;°
None but chains, gowns, and coifs shall have their places,°
Their chit-chat news, stockjobbing, and law causes.°
The middle-fry shall in the gall'ry sit,°   25
And *humh* whatever against cuckolds writ.°
And city wives from lectures throng the pit:°
Their daughters fair with prentice trudge it hither,
And throng as they do Lambeth Wells this weather.°
Then all thus stored, though money's scarce this age,°   30
We need not fear t' have a beau-crowded stage.°
So, for new guests we'll change, just as our beaux°
Wear doily-stuff, for want of better clothes.°

THE BUSYBODY

SUSANNA CENTLIVRE

Quem tulit ad scenam ventoso gloria curru;
Exanimat lentus spectator, sedulus inflat.
Sic leve, sic parvum est, animum quod laudis avarum
Subruit aut reficit—

Horat. Epist. Lib. II. Ep. I°

To the Right Honourable John, Lord Somers,° Lord-President of her Majesty's most honourable Privy-Council.

May it please your lordship,

As it's an established custom in these latter ages for all writers, particularly the poetical, to shelter their productions under the protection of the most distinguished, whose approbation produces a kind of inspiration much superior to that which the heathenish poets° pretended to derive from their fictitious Apollo, so it was my ambition to address one of my weak performances to your lordship, who, by universal consent,° are justly allowed to be the best judge of all kinds of writing.

I was indeed at first deterred from my design by a thought that it might be accounted unpardonable rudeness to obtrude a trifle of this nature to° a person whose sublime wisdom moderates that council° which, at this critical juncture, overrules the fate of all Europe.° But then I was encouraged by reflecting that Lelius° and Scipio,° the two greatest men in their time, among the Romans, both for political and military virtues, in the height of their important affairs, thought the perusal and improving of Terence's° comedies the noblest way of unbinding° their minds. I own I were guilty of the highest vanity should I presume to put my composures in parallel with those° of that celebrated dramatist. But then again, I hope that your lordship's native goodness and generosity, in condescension to the taste of the best and fairest° part of the town, who have been pleased to be diverted by the following scenes, will excuse and overlook such faults as your nicer° judgement might discern.

And here, my lord, the occasion seems fair for me to engage in a panegyric upon those natural and acquired abilities which so brightly adorn your person. But I shall resist that temptation, being conscious of the inequality of a female pen to so masculine an attempt, and having no other ambition than to subscribe myself,

> My lord,
> Your lordship's most humble and most obedient servant,
> Susanna Centlivre

THE CHARACTERS OF THE PLAY

Sir George Airy,° *a gentleman of four thousand a year, in love with Miranda* — Mr Wilks

Sir Francis Gripe,° *guardian to Miranda and Marplot, father to Charles, in love with Miranda* — Mr Estcourt

Charles, *friend to Sir George, in love with Isabinda* — Mr Mills

Sir Jealous Traffick,° *a merchant that had lived sometime in Spain, a great admirer of the Spanish customs, father to Isabinda* — Mr Bullock

Marplot,° *a sort of a silly fellow, cowardly, but very inquisitive to know everybody's business; generally spoils all he undertakes, yet without design* — Mr Pack

Whisper,° *servant to Charles* — Mr Bullock, jun.

[Servants to Sir Jealous Traffick]

Miranda,° *an heiress, worth thirty thousand pound, really in love with Sir George, but pretends to be so with her guardian, Sir Francis* — Mrs Cross

Isabinda,° *daughter to Sir Jealous, in love with Charles, but designed for a Spanish merchant by her father, and kept up° from the sight of all men* — Mrs Rogers

Patch,° *woman to Isabinda* — Mrs Saunders

Scentwell,° *woman to Miranda* — Mrs Mills

PROLOGUE

BY THE AUTHOR OF *Tunbridge-Walks*°

Though modern prophets were exposed of late,°
The author could not prophesy his fate;°
If with such scenes an audience had been fired,°
The poet must have really been inspired.
But these, alas! are melancholy days   5
For modern prophets, and for modern plays.
Yet since prophetic lies please fools o'fashion,
And women are so fond of agitation,
To men of sense, I'll prophesy anew,
And tell you wondrous things that will prove true: 10
Undaunted colonels will to camps repair,°
Assured there'll be no skirmishes this year.
On our own terms will flow the wished-for peace;°
All wars, except 'twixt man and wife, will cease.
The grand monarch may wish his son a throne,   15
But hardly will advance to lose his own.°
This season most things bear a smiling face;°
But players in summer have a dismal case,°
Since your appearance only is our act of grace.°
Court ladies will to country seats be gone   20
(My lord can't all the year live great in town),°
Where wanting operas, basset, and a play,°
They'll sigh and stitch a gown to pass the time away.
Gay city-wives at Tunbridge will appear,°
Whose husbands long have laboured for an heir;   25
Where many a courtier may their wants relieve,
But by the waters only they conceive.°
The Fleet Street sempstress, toast of Temple sparks,°
That runs spruce neckcloths for attorneys' clerks,°
At Cupid's Gardens will her hours regale,°   30
Sing 'Fair Dorinda', and drink bottled ale.°
At all assemblies, rakes are up and down,
And gamesters, where they think they are not known.
　　Should I denounce our author's fate today,°
To cry down prophecies, you'd damn the play.°   35

Yet whims like these have sometimes made you laugh;
'Tis tattling all, like Isaac Bickerstaff.°
   Since war, and places, claim the bards that write,°
Be kind, and bear a woman's treat tonight;
Let your indulgence all her fears allay,   40
And none but woman-haters damn this play.

1.1

The Park°
Sir George Airy meeting Charles

CHARLES Ha! Sir George Airy! A-birding° thus early? What forbidden
game roused you so soon? For no lawful occasion could invite a
person of your figure° abroad at such unfashionable hours.°

SIR GEORGE There are some men, Charles, whom fortune has left free
from inquietudes, who are diligently studious to find out ways and 5
means to make themselves uneasy.

CHARLES Is it possible that anything in nature can ruffle the temper
of a man whom the four seasons of the year compliment with
as many thousand pounds? Nay, and a father at rest with his
ancestors? 10

SIR GEORGE Why, there 'tis now! A man that wants money thinks
none can be unhappy that has it; but my affairs are in such a
whimsical° posture, that it will require a calculation of my nativity°
to find if my gold will relieve me or not.

CHARLES Ha, ha, ha! Never consult the stars about that; gold has a 15
power beyond them. Gold unlocks the midnight councils;° gold
outdoes the wind, becalms the ship, or fills her sails; gold is
omnipotent below;° it makes whole armies fight, or fly; it buys even
souls, and bribes the wretches to betray their country. Then what
can thy business be that gold won't serve thee in? 20

SIR GEORGE Why, I'm in love.

CHARLES In love! Ha, ha, ha, ha! In love! Ha, ha, ha! With what,
prithee, a cherubim?

SIR GEORGE No, with a woman.

CHARLES A woman, good! Ha, ha, ha! And gold not help thee? 25

SIR GEORGE But suppose I'm in love with two—

CHARLES Ay, if thou'rt in love with two hundred, gold will fetch 'em, I
warrant thee, boy. But who are they? Who are they? Come.

SIR GEORGE One is a lady whose face I never saw, but witty as an angel;
the other beautiful as Venus— 30

CHARLES And a fool—

SIR GEORGE For aught I know, for I never spoke to her, but you can
inform me. I am charmed by the wit of one, and die for the beauty
of the other.

CHARLES And, pray, which are you in quest of now? 35

SIR GEORGE I prefer the sensual pleasure. I'm for her I've seen, who is
thy father's ward Miranda.

CHARLES Nay then, I pity you; for the Jew my father° will no more
part with her and thirty thousand pound,° than he would with a
guinea to keep me from starving.   40

SIR GEORGE Now you see gold can't do everything, Charles.

CHARLES Yes, for 'tis her gold that bars my father's gate against you.

SIR GEORGE Why, if he is this avaricious wretch, how cam'st thou by
such a liberal education?

CHARLES Not a souse° out of his pocket, I assure you. I had an uncle   45
who defrayed that charge, but for some little wildnesses of youth,°
though he made me his heir, left Dad my guardian till I came to
years of discretion, which I presume the old gentleman will never
think I am. And now he has got the estate into his clutches, it does
me no more good than if it lay in Prester John's dominions.°   50

SIR GEORGE What, canst thou find no stratagem to redeem it?

CHARLES I have made many essays to no purpose. Though Want, the
mistress of invention, still tempts me on, yet still the old fox is too
cunning for me. I am upon my last project, which if it fails, then for
my last refuge, a brown musket.°   55

SIR GEORGE What is't? Can I assist thee?

CHARLES Not yet. When you can, I have confidence enough in you to
ask it.

SIR GEORGE I am always ready. But what does he intend to do with
Miranda? Is she to be sold in private? Or will he put her up by way   60
of auction at who bids most? If so, egad, I'm for him; my gold, as
you say, shall be subservient to my pleasure.

CHARLES To deal ingeniously° with you, Sir George, I know very little
of her, or home; for since my uncle's death, and my return from
travel, I have never been well with my father. He thinks my   65
expenses too great, and I his allowance too little. He never sees me,
but he quarrels; and to avoid that, I shun his house as much as
possible. The report is, he intends to marry her himself.

SIR GEORGE Can she consent to it?

CHARLES Yes faith, so they say; but I tell you, I am wholly ignorant of   70
the matter. Miranda and I are like two violent members of a contrary party: I can scarce allow her beauty, though all the world does;
nor she me civility, for that contempt.° I fancy she plays the
mother-in-law already and sets the old gentleman on to do
mischief.   75

SIR GEORGE Then I've your free consent to get her.

CHARLES Ay, and my helping hand, if occasion be.

SIR GEORGE Pugh, yonder's a fool coming this way; let's avoid him.

CHARLES What, Marplot? No, no, he's my instrument. There's a thousand conveniences in him. He'll lend me his money when he has any, run of my errands and be proud on't; in short, he'll pimp for me, lie for me, drink for me, do anything but fight for me, and that I trust to my own arm for.

SIR GEORGE Nay then he's to be endured; I never knew his qualifications before.

Enter Marplot with a patch across his face

MARPLOT Dear Charles, yours. (*Aside*) Ha! Sir George Airy, the man in the world I have an ambition to be known to. [*To Charles*] Give me thy hand, dear boy—

CHARLES A good assurance!° But hark ye, how came your beautiful countenance clouded in the wrong place?

MARPLOT I must confess 'tis a little malapropos, but no matter for that; a word with you, Charles. [*Takes Charles aside*] Prithee, introduce me to Sir George. He is a man of wit, and I'd give ten guineas to—

CHARLES When you have 'em, you mean.

MARPLOT Ay, when I have 'em. Pugh, pox, you cut the thread of my discourse. I would give ten guineas, I say, to be ranked in his acquaintance. Well, 'tis a vast addition to a man's fortune, according to the rout of the world,° to be seen in the company of leading men; for then we are all thought to be politicians, or Whigs,° or Jacks,° or High-Flyers,° or Low-Flyers,° or Levellers° and so forth; for you must know, we all herd in parties now.

CHARLES Then a fool for diversion is out of fashion, I find.

MARPLOT Yes, without° it be a mimicking fool, and they are darlings everywhere. But prithee introduce me.

CHARLES Well, on condition you'll give us a true account how you came by that mourning nose,° I will.

MARPLOT I'll do it.

CHARLES Sir George, here's a gentleman has a passionate desire to kiss your hand.

SIR GEORGE Oh, I honour men of the sword; and I presume this gentleman is lately come from Spain or Portugal° by his scars.

MARPLOT No, really, Sir George, mine sprung from civil fury. Happening last night into the Groom Porters,° I had a strong inclination to go ten guineas with a sort of a, sort of a—kind of a milksop, as I thought. A pox of the dice he flung out; and, my pockets being empty as Charles knows they sometimes are, he proved a surly North Briton,° and broke my face for my deficiency.

SIR GEORGE Ha, ha! And did not you draw?

MARPLOT Draw, sir! Why, I did but lay my hand upon my sword to make a swift retreat, and he roared out, 'Now the deel a ma sol, sir, gin ye touch yer steel, Ise whip mine through yer wem.'°

SIR GEORGE Ha, ha, ha!

CHARLES Ha, ha, ha, ha! Safe was the word, so you walked off, I suppose.

MARPLOT Yes, for I avoid fighting, purely to be serviceable to my friends, you know—

SIR GEORGE Your friends are much obliged to you, sir; I hope you'll rank me in that number.

MARPLOT Sir George, a bow from the side box, or to be seen in your chariot, binds me ever yours.°

SIR GEORGE Trifles; you may command 'em when you please.

CHARLES Provided he may command you—

MARPLOT Me! Why, I live for no other purpose. Sir George, I have the honour to be caressed by most of the reigning toasts of the town.° I'll tell 'em you are the finest gentleman—

SIR GEORGE No, no, prithee let me alone to tell the ladies my parts. Can you convey a letter upon occasion, or deliver a message with an air of business?° Ha?

MARPLOT With the assurance of a page and the gravity of a statesman.

SIR GEORGE You know Miranda!

MARPLOT What, my sister ward? Why, her guardian is mine; we are fellow sufferers. Ah, he is a covetous, cheating, sanctified curmudgeon; that Sir Francis Gripe is a damned old—

CHARLES I suppose, friend, you forget that he is my father?

MARPLOT I ask your pardon, Charles, but it is for your sake I hate him. Well, I say, the world is mistaken in him; his outside piety makes him every man's executor, and his inside cunning makes him every heir's jailer. Egad, Charles, I'm half persuaded that thou'rt some ward too, and never of his getting, for thou art as honest a debauchee as ever cuckolded a man of quality.

SIR GEORGE A pleasant fellow.

CHARLES The dog is diverting sometimes, or there would be no enduring his impertinence. He is pressing to be employed and willing to execute, but some ill fate generally attends all he undertakes, and he oftener spoils an intrigue than helps it.

MARPLOT If I miscarry 'tis none of my fault; I follow my instructions.

CHARLES Yes, witness the merchant's wife.

MARPLOT Pish, pox, that was an accident.

SIR GEORGE What was it, prithee?   160

CHARLES Why, you must know, I had lent a certain merchant my
hunting horses, and was to have met his wife in his absence. Sending him along with my groom to make the compliment,° and to
deliver a letter to the lady at the same time, what does he do but
gives the husband the letter, and offers her the horses.   165

MARPLOT I remember you was even with me, for you denied the letter
to be yours, and swore I had a design upon her, which my bones
paid for.

CHARLES Come, Sir George, let's walk round, if you are not engaged,
for I have sent my man upon a little earnest business, and have   170
ordered him to bring me the answer into the park.

MARPLOT [aside] Business, and I not know it. Egad I'll watch him.

SIR GEORGE I must beg your pardon, Charles. I am to meet your father
here.

CHARLES My father!   175

SIR GEORGE Aye! And about the oddest bargain perhaps you ever
heard of, but I'll not impart till I know the success.

MARPLOT (aside) What can his business be with Sir Francis? Now
would I give all the world to know it. Why the devil should not one
know every man's concern?   180

CHARLES Prosperity to't, whate'er it be. I have private affairs too.
Over a bottle we'll compare notes.

MARPLOT (aside) Charles knows I love a glass as well as any man; I'll
make one.° Shall it be tonight? And I long to know their secrets.
        Enter Whisper

WHISPER [aside to Charles]° Sir, sir, Miss Patch says Isabinda's Span- 185
ish° father has quite spoiled the plot, and she can't meet you in the
park, but he infallibly will go out this afternoon, she says; but I
must step again to know the hour.

MARPLOT (aside) What did Whisper say now? I shall go stark mad, if
I'm not let into this secret.   190

CHARLES [aside to Whisper] Cursed misfortune! Come along with me.
My heart feels pleasure at her name. [To Sir George] Sir George,
yours; we'll meet at the old place the usual hour.

SIR GEORGE Agreed; I think I see Sir Francis yonder.
        Exit [Sir George Airy]

CHARLES Marplot, you must excuse me, I am engaged.   195
        Exeunt [Charles and Whisper]

MARPLOT Engaged? Egad, I'll engage my life I'll know what your
engagement is.

    Exit [*Marplot.*] [*Enter Miranda*]

MIRANDA ([*as if*] *coming out of a chair.*° [*To chair carriers*]) Let the
chair wait. [*Aside*] My servant that dogged° Sir George said he was
in the park.   200

    Enter Patch

[*To Patch*] Ha! Miss Patch alone? Did not you tell me you had
contrived a way to bring Isabinda to the park?

PATCH Oh, madam, your ladyship can't imagine what a wretched disappointment we have met with. Just as I had fetched a suit of my
clothes for a disguise, comes my old master into his closet, which is   205
right against her chamber door. This struck us into a terrible fright.
At length I put on a grave face and asked him if he was at leisure for
his chocolate, in hopes to draw him out of his hole, but he snapped
my nose off, 'No, I shall be busy here this two hours'; at which my
poor mistress, seeing no way of escape, ordered me to wait on your   210
ladyship with the sad relation.

MIRANDA Unhappy Isabinda! Was ever anything so unaccountable as
the humour of Sir Jealous° Traffick.

PATCH Oh, madam, it's his living so long in Spain. He vows he'll
spend half his estate, but he'll be a parliament-man on purpose to   215
bring in a bill for women to wear veils, and the other odious Spanish customs.° He swears it is the height of impudence to have a
woman seen bare-faced even at church, and scarce believes there's a
true begotten child in the city.

MIRANDA Ha, ha, ha! How the old fool torments himself! Suppose he   220
could introduce his rigid rules, does he think we could not match
them in contrivance? No, no, let the tyrant Man make what laws he
will; if there's a woman under the government, I warrant she finds
a way to break 'em. Is his mind set upon the Spaniard for his son-
in-law still?   225

PATCH Ay, and he expects him by the next fleet, which drives his
daughter to melancholy and despair. But, madam, I find you retain
the same gay, cheerful spirit you had when I waited on your ladyship. My lady is mighty good-humoured too, and I have found a
way to make Sir Jealous believe I am wholly in his interest, when   230
my real design is to serve her. He makes me her jailer, and I set her
at liberty.

MIRANDA I knew thy prolific brain would be of singular service to her,
or I had not parted with thee to her father.

PATCH But, madam, the report is that you are going to marry your   235
guardian.

MIRANDA It is necessary such a report should be, Patch.

PATCH But is it true, madam?

MIRANDA That's not absolutely necessary.

PATCH I thought it was only the old strain, coaxing him still for your   240
own, and railing at all the young fellows about town. In my mind
now, you are as ill-plagued with your guardian, madam, as my lady
is with her father.

MIRANDA No, I have liberty, wench; that she wants.° What would she
give now to be in this deshabille° in the open air, nay more, in   245
pursuit of the young fellow she likes; for that's my case, I assure
thee.

PATCH As for that, madam, she's even with you; for though she can't
come abroad, we have a way to bring him home in spite of old
Argus.°   250

MIRANDA Now, Patch, your opinion of my choice, for here he comes.
Ha, my guardian with him! What can be the meaning of this? I'm
sure Sir Francis can't know me in this dress. Let's observe 'em.
*Miranda and Patch withdraw.° Enter Sir Francis Gripe and Sir
George Airy*

SIR FRANCIS Verily, Sir George, thou wilt repent throwing away thy
money so, for I tell thee sincerely, Miranda, my charge, does not   255
love a young fellow. They are all vicious° and seldom make good
husbands. In sober sadness° she cannot abide 'em.

MIRANDA (*peeping*)° In sober sadness you are mistaken. What can this
mean?

SIR GEORGE Look ye, Sir Francis, whether she can or cannot abide   260
young fellows is not the business; will you take the fifty guineas?

SIR FRANCIS In good truth, I will not, for I knew thy father; he was
a hearty wary man, and I cannot consent that his son should
squander away what he saved, to no purpose.

MIRANDA (*peeping*) Now, in the name of wonder, what bargain can he   265
be driving about me for fifty guineas?

PATCH [*peeping*] I wish it ben't for the first night's lodging,° madam.

SIR GEORGE Well, Sir Francis, since you are so conscientious for my
father's sake, then permit me the favour, gratis.

MIRANDA (*peeping*) The favour!° Oh my life! I believe 'tis as you said,   270
Patch.

SIR FRANCIS No, verily, if thou dost not buy thy experience, thou
would never be wise; therefore give me a hundred and try fortune.

SIR GEORGE [*aside*] The scruples arose, I find, from the scanty sum. [*Aloud*] Let me see, a hundred guineas. (*Takes them out of a purse and chinks them*) Ha! They have a very pretty sound, and a very pleasing look—but then, Miranda—but, if she should be cruel— 275

MIRANDA (*peeping*) As ten to one I shall.

SIR FRANCIS Ay, do consider on't. He, he, he, he!

SIR GEORGE No, I'll do't. 280

PATCH [*peeping*] Do't! What, whether you will or no, madam?

SIR GEORGE Come to the point. Here's the gold; sum up the conditions.

MIRANDA (*peeping*) Ay, for heaven's sake do, for my expectation is on the rack. 285

SIR FRANCIS (*pulling out a paper*) Well, at your own peril be it.

SIR GEORGE Aye, aye, go on.

SIR FRANCIS [*reading the paper*] Imprimis,° you are to be admitted into my house in order to move your suit to Miranda, for the space of ten minutes, without let° or molestation, provided I remain in 290 the same room.

SIR GEORGE But out of earshot—

SIR FRANCIS Well, well, I don't desire to hear what you say. Ha, ha, ha! In consideration, I am to have that purse and a hundred guineas.

SIR GEORGE (*gives him the purse*) Take it. 295

MIRANDA (*peeping*) So, 'tis well it's no worse. I'll fit° you both.

SIR GEORGE And this agreement is to be performed today.

SIR FRANCIS Aye, aye, the sooner the better. [*Aside*] Poor fool, how Miranda and I shall laugh at him. [*To Sir George*] Well, Sir George, ha, ha, ha, take the last sound of your guineas, ha, ha, ha! (*Chinks* 300 *them*)

    Exit [*Sir Francis Gripe*]

MIRANDA (*peeping*) Sure he does not know I am Miranda.

SIR GEORGE A very extraordinary bargain I have made truly. If she should be really in love with this old cuff now. Pshaw, that's morally impossible. But then, what hopes have I to succeed? I never spoke 305 to her.

MIRANDA (*peeping*) Say you so? Then I am safe.

SIR GEORGE What though my tongue never spoke, my eyes said a thousand things, and my hopes flattered me hers answered 'em. If I'm lucky—if not, 'tis but a hundred guineas thrown away. 310

    [*Miranda puts on her mask.*] *Miranda and Patch come forward*

MIRANDA Upon what, Sir George?

SIR GEORGE Ha, my incognita!° Upon a woman, madam.

MIRANDA They are the worst things you can deal in, and damage the soonest; your very breath destroys 'em, and I fear you'll never see your return, Sir George. Ha, ha!   315

SIR GEORGE Were they more brittle than china and dropped to pieces with a touch, every atom of her I have ventured at, if she is but mistress of thy wit, balances ten times the sum. Prithee, let me see thy face.

MIRANDA By no means! That may spoil your opinion of my sense.   320

SIR GEORGE Rather confirm it, madam.

PATCH So rob the lady° of your gallantry, sir.

SIR GEORGE No, child, a dish of chocolate in the morning never spoils my dinner; the other lady I design a set meal;° so there's no danger—   325

MIRANDA Matrimony! Ha, ha, ha! What crimes have you committed against the god of love that he should revenge 'em so severely to stamp husband upon your forehead?

SIR GEORGE For my folly in having so often met you here, without pursuing the laws of nature and exercising her command. But I   330
resolve, ere we part now, to know who you are, where you live, and what kind of flesh and blood your face is; therefore unmask and don't put me to the trouble of doing it for you.

MIRANDA My face is the same flesh and blood with my hand, Sir George, which if you'll be so rude to provoke—   335

SIR GEORGE You'll apply it to my cheek. The ladies' favours are always welcome; but I must have that cloud° withdrawn. (*Taking hold of her*) Remember, you are in the park,° child, and what a terrible thing would it be to lose this pretty white hand.

MIRANDA And how will it sound in a chocolate-house, that Sir George   340
Airy rudely pulled off a lady's mask when he had given her his honour that he never would, directly or indirectly, endeavour to know her till she gave him leave.

PATCH (*aside*) I wish we were safe out.

SIR GEORGE But if that lady thinks fit to pursue and meet me at every   345
turn like some troubled spirit, shall I be blamed if I inquire into the reality? I would have nothing dissatisfied in a female shape.

MIRANDA [*aside*] What shall I do? (*Pause*)

SIR GEORGE Ay, prithee consider, for thou shalt find me very much at thy service.   350

PATCH Suppose, sir, the lady° should be in love with you.

SIR GEORGE Oh! I'll return the obligation in a moment.

PATCH And marry her?

SIR GEORGE Ha, ha, ha! That's not the way to love her, child.

MIRANDA [*aside*] If he discovers me I shall die. Which way shall I   355
escape? Let me see. (*Pauses*)

SIR GEORGE Well, madam?

MIRANDA [*aside*] I have it. [*To Sir George*] Sir George, 'tis fit you
should allow something. If you'll excuse my face and turn your
back—if you look upon me I shall sink, even masked as I am—I will   360
confess why I have engaged you so often, who I am, and where I
live.

SIR GEORGE Well, to show you I'm a man of honour I accept the
conditions. (*Aside*) Let me but once know those and the face won't
be long a secret to me.   365

PATCH [*aside to Miranda*] What mean you, madam?

MIRANDA [*aside to Patch*] To get off.

SIR GEORGE 'Tis something indecent to turn one's back upon a lady,
but you command and I obey. (*Turns his back*) Come, madam,
begin.   370

MIRANDA (*draws back a little while and speaks*) First then, it was my
unhappy lot to see you at Paris at a ball upon a birthday. Your shape
and air charmed my eyes; your wit and complaisance my soul, and
from that fatal night I loved you. (*Drawing back*)

> And when you left the place, grief seized me so,   375
> No rest my heart, no sleep my eyes could know.
> Last I resolved a hazardous point to try,
> And quit the place in search of liberty.

> *Exeunt* [*Miranda and Patch*]

SIR GEORGE Excellent. [*Aside*] I hope she's handsome. [*Aloud*] Well,
now, madam, to the other two things: Your name, and where you   380
live.—I am a gentleman, and this confession will not be lost upon
me.—Nay, prithee don't weep, but go on, for I find my heart melts
in thy behalf.—Speak quickly or I shall turn about.—Not yet?
[*Aside*] Poor lady, she expects I should comfort her; and to do her
justice, she has said enough to encourage me. (*Turns about*) [*Aloud*]   385
Ha? Gone! The devil, jilted? Why, what a tale has she invented, of
Paris, balls, and birthdays! Egad, I'd give ten guineas to know who
this gypsy° is. A curse of my folly! I deserve to lose her; what
woman can forgive a man that turns his back?

> The bold and resolute, in love and war,   390
> To conquer, take the right and swiftest way;
> The boldest lover soonest gains the fair,

As courage makes the rudest force obey.
Take no denial and the dames adore ye;
Closely pursue them and they fall before ye.   395
[*Exit*]

2.1

[Sir Francis Gripe's house]
Enter Sir Francis Gripe and Miranda

SIR FRANCIS Ha, ha, ha, ha, ha, ha, ha!

MIRANDA Ha, ha, ha, ha, ha, ha, ha! Oh, I shall die with laughing. The most romantic adventure! Ha, ha! What does the odious young fop mean? A hundred pieces° to talk an hour with me? Ho, ha!

SIR FRANCIS And I'm to be by, too; there's the jest. Adod, if it had been in private, I should not have cared to trust the young dog.

MIRANDA Indeed and indeed, but you might, Gardee.° Now, methinks there's nobody handsomer than you: so neat, so clean, so good-humoured, and so loving.

SIR FRANCIS Pretty rogue, pretty rogue, and so thou shalt find me, if thou dost prefer thy Gardee before these caperers of the age. Thou shalt outshine the queen's box on an opera night;° thou shalt be the envy of the ring,° for I will carry thee to Hyde Park, and thy equipage shall surpass the, what-d'ye call 'em, ambassadors.

MIRANDA Nay, I'm sure the discreet part of my sex will envy me more for the inside furniture, when you are in it, than my outside equipage.

SIR FRANCIS A cunning baggage, a-faith thou art, and a wise one too; and to show thee thou hast not chose amiss, I'll this moment disinherit my son, and settle my whole estate upon thee.

MIRANDA (*aside*) There's an old rogue now. [*To Sir Francis*] No, Gardee, I would not have your name be so black in the world. You know my father's will runs that I am not to possess my estate without your consent till I'm five and twenty; you shall only abate the odd seven years, and make me mistress of my estate today, and I'll make you master of my person tomorrow.

SIR FRANCIS Humph? That may not be safe. No, Chargee,° I'll settle it upon thee for pin-money,° and that will be every bit as well, thou know'st.

MIRANDA (*aside*) Unconscionable old wretch! Bribe me with my own money. Which way shall I get out of his hands?

SIR FRANCIS Well, what art thou thinking on, my girl, ha? How to banter Sir George?

MIRANDA (*aside*) I must not pretend to banter: he knows my tongue

too well. [*To Sir Francis*] No, Gardee, I have thought of a way will
confound him more than all I could say if I should talk to him seven
years.

SIR FRANCIS How's that? Oh, I'm transported; I'm ravished; I'm
mad—

MIRANDA (*aside*) It would make you mad, if you knew all. [*To Sir
Francis*] I'll not answer him one word, but be dumb to all he says.

SIR FRANCIS Dumb, good! Ha, ha, ha! Excellent, ha, ha! I think I have
you now, Sir George. Dumb! He'll go distracted. [*Aside*] Well, she's
the wittiest rogue.—Ha, ha, dumb! I can but laugh, ha, ha, to think
how damned mad he'll be when he finds he has given his money
away for a dumb show. Ha, ha, ha!

MIRANDA Nay, Gardee, if he did but know my thoughts of him, it
would make him ten times madder! Ha, ha, ha!

SIR FRANCIS Ay, so it would, Chargee. To hold him in such derision,
to scorn to answer him, to be dumb! Ha, ha, ha, ha!

Enter Charles

SIR FRANCIS How now, sirrah, who let you in?

CHARLES My necessity, sir.

SIR FRANCIS Sir, your necessities are very impertinent, and ought to
have sent before they entered.°

CHARLES Sir, I knew 'twas a word would gain admittance nowhere.

SIR FRANCIS Then, sirrah, how durst you rudely thrust that upon
your father which nobody else would admit?

CHARLES Sure the name of a son is a sufficient plea. I ask this lady's
pardon if I have intruded.

SIR FRANCIS Ay, ay, ask her pardon, and her blessing too, if you expect
anything from me.

MIRANDA I believe yours, Sir Francis, in a purse of guineas would be
more material. Your son may have business with you; I'll retire.

SIR FRANCIS I guess his business, but I'll dispatch him. I expect the
knight every minute: you'll be in readiness.

MIRANDA Certainly! [*Aside*]° My expectation is more upon the wing
than yours, old gentleman.

Exit [Miranda]

SIR FRANCIS Well, sir?

CHARLES Nay, it is very ill, sir; my circumstances are, I'm sure.

SIR FRANCIS And what's that to me, sir? Your management should
have made them better.

CHARLES If you please to entrust me with the management of my
estate, I shall endeavour it, sir.

SIR FRANCIS What, to set upon a card,° and buy a lady's favour at the   75
    price of a thousand pieces? To rig out an equipage for a wench, or
    by your carelessness enrich your steward? To fine for sheriff,° or
    put up for parliament-man?°
CHARLES I hope I should not spend it this way. However, I ask only for
    what my uncle left me; yours you may dispose of as you please, sir.   80
SIR FRANCIS That I shall, out of your reach, I assure you, sir. Adod,
    these young fellows think old men get estates for nothing but them
    to squander away in dicing, wenching, drinking, dressing, and so
    forth.
CHARLES I think I was born a gentleman, sir; I'm sure my uncle bred   85
    me like one.
SIR FRANCIS From which you would infer, sir, that gaming, whoring,
    and the pox° are requisites to a gentleman.
CHARLES (aside) Monstrous! When I would ask him only for a sup-
    port, he falls into these unmannerly reproaches. I must, though   90
    against my will, employ invention, and by stratagem relieve myself.
SIR FRANCIS Sirrah, what is it you mutter? Sirrah, ha? (Holds up his
    cane.) I say, you shan't have a groat out of my hands till I please—
    and maybe I'll never please, and what's that to you?
CHARLES Nay, to be robbed, or have one's throat cut is not much—   95
SIR FRANCIS What's that, sirrah? Would you rob me, or cut my throat,
    ye rogue?
CHARLES Heaven forbid, sir! I said no such thing.
SIR FRANCIS Mercy on me! What a plague it is to have a son of one
    and twenty who wants to elbow one out of one's life, to edge him-   100
    self into the estate.
        Enter Marplot
MARPLOT [aside] Egad, he's here! I was afraid I had lost him. His
    secret could not be with his father; his wants are public there.
    [Aloud] Guardian, your servant. Charles. [Aside to Charles] I know
    by that sorrowful countenance of thine. The old man's fist is as   105
    close as his strong box, but I'll help thee.°
SIR FRANCIS [aside] So: Here's another extravagant coxcomb that will
    spend his fortune before he comes to't; but he shall pay swingeing
    interest, and so let the fool go on. [Aloud] Well, what? Does
    necessity bring you too, sir?   110
MARPLOT You have hit it, guardian: I want a hundred pound.
SIR FRANCIS For what?
MARPLOT Pugh, for a hundred things; I can't for my life tell you for
    what.

CHARLES Sir, I suppose I have received all the answer I am like to have.   115

MARPLOT [aside] Oh, the devil, if he gets out before me, I shall lose him again.

SIR FRANCIS Ay, sir, and you may be marching as soon as you please. I must see a change in your temper ere you find one in mine.

MARPLOT Pray, sir, dispatch me; the money, sir, I'm in mighty haste.   120

SIR FRANCIS (gives him a note) Fool, take this and go to the cashier. I shan't be long plagued with thee.

MARPLOT [aside] Devil take the cashier, I shall certainly have Charles gone before I come back again. (Runs out)

CHARLES Well, sir, I take my leave, but remember, you expose an only   125
son to all the miseries of wretched poverty, which too often lays the plan for scenes of mischief.

SIR FRANCIS Stay, Charles. I have a sudden thought come into my head may prove to thy advantage.

CHARLES [aside] Ha, does he relent?   130

SIR FRANCIS My Lady Wrinkle, worth forty thousand pound, sets up for a handsome young husband; she praised thee t'other day. Though the matchmakers can get twenty guineas for a sight of her, I can introduce thee for nothing.

CHARLES My Lady Wrinkle, sir? Why, she has but one eye.   135

SIR FRANCIS Then she'll see but half your extravagance, sir.

CHARLES Condemn me to such a piece of deformity! Toothless, dirty, wry-necked, hunchbacked hag!

SIR FRANCIS Hunchbacked! So much the better! Then she has a rest for her misfortunes, for thou wilt load her swingeingly. Now I   140
warrant you think this is no offer of a father;° forty thousand pound is nothing with you.

CHARLES Yes, sir, I think it is too much. A young beautiful woman with half the money would be more agreeable. I thank you, sir; but you chose better for yourself, I find.   145

SIR FRANCIS Out of my doors, you dog! You pretend to meddle with my marriage, sirrah!

CHARLES Sir, I obey, but—

SIR FRANCIS But me no buts! Be gone, sir! Dare to ask me for money again—refuse forty thousand pound! Out of my doors, I say,   150
without reply.

Exit Charles. Enter Servant

SERVANT One Sir George Airy enquires for you, sir.

Enter Marplot running

MARPLOT Ha? Gone! Is Charles gone, guardian?

SIR FRANCIS Yes, and I desire your wise worship to walk after him.

MARPLOT Nay, egad, I shall run, I tell you but that. [*Aside*] Ah, pox of 155
the cashier for detaining me so long! Where the devil shall I find
him now? I shall certainly lose this secret.

> *Exit [Marplot] hastily*

SIR FRANCIS What, is the fellow distracted?—Desire Sir George to
walk up.

> [*Exit Servant*]

Now for a trial of skill that will make me happy, and him a fool. Ha, ha, 160
ha! In my mind he looks like an ass already.

> *Enter Sir George Airy*

SIR FRANCIS Well, Sir George, do ye hold in the same mind? Or would
you capitulate? Ha, ha, ha! Look, here are the guineas. (*Chinks
them*) Ha, ha, ha!

SIR GEORGE Not if they were twice the sum, Sir Francis. Therefore be 165
brief, call in the lady, and take your post. (*Aside*) If she's a woman,
and not seduced by witchcraft to this old rogue, I'll make his heart
ache; for if she has but one grain of inclination about her, I'll vary a
thousand shapes,° but find it.

> *Enter Miranda*

SIR FRANCIS Agreed.—Miranda. There, Sir George, try your fortune. 170
(*Takes out his watch*)

SIR GEORGE   So from the eastern chambers breaks the sun,
                    Dispels the clouds, and gilds the vales below.

(*Salutes Miranda*)°

SIR FRANCIS Hold, sir! Kissing was not in our agreement. 175

SIR GEORGE Oh, that's by way of prologue. Prithee, old Mammon,° to
thy post.

SIR FRANCIS Well, young Timon,° 'tis now four exactly: one hour,°
remember, is your utmost limit, not a minute more. (*Retires to the
bottom of the stage*)° 180

SIR GEORGE Madam, whether you will excuse or blame my love, the
author of this rash proceeding depends upon your pleasure, as also
the life of your admirer. Your sparkling eyes speak a heart suscep-
tible of love; your vivacity a soul too delicate to admit the embraces
of decayed mortality. 185

MIRANDA (*aside*) Oh, that I durst speak—

SIR GEORGE Shake off this tyrant guardian's yoke, assume yourself,
and dash his bold aspiring hopes. The deity of his desires is Avarice, a heretic in love, and ought to be banished by the Queen of
Beauty. See, madam [*kneels*], a faithful servant kneels and begs to be 190

admitted in the number of your slaves. (*Miranda gives him her hand to raise him*)

SIR FRANCIS [*aside*] I wish I could hear what he says now. (*Running up*)° [*Aloud*] Hold, hold, hold! No palming!° That's contrary to articles—

SIR GEORGE Death, sir, keep your distance (*lays his hand to his sword*), or I'll write another article in your guts.

SIR FRANCIS (*going back*) A bloody-minded fellow!

SIR GEORGE [*aside*] Not answer me! Perhaps she thinks my address too grave. I'll be more free. [*To Miranda*] Can you be so unconscionable, madam, to let me say all these fine things to you without one single compliment in return? View me well. Am I not a proper handsome fellow, ha? Can you prefer that old, dry, withered, sapless log of sixty-five to the vigorous, gay, sprightly love of twenty-four? With snoring only he'll awake thee, but I, with ravishing delight, would make thy senses dance in consort with the joyful minutes. [*Aside*] Ha? Not yet? Sure she is dumb. [*To Miranda*] Thus would I steal and touch thy beauteous hand (*takes hold of her hand*), till by degrees I reached thy snowy breasts, then ravish kisses thus. (*Embraces her in ecstasy*)

MIRANDA (*struggles and flings from him*) (*aside*) Oh heavens! I shall not be able to contain myself.

SIR FRANCIS (*running up with his watch in his hand*) [*aside*] Sure she did not speak to him. [*To Sir George*] There's three quarters of the hour gone, Sir George. [*Aside*] Adod, I don't like those close conferences—

SIR GEORGE More interruptions! You will have it, sir. (*Lays his hand to his sword*)

SIR FRANCIS (*going back*) (*aside*) No, no, you shan't have her neither.

SIR GEORGE [*aside*] Dumb still! Sure this old dog has enjoined her silence. I'll try another way. [*To Miranda*] I must conclude, madam, that, in compliance to your guardian's humour, you refuse to answer me. Consider the injustice of his injunction. This single hour cost me a hundred pound; and, would you answer me, I could purchase the twenty-four so. However, madam, you must give me leave to make the best interpretation I can for my money and take the indication of your silence for the secret liking of my person. Therefore, madam, I will instruct you how to keep your word inviolate to Sir Francis, and yet answer me to every question. As for example, when I ask anything, to which you would reply in the affirmative, gently nod your head thus [*nods his head*]; and when in

the negative thus (*shakes his head*); and in the doubtful a tender
sigh, thus. (*Sighs*)

MIRANDA (*aside*) How every action charms me, but I'll fit° him for   235
signs, I warrant him.

SIR FRANCIS (*aside*) Ha, ha, ha, ha! Poor Sir George! Ha, ha, ha, ha!

SIR GEORGE Was it by his desire that you are dumb, madam, to all that
I can say?

    Miranda nods

SIR GEORGE [*aside*] Very well! She's tractable I find. [*To Miranda*]
And is it possible that you can love him? (*Miranda nods*) Miracu-   240
lous! Pardon the bluntness of my questions, for my time is short;
may I not hope to supplant him in your esteem? (*Miranda sighs*)
[*Aside*] Good! She answers me as I could wish. [*To Miranda*] You'll
not consent to marry him then? (*Miranda sighs*) [*Aside*] How?
Doubtful in that? Undone again. Humph! But that may proceed   245
from his power to keep her out of her estate till twenty-five; I'll try
that. [*To Miranda*] Come, madam, I cannot think you hesitate in
this affair out of any motive but your fortune. Let him keep it till
those few years are expired: make me happy with your person, let
him enjoy your wealth. (*Miranda holds up her hands*) Why, what sign   250
is that now? Nay, nay, madam, except you observe my lesson, I can't
understand your meaning.

SIR FRANCIS [*aside*] What a vengeance! Are they talking by signs? Ad,
I may be fooled here. [*To Sir George*] What do you mean, Sir
George?   255

SIR GEORGE To cut your throat if you dare mutter another syllable.

SIR FRANCIS Od! I wish he were fairly out of my house.

SIR GEORGE Pray, madam, will you answer me to the purpose?
(*Miranda shakes her head and points to Sir Francis*) [*Aside*] What!
Does she mean she won't answer me to the purpose, or is she afraid   260
yon old cuff should understand her signs? Aye, it must be that. [*To
Miranda*] I perceive, madam. You are too apprehensive of the prom-
ise° you have made to follow my rules. Therefore I'll suppose your
mind and answer for you. First, for' myself, madam, that I am in
love with you is an infallible truth. Now for you. (*Turns on her side*)°   265
Indeed, sir, and may I believe it? [*Re-turning to his own side*] As
certainly, madam, as that 'tis daylight, or that I die if you persist in
silence. Bless me with the music of your voice and raise my spirits
to their proper heaven. Thus low let me entreat: ere I'm obliged to
quit this place, grant me some token of a favourable reception to   270
keep my hopes alive. (*Arises hastily, turns of her side*) Rise, sir, and

since my guardian's presence will not allow me privilege of tongue, read that (*offers her a letter*), and rest assured you are not indifferent to me. (*Miranda strikes down the letter*) Ha! Right woman! But no matter, I'll go on.   275

SIR FRANCIS Ha! What's that, a letter? Ha, ha, ha! Thou art balked.

MIRANDA (*aside*) The best assurance° I ever saw.

SIR GEORGE Ha? A letter! Oh, let me kiss it with the same raptures that I would do the dear hand that touched it! (*Opens it*) [*Aside*] Now for a quick fancy and a long extempore!° [*To Miranda*] What's   280
here? (*Reads*) 'Dear Sir George, this virgin muse I consecrate to you, which, when it has received the addition of your voice, 'twill charm me into desire of liberty to love, which you, and only you, can fix.' My angel! Oh, you transport me! (*Kisses the letter*) And see the power of your command. The god of love has set the verse   285
already; the flowing numbers° dance into a tune, and I'm inspired with a voice to sing it.

MIRANDA [*aside*] I'm sure thou art inspired with impudence enough.

SIR GEORGE (*sings*)

> Great love inspire him;
> Say I admire him.   290
> Give me the lover
> That can discover
> Secret devotion
> From silent motion;
> Then don't betray me,   295
> But hence convey me.

(*Sir George takes hold of Miranda*) With all my heart, this moment let's retire.

SIR FRANCIS (*coming up hastily*) The hour is expired, sir, and you must take your leave. There, my girl, there's the hundred pound   300
which thou hast won. Go, I'll be with you presently. Ha, ha, ha, ha!
      Exit Miranda

SIR GEORGE Adsheart, madam, you won't leave me just in the nick,° will you?

SIR FRANCIS Ha, ha, ha! She has nicked° you, Sir George, I think! Ha, ha, ha! Have you any more hundred pounds to throw away upon   305
courtship? Ha, ha, ha!

SIR GEORGE He, he, he, he! A curse of your fleering° jests. Yet, however ill I succeeded, I'll venture the same wager she does not value thee a spoonful of snuff.° Nay more, though you enjoined her

silence to me, you'll never make her speak to the purpose with   310
yourself.

SIR FRANCIS Ha, ha, ha! Did not I tell thee thou wouldst repent thy
money? Did not I say she hated young fellows? Ha, ha, ha!

SIR GEORGE And I'm positive she's not in love with age.

SIR FRANCIS Ha, ha! No matter for that! Ha, ha! She's not taken with   315
your youth, nor your rhetoric to boot. Ha, ha!

SIR GEORGE Whate'er her reasons are for disliking of me, I am certain
she can be taken with nothing about thee.

SIR FRANCIS Ha, ha, ha! [*Aside*] How he swells with envy! Poor man,
poor man. [*To Sir George*] Ha, ha! I must beg your pardon, Sir   320
George. Miranda will be impatient to have her share of mirth.
Verily we shall laugh at thee most egregiously. Ha, ha, ha!

SIR GEORGE With all my heart. Faith, I shall laugh in my turn too, for,
if you dare marry her, old Beelzebub,° you would be cuckolded
most egregiously. Remember that, and tremble.   325

> She that to age her beauteous self resigns,
> Shows witty management for close designs.
> Then if thou'rt graced with fair Miranda's bed,
> Actaeon's horns,° she means, shall crown thy head.
>
> *Exit [Sir George Airy]*

SIR FRANCIS Ha, ha, ha! He is mad.   330

> These fluttering fops imagine they can wind,
> Turn, and decoy to love, all womenkind.
> But here's a proof of wisdom in my charge:
> Old men are constant, young men live at large.°
> The frugal hand can bills at sight defray,   335
> When he that lavish is, has nought to pay.

Exit

2.2

*Sir Jealous Traffick's house [and the doorway leading to the
street]*°
*Enter Sir Jealous Traffick and Isabinda [from another room].
Patch following*

SIR JEALOUS What, in the balcony° again, notwithstanding my

positive commands to the contrary! Why don't you write a bill°
upon your forehead to show passengers° there's something to be
let?

ISABINDA What harm can there be in a little fresh air, sir?   5

SIR JEALOUS Is your constitution so hot, mistress, that it wants cool-
ing, ha? Apply the virtuous Spanish rules:° banish your taste° and
thoughts of flesh;° feed upon roots, and quench your thirst with
water.

ISABINDA That and a close° room would certainly make me die of the   10
vapours.

SIR JEALOUS No, mistress, 'tis your high-fed, lusty, rambling, ram-
pant° ladies that are troubled with the vapours; 'tis your ratafia,
persico, cinnamon, citron, and spirit of claret° cause such swim-
ming in the brain, that carries many a guinea full tide to the doc-   15
tor.° But you are not to be bred this way. No galloping abroad, no
receiving visits at home, for, in our loose country, the women are as
dangerous as the men.

PATCH So I told her, sir; and that it was not decent to be seen in a
balcony, but she threatened to slap my chaps and told me I was her   20
servant, not her governess.

SIR JEALOUS Did she so? But I'll make her to know that you are her
duenna. Oh, that incomparable custom of Spain! Why, here's no
depending upon old women in my country, for they are as wanton
at eighty as a girl of eighteen, and a man may as safely trust to   25
Asgill's translation° as to his great-grandmother's not marrying
again.

ISABINDA Or to the Spanish ladies' veils, and duenna's, for the safe-
guard of their honour.

SIR JEALOUS Dare to ridicule the cautious conduct of that wise nation   30
and I'll have you locked up this fortnight, without a peephole.

ISABINDA [aside] If we had but the ghostly helps in England, which
they have in Spain,° I might deceive you if you did. [To Sir Jealous]
Sir, 'tis not the restraint, but the innate principles, secures the
reputation and honour of our sex. Let me tell you, sir, confinement   35
sharpens the invention, as want of sight strengthens the other
senses, and is often more pernicious than the recreation innocent
liberty allows.

SIR JEALOUS Say you so, mistress? Who the devil taught you the art of
reasoning? I assure you, they must have a greater faith than I pre-   40
tend to that can think any woman innocent who requires liberty.
Therefore, Patch, to your charge I give her. Lock her up till I come

back from Change.° I shall have some sauntering coxcomb, with
nothing but a red coat and a feather,° think, by leaping into her
arms, to leap into my estate. But I'll prevent them; she shall be only   45
Senior Barbinetto's.°

PATCH Really, sir, I wish you would employ anybody else in this affair;
I lead a life like a dog with obeying your commands. Come, madam,
will you please to be locked up?

ISABINDA (*aside*) Ay, to enjoy more freedom than he is aware of.   50
        Exit [Isabinda] with Patch

SIR JEALOUS I believe this wench is very true to my interest. I am
happy I met with her. If I can but keep my daughter from being
blown upon° till Senior Barbinetto arrives, who shall marry her as
soon as he comes and carry her to Spain as soon as he has married
her. She has a pregnant wit,° and I'd no more have her an English   55
wife, than the Grand Signior's° mistress.
        Exit [Sir Jealous Traffick.] Enter Whisper

WHISPER So, I see Sir Jealous go out. Where shall I find Mrs Patch
now?
        Enter Patch

PATCH Oh, Mr Whisper, my lady saw you out at the window and
ordered me to bid you fly and let your master know she's now alone.   60

WHISPER Hush, speak softly! I go, go. But harkee, Mrs Patch, shall not
you and I have a little confabulation,° when my master and your
lady is engaged?

PATCH Ay, ay, farewell.
        Patch goes in and shuts the door.° Enter Sir Jealous Traffick
        meeting Whisper

SIR JEALOUS Sure whilst I was talking with Mr Tradewell, I heard my   65
door clap. (*Seeing Whisper*) Ha! A man lurking about my house.
Who do you want there, sir?

WHISPER Want—(*Aside*) Want, a pox, Sir Jealous! What must I say
now?—

SIR JEALOUS Ay, want. Have you a letter or message for anybody   70
there? [*Aside*] O my conscience, this is some he-bawd.°

WHISPER Letter or message, sir!

SIR JEALOUS Ay, letter or message, sir.

WHISPER No, not I, sir.

SIR JEALOUS Sirrah, sirrah, I'll have you set in the stocks° if you don't   75
tell me your business immediately.

WHISPER Nay, sir, my business—is no great matter of business
neither; and yet 'tis business of consequence too.

SIR JEALOUS Sirrah, don't trifle with me.

WHISPER Trifle, sir! Have you found him, sir?   80

SIR JEALOUS Found what, you rascal?

WHISPER Why, Trifle is the very lap-dog my lady lost, sir. I fancied I
see him run into this house. I'm glad you have him. Sir, my lady
will be overjoyed that I have found him.

SIR JEALOUS Who is your lady friend?   85

WHISPER My Lady Love-puppy,° sir.

SIR JEALOUS My Lady Love-puppy! Then prithee carry thyself to her,
for I know no other whelp that belongs to her, and let me catch ye
no more puppy-hunting about my doors, lest I have you pressed
into the service,° sirrah.   90

WHISPER By no means, sir. Your humble servant. [*Aside*] I must watch
whether he goes or no before I can tell my master.
        Exit [*Whisper*]

SIR JEALOUS This fellow has the officious leer of a pimp, and I half
suspect a design, but I'll be upon them before they think on me, I
warrant 'em.   95
        Exit

2.3

Charles's lodging
Enter Charles and Marplot

CHARLES Honest Marplot, I thank thee for this supply. I expect my
lawyer with a thousand pound I have ordered him to take up,° and
then you shall be repaid.

MARPLOT Foh, foh, no more of that. Here comes Sir George Airy—
        Enter Sir George Airy
cursedly out of humour at his disappointment! See how he looks!   5
Ha, ha, ha!

SIR GEORGE Ah, Charles, I am so humbled in my pretensions to plots
upon women that I believe I shall never have courage enough to
attempt a chambermaid again, I'll tell thee.

CHARLES Ha, ha! I'll spare you the relation by telling you: impatient to   10
know your business with my father, when I saw you enter, I slipped
back into the next room, where I overheard every syllable.

SIR GEORGE That I said—but I'll be hanged if you heard her answer!
But prithee, tell me, Charles, is she a fool?

CHARLES I ne'er suspected her for one; but Marplot can inform you   15
better, if you'll allow him a judge.

MARPLOT A fool? I'll justify she has more wit than all the rest of her
sex put together! Why, she'll rally me till I han't one word to say for
myself.

CHARLES A mighty proof of her wit, truly.   20

MARPLOT There must be some trick in't, Sir George. Egad, I'll find it
out if it cost me the sum you paid for't.

SIR GEORGE Do and command me.

MARPLOT Enough! Let me alone to trace a secret.

Enter Whisper, and speaks aside to Charles

[*Aside*] The devil! Whisper here again! That fellow never speaks   25
out. Is this the same, or a new, secret? [*Aloud*] Sir George, won't
you ask Charles what news Whisper brings?

SIR GEORGE Not I, sir; I suppose it does not relate to me.

MARPLOT Lord, lord, how little curiosity some people have! Now, my
chief pleasure lies in knowing everybody's business.   30

SIR GEORGE I fancy, Charles, thou hast some engagement upon thy
hands. I have a little business, too.—Marplot, if it falls in your way
to bring me any intelligence from Miranda, you'll find me at the
Thatched House° at six.

MARPLOT You do me much honour.   35

CHARLES You guess right, Sir George. Wish me success.

SIR GEORGE Better than attended me. Adieu.

Exit [Sir George Airy]

CHARLES Marplot, you must excuse me.

MARPLOT Nay, nay, what need of any excuse amongst friends! I'll go
with you.   40

CHARLES Indeed, you must not.

MARPLOT No, then I suppose 'tis a duel, and I will go to secure ye.

CHARLES Secure me? Why, you won't fight!

MARPLOT What then? I can call people to part ye.

CHARLES Well, but it is no duel; consequently, no danger. Therefore,   45
prithee, be answered.

MARPLOT What, is't a mistress then? Mum! You know I can be silent
upon occasion.

CHARLES I wish you could be civil° too. I tell you, you neither must
nor shall go with me. Farewell.   50

Exeunt [Charles and Whisper]

MARPLOT Why, then, I must and will follow you.

Exit

3.1

[*Outside Sir Jealous Traffick's house*]
Enter Charles

CHARLES Well, here's the house which holds the lovely prize quiet and serene. Here no noisy footmen throng to tell the world that beauty dwells within; no ceremonious visit makes the lover wait; no rival to give my heart a pang. Who would not scale the window at midnight, without fear of the jealous father's pistol, rather than fill up 5 the train of a coquette, where every minute he is jostled out of place? (*Knocks softly*) Mrs Patch, Mrs Patch.

Enter Patch

PATCH Oh, are you come, sir? All's safe.

CHARLES So in, in then.

[*Exeunt Charles and Patch*] *Enter Marplot*

MARPLOT There he goes. Who the devil lives here? Except I can find 10 out that, I am as far from knowing his business as ever. Gad, I'll watch. It may be a bawdy-house, and he may have his throat cut; if there should be any mischief, I can make oath he went in. Well, Charles, in spite of your endeavour to keep me out of the secret, I may save your life, for aught I know. At that corner I'll plant myself: 15 there I shall see whoever goes in, or comes out. Gad, I love discoveries.

Exit

3.2

Scene draws,° [*discovering a room in Sir Jealous Traffick's house*]

Charles, Isabinda and Patch

ISABINDA Patch, look out sharp; have a care of Dad.

PATCH I warrant you.

Exit [*Patch*]

ISABINDA Well, sir, if I may judge your love by your courage, I ought to believe you sincere; for you venture into the lion's den when you come to see me. 5

104

CHARLES If you'd consent whilst the furious beast is abroad, I'd free you from the reach of his paws.

ISABINDA That would be but to avoid one danger by running into another, like the poor wretches who fly the burning ship and meet their fate in the water. Come, come, Charles, I fear if I consult my reason, confinement and plenty is better than liberty and starving. I know you'd make the frolic pleasing for a little time by saying and doing a world of tender things, but when our small substance is once exhausted, and a thousand requisites for life are wanting, love, who rarely dwells with poverty, would also fail us.

CHARLES Faith, I fancy not! Methinks my heart has laid up a stock will last for life, to back which I have taken a thousand pound upon° my uncle's estate. That surely will support us till one of our fathers relent.

ISABINDA There's no trusting to that, my friend. I doubt your father will carry his humour to the grave, and mine till he sees me settled in Spain.

CHARLES And can ye then cruelly resolve to stay till that cursed don arrives, and suffer that youth, beauty, fire and wit to be sacrificed to the arms of a dull Spaniard? To be immured and forbid the sight of anything that's humane?

ISABINDA No, when it comes to the extremity and no stratagem can relieve us, thou shalt list for a soldier, and I'll carry thy knapsack after thee.

CHARLES Bravely resolved! The world cannot be more savage than our parents, and Fortune generally assists the bold;° therefore consent now. Why should we put it to a future hazard? Who knows when we shall have another opportunity?

ISABINDA Oh, you have your ladder of ropes, I suppose, and the closet window stands just where it did; and if you haven't forgot to write in characters,° Patch will find a way for our assignations. Thus much of the Spanish contrivance my father's severity has taught me, I thank him. Though I hate the nation, I admire their management in these affairs.

Enter Patch

PATCH Oh, madam, I see my master coming up the street.

CHARLES Oh, the devil! Would I had my ladder now! I thought you had not expected him till night. Why, why, why, why? What shall I do, madam?

ISABINDA Oh, for heaven's sake, don't go that way, you'll meet him full in the teeth.° Oh, unlucky moment!

CHARLES Adsheart, can you shut me into no cupboard; ram me into no chest, ha?

PATCH Impossible, sir; he searches every hole in the house.

ISABINDA Undone forever! If he sees you, I shall never see you more.

PATCH I have thought on't. Run you to your chamber, madam. And sir, 50
come you along with me. I'm certain you may easily get down from the balcony.

CHARLES My life, adieu!—Lead on, guide.

    Exeunt [Charles and Patch]

ISABINDA Heaven preserve him.

    Exit

3.3

The street [outside Sir Jealous Traffick's house]
Enter Sir Jealous Traffick, with Marplot behind him

SIR JEALOUS I don't know what's the matter, but I have a strong suspicion all is not right within. That fellow's sauntering about my door,° and his tale of a puppy, had the face of a lie, methought. By St Iago,° if I should find a man in the house, I'd make mincemeat of him. 5

MARPLOT [*aside*] Ah, poor Charles! Ha? Agad, he is old; I fancy I might bully him and make Charles have an opinion of my courage.

SIR JEALOUS (*feeling for his key*) My own key shall let me in. I'll give them no warning. 10

MARPLOT (*going up to Sir Jealous*) What's that you say, sir?

SIR JEALOUS (*turns quick upon him*) What's that to you, sir?

MARPLOT Yes, 'tis to me, sir; for the gentleman you threaten is a very honest gentleman. Look to't, for if he comes not as safe out of your house as he went in, I have half a dozen myrmidons° hard by shall 15
beat it about your ears.

SIR JEALOUS Went in? What, is he in then? Ah, a combination to undo me! I'll myrmidon you, ye dog you. (*Beats Marplot*) Thieves, thieves!

MARPLOT Murder, murder! I was not in your house, sir! 20

    Enter Servant[s]

SERVANT What's the matter, sir?

SIR JEALOUS The matter, rascals? Have you let a man into my house?

But I'll flea° him alive; follow me! I'll not leave a mousehole
unsearched. If I find him, by St Iago, I'll equip him for the opera.°

Exeunt [Sir Jealous Traffick and Servants]

MARPLOT A deuce of his cane! There's no trusting to age. What shall I   25
do to relieve Charles? Egad, I'll raise the neighbourhood.—
Murder, murder!

Charles drops down upon him from the balcony

Charles! Faith, I'm glad to see thee safe out with all my heart.

CHARLES A pox of your bawling! How the devil came you here?

MARPLOT Here? Gad, I have done you a piece of service: I told the old   30
thunderbolt that the gentleman that was gone in was—

CHARLES Was it you that told him, sir? (*Laying hold of him*) 'Sdeath, I
could crush thee into atoms.

Exit [Charles]

MARPLOT What, will you choke me for my kindness?—Will my
enquiring soul never leave searching into other people's affairs till it   35
gets squeezed out of my body? I dare not follow him now, for my
blood, he's in such a passion! I'll to Miranda; if I can discover aught
that may oblige Sir George, it may be a means to reconcile me again
to Charles.

Exit [Marplot.] Enter Sir Jealous Traffick and Servants

SIR JEALOUS Are you sure you have searched everywhere?   40

SERVANT Yes, from the top of the house to the bottom.

SIR JEALOUS Under the beds, and over the beds?

SERVANT Yes, and in them too, but found nobody, sir.

SIR JEALOUS Why, what could this rogue mean?

Enter Isabinda and Patch

PATCH (*aside to Isabinda*) Take courage, madam, I saw him safe out.   45

ISABINDA Bless me! What's the matter, sir?

SIR JEALOUS You know best. Pray where's the man that was here just
now?

ISABINDA What man, sir? I saw none!

PATCH Nor I, by the trust you repose in me. Do you think I would let a   50
man come within these doors when you were absent?

SIR JEALOUS Ah, Patch, she may be too cunning for thy honesty. The
very scout that he had set to give warning discovered it to me, and
threatened me with half a dozen myrmidons. But I think I mauled
the villain. These afflictions you draw upon me, mistress!   55

ISABINDA Pardon me, sir, 'tis your own ridiculous humour draws you
into these vexations, and gives every fool pretence to banter you.

SIR JEALOUS No, 'tis your idle conduct, your coquettish flirting into°

the balcony. Oh, with what joy shall I resign thee into the arms of
Don Diego Barbinetto!   60

ISABINDA (*aside*) And with what industry shall I avoid him!

SIR JEALOUS Certainly that rogue had a message from somebody or
other, but being balked by my coming, popped that sham upon me.
[*To Servants*] Come along, ye sots, let's see if we can find the dog
again.—Patch, lock her up, d'ye hear?   65

PATCH Yes, sir.

      Exeunt [*Sir Jealous Traffick*] *with Servants*

Ay, walk till your heels ache, you'll find nobody, I promise you.

ISABINDA Who could that scout be which he talks of?

PATCH Nay, I can't imagine, without° it was Whisper.

ISABINDA Well, dear Patch, let's employ all our thoughts how to escape   70
this horrid Don Diego. My very heart sinks at his terrible name.

PATCH Fear not, madam, Don Carlo° shall be the man, or I'll lose the
reputation of contriving, and then what's a chambermaid good for?

ISABINDA Say'st thou so, my girl? Then

     Let Dad be jealous, multiply his cares;   75
     While love instructs me to avoid the snares,
     I'll, spite of all his Spanish caution, show
     How much for love a British maid can do.

    Exeunt

3.4

Sir Francis Gripe's house
Sir Francis Gripe and Miranda meeting

MIRANDA Well, Gardee, how did I perform my dumb scene?

SIR FRANCIS To admiration! Thou dear little rogue, let me buss thee
for it! (*Hugging and kissing her*) Nay, adod, I will, Chargee, so
muzzle,° and tuzzle,° and hug thee; I will, i' faith, I will.

MIRANDA Nay, Gardee, don't be so lavish.° Who would ride post°   5
when the journey lasts for life?

SIR FRANCIS Ah wag, ah wag, I'll buss thee again for that.

MIRANDA (*aside*) Foh! How he stinks of tobacco! What a delicate°
bedfellow I should have!

SIR FRANCIS Oh, I'm transported! When, when, my dear, wilt thou   10
convince the world of thy happy day? When shall we marry, ha?

MIRANDA There's nothing wanting but your consent, Sir Francis.

SIR FRANCIS My consent! What does my charmer mean?

MIRANDA Nay, 'tis only a whim, but I'll have everything according to
form; therefore, when you sign an authentic paper, drawn up by an 15
able lawyer, that I have your leave to marry, the next day makes me
yours, Gardee.

SIR FRANCIS Ha, ha, ha! A whim indeed! Why, is it not demonstration
I give my leave when I marry thee?

MIRANDA Not for your reputation, Gardee. The malicious world will 20
be apt to say you tricked me into marriage, and so take the merit
from my choice. Now I will have the act for my own, to let the idle
fops see how much I prefer a man loaded with years and wisdom.

SIR FRANCIS Humph! Prithee leave out years, Chargee; I'm not so old,
as thou shalt find. Adod, I'm young; there's a caper for ye. (*Jumps*) 25

MIRANDA Oh never excuse° it! Why, I like you the better for being old.
But I shall suspect you don't love me if you refuse me this
formality.

SIR FRANCIS Not love thee, Chargee! Adod, I do love thee better than,
than, than, better than—what shall I say? Egad, better than money, 30
i' faith I do.

MIRANDA (*aside*) That's false I'm sure. [*To Sir Francis*] To prove it,
do this then.

SIR FRANCIS Well, I will do it, Chargee, provided I bring a licence° at
the same time. 35

MIRANDA Ay, and a parson too, if you please. Ha, ha, ha! I can't help
laughing to think how all the young coxcombs about town will be
mortified when they hear of our marriage.

SIR FRANCIS So they will, so they will. Ha, ha, ha!

MIRANDA Well, I fancy I shall be so happy with my Gardee! 40

SIR FRANCIS If wearing pearls and jewels, or eating gold, as the old
saying is, can make thee happy,° thou shalt be so, my sweetest, my
lovely, my charming, my—verily I know not what to call thee.

MIRANDA You must know, Gardee, that I am so eager to have this
business concluded that I have employed my woman's brother, who 45
is a lawyer in the Temple,° to settle matters just to your liking. You
are to give your consent to my marriage, which is to yourself, you
know. But mum: you must take no notice of that. So then I will—
that is, with your leave—put my writings° into his hands. Then
tomorrow we come slap upon them with a wedding that nobody 50
thought on,° by which you seize me and my estate and, I suppose,
make a bonfire of your own act and deed.°

SIR FRANCIS Nay, but, Chargee, if—

MIRANDA Nay, Gardee, no ifs! Have I refused three northern lords, two British peers, and half a score knights to have you put in your ifs? 55

SIR FRANCIS So thou hast indeed, and I will trust to thy management. Od, I'm all of a fire.

MIRANDA [*aside*] 'Tis a wonder the dry stubble° does not blaze.
    Enter Marplot

SIR FRANCIS How now! Who sent for you, sir? What's° the hundred pound gone already? 60

MARPLOT No, sir, I don't want money now.

SIR FRANCIS No? That's a miracle! But there's one thing you want, I'm sure.

MARPLOT Ay, what's that, guardian? 65

SIR FRANCIS Manners. What, had I no servants without?

MARPLOT None that could do my business, guardian, which is at present with this lady.

MIRANDA With me, Mr Marplot! What is it, I beseech you?

SIR FRANCIS Ay, sir, what is it? Anything that relates to her may be delivered to me. 70

MARPLOT I deny that.

MIRANDA That's more than I do, sir.

MARPLOT Indeed, madam. Why then, to proceed. Fame says that you and my most conscionable° guardian here designed, contrived, plotted and agreed to chouse a very civil, honourable, honest gentleman out of a hundred pound. 75

MIRANDA That I contrived it!

MARPLOT Ay, you: you never said a word against it, so far you are guilty. 80

SIR FRANCIS Pray tell that civil, honourable, honest gentleman that, if he has any more such sums to fool away, they shall be received like the last. Ha, ha, ha, ha! Choused, quotha!° But hark ye, let him know at the same time, that if he dare to report I tricked him of it, I shall recommend a lawyer to him shall show him a trick for twice as much. D'ye hear, tell him that. 85

MARPLOT So, and this is the way you use a gentleman, and my friend.

MIRANDA Is the wretch thy friend?

MARPLOT The wretch! Look ye, madam, don't call names. Egad, I won't take it. 90

MIRANDA Why, you won't beat me, will you? Ha, ha!

MARPLOT I don't know whether I will or no.

SIR FRANCIS Sir, I shall make a servant show you out at the window if you are saucy.

MARPLOT I am your most humble servant, guardian. I design to go out the same way I came in. I would only ask this lady if she does not think in her soul Sir George Airy is not a fine° gentleman.

MIRANDA He dresses well.

SIR FRANCIS Which is chiefly owing to his tailor and *valet de chambre*.°

MIRANDA And, if you allow that a proof of his being a fine gentleman, he is so.

MARPLOT The judicious part of the world allow him wit, courage, gallantry and management; though I think he forfeited that character when he flung away a hundred pound upon your dumb ladyship.

SIR FRANCIS Does that gall him? Ha, ha, ha!

MIRANDA So, Sir George, remaining in deep discontent, has sent you, his trusty squire, to utter his complaint? Ha, ha, ha!

MARPLOT Yes, madam, and you, like a cruel, hard-hearted Jew,° value it no more than I would your ladyship, were I Sir George, you, you, you—

MIRANDA Oh, don't call names. I know you love to be employed, and I'll oblige you; and you shall carry him a message from me.

MARPLOT According as I like it. What is it?

MIRANDA Nay, a kind one you may be sure. First tell him I have chose this gentleman (*clapping her hand into Sir Francis's*) to have and to hold, and so forth.°

SIR FRANCIS (*aside*) Oh, the dear rogue, how I dote on her!

MIRANDA And advise his impertinence to trouble me no more, for I prefer Sir Francis for a husband before all the fops in the universe.

MARPLOT Oh lord, oh lord! She's bewitched, that's certain. Here's a husband for eighteen!° (*Turning Sir Francis about*) Here's a shape! Here's bones rattling in a leather bag!° Here's buckram° and canvas° to scrub you to repentance!°

SIR FRANCIS Sirrah, my cane shall teach you repentance presently.

MARPLOT No, faith, I have felt its twin brother from just such a withered hand too lately.

MIRANDA One thing more: advise him to keep from the garden-gate on the left hand; for if he dares to saunter there, about the hour of eight, as he used to do, he shall be saluted with a pistol or a blunderbuss.°

SIR FRANCIS Oh monstrous! Why, Chargee, did he use to come to the garden-gate?

MIRANDA° The gardener described just such another man that always
watched his coming out and fain would have bribed him for his   13.
entrance.—Tell him that he shall find a warm reception if he comes
this night.

MARPLOT Pistols and blunderbusses! Egad, a warm reception indeed!
I shall take care to inform him of your kindness and advise him to
keep farther off.   14

MIRANDA (*aside*) I hope he will understand my meaning better than to
follow your advice.

SIR FRANCIS Thou hast signed, sealed, and taken possession of my
heart forever, Chargee. Ha, ha, ha! And for you, Mr Saucebox,° let
me have no more of your messages, if ever you design to inherit   14
your estate, gentleman.

MARPLOT Why, there 'tis now. Sure I shall be out of your clutches one
day. Well, guardian, I say no more; but if you be not as errant a
cuckold as e'er drove bargain upon the Exchange° or paid attendance to a court, I am the son of a whetstone.° And so, your humble   15
servant.

MIRANDA Don't forget the message! Ha, ha!

Exit [Marplot]

SIR FRANCIS I am so provoked! 'Tis well he's gone.

MIRANDA Oh mind him not, Gardee, but let's sign articles, and then—

SIR FRANCIS And then—adod, I believe I am metamorphosed; my   15
pulse beats high, and my blood boils, methinks. (*Kissing and hugging
her*)

MIRANDA Oh fie, Gardee, be not so violent. Consider the market lasts
all the year.° Well, I'll in and see if the lawyer be come. You'll
follow?   16

SIR FRANCIS Ay, to the world's end, my dear.

Exit [Miranda]

Well, Frank, thou art a lucky fellow in thy old age to have such a
delicate morsel, and thirty thousand pound, in love with thee. I
shall be the envy of bachelors, the glory of married men, and the
wonder of the town. Some guardians would be glad to compound   16
for part of the estate at dispatching an heiress,° but I engross the
whole: *O! Mihi praeteritos referet si Jupiter Annos.*°

Exit

3.5

A tavern
Discovers Sir George Airy and Charles with wine before them,
and Whisper waiting°

SIR GEORGE Nay, prithee don't be grave, Charles. Misfortunes will happen. Ha, ha, ha! 'Tis some comfort to have a companion in our sufferings.

CHARLES I am only apprehensive for Isabinda; her father's humour is implacable, and how far his jealousy may transport him° to her undoing shocks my soul to think. 5

SIR GEORGE But since you escaped undiscovered by him, his rage will quickly lash° into calm, never fear it.

CHARLES But who knows what that unlucky dog, Marplot, told him? Nor can I imagine what brought him thither. That fellow is ever 10 doing mischief, and yet, to give him his due, he never designs it. This is some blundering adventure, wherein he thought to show his friendship, as he calls it. A curse on him.

SIR GEORGE Then you must forgive him. What said he?

CHARLES Said! Nay, I had more mind to cut his throat than hear his 15 excuses.

SIR GEORGE Where is he?

WHISPER Sir, I saw him go into Sir Francis Gripe's just now.

CHARLES Oh! Then he is upon your business, Sir George! A thousand to one, but he makes some mistake there too. 20

SIR GEORGE Impossible, without he huffs° the lady and makes love to Sir Francis.

Enter Drawer

DRAWER Mr Marplot is below, gentlemen, and desires to know if he may have leave to wait upon ye.

CHARLES How civil the rogue is when he has done a fault! 25

SIR GEORGE Ho! Desire him° to walk up.

[Exit Drawer]

Prithee, Charles, throw off this chagrin° and be good company.

CHARLES Nay, hang him, I'm not angry with him. Whisper, fetch me pen, ink and paper.

WHISPER Yes, sir. 30

Exit [Whisper.] Enter Marplot

CHARLES Do but mark his sheepish look, Sir George.

MARPLOT Dear Charles, don't o'erwhelm a man already under

insupportable affliction. I'm sure I always intend to serve my
friends, but if my malicious stars deny the happiness, is the fault
mine?   35

SIR GEORGE Never mind him, Mr Marplot; he is eat up with spleen.°
But tell me, what says Miranda?

MARPLOT Says? Nay, we are all undone there too.

CHARLES I told you so; nothing prospers that he undertakes.

MARPLOT Why, can I help her having chose your father for better for   40
worse?

CHARLES So. There's another of Fortune's strokes. I suppose I shall be
edged out of my estate, with twins every year, let who will get° 'em.

SIR GEORGE What, is the woman really possessed?°

MARPLOT Yes, with the spirit of contradiction; she railed at you most   45
prodigiously.

SIR GEORGE That's no ill sign.

    Enter Whisper, with pen, ink, and paper

MARPLOT You'd say it was no good sign, if you knew all.

SIR GEORGE Why, prithee?

MARPLOT Harkee, Sir George. Let me warn you, pursue your old   50
haunt no more; it may be dangerous.

    Charles sits down to write

SIR GEORGE My old haunt? What d'you mean?

MARPLOT Why, in short then, since you will have it, Miranda vows if
you dare approach the garden-gate at eight o'clock, as you used,
you shall be saluted with a blunderbuss, sir. These were her words.   55
Nay, she bid me tell you so too.

SIR GEORGE Ha! The garden-gate at eight, as I used to do! There must
be a meaning in this. Is there such a gate, Charles?

CHARLES Yes, yes. It opens into the park. I suppose her ladyship has
made many a scamper through it.   60

SIR GEORGE It must be an assignation° then. Ha! My heart springs
with joy; 'tis a propitious omen. My dear Marplot, let me embrace
thee! Thou art my friend, my better angel—

MARPLOT What do you mean, Sir George?

SIR GEORGE No matter what I mean. [*Giving Marplot a glass of wine*]   65
Here, take a bumper° to the garden-gate, ye dear rogue, you.

MARPLOT You have reason to be transported, Sir George. I have saved
your life.

SIR GEORGE My life! Thou hast saved my soul, man. Charles, if thou
dost not pledge this health,° may'st thou never taste the joys of   70
love.

CHARLES Whisper, be sure you take care how you deliver this. (*Gives him the letter*) Bring me the answer to my lodgings.

WHISPER I warrant you, sir.

    Exit [Whisper]

MARPLOT [*aside*] Whither does that letter go? Now dare I not ask for   75
my blood.

CHARLES Now I'm for you.

SIR GEORGE To the garden-gate at the hour of eight, Charles. Along,
huzza!°

CHARLES I begin to conceive you.   80

MARPLOT That's more than I do. Egad, to the garden-gate, huzza!
(*Drinks*) But I hope you design to keep far enough off on't, Sir
George.

SIR GEORGE Ay, ay, never fear that. She shall see I despise her frowns.
Let her use her blunderbuss against the next fool. She shan't reach   85
me with the smoke, I warrant her. Ha, ha, ha!

MARPLOT Ah, Charles, if you could receive a disappointment thus *en
cavalier*,° one should have some comfort in being beat for you.

CHARLES [*to Sir George*] The fool comprehends nothing.

SIR GEORGE [*to Charles*] Nor would I have him; prithee take him   90
along with thee.

CHARLES Enough! Marplot, you shall go home with me.

MARPLOT [*aside*] I'm glad I'm well with him however. [*Aloud*] Sir
George, yours. [*Aside*] Egad, Charles asking me to go home with
him gives me a shrewd suspicion there's more in the garden-gate   95
than I comprehend. Faith, I'll give him the drop° and away to
guardian's and find it out.

SIR GEORGE I kiss both your hands.

    [*Exeunt Charles and Marplot*]

—And now for the garden-gate.

        It's beauty gives the assignation there,   100
        And love too powerful grows t'admit of fear.

    Exit

4.1

The outside of Sir Jealous Traffick's house
Patch, peeping out of door. Enter Whisper

WHISPER Ha, Mrs Patch! This is a lucky minute to find you so readily. My master dies with impatience.

PATCH My lady imagined so, and by her orders I have been scouting this hour in search of you to inform you that Sir Jealous has invited some friends to supper with him tonight, which gives an opportunity to your master to make use of his ladder of ropes. The closet window shall be open, and Isabinda ready to receive him. Bid him come immediately.

WHISPER Excellent! He'll not disappoint, I warrant him. But hold, I have a letter here, which I'm to carry an answer of. I can't think what language the direction is.

PATCH Foh, 'tis no language, but a character which the lovers invented to avert discovery. Ha, I hear my old master coming downstairs. It is impossible you should have an answer. Away, and bid him come himself for that. Begone, we are ruined if you're seen, for he has doubled his care since the last accident.

WHISPER I go, I go.
           Exit [Whisper]

PATCH There, go thou into my pocket. (*Puts it besides,*° *and it falls down*) Now I'll up the backstairs, lest I meet him. Well, a dextrous chambermaid is the ladies' best utensil,° I say.
           Exit [Patch.] Enter Sir Jealous Traffick, with a letter in his hand

SIR JEALOUS So, this is some comfort. This tells me that Senior Don Diego Barbinetto is safely arrived. He shall marry my daughter the minute he comes. Ha! What's here? (*Takes up the letter Patch dropped*) A letter! I don't know what to make of the superscription. I'll see what's within side. (*Opens it*) Humph, 'tis Hebrew I think. What can this mean? There must be some trick in it. This was certainly designed for my daughter, but I don't know that she can speak any language but her mother tongue. No matter for that; this may be one of love's hieroglyphics, and I fancy I saw Patch's tail sweep by. That wench may be a slut, and instead of guarding my honour, betray it. I'll find it out, I'm resolved. Who's there?
           [Enter Servant]
What answer did you bring from the gentlemen I sent you to invite?

RVANT That they'd all wait of° you, sir, as I told you before; but I
  suppose you forget, sir.

R JEALOUS Did I so, sir? But I shan't forget to break your head if any   35
  of 'em come, sir.

RVANT Come, sir? Why, did you not send me to desire their
  company, sir?

R JEALOUS But I send you now to desire their absence. Say I have
  something extraordinary fallen out which calls me abroad, contrary   40
  to expectation, and ask their pardon, and, d'ye hear, send the butler
  to me.

RVANT Yes, sir.
      Exit [Servant.] Enter Butler

R JEALOUS If this paper has a meaning I'll find it.—Lay the cloth° in
  my daughter's chamber, and bid the cook send supper thither   45
  presently.

JTLER Yes, sir. [*Aside*] Heyday, what's the matter now?
      Exit [Butler]

R JEALOUS He wants the eyes of Argus° that has a young handsome
  daughter in this town; but my comfort is, I shall not be troubled
  long with her. He that pretends to rule a girl once in her teens had   50
  better be at sea in a storm, and would be in less danger.

   For let him do, or counsel, all he can,
   She thinks and dreams of nothing else but man.

  Exit

4.2

  Isabinda's chamber
  Isabinda and Patch

ABINDA Are you sure nobody saw you speak to Whisper?

TCH Yes, very sure, madam; but I heard Sir Jealous coming
  downstairs, so I clapped° this letter into my pocket. (*Feels for the
  letter*)

ABINDA A letter! Give it me quickly.   5

TCH (*searching still*) Bless me! What's become on't? I'm sure I put
  it—

ABINDA Is it possible thou couldst be so careless? Oh! I'm undone
  forever if it be lost.

PATCH I must have dropped it upon the stairs. But why are you so much alarmed? If the worst happens, nobody can read it, madam, nor find out whom it was designed for.

ISABINDA If it falls into my father's hands, the very figure of a letter will produce ill consequences. Run and look for it upon the stairs this moment.

PATCH Nay, I'm sure it can be nowhere else.

As Patch is going out of the door, she meets the Butler

How now, what do you want?

BUTLER My master ordered me to lay the cloth here for his supper.

ISABINDA (*aside*) Ruined past redemption!

PATCH You mistake sure.—What shall we do?

ISABINDA I thought he expected company tonight. [*Aside*] Oh, poor Charles! Oh, unfortunate Isabinda!

BUTLER I thought so too, madam, but I suppose he has altered his mind. (*Lays the cloth*)

Exit [Butler]

ISABINDA The letter is the cause. This heedless action has undone me. Fly and fasten the closet-window, which will give Charles notice to retire.

Enter Sir Jealous Traffick

Ha, my father! Oh, confusion!

SIR JEALOUS Hold, hold, Patch. Whither are you going? I'll have nobody stir out of the room till after supper.

PATCH Sir, I was only going to reach your easy chair.° [*Aside*] Oh, wretched accident!

SIR JEALOUS I'll have nobody stir out of the room. I don't want my easy chair.

ISABINDA (*aside*) What will be the event° of this?

SIR JEALOUS Hark ye, daughter, do you know this hand?

ISABINDA [*aside*] As I suspected. [*To Sir Jealous*] Hand do you call it, sir? 'Tis some school-boy's scrawl.

PATCH (*aside*) O Invention, thou chambermaid's best friend, assist me.

SIR JEALOUS Are you sure you don't understand it?

Patch feels in her bosom and shakes her coats°

ISABINDA Do you understand it, sir?

SIR JEALOUS I wish I did.

ISABINDA (*aside*) Thank heaven you do not. [*To Sir Jealous*] Then I know no more of it than you do, indeed, sir.

PATCH Oh lord, oh lord! What have you done, sir? Why, the paper is mine. I dropped it out of my bosom. (*Snatching it from him*)

SIR JEALOUS Ha! Yours, mistress?

SABINDA (*aside*) What does she mean by owning it?°

PATCH Yes, sir, it is.

SIR JEALOUS What is it? Speak.   50

PATCH Why, sir, it is a charm for the toothache. I have worn it this
seven year. 'Twas given me by an angel, for aught I know, when I
was raving with the pain, for nobody knew from whence he came
nor whither he went. He charged me never to open it, lest some
dire vengeance befall me, and heaven knows what will be the event.   55
Oh, cruel misfortune that I should drop it, and you should open it!
If you had not opened it—

SABINDA (*aside*) Excellent wench.

SIR JEALOUS Pox of your charms and whims for me! If that be all 'tis
well enough. There, there, burn it, and I warrant you no vengeance   60
will follow.

PATCH (*aside*) So, all's right again thus far.

SABINDA (*aside*) I would not lose Patch for the world. I'll take courage a little. [*To Sir Jealous*] Is this usage for your daughter, sir?
Must my virtue and conduct be suspected? For every trifle, you   65
immure me like some dire offender here, and deny me all recre-
ations which my sex enjoy, and the custom of the country and
modesty allow. Yet, not content with that, you make my confinement more intolerable by your mistrusts and jealousies. Would I
were dead, so I were free from this. (*Weeps*)   70

SIR JEALOUS Tomorrow rids you of this tiresome load. Don
Diego Barbinetto will be here, and then my care ends and his
begins.

SABINDA (*aside*) Is he come then! Oh, how shall I avoid this hated
marriage?   75

    Enter Servants with supper

SIR JEALOUS Come, will you sit down?

SABINDA I can't eat, sir.

PATCH (*aside*) No, I dare swear he has given her supper enough. I wish
I could get into the closet.

SIR JEALOUS Well, if you can't eat, then give me a song whilst I do.   80

SABINDA I have such a cold I can scarce speak, sir; much less sing.
(*Aside*) How shall I prevent Charles coming in?

SIR JEALOUS I hope you have the use of your fingers, madam. Play a
tune upon your spinet,° whilst your woman sings me a song.

PATCH (*aside*) I'm as much out of tune as my lady, if he knew all.   85

SABINDA (*sits down to play*) I shall make excellent music.

PATCH Really, sir, I'm so frighted about your opening this charm that I
can't remember one song.

SIR JEALOUS Pish, hang your charm. Come, come, sing anything.

PATCH (*aside*) Yes, I'm likely to sing° truly. [*To Sir Jealous*] Humph,   90
humph.° Bless me, sir, I cannot raise my voice, my heart pants so.

SIR JEALOUS [*to Isabinda*] Why, what? Does your heart pant so that
you can't play neither? Pray what key are you in, ha?

PATCH (*aside*) Ah, would the key was turned of you once.°

SIR JEALOUS Why don't you sing, I say?   95

PATCH When madam has put her spinet in tune, sir. Humph, humph.

ISABINDA (*rising*) I cannot play, sir, whatever ails me.

SIR JEALOUS Zounds! Sit down, and play me a tune or I'll break the
spinet about your ears.

ISABINDA [*aside*] What will become of me? (*Sits down and plays*)   100

SIR JEALOUS (*to Patch*) Come, mistress.

PATCH Yes, sir. (*Sings, but horribly out of tune*)

SIR JEALOUS Hey, hey! Why, you are atop of the house, and you are
down in the cellar.° What is the meaning of this? Is it on purpose to
cross me, ha?   105

PATCH Pray, madam, take it a little lower; I cannot reach that note—
nor any note, I fear.

ISABINDA Well, begin. [*Aside*] Oh, Patch, we shall be discovered.

PATCH [*aside*] I sink with the apprehension, madam. [*Aloud*] Humph,
humph. (*Sings*)   110

> 'Tis thus the bright celestial court above,
> Beguiles the hours with music and with love.

CHARLES (*pulls open the closet door*) [*aside*] Music and singing.
      Isabinda and Patch shriek
Death! Her father there! Then I must fly.
      *Exit [Charles] into the closet. Sir Jealous rises up hastily, seeing
      Charles slip back into the closet*

SIR JEALOUS Hell and furies, a man in the closet!   115

PATCH Ah! A ghost, a ghost! [*Aside*] He must not enter the closet!
      Isabinda throws herself down before the closet door as in a sound°

SIR JEALOUS (*strives to get by*) The devil! I'll make a ghost of him, I
warrant you.

PATCH Oh hold, sir, have a care. You'll tread upon my lady. [*Calling
offstage*] Who waits there? Bring some water. (*Weeps aloud*) Oh, this   120
comes of your opening the charm. Oh, oh, oh, oh!

SIR JEALOUS I'll charm you, housewife. Here lies the charm° that

conjured this fellow in, I'm sure on't.—Come out, you rascal, do
so! [*To Patch*] Zounds, take her from the door, or I'll spurn her
from it and break your neck downstairs.

SABINDA Oh, oh, where am I? (*Aside to Patch*) He's gone. I heard him
leap down.

ATCH [*aside to Isabinda*] Nay, then let him enter. [*Aloud*] Here, here,
madam, smell to this.° Come, give me your hand. Come nearer to
the window. The air will do you good.

IR JEALOUS I would she were in her grave.—Where are you, sirrah,
villain, robber of my honour? I'll pull you out of your nest.

> *Sir Jealous goes into the closet*

ATCH [*aside*] You'll be mistaken, old gentleman; the bird is flown.

SABINDA [*aside*] I'm glad I have 'scaped so well. I was almost dead in
earnest with the fright.

> *Enter Sir Jealous out of the closet*

IR JEALOUS Whoever the dog were, he has escaped out of the window, for the sash is up. But though he is got out of my reach, you
are not. And first, Mrs Pander,° with your charms for toothache,
get out of my house. Go, troop!° Yet hold, stay. I'll see you out of
my doors myself, but I'll secure your charge ere I go.

SABINDA What do you mean, sir? Was she not a creature of your own
providing?

IR JEALOUS She was of the devil's providing for aught I know.

ATCH What have I done, sir, to merit your displeasure?

IR JEALOUS I don't know which of you have done it, but you shall
both suffer for it till I can discover whose guilt it is. [*To Isabinda*]
Go, get in there. I'll move you from this side of the house.

> *Sir Jealous pushes Isabinda in at the other door and locks it; puts
> the key in his pocket*

I'll keep the key myself. I'll try what ghost will get into that room.
[*To Patch*] And now, forsooth, I'll wait on you downstairs.

ATCH Ah, my poor lady! Downstairs, sir? But I won't go out, sir, till I
have looked up° my clothes.

IR JEALOUS If thou wert as naked as thou wert born, thou shouldst
not stay to put on a smock. Come along, I say. When your mistress
is married you shall have your rags, and everything that belongs to
you, but till then—

> *Exeunt [Sir Jealous Traffick], pulling Patch out*

ATCH [*calling as she is pulled out*] Oh! Barbarous usage for nothing!

4.3

[Outside Sir Jealous Traffick's house]
Enter [Sir Jealous Traffick and Patch] at the lower door°

SIR JEALOUS There! Go, and come no more within sight of my habitation these three days, I charge you.

[Exit Sir Jealous Traffick, and] slaps the door after [him]

PATCH Did ever anybody see such an old monster!

Enter Charles

Oh, Mr Charles! Your affairs and mine are in an ill posture.°

CHARLES I am inured° to the frowns of fortune, but what has befallen thee?

PATCH Sir Jealous, whose suspicious nature's always on the watch— nay, even whilst one eye sleeps, the other keeps sentinel—upon sight of you flew into such a violent passion that I could find no stratagem to appease him, but, in spite of all arguments, locked his daughter into his own apartment and turned me out of doors.

CHARLES Ha! Oh, Isabinda!

PATCH And swears she shall neither see sun nor moon till she is Don Diego Barbinetto's wife, who arrived last night and is expected with impatience.

CHARLES He dies! Yes, by all the wrongs of love he shall! Here will I plant myself, and through my breast he shall make his passage, if he enters.

PATCH A most heroic resolution. There might be ways found out more to your advantage. Policy° is often preferred to open force.

CHARLES I apprehend° you not.

PATCH What think you of personating° this Spaniard, imposing upon the father, and marrying your mistress by his own consent?

CHARLES Say'st thou so, my angel? Oh, could that be done, my life to come would be too short to recompense thee. But how can I do that when I neither know what ship he came in, nor from what part of Spain, who recommends him, nor how attended?°

PATCH I can solve all this. He is from Madrid; his father's name Don Pedro Questo Portento Barbinetto.° Here's a letter of his to Sir Jealous which he dropped one day. You understand Spanish, and the hand may be counterfeited. You conceive° me, sir.

CHARLES My better genius, thou hast revived my drooping soul. I'll about it instantly. Come to my lodgings and we'll concert° matters.

Exeunt

4.4

A garden-gate, open
Scentwell waiting offstage.° Enter Sir George Airy

SIR GEORGE So, this is the gate, and most invitingly open. If there
should be a blunderbuss here now, what a dreadful ditty° would my
fall make for fools, and what a jest for the wits; how my name would
be roared about streets. Well, I'll venture all.
  [*Scentwell peeps her head out through the garden-gate*]

SCENTWELL Hist, hist, Sir George Airy—   5

SIR GEORGE A female voice!—Thus far I'm safe, my dear.

SCENTWELL No, I'm not your dear, but I'll conduct you to her. Give
me your hand; you must go through many a dark passage and dirty
step before you arrive.

SIR GEORGE I know I must before I arrive at Paradise; therefore be   10
quick, my charming guide.

SCENTWELL For aught you know.° Come, come, your hand and away.

SIR GEORGE Here, here, child; you can't be half so swift as my desires.
  Exeunt

4.5

[*Sir Francis Gripe's*] *house*
Enter Miranda

MIRANDA Well, let me reason a little with my mad self. Now, don't I
transgress all rules to venture upon a man without the advice of the
grave and wise? But then° a rigid knavish guardian who would have
married me? To whom? Even to his nauseous self, or nobody. Sir
George is what I have tried in conversation, inquired into his char-   5
acter, am satisfied in both. Then his love: who would have given a
hundred pound only to have seen a woman he had not infinitely
loved? So I find my liking him has furnished me with arguments
enough of his side, and now the only doubt remains whether he will
come or no.   10
  Enter Scentwell [*and Sir George Airy*]

SCENTWELL That's resolved, madam, for here's the knight.
  Exit Scentwell

SIR GEORGE And do I once more behold that lovely object whose idea
fills my mind and forms my pleasing dreams?

MIRANDA What, beginning again in heroics! Sir George, don't you
remember how little fruit your last prodigal oration produced? Not
one bare single word in answer.

SIR GEORGE Ha! The voice of my incognita. Why did you take
ten thousand ways to captivate a heart your eyes alone had
vanquished?

MIRANDA Prithee, no more of these flights, for our time's but short
and we must fall into business. Do you think we can agree on that
same terrible bugbear, matrimony, without heartily repenting on
both sides?

SIR GEORGE It has been my wish since first my longing eyes beheld ye.

MIRANDA And your happy ears drank in the pleasing news I had thirty
thousand pound.

SIR GEORGE Unkind! Did I not offer you in those purchased minutes
to run the risk of your fortune, so° you would but secure that lovely
person to my arms?

MIRANDA Well, if you have such love and tenderness, since our wooing
has been short, pray reserve it for our future days to let the world
see we are lovers after wedlock. 'Twill be a novelty.

SIR GEORGE Haste then, and let us tie the knot and prove the envied
pair—

MIRANDA Hold! Not so fast! I have provided better than to venture on
dangerous experiments headlong. My guardian, trusting to my dis-
sembled love, has given up my fortune to my own dispose, but with
this proviso: that he tomorrow morning weds me. He is now gone
to Doctors' Commons° for a licence.

SIR GEORGE Ha, a licence!

MIRANDA But I have planted emissaries that infallibly take him down
to Epsom° under pretence that a brother usurer of his is to make
him his executor;° the thing on earth he covets.

SIR GEORGE 'Tis his known character.

MIRANDA Now, my instruments° confirm him this man is dying, and
he° sends me word he goes this minute. It must be tomorrow ere he
can be undeceived. That time is ours.

SIR GEORGE Let us improve it then, and settle on our coming years
endless, endless happiness.

MIRANDA I dare not stir till I hear he's on the road; then I and my
writings, the most material point, are soon removed.

SIR GEORGE I have one favour to ask, if it lies in your power: you
would be a friend to poor Charles, though the son of this tenacious
man. He is as free from all his° vices as nature and a good education

can make him, and, what now I have vanity enough to hope will   55
induce you, he is the man on earth I love.

MIRANDA I never was his enemy, and only put it on as it helped my
designs on his father. If his uncle's estate ought to be in his possession, which I shrewdly suspect, I may do him a singular piece of
service.   60

SIR GEORGE You are all goodness.

　　　Enter Scentwell

SCENTWELL Oh, madam, my master and Mr Marplot are just coming
into the house.

MIRANDA Undone, undone! If he finds you here in this crisis, all my
plots are unravelled.   65

SIR GEORGE What shall I do? Can't I get back into the garden?

SCENTWELL Oh, no! He comes up those stairs.

MIRANDA Here, here, here! Can you condescend to stand behind this
chimney-board,° Sir George?

SIR GEORGE Anywhere, anywhere, dear madam, without ceremony.   70

SCENTWELL Come, come, sir; lie close.°

　　　Miranda and Scentwell put Sir George behind the chimney-
　　　board. Enter Sir Francis Gripe and Marplot, Sir Francis Gripe
　　　peeling an orange

SIR FRANCIS I could not go, though 'tis upon life and death, without
taking leave of dear Chargee. Besides, this fellow buzzed in my ears
that thou might'st be so desperate to° shoot that wild rake which
haunts the garden-gate, and that would bring us into trouble, dear.   75

MIRANDA So, Marplot brought you back then. I am obliged to him for
that, I'm sure. (*Frowning at Marplot aside*)

MARPLOT [*aside*] By her looks, she means she is not obliged to me. I
have done some mischief now, but what I can't imagine.

SIR FRANCIS Well, Chargee, I have had three messengers to come° to   80
Epsom to my neighbour Squeezum's,° who, for all his vast riches,
is departing. (*Sighs*)

MARPLOT Ay, see what all you usurers must come to.

SIR FRANCIS Peace, ye young knave! Some forty years hence I may
think on't.—But, Chargee, I'll be with thee tomorrow, before those   85
pretty eyes are open. I will, I will, Chargee; I'll rouse you, i'faith.—
Here, Mrs Scentwell, lift up your lady's chimney-board, that I may
throw my peel in and not litter her chamber.

MIRANDA [*aside*] Oh my stars! What will become of us now?

SCENTWELL Oh, pray sir, give it me; I love it above all things in   90
nature, indeed I do.

SIR FRANCIS No, no, hussy; you have the green pip° already. I'll have no more apothecary's bills. (*Goes towards the chimney*)

MIRANDA Hold, hold, hold, dear Gardee! I have a . . . a . . . a . . . a . . . a monkey° shut up there, and if you open it before the man comes   95
that is to tame it,° 'tis so wild 'twill break all my china,° or get away; and that would break my heart, for I am fond on't to distraction, (*in a flattering tone*) next thee,° dear Gardee.

SIR FRANCIS Well, well, Chargee, I won't open it. She shall have her monkey, poor rogue.—Here, throw this peel out of the window.   100
   Exit Scentwell [with peel]

MARPLOT A monkey, dear madam? Let me see it. I can tame a monkey as well as the best of them all. Oh, how I love the little miniatures of man!°

MIRANDA Be quiet, mischief, and stand farther from the chimney. You shall not see my monkey. (*Striving with him*) Why, sure—   105

MARPLOT For heaven's sake, dear madam, let me but peep, to see if it be as pretty as my Lady Fiddle-Faddle's. Has it got a chain?

MIRANDA Not yet, but I design it one shall last its lifetime. Nay, you shall not see it.—Look, Gardee, how he teases me!   110

SIR FRANCIS (*getting between Marplot and the chimney*) Sirrah, sirrah, let my Chargee's monkey alone or bamboo° shall fly about your ears. What, is there no dealing with you?

MARPLOT Pugh, pox of the monkey! Here's a rout;° I wish he may rival you.   115
   Enter Servant

SERVANT Sir, they put two more horses in the coach, as you ordered, and 'tis ready at the door.

SIR FRANCIS Well, I'm going to be executor; better for thee, jewel. Bye, Chargee, one buss! I'm glad thou hast got a monkey to divert thee a little.   120

MIRANDA Thank'ee, dear Gardee.—Nay, I'll see you to the coach.

SIR FRANCIS That's kind, adod.

MIRANDA (*to Marplot*) Come along, impertinence.
   [*Exeunt Miranda, Sir Francis Gripe and Servant. Marplot makes as to go with them*]

MARPLOT (*stepping back*) Egad, I will see the monkey. Now (*Lifts up the board, and discovers Sir George*) Oh, lord! Oh, lord! Thieves,   125
thieves, murder!

SIR GEORGE Damn'ee, you unlucky dog! 'Tis I! Which way shall I get out? Show me instantly or I'll cut your throat.

MARPLOT Undone, undone! At that door there. But hold, hold, break
    that china, and I'll bring you off.   130
       Sir George Airy runs off at the corner and throws down some
       china.° Enter Sir Francis Gripe, Miranda, and Scentwell
SIR FRANCIS Mercy on me! What's the matter?
MIRANDA Oh, you toad! What have you done?
MARPLOT No great harm. I beg of you to forgive me. Longing to see
    the monkey, I did but just raise up the board, and it flew over my
    shoulders, scratched all my face, broke yon china, and whisked out   135
    of the window.
SIR FRANCIS Was ever such an unlucky rogue! Sirrah, I forbid you my
    house. Call the servants to get the monkey again. I would stay
    myself to look it,° but that you know my earnest business.
SCENTWELL Oh, my lady will be the best to lure it back. All them   140
    creatures love my lady extremely.
MIRANDA Go, go, dear Gardee. I hope I shall recover it.
SIR FRANCIS Bye, bye, dear'ee. Ah, mischief, how you look now! Bye,
    bye.
       Exit [Sir Francis Gripe]
MIRANDA Scentwell, see him in the coach and bring me word.   145
SCENTWELL Yes, madam.
      [Exit Scentwell]
MIRANDA So, sir, you have done your friend a signal piece of service, I
    suppose.
MARPLOT Why, look you, madam, if I have committed a fault, thank
    yourself. No man is more serviceable° when I am let into a secret,   150
    nor none more unlucky at finding it out. Who could divine your
    meaning? When you talked of a blunderbuss, who thought of a
    rendezvous? And when you talked of a monkey, who the devil
    dreamt of Sir George?
MIRANDA A sign you converse° but little with our sex when you can't   155
    reconcile contradictions.
      Enter Scentwell
SCENTWELL He's gone, madam, as fast as the coach and six can carry
    him.
      Enter Sir George Airy
SIR GEORGE Then I may appear.
MARPLOT Dear, Sir George, make my peace! On my soul, I did not   160
    think of you.
SIR GEORGE I dare swear thou didst not. Madam, I beg you to forgive
    him.

MIRANDA Well, Sir George, if he can be secret.

MARPLOT Ods heart, madam, I'm as secret as a priest when I'm   165
trusted.

SIR GEORGE Why 'tis with a priest our business is at present.

SCENTWELL Madam, here's Mrs Isabinda's woman to wait on you.

MIRANDA Bring her up.

Enter Patch

How do'ee, Mrs Patch? What news from your lady?   170

PATCH That's for your private ear, madam.—Sir George, there's a
friend of yours has an urgent occasion for your assistance.

SIR GEORGE His name.

PATCH Charles.

MARPLOT [*aside*] Ha! Then there is something afoot that I know   175
nothing of. [*To Sir George*] I'll wait on you, Sir George.

SIR GEORGE A third person may not be proper perhaps. As soon as I
have dispatched my own affairs, I am at his service. I'll send my
servant to tell him I'll wait upon him in half an hour.

MIRANDA How come you employed in this message, Mrs Patch?   180

PATCH Want of business, madam. I am discharged by my master, but
hope to serve my lady still.

MIRANDA How, discharged? You must tell me the whole story within.

PATCH With all my heart, madam.

MARPLOT (*aside*) Pish! Pox, I wish I were fairly out of the house. I   185
find marriage is the end of this secret. And now I am half mad to
know what Charles wants him for.

SIR GEORGE Madam, I'm doubly pressed, by love and friendship. This
exigence admits of no delay. Shall we make Marplot of the party?

MIRANDA If you'll run the hazard, Sir George. I believe he means well.   190

MARPLOT Nay, nay, for my part, I desire to be let in to nothing. I'll be
gone, therefore pray don't mistrust me. (*Going*)

SIR GEORGE [*aside*] So now has he a mind to be gone to Charles. But,
not knowing what affairs he may have upon his hands at present,
I'm resolved he shan't stir. [*To Marplot*] No, Mr Marplot, you must   195
not leave us. We want a third person. (*Takes hold of him*)

MARPLOT [*aside*] I never had more mind to be gone in my life.

MIRANDA Come along then. If we fail in the voyage, thank yourself for
taking this ill-starred gentleman on board.

SIR GEORGE   That vessel ne'er can unsuccessful prove,   200
　　　　　　Whose freight is beauty, and whose pilot love.

[*Exeunt*]

5.1

[*Sir Francis Gripe's house*]
Enter Miranda, Patch, and Scentwell

MIRANDA Well, Patch, I have done a strange bold thing! My fate is determined, and expectation is no more. Now, to avoid the impertinence and roguery of an old man, I have thrown myself into the extravagance of a young one. If he should despise, slight or use me ill, there's no remedy from a husband but the grave, and that's a terrible sanctuary to one of my age and constitution. 5

PATCH O fear not, madam, you'll find your account in° Sir George Airy. It is impossible a man of sense should use a woman ill, indued with° beauty, wit and fortune. It must be the lady's fault, if she does not wear the unfashionable name of wife easy, when nothing but complaisance and good humour is requisite on either side to make them happy. 10

MIRANDA I long till I am out of this house, lest any accident should bring my guardian back. Scentwell, put my best jewels into the little casket, slip them into thy pocket, and let us march off to Sir Jealous's. 15

SCENTWELL It shall be done, madam.

Exit Scentwell

PATCH Sir George will be impatient, madam. If their plot succeeds, we shall be well received; if not, he will be able to protect us. Besides, I long to know how my young lady fares. 20

MIRANDA Farewell, old Mammon, and thy detested walls. 'Twill be no more 'sweet Sir Francis'; I shall be compelled to the odious talk of dissembling no longer to get my own, and coax him with the wheedling names of my *precious*, my *dear*, dear Gardee.

Enter Sir Francis Gripe behind. [Miranda] starts

Oh heavens! 25

SIR FRANCIS Ah, my sweet Chargee, don't be frighted. But thy poor Gardee has been abused, cheated, fooled, betrayed, but nobody knows by whom.

MIRANDA (*aside*) Undone! Past redemption.

SIR FRANCIS What, won't you speak to me, Chargee! 30

MIRANDA I'm so surprised with joy to see you, I know not what to say.

SIR FRANCIS Poor, dear girl! But do'ee know that my son, or some such rogue, to rob or murder me, or both, contrived this journey?

For upon the road I met my neighbour Squeezum, well and coming
to town.   35

MIRANDA Good lack, good lack! What tricks are there in this
world!

> *Enter Scentwell, with a diamond necklace in her hand, not seeing
> Sir Francis*

SCENTWELL Madam, be pleased to tie this necklace on; for I can't get
it into the—(*Sees Sir Francis*)

MIRANDA The wench is a fool, I think! Could you not have carried it to   40
be mended, without putting it in the box?

SIR FRANCIS What's the matter?

MIRANDA Only, dearee, I bid her, I bid her—your ill usage has put
everything out of my head! But won't you go, Gardee, and find out
these fellows, and have them punished! And, and—   45

SIR FRANCIS Where should I look them,° child? No, I'll sit me down
contented with my safety, nor stir out of my own doors till I go with
thee to a parson.

MIRANDA (*aside*) If he goes into his closet I am ruined.—Oh! Bless
me, in this fright I had forgot Mrs Patch.   50

PATCH [*aside to Miranda*] Ay, madam, and I stay for your speedy
answer.

MIRANDA (*aside*) I must get him out of the house. Now assist me,
Fortune.

SIR FRANCIS Mrs Patch, I profess I did not see you. How dost thou do,   55
Mrs Patch? Well, don't you repent leaving my Chargee?

PATCH Yes, everybody must love her; but I came now—(*Aside to
Miranda*) Madam, what did I come for? My invention is at the last
ebb.

SIR FRANCIS Nay, never whisper, tell me.   60

MIRANDA She came, dear Gardee, to invite me to her lady's wedding,
and you shall go with me, Gardee. 'Tis to be done this moment to a
Spanish merchant. Old Sir Jealous keeps on his humour: the first
minute he sees her, the next he marries her.

SIR FRANCIS Ha, ha, ha! I'd go if I thought the sight of matrimony   65
would tempt Chargee to perform her promise. There was a smile,
there was a consenting look with those pretty twinklers, worth a
million. Ods precious, I am happier than the great Mogul,° the
emperor of China, or all the potentates that are not in wars.° Speak,
confirm it, make me leap out of my skin.   70

MIRANDA When one has resolved, 'tis in vain to stand 'Shall I, shall
I?', 'If I ever marry'. Positively this is my wedding day.

SIR FRANCIS Oh! Happy, happy man! Verily I will beget a son; the first
night shall disinherit that dog, Charles. I have estate enough to
purchase a barony, and be the immortalizing the whole family of   75
the Gripes.

MIRANDA Come then, Gardee, give me thy hand. Let's to this house of
Hymen.°
        My choice is fixed, let good or ill betide.

SIR FRANCIS   The joyful bridegroom, I—

MIRANDA   And I the happy bride.   80
    Exeunt

5.2

[*Sir Jealous Traffick's house*]
Enter Sir Jealous Traffick, meeting a Servant

SERVANT Sir, here's a couple of gentlemen enquire for you. One of 'em
calls himself Señor Diego Barbinetto.

SIR JEALOUS Ha! Senior Barbinetto! Admit 'em instantly. Joyful
minute. I'll have my daughter married tonight.
    Enter Charles, in Spanish habit, with Sir George Airy, dressed
    like a merchant

SIR JEALOUS *Senior, beso las manos. Vuestra merced es muy bienvenido en*   5
esta tierra.°

CHARLES *Señor, soy el muy humilde y muy obligado criado de vuestra*
merced. Mi padre envia a vuestra merced los más profondos de sus
respetos, y ha commissionado este mercader inglés de concluir un negocio
que me hace el más dischoso hombre del mundo, haciéndome su yerno.°   10

SIR JEALOUS I am glad on't,° for I find I have lost much of my
Spanish. [*To Sir George*] Sir, I am your most humble servant.
Senior Don Diego Barbinetto has informed me that you are
commissioned by Senior Don Pedro, etc., his worthy father.

SIR GEORGE To see an affair of marriage consummated between a   15
daughter of yours and Señor Diego Barbinetto, his son here. True,
sir; such a trust is reposed in me as that letter will inform you.
(*Gives him a letter*) (*Aside*) I hope 'twill pass upon him.

SIR JEALOUS Ay, 'tis his hand. (*Seems to read*)°

SIR GEORGE [*aside*] Good. (*Aside to Charles*) You have counterfeited to   20
a nicety, Charles.

131

CHARLES [*aside*] If the whole plot succeeds as well, I'm happy.

SIR JEALOUS Sir, I find by this that you are a man of honour and probity. I think, sir, he calls you Meanwell.

SIR GEORGE Meanwell is my name, sir.

SIR JEALOUS A very good name, and very significant.

CHARLES (*aside*) Yes, faith, if he knew all.

SIR JEALOUS For to mean well is to be honest, and to be honest is the virtue of a friend, and a friend is the delight and support of human society.

SIR GEORGE You shall find that I'll discharge the part of a friend in what I have undertaken, Sir Jealous.

CHARLES (*aside*) But little does he think to whom.

SIR GEORGE Therefore, sir, I must entreat the presence of your fair daughter and the assistance of your chaplain, for Señor Don Pedro strictly enjoined me to see the marriage rites performed as soon as we should arrive, to avoid the accidental overtures of Venus.

SIR JEALOUS Overtures of Venus!

SIR GEORGE Ay, sir—that is, those little hawking females° that traverse the park and the playhouse to put off their damaged ware.° They fasten upon foreigners like leeches and watch their arrival as carefully as the Kentish men° do a shipwreck. I warrant you they have heard of him already.

SIR JEALOUS Nay, I know this town swarms with them.

SIR GEORGE Ay, and then you know the Spaniards are naturally amorous, but very constant; the first face fixes 'em, and it may be dangerous to let him ramble ere he is tied.

CHARLES (*aside*) Well hinted.

SIR JEALOUS Pat to my purpose. Well, sir, there is but one thing more, and they shall be married instantly.

CHARLES (*aside*) Pray heaven, that one thing more don't spoil all.

SIR JEALOUS Don Pedro wrote me word in his last but one° that he designed the sum of five thousand crowns by way of jointure° for my daughter, and that it should be paid into my hand upon the day of marriage—

CHARLES (*aside*) Oh, the devil!

SIR JEALOUS —In order to lodge it in some of our funds,° in case she should become a widow and return for° England.

SIR GEORGE (*aside*) Pox on't, this is an unlucky turn. What shall I say?

SIR JEALOUS And he does not mention one word of it in this letter.

CHARLES (*aside*) I don't know how he should.

SIR GEORGE Humph! True, Sir Jealous, he told me such a thing, but

... but ... but ... but he ... he ... he ... he—he did not imagine
that you would insist upon the very day, for ... for ... for
money you know is dangerous returning by sea, an ... an ... an   65
... an—

CHARLES (*aside to Sir George*) Zounds, say we have brought it in
commodities.

SIR GEORGE And so sir, he has sent it in merchandise: tobacco, sugars,
spices, lemons, and so forth, which shall be turned into money with   70
all expedition.° In the meantime, sir, if you please to accept of my
bond for performance.

SIR JEALOUS It is enough, sir. I am so pleased with the countenance of
Senior Diego and the harmony of your name that I'll take your
word and will fetch my daughter this moment. [*Calling offstage*]   75
Within there!

> (*Enter Servant*)

Desire Mr Tackum,° my neighbour's chaplain, to walk hither.

SERVANT Yes, sir.

> *Exit Servant*

SIR JEALOUS Gentlemen, I'll return in an instant.

> *Exit* [*Sir Jealous Traffick*]

CHARLES Wondrous well. Let me embrace thee.   80

SIR GEORGE Egad, that five thousand pounds° had like to have ruined
the plot.

CHARLES But that's over! And if Fortune throws no more rubs° in our
way—

SIR GEORGE Thou'lt carry the prize. But hist, here he comes.   85

> *Enter Sir Jealous, dragging in Isabinda*

SIR JEALOUS Come along, you stubborn baggage you, come
along.

ISABINDA Oh, hear me, sir! Hear me but speak one word:
> Do not destroy my everlasting peace.
> My soul abhors this Spaniard you have chose;   90
> Nor can I wed him without being cursed.

SIR JEALOUS How's that?°

ISABINDA (*kneels*) Let this posture move your tender nature.
> Forever will I hang upon these knees;
> Nor loose my hands till you cut off my hold,   95
> If you refuse to hear me, sir.

CHARLES (*aside*) Oh, that I could discover myself to her!

SIR GEORGE (*aside*) Have a care what you do. You had better trust to
his obstinacy.

SIR JEALOUS Did you ever see such a perverse slut?—Off, I say.—Mr   100
Meanwell, pray help me a little.

SIR GEORGE Rise, madam, and do not disoblige your father, who has
provided a husband worthy of you, one that will love you equal
with his soul, and one that you will love, when once you know him.

ISABINDA Oh! Never, never!   105
Could I suspect that falsehood in my heart,
I would this moment tear it from my breast,
And straight present him with the treacherous part.°

CHARLES (aside) Oh, my charming faithful dear!

SIR JEALOUS Falsehood! Why, who the devil are you in love with? Ha!   110
Don't provoke me, for, by St Iago, I shall beat you, housewife.

CHARLES (aside) Heaven forbid, for I shall infallibly discover myself if
he should.

SIR GEORGE Have patience, madam, and look at him!° Why will you
prepossess yourself against a man that is master of all the charms   115
you would desire in a husband?

SIR JEALOUS Ay, look at him, Isabinda. Senior, pase usted adelante.°

CHARLES [aside] My heart bleeds to see her grieve, whom I imagined
would with joy receive me. [To Isabinda] Señora, obligue me, vuestra
merced, de su mano.°   120

SIR JEALOUS (pulling up her head) Hold up your head, hold up your
head, housewife, and look at him: is there a properer, handsomer,
better-shaped fellow in England, ye jade you? Ha! See, see, the
obstinate baggage shuts her eyes! By St Iago, I have a good mind to
beat 'em out. (Pushes her down)   125

ISABINDA Do then, sir, kill me, kill me instantly.
'Tis much the kinder action of the two,
For 'twill be worse than death to wed him.

SIR GEORGE Sir Jealous, you are too passionate. Give me leave; I'll try
by gentle words to work her to your purpose.   130

SIR JEALOUS (weeps) I pray do, Mr Meanwell, I pray do. She'll break
my heart. There is in that° jewels of the value of three thousand
pounds which were her mother's, and a paper wherein I have settled one half of my estate upon her now, and the whole when I die.
But provided she marries this gentleman! Else, by St Iago, I'll turn   135
her out of doors to beg or starve. Tell her this, Mr Meanwell, pray
do. (Walks off)°

SIR GEORGE [aside] Ha! This is beyond expectation! [To Sir Jealous]
Trust to me, sir. I'll lay the dangerous consequence of disobeying
you at this juncture before her, I warrant you.   140

CHARLES (*aside*) A sudden joy runs through my heart like a propitious omen.

SIR GEORGE Come, madam, do not blindly cast your life away just in the moment you would wish to save it.

ISABINDA Pray cease your trouble, sir. I have no wish but sudden death to free me from this hated Spaniard. If you are his friend, inform him what I say: my heart is given to another youth, whom I love with the same strength of passion that I hate this Diego, with whom if I am forced to wed, my own hand shall cut the Gordian knot.°

SIR GEORGE Suppose this Spaniard, which you strive to shun, should be the very man to whom you'd fly?

ISABINDA Ha!

SIR GEORGE Would you not blame your rash result, and curse those eyes that would not look on Charles?

ISABINDA On Charles? Oh, you have inspired new life and collected every wandering sense. Where is he? Oh, let me fly into his arms. (*Rises*)

SIR GEORGE Hold, hold, hold. 'Sdeath, madam, you'll ruin all. Your father believes him to be Señor Barbinetto. Compose yourself a little, pray, madam.

  Sir George runs to Sir Jealous

CHARLES (*aside*) Her eyes declare she knows me.

SIR GEORGE She begins to hear reason, sir. The fear of being turned out of doors has done it.

  Sir George runs back to Isabinda

ISABINDA 'Tis he! Oh, my ravished soul!

SIR GEORGE Take heed, madam, you don't betray yourself. Seem with reluctance to consent, or you are undone. (*Runs to Sir Jealous*) Speak gently to her, sir; I'm sure she'll yield. I see it in her face.

SIR JEALOUS [*returning to Isabinda*] Well, Isabinda, can you refuse to bless a father, whose only care is to make you happy, as Mr Meanwell has informed you? Come, wipe thy eyes; nay, prithee do, or thou wilt break thy father's heart. (*Weeps*) See, thou bring'st the tears in mine to think of thy undutiful carriage to me.

ISABINDA Oh, do not weep, sir! Your tears are like a poniard to my soul. Do with me what you please; I am all obedience.

SIR JEALOUS Ha! Then thou art my child again.

SIR GEORGE [*aside to Charles*] 'Tis done, and now, friend, the day's thy own.

CHARLES [*aside to Sir George*] The happiest of my life, if nothing intervene.

SIR JEALOUS And wilt thou love him?   180
ISABINDA I will endeavour it, sir.
          Enter Servant
SERVANT Sir, here is Mr Tackum.
SIR JEALOUS Show him into the parlour.—*Senior, tome usted su esposa;
          este momento les junta las manos.*° (*Gives her to Charles*)
CHARLES [*aside*] Oh, transport! [*To Sir Jealous*] *Señor, yo la recibo*   185
          como se debe un tesoro tan grande.° [*To Isabinda*]—Oh, my joy, my
          life, my soul! ([*Charles and Isabinda*] *embrace*)
ISABINDA [*To Charles*] My faithful, everlasting comfort.
SIR JEALOUS Now, Mr Meanwell, let's to the parson,
          Who, by his art, will join this pair for life: 190
          Make me the happiest father; her the happiest wife.

          Exeunt

5.3

The street before Sir Jealous Traffick's door°
Enter Marplot, solus
MARPLOT I have hunted all over the town for Charles, but can't find
          him. And by Whisper's scouting at the end of the street I suspect
          he must be in this house again. I'm informed too that he has
          borrowed a Spanish habit out of the playhouse. What can it
          mean?   5
          Enter a Servant of Sir Jealous's to Marplot, out of the house
          Harkee, sir, do you belong to this house?
SERVANT Yes, sir.
MARPLOT Pray can you tell if there be a gentleman in it in Spanish
          habit?
SERVANT There is a Spanish gentleman within that is just a-going to   10
          marry my young lady, sir.
MARPLOT Are you sure he is a Spanish gentleman?
SERVANT I'm sure he speaks no English that I hear of.
MARPLOT Then that can't be him I want; for 'tis an English gentle-
          man, though I suppose he may be dressed like a Spaniard, that I   15
          enquire after.
SERVANT (*aside*) Ha! Who knows but this may be an impostor? I'll
          inform my master; for if he should be imposed upon, he'll beat us

all round. [*To Marplot*] Pray, come in, sir, and see if this be the
person you enquire for.   20
    [*Exeunt*]

5.4

    Inside [Sir Jealous Traffick's] house°
    Enter Marplot

MARPLOT So, this was a good contrivance. If this be Charles, now will
he wonder how I found him out.
    Enter Servant and [Sir] Jealous Traffick

SIR JEALOUS [*to Servant*] What is your earnest business, blockhead,
that you must speak with me before the ceremony's past? Ha!
Who's this?   5

SERVANT Why, this gentleman, sir, wants another gentleman in Spanish habit, he says.

SIR JEALOUS In Spanish habit! 'Tis some friend of Senior Don
Diego's, I warrant. [*To Marplot*] Sir, I suppose you would speak
with Senior Barbinetto.   10

MARPLOT Heyday! What the devil does he say now?—Sir, I don't
understand you.°

SIR JEALOUS Don't you understand Spanish, sir?

MARPLOT Not I indeed, sir.

SIR JEALOUS I thought you had known Senior Barbinetto.   15

MARPLOT Not I, upon my word, sir.

SIR JEALOUS What, then you'd speak with his friend, the English
merchant, Mr Meanwell?

MARPLOT Neither, sir; not I.

SIR JEALOUS (*in an angry tone*) Why, who are you then, sir? And what   20
do you want?

MARPLOT Nay, nothing at all, not I, sir. [*Aside*] Pox on him! I wish I
were out. He begins to exalt° his voice. I shall be beaten again.

SIR JEALOUS Nothing at all, sir! Why then, what business have you in
my house? Ha?   25

SERVANT You said you wanted a gentleman in Spanish habit.

MARPLOT Why, ay, but his name is neither Barbinetto nor Meanwell.

SIR JEALOUS What is his name then, sirrah? Ha? Now I look at you
again, I believe you are the rogue° threatened me with half a dozen
myrmidons. Speak, sir who is it you look for or, or—   30

MARPLOT [*aside*] A terrible old dog! [*To Sir Jealous*] Why, sir, only an
honest young fellow of my acquaintance. I thought that here might
be a ball, and that he might have been here in a masquerade. 'Tis
Charles, Sir Francis Gripe's son, because I know he used to come
hither sometimes.   35

SIR JEALOUS Did he so? Not that I know of, I'm sure. Pray heaven that
this be Don Diego. If I should be tricked now! Ha! My heart
misgives me plaguily. [*Calling offstage*] Within there! Stop the
marriage! [*To Servant*] Run, sirrah, call all my servants!
        [*Exit Servant*]
I'll be satisfied that this is Senior Pedro's son ere he has my daughter.   40

MARPLOT [*aside*] Ha, Sir George!
    What have I done now?
        Enter Sir George Airy with a drawn sword between the scenes°

SIR GEORGE [*aside*] Ha! Marplot, here. Oh, the unlucky dog! [*To Sir
Jealous*] What's the matter, Sir Jealous?

SIR JEALOUS Nay, I don't know the matter, Mr Meanwell.   45

MARPLOT (*going up to Sir George*) Upon my soul, Sir George—

SIR JEALOUS Nay then, I'm betrayed, ruined, undone. Thieves,
traitors, rogues! (*Offers to go in*) Stop the marriage, I say—

SIR GEORGE I say, go on, Mr Tackum! [*To Sir Jealous*] Nay, no entering here. I guard this passage, old gentleman. The act and deed°   50
were both your own, and I'll see 'em signed, or die for't.
        Enter Servants

SIR JEALOUS A pox on the act and deed! [*To Servants*] Fall on! Knock
him down.

SIR GEORGE Ay, come on, scoundrels! I'll prick your jackets for you.

SIR JEALOUS [*to Marplot*] Zounds, sirrah, I'll be revenged on you.   55
(*Beats Marplot*)

SIR GEORGE Ay, there your vengeance is due. Ha, ha!

MARPLOT Why, what do you beat me for? I han't married your
daughter.

SIR JEALOUS Rascals! Why don't you knock him down?   60

SERVANTS We are afraid of his sword, sir. If you'll take that from him,
we'll knock him down presently.
        Enter Charles and Isabinda

SIR JEALOUS Seize her then.

CHARLES Rascals, retire. She's my wife. Touch her if you dare; I'll
make dog's meat of you.   65

SIR JEALOUS Ah, downright English! Oh, oh, oh, oh!
        Enter Sir Francis Gripe, Miranda, Patch, Scentwell, and Whisper

IR FRANCIS Into the house of joy we enter without knocking. Ha! I think 'tis the house of sorrow, Sir Jealous.

IR JEALOUS Oh, Sir Francis! Are you come? What? Was this your contrivance to abuse, trick, and chouse me of my child?   70

IR FRANCIS My contrivance! What do you mean?

IR JEALOUS No, you don't know your son there in Spanish habit.

IR FRANCIS How! My son in Spanish habit? Sirrah, you'll come to be hanged. Get out of my sight, ye dog! Get out of my sight.

IR JEALOUS Get out of your sight, sir? Get out with your bags.° Let's   75
see what you'll give him now to maintain my daughter on.

IR FRANCIS Give him? He shall be never the better for a penny of mine—and you might have looked after your daughter better, Sir Jealous. Tricked, quotha? Egad, I think you designed to trick me. But look ye, gentlemen, I believe I shall trick you both. This lady is   80
my wife, do you see? And my estate shall descend only to the heirs of her body.

IR GEORGE Lawfully begotten by me. I shall be extremely obliged to you, Sir Francis.

IR FRANCIS Ha, ha, ha, ha! Poor Sir George! You see your project was   85
of no use. Does not your hundred pound stick in your stomach?° Ha, ha, ha!

SIR GEORGE No, faith, Sir Francis, this lady has given me a cordial for that. (*Takes Miranda by the hand*)

SIR FRANCIS Hold, sir! You have nothing to say to this lady.   90

SIR GEORGE Nor you nothing to do with my wife, sir.

SIR FRANCIS Wife, sir!

MIRANDA Ay, really, guardian, 'tis even so. I hope you'll forgive my first offence.

SIR FRANCIS What, have you choused me out of my consent and your   95
writings then, mistress? Ha?

MIRANDA Out of nothing but my own, guardian.

SIR JEALOUS Ha, ha, ha! 'Tis some comfort at least to see you are overreached as well as myself. Will you settle your estate upon your son now?   100

SIR FRANCIS He shall starve first.

MIRANDA That I have taken care to prevent. There, sir, is the writings of your uncle's estate, which has been your due these three years. (*Gives Charles papers*)

CHARLES I shall study to deserve this favour.   105

SIR FRANCIS What, have you robbed me too, mistress! Egad, I'll make you restore 'em. Huswife, I will so.

SIR JEALOUS Take care I don't make you pay the arrears, sir. 'Tis well it's no worse, since 'tis no better.—Come, young man, seeing thou hast outwitted me, take her, and bless you both.°   110

CHARLES I hope, sir, you'll bestow your blessing too. 'Tis all I'll ask.
(*Kneels*)

SIR FRANCIS Confound you all!
Exit [Sir Francis Gripe]

MARPLOT Mercy upon us! How he looks!

SIR GEORGE Ha, ha! Ne'er mind his curses, Charles. Thou'lt thrive   115
not one jot the worse for 'em. Since this gentleman° is reconciled, we are all made happy.

SIR JEALOUS I always loved precaution, and took care to avoid dangers. But when a thing was past, I ever had philosophy to be easy.   120

CHARLES Which is the true sign of a great soul. I loved your daughter, and she me, and you shall have no reason to repent her choice.

ISABINDA You will not blame me, sir, for loving my own country best.

MARPLOT So here's everybody happy, I find, but poor Pilgarlic.° I wonder what satisfaction I shall have, for being cuffed, kicked, and   125
beaten in your service.

SIR JEALOUS I have been a little too familiar with you, as things are fallen out, but since there's no help for't, you must forgive me.

MARPLOT Egad, I think so. But provided that you be not so familiar for the future.   130

SIR GEORGE Thou hast been an unlucky rogue.

MARPLOT But very honest.

CHARLES That I'll vouch for, and freely forgive thee.

SIR GEORGE And I'll do you one piece of service more, Marplot. I'll take care that Sir Francis make you master of your estate.   135

MARPLOT That will make me as happy as any of you.

PATCH [*To Isabinda*] Your humble servant begs leave to remind you, madam.

ISABINDA Sir, I hope you'll give me leave to take Patch into favour again.   140

SIR JEALOUS Nay, let your husband look to that; I have done with my care.

CHARLES Her own liberty shall always oblige me. Here's nobody but honest Whisper and Mrs Scentwell to be provided for now. It shall be left to their choice to marry, or keep their services.   145

WHISPER Nay then, I'll stick to my master.

SCENTWELL Coxcomb! And I prefer my lady before a footman.

SIR JEALOUS Hark, I hear music! The fiddlers smell a wedding. What
    say you, young fellows? Will ye have a dance?
SIR GEORGE With all my heart! Call 'em in.   150
       [*Enter Musicians.*] *A dance*
SIR JEALOUS Now let us in and refresh ourselves with a cheerful
    glass, in which we'll bury all animosities, and
       By my example, let all parents move,°
       And never strive to cross their children's love;
       But still submit that care to Providence above.   155
       [*Exeunt*]

EPILOGUE°

In me you see one busybody more,
Though you may have enough of one before.
With epilogues, the busybody's way,
We strive to help, but sometimes mar a play.
At this mad sessions, half-condemned ere tried,°   5
Some, in three days, have been turned off, and died.°
In spite of parties, their attempts are vain,°
For, like false prophets, they ne'er rise again.°
Too late, when cast, your favour one beseeches,°
And epilogues prove execution speeches.°   10
Yet sure I spy no busybodies here;
And one may pass, since they do everywhere.
Sour critics, time and breath, and censures, waste,
And balk your pleasure to refine your taste.
One busy don ill-timed high tenets preaches,   15
Another yearly shows himself in speeches.
Some snivelling cits would have a peace for spite,
To starve those warriors who so bravely fight,°
Still of a foe upon his knees afraid,
Whose well-banged troops want money, heart, and bread.   20
Old beaux, who none, not even themselves, can please,
Are busy still, for nothing but to tease.°
The young, so busy to engage a heart,
The mischief done, are busy most to part.
Ungrateful wretches, who still cross one's will,   25
When they more kindly might be busy still!
One to a husband, who ne'er dreamt of horns,
Shows how dear spouse, with friend, his brows adorns.°
Th'officious tell-tale fool—he should repent it—
Parts three kind souls that lived at peace contented.   30
Some with law quirks set houses by the ears;°
With physic one what he would heal impairs,°
Like that dark mobbed up fry, that neighbouring curse,°
Who to remove Love's pain, bestow a worse.°

Since then this meddling tribe infest the age,°   35
Bear one awhile exposed upon the stage.
Let none but busybodies vent their spite!
And with good humour, pleasure crown the night!°

THE TIMES

ELIZABETH GRIFFITH

The favourable reception which the following comedy has met with
from a candid and generous public calls for my warmest acknowledgements; and though it may be of little consequence to them to
know the source of so slight an amusement, I think myself bound
by truth and gratitude to own that the first idea of this piece was
hinted to me by my ever-respected and lamented friend, Mr
Garrick,° who mentioned Goldoni's *Bourru bienfaisant*° as a sketch
that, if adapted to our times and manners, might be rendered pleasing to an English audience. Those who have read the French piece
must judge how far I have profited by Goldoni's work,° but of this
I am certain, that had Mr Garrick lived to afford me that friendly
assistance which he has done on former occasions, my comedy
would have been more worthy of the reception with which it has
been honoured.° I will, however, hope that, 'with all its imper-
fections on its head',° the same indulgence which attended its
representation will follow it into the closet,° and that the reader
will allow me the only merit I presume to claim, that of meaning
well.

I gladly take this opportunity of returning my thanks to my much-
esteemed friend, Mr Sheridan, senior,° for his kind attention to the
getting up my play, my ill health not permitting me to attend one
rehearsal. But Mr Sheridan's friendship, wherever professed, is not of
modern growth.°

I have more than common acknowledgements to make to all the
performers in my comedy, particularly to Mrs Abington° and Miss
Pope,° who both cheerfully undertook parts out of their usual line of
acting, and in which they have both excelled. I should be utterly
unable to express my sentiments of Mr King,° in the character of Sir
William Woodley, if I were not at liberty seriously to adopt the very
words which he humorously, but justly, speaks of himself, under a
personated character in *The Critic*:° 'But it is impossible for language
to do justice to Mr King! Indeed, he more than merited those repeated
bursts of applause which he drew from a most brilliant and judicious
audience.'°

I flatter myself, this little tribute to distinguished merit will not be

deemed tedious or impertinent by the public, for whose opinion I have
the sincerest respect, and to whom I have the honour to be

A most obliged,

And most obedient servant,

The Author   40

London, December 18, 1779

THE CHARACTERS OF THE PLAY

Sir William Woodley° · *Mr King*
Mr Woodley · *Mr Brereton*
Colonel Mountfort° · *Mr Palmer*
Counsellor Belford° · *Mr Bensley*
Mr Bromley° · *Mr Aickin*
Forward,° *servant to Mr Woodley* · *Mr Baddeley*
Waters,° *servant to Sir William* · *Mr Wrighten*
[Footman]
[Servant to Mr Woodley]

Lady Mary Woodley · *Mrs Abington*
Mrs Bromley · *Miss Pope*
Louisa · *Mrs Brereton*
Mrs Williams, *woman to Lady Mary* · *Mrs Colles*

Gentlemen and Ladies, Players at
    whist, loo, and quadrille

PROLOGUE

SPOKEN BY MR KING

To glow with ardour and attempt with zeal
The reformation of the public weal°
Is the high duty of the comic muse;
And though keen Attic salt allowed to use°
To season precept, and with art to tickle   5
The sores she means to wash with sharpest pickle,°
Yet not the rosy, pulpited divine,°
Nor lank-haired Methodist with rueful whine,°
Is more intent to root out vice and folly,
And make ye all lead lives discreet and holy.   10
    Yet why to clear the field were all their toil,
If weeds o'erspread not the luxuriant soil?
Congreve or Wesley, Whitfield or Molière,°
In vain might prompt the laugh or bribe the tear
If no man felt, or in himself or neighbour,°   15
Some failing to call forth the zealot's labour;
If no fair dame descried, 'midst her acquaintance,°
Some few who might be mended by repentance.
    Loose as the buxom air, the youth from college
Comes, fraught with all Newmarket's hopeful knowledge,°   20
In haste to spend the estate not yet his own,
Completes his ruin ere his beard is grown.
And when to foreign climes he spreads the sail,
'Tis not to enlarge his mind, but 'scape a jail.°
    Then blessed the poet, happy the divine,   25
When folly gives the *ton* from fashion's shrine!°
But whilst the priest and satirist reprove
Those vices which provoke the wrath of Jove,
Our author, like the patient angler sitting
To catch small fry, for humbler palates fitting,°   30
Has served a meal, not seasoned high with crimes.—
Taste it, and if approved, applaud *The Times*.

1.1

A dressing-room, books, music, clothes scattered about
Woodley, dressing; Forward at a distance

WOODLEY Sure never man was so suddenly involved° as I have been! And yet I cannot charge either my wife or myself with any particular extravagance. We do but live like other people of our rank; and yet, in less than four years that we have been married, an estate of four thousand pounds a year has dwindled into nothing! Heigh-ho!° (*Observing Forward listening, [Woodley] hums a tune*)—I can neither get this air into my head or out of it.

FORWARD I am often plagued so myself, sir, after the first night of a new opera, though I have a tolerable ear and catch a tune pretty readily.

Enter Footman, and delivers a letter to Woodley. [Exit
Footman.] [Woodley] reads it and appears agitated

WOODLEY What a proposal! I would die first. [*To Forward*] Get me pen, ink, and paper.

[Woodley] throws the letter on the table

FORWARD (*going*) I'll fetch them instantly from the library, sir.

WOODLEY You need not. I'll write there.

Exit [Woodley]

FORWARD He seems devilishly flurried by that same letter. I wish I could come fairly at its contents. 'Tis no billet-doux, I am certain, for I have never found him tripping° that way since I have been in the family. It must be some matter of business,° and if it is, it may concern me as well as my master. I have had my doubts that our affairs were going wrong for some months past. Our hall has been crowded with sturdy tradesmen, and we have had sneaking Jews° closeted in the library. Egad, I'll venture; for where interest is concerned, even my honour must give way. (*Takes up the letter*) He may surprise me though. I wish his shoes creaked. (*Looks out and listens*) No. All's safe yet. And now for the indulgence of a reasonable curiosity. (*Reads*) 'I find it impossible to trifle any longer with your creditors. The executions will therefore immediately be laid on° unless you can prevail on Lady Mary to release her jointure;° for there is not even a Jew in Duke's Place° that will advance a guinea more on your estate whilst that encumbrance remains. I am

your humble servant, John Fleec'em.° P.S. I have scarce cash
enough in my hands to discharge the enclosed small bill of costs.'°
Here's a bill as long as his tailor's!

    Enter Woodley°

WOODLEY Puppy! What are you meddling with those papers for? Give
    this letter to James, and order him to carry it instantly.   35

FORWARD Must I not put the things to rights first, sir?

WOODLEY Do as I order you, and leave the room.

FORWARD (*aside*) Ay, and the place, too, as soon as your honour can
    provide yourself.° I should not choose to depend upon a *post-obit*°
    for my wages.   40

    Exit [*Forward*]

WOODLEY How shall I be able to reveal my situation to Lady Mary?
    My heart bleeds for what she must suffer!

    Enter Footman

FOOTMAN Colonel Mountfort, sir.

WOODLEY Desire him to walk in.

    [*Exit Footman.*] *Enter Colonel Mountfort*

COL. MOUNTFORT Good morrow, Woodley! What, not dressed yet? I   45
    expected to find you booted and ready to set out for Newmarket.°
    You'll be late on the turf. Your horses run, I suppose? What
    matches° have you made?

WOODLEY None, colonel. I shall not be there this meeting.°

COL. MOUNTFORT You amaze me.   50

WOODLEY (*aside*) Would I had never been there! [*To Colonel Mountfort*] I am sick of the diversion and shall never make another bet on
    the turf while I live.

COL. MOUNTFORT Why don't you dispose of your stud, then? It must
    be an enormous, and now an useless, expense.   55

WOODLEY Horses are the least part of the extravagances incident to°
    racing.

COL. MOUNTFORT That is *selon*,° Woodley, for I have known several
    fortunes made on the turf.

WOODLEY True, but by those only who had none to lose. They are   60
    surest to win who carry least weight.°

COL. MOUNTFORT Take my advice, then, and sell your horses.

WOODLEY Why, faith, I wish they were disposed of. But yet, I don't
    know, I should be ashamed, I think, to advertise them, as it
    might look somehow as if one could not afford to keep them. Ha,   65
    ha, ha!

COL. MOUNTFORT Ridiculous supposition!

WOODLEY Ridiculous, indeed! That you know, Mountfort, is far from the case, but I really am tired of the sport; and the meeting, too, is at a time of the year when there are so many more agreeable amusements to be met with in London, so that I should be glad to get rid of them with all my heart.   70

COL. MOUNTFORT Let me dispose of them for you, then. I'll be your auctioneer, and try if I can't emblazon their pedigree with a little of that true humour which Charles Surface° bestows on his ancestors when he sets up their pictures to sale. 'Bucephalus,° the famous Bucephalus, gentlemen, descended in a right line° from the renowned quadruped of that name which had the honour of carrying a greater brute than himself, the immortal Alexander—'   75

WOODLEY Bravo, colonel!   80

COL. MOUNTFORT 'Or shall we deduce his lineage from—'

WOODLEY You had better consult Tattersall° for their pedigree, as he is your only herald in those points. Heigh-ho!

COL. MOUNTFORT Heigh-ho? This is but poor encouragement for me to enter on my new profession. Surely there is something malignant in the air at present, for every man I have conversed with this morning seems rather to be depressed with the gloom of November than enlivened by the sunshine of April. I have just now left Jack Knightly and Will Careless calculating, not their nativities, but their deaths.°   85   90

WOODLEY I saw them both at Boodle's° yesterday, in good health.

COL. MOUNTFORT Not the more likely to live for that, I assure you. However, it was not their natural existence, but their necessary subsistence that employed their mathematics.

WOODLEY You astonish me! Why, it is but lately they came into possession of great estates.   95

COL. MOUNTFORT True, but then they have travelled the modern short and easy road to ruin, of granting annuities for this twelve-month past,° and are now so nearly arrived at the last stage of their journey that I think Jack said he had but two months to run, and Will flattered himself that, as the summer was approaching, he might be able to hold out four. I advised their compounding the terms and running together for three months each.°   100

WOODLEY Poor fellows! I am sorry for them. (*Aside*) Would I could promise myself even so long a reprieve.   105

COL. MOUNTFORT What! Moping again, Woodley? You'll infect me, if I stay. Where are the ladies? In truth, my visit was to them, for I scarce hoped to find you here. Are Lady Mary and your sister visible?° Or shall I pass on to your uncle's apartment and pay my respects to him? I think there is a door of communication to his house from this room. Shall I go this way?

WOODLEY That may be a service of danger, colonel; for I fear Sir William is not at present much delighted either with his vicinity, or affinity, to any of this family, except my sister.

COL. MOUNTFORT I am glad to hear you can except my sweet Louisa, for, notwithstanding the brusqueness of his manners, I have such an opinion of the old knight's good sense and good nature that I cannot readily acquit those he is offended with as wholly free from blame.

WOODLEY I subscribe to your censure as far as it relates to myself, but the asperity of his behaviour to Lady Mary renders me extremely unhappy; and not even my past obligations, or future prospects, shall ever make me acquiesce in his treating my wife with disrespect.

COL. MOUNTFORT Allow me to say, Woodley, that persons so nearly connected ought to dispense with ceremony in favour of sincerity.

WOODLEY That's a dangerous tenet, colonel, and may be extended till downright rudeness may be considered but as the privilege of family chat.

COL. MOUNTFORT I think you have no cause for such an apprehension in this case, as Sir William is quite as singular for goodness of heart as for a deficiency in that outward varnish which too often supplies the place of it. But to compound the argument, let us admit there may be faults on both sides.

Enter Lady Mary and Louisa

LADY MARY My dear Woodley, don't I look like a hag today? Do you know that I have not slept an hour the whole night!

WOODLEY I'm sorry for it, my dear. I hope it was not any illness that prevented your rest.

LADY MARY No, I was not the least ill, but the uncommon brilliancy of Lady Mushroom's° earrings, that I saw at the opera in the evening, twinkled all night before my eyes and would not suffer me to close them.

COL. MOUNTFORT Vanity has her vigils, I perceive, ladies.

LOUISA That's but fair, colonel, as her festivals seem to bestow such supreme delight on her votaries of both sexes.

LADY MARY I think, now, that a thousand pounds added to my own would make them outblaze Lady Mushroom's; and I am sure my dear Woodley won't refuse me such a trifle.

WOODLEY I can refuse you nothing, but we'll talk of it some other time.   150

    Enter Servant and delivers a letter to Woodley, which he just runs his eye over and puts up. [*Exit Servant*]

LADY MARY What makes you look so grave, my love? I should almost suppose that letter was from your uncle, if he did not live in the same house and had not a peculiar delight in seeing the effect of his own ill temper.

LOUISA The reprehensions of sincere friends proceed oftener from   155
kindness than ill-nature.

LADY MARY (*to Woodley*) Will you send for Setwell° tomorrow, my dear, if you are not at leisure today? I must have this bar taken out, the middle stone larger, and the drop° at least twice this size. And pray hurry him, for I must positively wear them at Court next   160
Sunday.°

WOODLEY (*musing*) It must be so.

LADY MARY You don't attend to me, Mr Woodley?

WOODLEY Oh, yes, my dear, I hear every word you say. Give me the earrings, I'll carry them myself to the jeweller.   165

LADY MARY Here they are. But don't be too extravagant; I would not have more than a thousand pounds added on any account.

COL. MOUNTFORT I give you credit for that last caution, Lady Mary, as 'tis uncommon to hear a wife restraining her husband's generosity to herself in this day.   170

LADY MARY His indulgence, colonel, has ever exceeded my wishes.

WOODLEY But never equalled my own. (*Aside*) My heart is breaking for her.

    Enter Servant, who gives a printed paper to Lady Mary

SERVANT With Mrs Bromley's compliments, madam, and requests you'll do her the honour to call on her.   175

LADY MARY Oh! 'Tis the catalogue she promised to mark for me. [*To Servant*] My compliments, and I shall be at her door in a few minutes.

    [*Exit Servant*]

Louisa, are you disposed for Christie's° rooms this morning? There are abundance of fine things, and, of course, fine people, to be   180
there. I delight in an auction; one meets with so many things there one never thought one wanted before.

LOUISA Though it is not my passion, I'll attend your ladyship with pleasure.

LADY MARY (*looking over the catalogue*) See, Woodley, what an   185

unconscionable creature Bromley is! She has marked a whole side
of the catalogue.—'A lustre that holds a hundred lights!'—I think I
should like that, now, for our grand saloon, in the country. I own I
should delight vastly to astonish our neighbours in Dorsetshire, if
ever we go there. Have you any objection, my dear?   190

OODLEY But one, my dear: I am to settle with my banker today.

ADY MARY No matter; Mrs Bromley shall be my banker. Her purse is
always at the service of her friends.—Oh, here's the sweetest set of
filigree dressing-plate!°—I must have that, Woodley, instead of the
one I have had these two years. 'Tis absolutely Gothic.°   195

OODLEY (aside) I cannot wound her by restraint.

ADY MARY Don't you think Mrs Bromley a delightful creature,
colonel?—'Two of the largest Sèvres° vases that have ever been
imported.'—I positively must have them. How good it was in dear
Bromley to note these articles! (To Colonel Mountfort) Why don't   200
you tell me how you like my friend?

OL. MOUNTFORT I have not the honour, madam, of knowing her
sufficiently to judge of her character, and therefore can only speak
of it as doubtful.°

ADY MARY Doubtful, colonel!   205

OUISA In some cases, Lady Mary, to doubt is rather to compliment
than to censure.

OL. MOUNTFORT And, in other cases, to doubt is to be certain.

ADY MARY You don't affect to be doubtful, I hope, Miss Woodley?

OUISA By no means, I assure you. Mrs Bromley's character is quite   210
clear to me.

ADY MARY If you talk in this style, Louisa, I shall certainly conclude
that you are jealous of the dear Bromley.

OUISA I know not on what account I should be so, except in your
good graces, for I hope you don't think me vain enough to attempt   215
rivalling her with her present cicisbeo,° Sir Harry Granger.

OL. MOUNTFORT That ridiculous compound of affectation and epi-
curism! Who ruminates upon every meal, and tries to preserve the
relish of his sauces by a repetition of their ingredients in every new
company that admits him.   220

ADY MARY You are monstrously censorious, colonel. But I will allow
that he is a little out of fashion, at present; and for that reason, I
have forbidden his ever coming into this house. (To Woodley) The
Bromleys dine here today, my dear. [To Louisa] But we lose time.
The auction may begin and some of the dear things I have set my   225
heart upon be gone before we get there. I shall never forget that old

frightful mandarin,° Lord Gobble, for whipping up the Sèvres
china *dejeuner*° from me at the last sale.

COL. MOUNTFORT Will your ladyship permit me to have the honour
of attending you?

LADY MARY There's a vacant seat in the coach, and you shall be
welcome, if you won't be spiteful. Good morrow, Woodley! Come,
Louisa.

Exeunt Lady Mary, Louisa, and Colonel Mountfort

WOODLEY So, I am once more left at leisure for my own reflection.
Solitude is said to be a relief to the unhappy, but thought only
serves to double my distress. Surely my poverty begins to be apparent or Knightly would not write so pressingly. His note surprises
me. (*Reads*) 'Dear Woodley, I desire you will, on receipt of this, let
me have the three hundred pieces° you lost to me at our last meeting, as I am just setting off for Newmarket, and must have some
weight of metal to balance the scales on the turf. I shall wait at
home for you exactly one hour, by the best-going watch in Europe,
and must have the cash by that time, pos. Yours ever, T. Knightly.'°
The peremptory style of this billet alarms me! Knightly used to be
a careless, liberal fellow, but Mountfort told me just now that he is
on the verge of ruin. His state, however, is to be envied, in comparison of mine. He falls alone. No wife, no family, at once to share
and aggravate his wretchedness. I'll go this moment and acquit me
of his demand by parting with these toys. (*Takes up the earrings*)
How much my Mary's beauty added to their lustre! Let me fly from
the thought. (*Going*)

Enter Bromley

BROMLEY Just on the wing, my dear friend! How lucky thus to catch
you flying, as it were!

WOODLEY The good fortune is rather mine, Mr Bromley.

BROMLEY No, no; you compliment. But where are the dear, the divine
ladies? Mayn't I hope to be cheered with one glance from their
bright eyes? What a beautiful creature is Lady Mary! Do you know
she wants but little, very little, my dear friend, to be the top of the
tree, the very paragon of fine taste and *bon ton*;° and I think she will
very soon acquire that little. My dame has an excellent hand at
touching up the last polish.

WOODLEY I allow Mrs Bromley to be perfectly elegant.

BROMLEY No, no; there you are wrong. She is pretty, lively, and so
forth, but somewhat fubsy, you know. But Lady Mary! Lady Mary
is the thing!—But what's here? (*Taking up the earrings*) A new

purchase, I presume? They are fine, very fine, indeed! What now
may the value be? Some thousands, I suppose.

WOODLEY They did cost a pretty large sum when they were bought.

BROMLEY Not new then, I perceive, but fine, very fine, indeed!

WOODLEY Lady Mary don't quite like the fashion—the setting, I   270
mean. And therefore I should not be sorry to part with them—and
buy others.

BROMLEY (*aside*) Oh, that alters the case considerably! [*To Woodley*]
Let us see . . . let's see. Why now, upon examining them closely,
they appear but middling, very middling, indeed. I don't wonder   275
Lady Mary should not like them—no lustre—very old-fashioned.
They'll sell for little or nothing, believe me.

WOODLEY They cost me fifteen hundred pounds about four years ago.

BROMLEY Fifteen hundred pounds! You amaze me! You must have
been sadly imposed upon! Very sadly indeed, my dear friend! What   280
monstrous cheats these tradesfolk are! Why, these jewels now will
not bring above three hundred.

WOODLEY That's more than the common disproportion between buying and selling, I should think, Mr Bromley.

BROMLEY I mean in the trade, Mr Woodley. Among the trade, dia-   285
monds are a drug,° a mere drug, indeed. And money is a rare jewel
in all trades now, I assure you. A gentleman, or a friend, perhaps,
might give more. Come, for the frolic's sake, I'll turn jeweller
myself and offer you a cool five hundred for them. What say you? Is
it a bargain, Woodley?   290

WOODLEY (*aside*) I cannot bear the thought of carrying them abroad
to sell! [*To Bromley*] Well, if you really think they are worth no
more—

BROMLEY Nay, I have over-rated them; but I never compute by
pounds, shillings, and pence when dealing with a friend. Diamonds   295
are, as I told you before, a mere drug, and cash, cash, my dear boy,
your only valuable commodity. Here, here it is. (*Looking in his
pocket-book*°) I have not quite so much about me, I find.

WOODLEY That's unlucky, (*looking at his watch*) for I want three hundred of it this very instant.   300

BROMLEY (*aside*) Does the wind sit in that point?° [*To Woodley*] I'll see
. . . I'll see. Oh! Here is just the three hundred, cut and dry,° my
boy. You shall have the other two this evening at Boodle's. We'll cut
a card, or throw a cast for it, or how you will.

WOODLEY I shan't go to Boodle's tonight—nor do I think I shall ever 305
play again.

BROMLEY (*aside*) The knowing ones are taken in.° I would not have given so much for the jewels if I had thought so. [*To Woodley*] What, not play? That's good, very good, indeed! You have a sort of lover's quarrel to the dice, I perceive. But though they have, I   31 confess, used you a little scurvily, they'll make you amends some other time. One lucky hit, you know, may repay all your losses.

WOODLEY They have so often, and so fatally, deceived me—

BROMLEY That you'll trust them again, for all that.

WOODLEY I think not. But shall we meet at dinner?   31

BROMLEY Yes, yes; I obey the dear, sweet Lady Mary's invitation. I shall bring the money with me. Besides, I recollect that you and I have a little matter of business to settle, but it shan't break in upon our pleasures, though. You shall have no trouble but just to set your name. A memorandum° is all I want, my boy.   32

WOODLEY I have a particular reason for desiring that you will not mention the transaction of the jewels to my wife, or even to yours.

BROMLEY Secret! Secret as the grave, my dear friend! Trusty as steel, my boy. You may always depend upon honest Bob Bromley. We shall be with you at five, though that's rather early.° (*Going*) Nay, no   32 ceremony.°

WOODLEY I am going out this moment.

Exeunt [Woodley and Bromley.] Enter Forward

FORWARD I have listened and pried to good purpose, I think, and am thoroughly confirmed in my resolution of shifting my quarters tomorrow morning. Up tents and away, then! But I cannot help   33 being a little concerned at leaving my master and lady because I am sure I shall never get so good place again. All masters, no servants; every one did as he liked. It grieves me to think what a hand the rest of the servants have made of them.° There's the lazy housekeeper, the drunken butler, the cribbing coachman! But what signifies mor-   335 alizing! Let me look about me a little and see if there be any small matters lying loose, that are of no farther use to my master, and may be of some to me. (*Takes up a pair of lace ruffles*°) These have been worn but never washed, and he may miss them. No, that's not probable, as he has at least twenty pair more than he knows any-   340 thing of. (*Puts them in his pocket*) This snuff-box, too, is but a bauble, of more curiosity than value. I shall accept of it as a keepsake.

Forward pockets it. [He continues to look for items to pilfer.]
Enter Sir William from the middle door

SIR WILLIAM [*aside*] By the quietness in the nest, the birds are flown;

and I am glad of it. My apartment smokes a little,° today. I'll have   345
the tables brought here and try if the game be recoverable, though,
to be sure, I have but little hopes, for sure there never was any man
so unlucky. [*Calling offstage*] Waters!

FORWARD (*aside*) What! Is old Square-Toes° ruined, too? Egad, I
should be glad of that.   350

SIR WILLIAM (*seeing Forward*) Why, hey, what are you doing here?—
Waters! I say—

FORWARD Only removing a few useless things of my master's, sir.

SIR WILLIAM Then you will certainly remove yourself; for I know
nothing half so useless as a pert, coxcombical, lazy *valet-de-*   355
chambre.

FORWARD As your honour chooses to be alone, I shall retire directly.
    Exit [Forward]

SIR WILLIAM Retire! There's a phrase now for a footman! But these
puppies all mimic their masters, even in their language and, what's
worse, in their vices. I'll answer for it that fellow now is as idle, as   360
dissipated, and extravagant as my nephew himself. But why do I
think of a man whose misconduct has so totally alienated my affections? Yet he was a sweet boy at Eton, and a fine youth at college.°
His indiscreet marriage has ruined him. A fine lady, a lady of quality,° forsooth, and without a fortune to support her vanity. But, no   365
matter now; I renounce them both.—Waters!—I wish Louisa was
removed from this scene of folly and extravagance and safely settled in the country. There is no other place for a woman to be
secure in.
    Enter Waters

I wish you would advance, Mr Slow-boots. I have called you at least a   370
dozen times.

WATERS I came the very moment—

SIR WILLIAM Well, well, well, apologies take up time. Bring the backgammon tables here; then go to Counsellor° Belford and desire him
to come to me, directly. (*Waters going through the middle door*) Why   375
don't you go the shortest way? (*Pointing to the side-door*)

WATERS Your honour bid me bring the tables first.

SIR WILLIAM Of what use are they when Belford is not here to play?
(*Waters going*) No, come back and fetch the tables, and I'll place the
men just to show you how I was gammoned,° and I think you'll   380
allow there never was such luck.

WATERS I am utterly ignorant of every point of the game, sir.

SIR WILLIAM Stupidity in the abstract! How often have you been in

the room while Belford and I have been playing? Had we been
saying or doing anything we ought not, you would have picked it up   38
fast enough, I warrant you.

WATERS Indeed, sir—

SIR WILLIAM No words! I hate prate. Fly to Mr Belford's.

Exit Waters

I'll go and show Jones how it was; for though she is my housekeeper
now, she is a parson's daughter and must understand backgammon.   39
I am sure she will be astonished at Belford's move.

Exit

2.1

[*Woodley's dressing-room*]
Enter, at opposite doors, Woodley and Belford

WOODLEY How truly do I rejoice to see my good friend Mr Belford! But may I flatter myself that the honour of this visit was intended for me?

BELFORD I am sorry, my dear sir, that there should be a necessity for discriminating° the person to whom my respects are paid in a family I so equally regard, and which was once so happily united.   5

WOODLEY If indeed you regard this family, or ever had any friendship for me—but I cannot speak.

BELFORD I am already apprized of your difficulties, and would spare you the pain of even hinting at them, were it in my power to redress them.   10

WOODLEY Then be assured it is; for amidst all my distresses, nothing affects me half so much as Sir William's implacable resentment against Lady Mary and me. If he were but reconciled—

BELFORD That is, in plain English, my young friend, if he could be   15
reconciled to your expensive mode of living, he ought in honour to assist in supporting it. But that, I doubt, will never be brought to pass, though Sir William is both rich and generous—

WOODLEY To all the world but me.

BELFORD In this case then, you should suspect your own conduct,   20
rather than his character. But remonstrances are useless now, and I promise to use my utmost interest to bring about a reconciliation. But I much fear that we shall not be able to get Lady Mary included in the family-compact,° for I know no man more resolute in what he conceives to be right than Sir William.   25

WOODLEY My honour, as well as my love, obliges me to vindicate her; and I here pledge them both that she is free from blame.

BELFORD I am glad to find you still a lover, Mr Woodley; but I, who am but a friend, in this question can't help thinking that if Lady Mary had spent more of her time in Dorsetshire, and less at Spa,°   30
Paris, and other places of dissipation and extravagance, she would have been more entitled to Sir William's esteem, and you would have had less need of his assistance.

WOODLEY The fault was mine alone. Vain of possessing such a treasure—   35

BELFORD You childishly exposed it to the gaze of fops and foreigners. And let me tell you, Mr Woodley, you are a lucky man, in these licentious times, to have preserved such a gem pure and entire,° even at the expense of your other possessions. But, prithee, why don't you now retreat into the country?   40

WOODLEY My wife is quite ignorant of my present circumstances. I have not resolution to acquaint her with them. And to propose quitting London, in this gay season, without assigning some cause—

BELFORD Would, in your situation, be extremely prudent.   45

WOODLEY I cannot bear the thought of giving her uneasiness—

BELFORD And so cruelly prefer the evil to the cure.

Enter Waters

WATERS I humbly beg your honour's pardon for my intrusion, but I have been at your chambers, and at the Temple Coffee-house° to look for you. My master is quite impatient to see you, sir, and one   50 of Mr Woodley's servants told me you were here.

WOODLEY This seems to fall out luckily. I will not detain you a moment. Dear Belford, remember what a cause you have in hand.

BELFORD Do not distrust my attention to my client, though I cannot warrant success to the suit.°   55

Exit Woodley

WATERS I cannot tell your honour how proud° I am to meet you. My good, dear master has been as angry with me for not finding you at home as if I had committed the greatest of faults; and I would die rather than vex him.

BELFORD I know my friend's hasty temper perfectly well, but I also   60 know that his good nature is an overmatch for it.

WATERS Oh, sir! You don't know how good and generous he is.

BELFORD You are mistaken, Waters; I am no stranger to Sir William's benevolence.

WATERS Indeed sir, with submission you are, for he takes as much   65 pains to conceal his goodness as others do to reveal theirs. He would never forgive me if he knew I mentioned it, but my heart is so glad I can't help telling your honour that he apprenticed my eldest boy° last week, and pays for the schooling of the two youngest.   70

BELFORD These are noble bounties, I confess, Waters, but I think your feelings on the occasion do as much honour to human nature as the knight's generosity; for a liberal hand is more frequently to be met with than a grateful heart. But where is Sir William?

WATERS I left him going to take a turn in the garden, and I don't in the   75
least doubt but he will come in cool as a cucumber, though, when
he went downstairs, he was as angry with me as if he had never
done me any good.

BELFORD Show me the way, and I'll go to him directly.

Exeunt through the middle door

2.2

A dressing-room, an elegant toilet°
Lady Mary and Mrs Bromley

LADY MARY (*taking up the dressing plate°*) They are pretty, I confess,
but even I think them rather dear.

MRS BROMLEY What an idea for my dear Lady Mary! Do you know
now, that the equipage of Mrs Stockwell's° toilet, the broker's wife,
cost thirteen hundred pounds?

LADY MARY I remember her at Paris—an over-dressed thing!   5
I thought she had been a jeweller's wife, and looked upon
her as a stalking show-glass° to expose her husband's goods
for sale. But the poor man, I suppose, was ruined by her extravagance.

MRS BROMLEY Yes, yes, he was done-up° very soon after. But   10
the woman had wit in her madness, however, for she secreted
her paraphernalia, and her chariot has rolled on her personal fortune ever since.° Women are much wiser nowadays than they used
to be.

Enter Mrs Williams   15

MRS WILLIAMS Your ladyship's masquerade dress is just come home,
ma'am.

LADY MARY Let me see! Let me see!

MRS BROMLEY How beautiful! My dear creature, 'You'll look a
goddess, and you'll move a queen!'°   20

LADY MARY Ah, Bromley, I have just recollected that I can't go as a
sultana. I have sent my earrings to be altered, and the rest of my
jewels will make no figure without them.

MRS BROMLEY Hire, hire, my dear.

LADY MARY I don't understand you.   25

MRS BROMLEY What a baby, Mrs Williams! But 'tis a sweet baby,
we must allow. Why, for fifty, or a hundred guineas at most, you

may hire as many diamonds as would outblaze the throne of
Delhi.°

LADY MARY A hundred guineas! What a sum for one night's vanity!   30
No, I'll go as a shepherdess.

MRS BROMLEY That would be a disguise, indeed, in these days of
martial ardour, when our whole sex have exchanged their old-
fashioned simplicity of dress and manners for the military air, the
smart cockade, and lively regimental.°   35

LADY MARY But one may be allowed to look innocent in masquerade, I
hope?

MRS BROMLEY Ha! My little sly one! Have I found you out? Nothing
but a Corydon° could have inspired such an idea.

LADY MARY All dresses, I fancy, are alike to Mr Woodley.   40

MRS BROMLEY Mr Woodley! Ridiculous! Why, surely, my dear, you
don't think of exposing yourself to be the jest of the whole town by
going *en groupe* with your husband to a masquerade! Would not the
dear, good-natured Sir Harry Granger, or even the wise Colonel
Mountfort, make a better Corydon for our sweet shepherdess, think   45
you?

LADY MARY How idly you talk! Mountfort is Louisa's cicisbeo,° and
Sir Harry, I fancy, would be proud to enlist under your banner in
the same capacity.

MRS BROMLEY This is wilful blindness, Lady Mary, for you can't   50
avoid seeing that Sir Harry is your slave. I pity him with all my
heart, and wish you would do so too. Poor soul, how he dotes upon
you!

LADY MARY You'll make me angry, Mrs Bromley. But prithee, why
must I be treated like a picture for a drawing-room, not to be   55
hung up without its companion? I want no Corydon, I assure
you.

MRS BROMLEY No, to be sure, quite lonely and discreet. Come, come,
my dear Lady Mary, you were not designed for a simple shepherdess. The sultana is your natural character: born to command and be   60
adored. But you must and shall be fine; for let the men say what
they will of native charms, our diamonds add considerably to the
lustre of our eyes. What say you, Mrs Williams?

MRS WILLIAMS There never was a truer word spoken, ma'am; for
though my lady wants no off-settings and looks like an angel in any   65
dress—

LADY MARY A truce with your flattery, Williams! Take away the dress.
I shall consider of it.

MRS WILLIAMS (*aside*) Nobody's flattery will go down now but Mrs
    Bromley's, it seems.   70
      Exit [*Mrs Williams*]

LADY MARY I should like the sultana, I confess; but—

MRS BROMLEY But what?

LADY MARY Can't you guess? You know I have been stripped at play,
    and have squandered a great deal of money this morning. I am
    sorry I bought these toys.°   75

MRS BROMLEY Bless me! How you talk! You that have the fondest,
    and the most indulgent, husband breathing!

LADY MARY For that very reason, my dear Bromley.

MRS BROMLEY You really talk like a wife of the last century. Here's a
    fuss indeed, about a poor hundred guineas! Do you know now, that   80
    I would not have this story told of you, in any polite circle, for
    treble the sum! If it should take wind,° you'd be sneered to death
    with encomiums on your ladyship's very uncommon prudence.

LADY MARY Why, I should not care to be thought too prudent neither,
    so I beg you'll not mention it to anyone.   85

MRS BROMLEY You may rely on my friendship. And now, my dear,
    what jewels would you have?

LADY MARY You can't imagine how much distressed I am upon this
    trifling subject. I'm resolved not to ask Mr Woodley for money
    today.   90

MRS BROMLEY Borrow, then. You may command thousands, to my
    knowledge. Sir Harry is as rich as all Duke's Place,° and I am sure
    he would be happy to lay all his treasures at your feet.

LADY MARY Borrow money from Sir Harry Granger! You cannot
    mean it!   95

MRS BROMLEY Ha, ha, ha! Sure never mortal was so easily taken in as
    my dear Lady Mary! You could not think me serious, I hope. Not
    but I know many wives—

LADY MARY Who are a reproach to their sex, perhaps.°

MRS BROMLEY No preaching, if you love me! I shall get the jewels for   100
    you on my own credit, for I am resolved that you shall not only be
    the loveliest, but the finest° woman in all that dear, gay, motley
    assembly tonight.

LADY MARY I thank you, my dear Bromley. I think the dress will
    become me. But I owe you a monstrous deal of money, I'm afraid,   105
    already. How much is it?

MRS BROMLEY A trifle, a very trifle indeed, and between such friends!
    And I shall be apt to quarrel with you if ever you mention it again.

Let the men settle it. I shall bring the jewels with me at five. Till
then, *adio, mia cara.*°   110

LADY MARY Mr Bromley comes, I hope?

MRS BROMLEY Lord! Who knows anything of a husband's engagements, my dear? But there is no doubt of his attending your summons on any occasion, for my poor Bromley dies for you. You are
quite a monopolizer, Lady Mary!   115

> *Exit* [*Mrs Bromley*]

LADY MARY What a rattle you are!

> *Exit*

2.3

> *Sir William Woodley's apartments*
> *Sir William and Belford at backgammon*

SIR WILLIAM I tell you, I will hear no more of him. If he has destroyed
his fortune, he shall not destroy my peace. (*Throws the dice*) Cinque
ace.°—Come, come, 'tis your throw.

BELFORD It is amazing, Sir William, that you can be so anxious about
this trifling game, and at the same time so indifferent about your   5
nephew!

SIR WILLIAM I am in earnest about everything, Mr Belford; consequently, in my resentment against my silly nephew, who is a slave
to his wife and a victim to his vanity. (*Hastily*°) Will you take the
box,° I say?   10

BELFORD Gently, gently, my good Sir William. You have put yourself
in a passion already. (*Rises*)

SIR WILLIAM No, sir, 'tis you that have put me in a passion. I hate
'gently', and all the phlegmatic people in the world.

BELFORD And yet you and I have been friends these twenty years.   15

SIR WILLIAM True, true, my dear Belford! And, perhaps, I am
indebted to your 'gently' for our continuing so. But don't put my
patience to any further trial at present. Sit down, I entreat you.

BELFORD But one word more and I have done.

SIR WILLIAM Well, I am patient, but don't harp again on the same   20
string; no more of Mr Woodley.

BELFORD You have a noble fortune, Sir William!

SIR WILLIAM Yes, thanks to Providence! More than I have occasion
for myself, and therefore I consider the overplus but as a bank for

my friends. Do you want money, Belford? Name the sum and take   25
it.

BELFORD Thank you, Sir William, but 'tis not my wants I wish you to
supply, but those of your nephew.

SIR WILLIAM What? At it again? I will not give him a doit—not a doit,
sir. My fortune shall not be lavished to indulge his vanity or supply   30
his prodigality.

BELFORD I am persuaded he has so thoroughly reflected upon his past
folly that he would make a proper use of your future kindness.

SIR WILLIAM Let him alter his conduct first if he expects I should
alter mine. His repentance may merit my bounty, but my liberality   35
shall not prevent his reformation.

BELFORD But if Mr Woodley should be undone, what will become of
your niece?

SIR WILLIAM Let her share his fate as she has done his folly; she has
earned it. An extravagant woman that could not be content to live   40
at one of the finest seats in England, but must frisk it to Spa and
Paris, forsooth, like the rest of the silly English, to squander their
money and be laughed at by foreigners!

BELFORD I understood Miss Woodley had remained in England.

SIR WILLIAM What, Louisa? I did not speak of her. She is the best girl   45
on earth. No, no, she shan't suffer for other people's faults. If he
has involved her fortune too, I shall take care of her.

BELFORD Do you intend she shall live with you?

SIR WILLIAM No, sir, no! I'll have no mistress in my house, but old
Jones. I would not displace her for a duchess; it would break the   50
poor woman's heart. But I shall take proper care of Louisa. (*Aside*) I
wish she was well married, out of the way.

BELFORD But now give me leave, Sir William—

SIR WILLIAM Neither now, nor then, Mr Belford. The matter is all
settled in my mind, and the game gone quite out of my head. I'll   55
send for Louisa directly and talk this matter over with her. [*Calling
offstage*] Waters!

    Enter Waters

Step in to Mr Woodley's and desire my niece to come to me
immediately.

    Exit Waters

BELFORD I am sorry I have been so unsuccessful in my suit, Sir   60
William, and wish you a good day.

SIR WILLIAM You are not angry with me, I hope, Belford? I am as
sorry for my nephew's indiscretion as you or anyone can be.

BELFORD If you are, you will certainly assist him. (*Aside*) But I know it
must be all done in your own way.   6

SIR WILLIAM Dine with me, and we'll play out our party° after dinner.

BELFORD With all my heart, but I shall be too many for you, as usual.
Exit [Belford]

SIR WILLIAM If I had not the greatest regard imaginable for my old
friend, I should hate him abominably for always beating me at
backgammon. But let me consider now: she has ten thousand   7
pounds of her own. I will give her as much more at present, and my
whole estate after my death.—No, no. That won't be acting justly.
Woodley may have children. They have not offended me, though
their father has, and if they should be half so pleasant as he was
when he was a child, I should love them dearly, as I once did him.   7
But I must strive to forget all that business, now.—Here comes
Louisa.
*Enter Lady Mary, who keeps at a distance without Sir William's
looking at her.*

SIR WILLIAM Well, child, you know, I suppose, that my hopeful
nephew is totally ruined—

LADY MARY Sir!   8

SIR WILLIAM Why don't you come nearer? I wouldn't have all the
house hear me. (*Lady Mary advances*) My nephew, I tell you, is
ruined.

LADY MARY I could not have imagined, sir, when you did me the
honour of sending for me, that you meant to alarm or insult me.   8

SIR WILLIAM (*looking at Lady Mary*) I send for you? I insult you?—
That blundering Waters!—No, madam, you are the last person
in the world, except your husband, that I should think of sending
for.

LADY MARY The respect I have for you, sir, as Mr Woodley's relation,   9
must make it extremely painful to me to know that I am so disagreeable to you.

SIR WILLIAM Respect for me, madam! I don't desire your respect, nor
deserve your respect. (*Aside*) If she talks in this way, she'll stagger
my resolution. [*To Lady Mary*] I wanted to speak with my niece,   9
madam, and my blundering servant—

LADY MARY Has brought you one that is proud of that title, sir.

SIR WILLIAM You have a title of your own, madam. I hate titles, and
one reason why I never married was because I would not have my
wife called 'my lady'.   10

LADY MARY I see, Sir William, that you are not inclined—

SIR WILLIAM To converse with *ladies*, madam. I would speak with
   Louisa upon business.

LADY MARY I shall no longer obtrude on you, sir, but before I go, must
   request you'll explain what you meant by saying that Mr Woodley   105
   was ruined.

SIR WILLIAM (*aside*) She knows nothing of the matter, I find, and I
   cannot bear to shock her. [*To Lady Mary*] I think, madam, you
   ought to understand that matter as well as I.—Ruined!°—Why, 'tis
   a common phrase, at present, madam. Dukes, lords, and com-   110
   mons,° nay the whole nation, are ruined, madam. 'Tis quite the
   ton; and I suppose that neither Mr Woodley nor you would choose
   to be out of the fashion.

LADY MARY I hope, sir, you'll allow that Mr Woodley's fortune, and
   my rank, entitles us—   115

SIR WILLIAM To be ruined in good company, madam. (*Aside*) She has
   touched the right key now. I'm no more afraid of her. Had she
   fallen a-crying, I might have been ruined too.

LADY MARY I am sorry to find, sir, that your prejudices against Mr
   Woodley and me are so strong that it would be in vain for us to   120
   attempt a justification of our conduct.

SIR WILLIAM Quite so, indeed, madam.

LADY MARY I shall therefore take my leave, sir. (*Going*)

SIR WILLIAM (*aside*) You have mine, with all my heart.

LADY MARY Shall I send Miss Woodley to you, sir?   125

SIR WILLIAM No, madam, no. I'll send for her when I am a little more
   composed. Your servant—your servant, madam.
        Exit Lady Mary
   [*Calling offstage*] Waters!—What a martyrdom has this fellow exposed
   me to!—Waters!—
        Enter Waters
   Thou eternal blockhead, dolt, dunderhead—   130

WATERS Does your honour speak to me?

SIR WILLIAM No, to the door, to the window, to this table! Matter
   itself has more intelligence than thou.
        Enter Servant

SERVANT Would your honour please to have dinner served? It is quite
   ready.   135

SIR WILLIAM Let it wait.

SERVANT Mr Belford is below, sir,

SIR WILLIAM Well, well, I'll go then. What a provoking blunder!
        Exeunt

2.4

Woodley's dressing-room
Woodley alone

WOODLEY If Belford should succeed with my uncle, all may yet be well. Something must be done, and quickly too. I can no longer endure the agony of endeavouring to impose upon° the world, and myself, by personating a borrowed character. But here she comes, who innocently adds to all my sufferings and tips the darts of poverty with anguish!

Enter Lady Mary

LADY MARY Oh, my dear Woodley! Such a trial ordeal as I have undergone! I declare I would rather be buried alive in Dorsetshire than endure such another *tête-à-tête*. He has done everything but beat me.   10

WOODLEY I don't comprehend you. Whom do you mean?

LADY MARY Nay, that's downright perverseness; for I am certain there is not such another creature upon earth as your precious uncle.

WOODLEY I hope you have not quarrelled with him, Lady Mary?

LADY MARY No, truly; he has spared me that trouble by quarrelling with me most outrageously.

WOODLEY (*aside*) Then all my hopes in Belford are at an end. [*To Lady Mary*] I am very sorry you happened to come in his way.

LADY MARY I'm sure so am I, Mr Woodley. The interview was not of my seeking, and, though I was as mild as a lamb, he was as rude as a   20 bear. The deuce take his blundering servant for bringing me into such a scrape!

WOODLEY I should hope that your regard for me would have prevented—

LADY MARY And so it did, I assure you; for I did not laugh, though he   25 said something so ridiculous, about your being ruined, the nation being ruined, and all the world being ruined, that I had much ado to keep my countenance. However, I behaved very decently all the while, and even condescended to entreat that he would give you leave to justify your conduct to him.   30

WOODLEY (*with eagerness*) And did my dear Mary obtain his permission?

LADY MARY Your earnestness startles me, Mr Woodley. Of what consequence can the old-fashioned opinion of an obstinate Don Choleric,° who hates us both, be of to us? I wish he would endow a   35

hospital with his fortune, that our solicitude to please might end
with our expectations.

WOODLEY Mine should not, I assure you.

LADY MARY That must be as you please, Mr Woodley; but I declare,
from this hour—   40

WOODLEY Make no rash vows, madam. You know not how much you
have been, or may be, indebted to Sir William.

LADY MARY I indebted to him! No, Mr Woodley, that I positively deny.
    Enter Mr and Mrs Bromley

BROMLEY (*entering*) And so do I, with both my hands and all my heart;
for, be the question in law, physic, or divinity, I'll pawn my life on't 45
that Lady Mary is right.

LADY MARY I am much obliged to you for your good opinion, Mr
Bromley.

MRS BROMLEY And I wager on Mr Woodley's side, were it only to
keep up the argument. The question, then?   50

BROMLEY Ay, ay, the question?

LADY MARY (*to Mrs Bromley*) There are secrets in all families, you
know, my dear Bromley.

WOODLEY And it is always prudent to keep them so, Lady Mary.

BROMLEY Very good, very good, indeed.   55

MRS BROMLEY Curiosity, thank heaven, is not one of my failings. 'Tis
ever a mark both of ignorance and ill-breeding. I am astonished
how anyone can be infected with such an impertinent weakness.

BROMLEY Yes, yes, my dame is quite above all silly curiosity. (*Aside*)
The veriest eavesdropper that ever existed. She'll not rest till she 60
has got the whole story, and I shall have it the moment we get home.
    Mrs Bromley shows a box of jewels to Lady Mary

LADY MARY They are quite charming, indeed! I shall outblaze the
Queen of Diamonds.

WOODLEY What jewels are these? I hope you have not bought them,
Lady Mary!   65

LADY MARY You hope I have not bought them? What an odd speech,
Mr Woodley! No; I have only borrowed them, and will lend you
part, if you will go *en Turc*.° I can spare enough to ornament his
turban, can't I, Bromley?

MRS BROMLEY Surely you don't persist in making a family party,   70
Lady Mary?

LADY MARY (*to Woodley*) You shall have these.

WOODLEY Prithee, don't tease me, Lady Mary. I shall not go to the
masquerade.

Exit [Woodley]

LADY MARY Don't tease me! Something extraordinary must have disturbed him.

BROMLEY You'll have a charming squeeze at your rout, Lady Mary! Not a vacant chair to be found in the whole house, I warrant you.

LADY MARY You flatter me. No; I believe there will hardly be anybody. Do you know that I have had a hundred and ninety-one excuses within these two days?°

MRS BROMLEY Ay, but you'll have nine hundred and ninety people for all that. I hope Lady Sitfast° won't come! That woman never orders her carriage till near one, though she plagues the servant to call it up every five minutes after eleven.

LADY MARY Then there's that poor, drooping Mrs Henpeck,° who always loses, and sits moaning over her losses and playing the aftergame,° till the servants are obliged to put her out along with the candles.

Enter Forward

LADY MARY No more excuses, I hope?

FORWARD Dinner is served, please your ladyship.

MRS BROMLEY Is Sir Harry Granger come?

LADY MARY Oh, no; he has no longer the *entrée* here.

BROMLEY I'm heartily sorry for it. No man tempers a salad° like Sir Harry. He is a perfect compendium° of the whole art of cookery, and has more good receipts in his pocket-book, than ever were published by the celebrated Hannah Glasse.°

LADY MARY Most excellent qualifications for a man of fashion!°

BROMLEY True, very true, indeed! Eating is the rage, the high *ton*, at present, and indeed is one of the most refined of our modern studies. Will your ladyship permit me the transcendent honour of your fair hand?

LADY MARY I attend Mrs Bromley.°

Exeunt

3.1

[Sir William Woodley's] dining-parlour
Sir William and Belford at a table with a bottle and glasses

SIR WILLIAM I am no drinking man myself, Belford, but yet I do
not approve of this water system of yours. It keeps the spirits too
low—

BELFORD To say or do anything mad or foolish, I grant it may. But if
water does not raise, it never depresses the spirits. Can you say as   5
much for your generous wine?

SIR WILLIAM Well, well, I won't dispute with you because I hate
argument, and, as you are an honest fellow, I can venture to take my
glass cheerfully in your company though you don't partake of my
liquor. But I'd give something, ay, more than I'll mention, that   10
you'd share only one pint of claret with me now.

BELFORD I have made no vows, Sir William, and to humour a friend
can easily dispense with rules of my own making. [*Takes glass*] So,
here's your fair niece, Louisa Woodley, in a bumper. [*Both drink*]

SIR WILLIAM Thank you, thank you, my good friend! She is a most   15
excellent girl, and I like to have her toasted by such a man as you. I
wish she was well-settled with all my heart.

BELFORD There can be no doubt of her marrying to advantage. She is
a fine young woman with a fine fortune.

SIR WILLIAM And so may be sacrificed to some fine young man that   20
may spend her fortune in finery, as her hopeful brother has done,
and leave her a beggar. No, no, I'll prevent that. I have thought of a
match for her—fill your glass, Belford!—a prudent, sober, sensible
man. (*Aside*) I wish he'd take the hint.

BELFORD Rare qualities, indeed, for a young man of fashion to possess   25
in these days, Sir William.

SIR WILLIAM Who told you that he was a 'young man of fashion'?
Why, sir, there have been no *men* born at least for these last thirty
years—all monkeys and macaronies.° No hearts of oak° now,
Belford; all dwindled into aspens!°   30

BELFORD Your sarcasm is rather too general, my good friend. Courage
is the birthright of an Englishman, and while one acre of our soil
remains, both the oak and the laurel° will thrive on it. We must not
prejudge the rising generation. And I have not the least doubt but
your niece will make a very proper choice.   35

SIR WILLIAM A choice! I hope she has been better educated than to have a choice, sir. I was not consulted in her brother's match, and you see the consequence. I shall dispose of Louisa in my own way. I have a husband now in my eye for her, Belford.

BELFORD Whoever obtains Miss Woodley will, I dare say, be a very happy man. 40

SIR WILLIAM Stick to that, my dear Belford. Yes, yes, whoever marries Louisa will be a very happy man, and I am extremely glad you think so. (*Aside*) I wish he'd come to the point.

BELFORD You know, Sir William, that I have long been acquainted with Miss Woodley's merit. 45

SIR WILLIAM You charm me, my dear Belford. I am glad you know her worth, and you will therefore cherish it. She is mild and timid, but you'll be kind and gentle to her even for my sake, my good old friend. 50

BELFORD *Kind and gentle to her?* and your *good old friend?*

SIR WILLIAM Why, are not you my friend?

BELFORD Most certainly.

SIR WILLIAM Then why all this reiteration? If you marry Louisa—

BELFORD I marry her, Sir William! 55

SIR WILLIAM Yes, sir! Did you not, this moment, allow that whoever married her would be a very happy man? And, I suppose, you can have no possible objection to being a very happy man, Mr Belford?

BELFORD Yes, sir, the strongest in the world, if my happiness is to be purchased at the expense of another's misery. But I am wrong for 60 being serious when I am certain you do but jest.

SIR WILLIAM In the first place, sir, I never said anything in jest since I was born. And, secondly, sir, I never was more in earnest in the whole course of my life. I therefore request from you a serious answer.—Jest, indeed! No, truly, counsellor, I am no joker. 65

BELFORD Why, then, sir, I should think myself highly honoured—

SIR WILLIAM Psha, psha, psha—

BELFORD Patience, my good friend—

SIR WILLIAM No, sir! I will have no patience with your nonsensical compliments; none of your honours, I say. 70

BELFORD In a word then, Sir William, the disparity of years between forty-eight and eighteen—

SIR WILLIAM Is just nothing at all. What need you tell her you are forty-eight?

BELFORD There will be no occasion, I grant you. Self-evident proposi- 75 tions need no proof.

SIR WILLIAM Hark ye, Belford, you fatigue me to death with your logic and sophistry. The point may be reduced to two words: Will you marry my niece, or no?

BELFORD It is a match so infinitely beyond my pretensions, Sir 80 William—

SIR WILLIAM I hope I may be allowed the best judge in that matter, Mr Belford.

BELFORD By no means, Sir William. Your partial kindness towards me— 85

SIR WILLIAM Is almost worn out by your tiresome, false modesty. And, if I thought I should have as much plague with Louisa as I have had with you, I'd renounce my project, and leave her to die an old maid.

BELFORD The proposal is so highly favourable to me— 90

SIR WILLIAM That you consent.

BELFORD Were I certain that Miss Woodley's inclinations—

SIR WILLIAM I told you before that I could dispose of them as I pleased; so that if you have no other objection, I shall carry my point and settle one of my family to my entire satisfaction at last. 95

BELFORD It is impossible that I can have any objection, if she has none.

SIR WILLIAM Your hand then, my dear Belford. 'Tis a match. Order your clerks to set about the writings directly.—Your estate lies in Staffordshire, I think.—You know I add ten thousand to her 100 fortune.

BELFORD But surely, my dear Sir William, Miss Woodley ought to be made acquainted—

SIR WILLIAM Why, has she not been acquainted with you ever since she was born? If I mistake not, you were present at her christening. 105 The wedding shall be next week. The sooner my dear girl is happily settled, the better.

BELFORD Your kindness overwhelms me, but still, Miss Woodley—

SIR WILLIAM Shall be made acquainted with her happiness this evening. I leave all the articles of settlement to your own honour. I know 110 you'll make a proper provision for my niece, because it is possible you may die before her—but no pin-money,° I charge you. 'Tis but a prelude to alimony, believe me.

BELFORD I shall endeavour to acquit myself as such generous confidence deserves. 115

SIR WILLIAM Hurry, hurry your clerks, and bring this happy event to a speedy conclusion, my dear nephew.

BELFORD I have the strongest motives to enforce their diligence, as well as the highest sense of my obligations to your friendship.

SIR WILLIAM No speeches! Hasten the business, and adieu.   12

    Exit Belford

I'll speak to Jones directly to prepare for the wedding-dinner. She can't bear to be hurried; and I'd have every thing magnificent on that day, which I shall deem the happiest of my whole life, because it will be the first time I could ever get any of my family to know their own interest and act as I would have them. (*Going off*)   12

    Enter Louisa

I am very glad to see you, my dear child. And now, what have you to say to me?

LOUISA I was informed, sir, by my sister,° that you desired to speak with me, and I am therefore come to receive your commands.

SIR WILLIAM Why, my dear, it will neither be questions nor com-   13
mands, but cross-purposes,° if you keep at such a distance as will make it impossible we should hear one another. Come nearer, I say. What are you afraid of?°

LOUISA (*advancing*) Sir—

SIR WILLIAM So, so. That will do. And now, my dear child, you can't   13
imagine what a heavenly temper I am in, and what favourable dis-positions I have towards you.°

LOUISA I am very happy, sir—

SIR WILLIAM So you'll say, my dear, when you know all. But you must deserve my kindness by your frankness. Therefore, first tell me   14
whether you have any particular objection to matrimony?

LOUISA It is a subject, sir, that I have never much thought upon.

SIR WILLIAM That's singular now, for I am told that the girls of these days think of nothing else. But, luckily, there is no occasion for your considering about the matter, as you have such a friend as I am to   14
consider for you, child.

LOUISA Sir!

SIR WILLIAM And so I shall make your mind easy at once by letting you know that I have provided a husband for you.

LOUISA (*aside*) Now, heaven forbid!   15

SIR WILLIAM And such a one as is not to be met with everyday, I assure you. A man after my own heart—has not a fault, Louisa, but that he is a water-drinker. But I won't anticipate by telling you his name. He shall surprise you with it himself.—Why, hey! What's the matter now? You don't seem at all overjoyed! You are not hankering   15
after a title, I hope, for, believe me, niece, if there be either

happiness or virtue left in the present world, they are only to be
met with in the middle ranks of life. What makes you tremble so?

LOUISA You are not unacquainted with my timidity, sir.

SIR WILLIAM Yes, yes, I understand the timidity of your whole sex.   160
(*Aside*) Doves before marriage, and kites° after. [*To Louisa*] You'll
soon get the better of your timidity, I'll answer for it.

LOUISA As I am certain, sir, that 'tis your wish to make me happy—

SIR WILLIAM You are right, my dear; but it must be my own way. Your
brother's want of respect to my opinion, you see, has been his ruin,   165
child. Don't attempt to copy him, Louisa.

LOUISA If you would but condescend to hear me, sir—

SIR WILLIAM Why, child, I know everything already that you would
wish to say. Your obligations to me, and your modesty, and your
timidity, and your settlement, and all that—   170

LOUISA Dear sir, I have not a thought about a settlement—

SIR WILLIAM Well, well, everything shall be taken care of, except a
provision for a separate maintenance.° I bar that; for if you can't live
happily with such a husband as I have chosen for you, I should think
you deserved to starve, though you were my niece a thousand times.   175

LOUISA But, my dear uncle—

SIR WILLIAM But, my dear niece, don't insist upon it; for a woman
who thinks of separation at the moment of her union, does not
intend to abide by her husband, as she ought to do, till death do
them part.   180

LOUISA I neither think of union nor separation, sir—

SIR WILLIAM Modest and virtuous that—

LOUISA Hear me but one word, sir—

SIR WILLIAM Enough's said, enough's said, my dear. Here, take this
bill to provide for your dress. I'd have everything handsome. The   185
ladies are great belles in Staffordshire, and I'd have my niece make
as good an appearance as any *private gentlewoman* among them.
Why don't you take the bill? 'Tis for five hundred pounds, and I
hope you think that sufficient.

LOUISA I have no sort of occasion for it, sir; and if you would but   190
indulge me with a moment's conversation—

SIR WILLIAM Psha, psha, psha! I hate all this affected delicacy. Take
money from the old man whenever you can get it. Hasten your
milliners and mantua-makers, and get all your matters ready by this
day se'nnight, for I won't have the wedding deferred an hour longer.   195
Delays are ever dangerous.

    Exit [*Sir William*], *throwing the bill on the table*

LOUISA What, in the name of wonder, can this dear, kind, cruel uncle of mine intend for me? I almost doubt whether I wake or not. Married in a week, to a man perhaps I never saw! No, that's impossible. He is too good to think of such an union. Possibly Mount- 20 fort may have applied for his consent before he asked mine! Too fond a hope, I fear. I wish I could see Counsellor Belford; my uncle keeps no secret from him, and he is a friend to all our family. I'll write to him to come to me instantly. (*Sits down to the table*) 20

Enter Belford, without seeing Louisa

BELFORD I cannot proceed on this business in earnest till Sir William has had some conference with his niece. It is possible she may dislike the match, or perhaps be otherwise engaged, and then I should become the standing jest of all my brother benchers.° I must speak to Sir William again. 21

LOUISA [*sees Belford*] My good Mr Belford, I never was so glad to see you in my whole life. I have been this moment writing to you.

BELFORD You make me the happiest of mortals, madam. (*Aside*) This brief° opens well! I need not be much afraid of being laughed at now. 21

LOUISA There is something so particular—(*Aside*) I know not how to mention it! [*To Belford*] Mr Belford, my good uncle has—

BELFORD I find, completed his kindness, and acquainted you, madam—

LOUISA No, sir, but as you share his confidence, I must entreat that 22 you'll inform me—(*Hesitates*)

BELFORD (*aside*) Her modesty distresses me vastly, but I like her the better for it! I wish I had a speech ready. [*To Louisa*] Did not Sir William, madam, say anything of matrimony to you?

LOUISA You can't imagine, sir, how he has surprised and terrified me 22 by talking of my being to be married in a week.

BELFORD You might be surprised, to be sure, madam, but I don't see any occasion for your being terrified, any more than for such a violent hurry. The writings can't be properly engrossed in that time. The law seldom keeps pace with a lover's wishes; and how- 23 ever impatient I may be to expedite this business, you shall not be hurried, fair lady, but be at liberty to name your own day.

LOUISA It shall be doomsday, then! However, I thank you, sir, for allowing me even a reprieve.

BELFORD (*aside*) Hey-dey! Where sits the wind now? [*To Louisa*] You 23 have no absolute aversion to marriage, I hope, Miss Woodley?

LOUISA I despise affectation, sir, and am above disguise with an old
friend like you: I have no aversion to marriage when I can bestow
my hand with my heart, but I would rather die than be sacrificed to
a frightful sordid wretch who has trepanned my uncle out of his   240
consent because he despaired of mine, and takes me merely as an
appendage to my fortune.

BELFORD (*aside*) How lucky was my coming back! [*To Louisa*] But why
should you suppose, madam, that your uncle should 'sacrifice you
to a frightful sordid wretch'? Your intended husband is a very   245
different kind of man, I'll assure you, madam.

LOUISA Let him be what he will, sir, I shall detest him.

BELFORD I never thought, Miss Woodley, that my conduct or character had in any instance merited your detestation, madam.

LOUISA Detest you, Mr Belford! No, that's impossible! But how are   250
you concerned in the matter?

BELFORD Not much at present, madam; for I scorn to take advantage
of your uncle's engagements unless ratified by your consent.

LOUISA Oh, Mr Belford!

BELFORD Nay, never whimper about it. I own, I suspected from the   255
first that it was rather too good news to be true. But don't make
yourself unhappy, Miss Woodley, for I would rather live and die a
bachelor than marry the finest woman in England, as is now the
case, (*bowing*) who was not equally ready 'to have and to hold'.

LOUISA Generous, worthy man!   260

BELFORD Not more generous than prudent, madam, on this occasion.
But as I hope I have now deserved your confidence, Miss Woodley,
tell me, then, if you have any particular attachment, and I shall
endeavour to serve you with Sir William, though I know I shall, for
a time, stand in the light of a culprit before him by declining the   265
honour he intended me.

LOUISA You overpower me with obligations, Mr Belford.

BELFORD No speeches, my dear madam. If I was not sufficiently
gratified by the honour of the act, no acknowledgments could make
me amends for the disappointment. So, frankly name the happy   270
man who is to raise my envy and complete your happiness.

LOUISA Though I think that a well-placed and mutual affection need
not raise a blush upon the chastest cheek, yet mine will glow when I
name Colonel Mountfort.

BELFORD Colonel Mountfort! I'm sorry for it.   275

LOUISA Why so, sir?

BELFORD Because he's a very pretty fellow, madam, and for that

179

reason may fall within your uncle's chapter of coxcombs and prevent his consent.

LOUISA Then I shall never give mine to marry any man else.   280

BELFORD That's somewhat in the knight's own style, Miss Woodley. But I heartily wish you success, and shall show myself a warmer friend than a lover by using my best pleadings in my rival's suit.

LOUISA Accept my warmest thanks, my good old friend.

  Exit [Louisa]

BELFORD Ay, ay, I knew she would always think of me as her *old*   285 friend.

  Exit

3.2

  [Woodley's] dining-room
  Woodley and Bromley at a table with a dice-box

WOODLEY I'll play no more.

BROMLEY Why, to be sure, my dear friend, luck has run confoundedly against you, but I never saw you give out° for such a trifling loss before.

WOODLEY Seven hundred pounds is no trifle, Mr Bromley!   5

BROMLEY A trifle, indeed, to a person of your immense fortune!

WOODLEY You have made a false estimate of my circumstances. I am rather a distressed man at present, Mr Bromley.

BROMLEY *(aside)* Are you so? Then 'tis time for me to take care of myself. [*To Woodley*] You surprise me vastly. Distressed did you   10 say?

WOODLEY I hate to repeat it, but 'tis so true that I had some thoughts of applying to your friendship to extricate me out of my present difficulties, Mr Bromley.

BROMLEY Command me, command me, my dear Woodley! Every-   15 thing that poor Bob Bromley has in the world—*(aside)* except his money—[*to Woodley*] is at your service. But let us clear° as we go; settle our little matters first. Just set your name to this paper; or will you take another throw, my friend, and let it be double or quit?

  Enter Colonel Mountfort

COL. MOUNTFORT For shame, Woodley! At hazard in your own   20 house! I thought you had enough of that at clubs.

BROMLEY Play among friends is wrong, very wrong, I confess,

colonel; but one can't be always grave and wise.—Come, my dear
Woodley, let us make an end of our business: the pen, or the box,
my dear boy?   25

WOODLEY (*aside*) Desperate situations require desperate remedies.
[*To Bromley*] Give me the box. (*Woodley and Bromley throw* [*the
dice*]) Damn the dice!

BROMLEY 'Tis double now, you know, my unlucky friend, which
makes upon the whole exactly the sum of seven thousand three   30
hundred and fifty-four pounds, including the dear Lady Mary's
trifling debt to Mrs Bromley.

WOODLEY True, sir.

BROMLEY Well, I have brought a bond with me, and when I have filled
up the blanks, if you please we'll perfect it in the next room.   35

WOODLEY With all my heart. (*Aside*) Sure never a man was so
unfortunate! [*To Colonel Mountfort and Bromley*] Never, by heaven,
will I touch a die again!

COL. MOUNTFORT Then I give you joy of your losses, for I know you
are too much a man of honour to break your vow.   40

BROMLEY Gamesters, like lovers,° you know, colonel! And, after all
now, this is but a matter of form between friends, and men of
honour, like you and me. Don't you think so, colonel?

COL. MOUNTFORT I consider all compulsive obligations between men
as a disgrace to human nature. But while there are such things as   45
knaves in the world, Mr Bromley, we must submit to the mean
securities of bars and bonds.° But between men of honour, as you
say—

BROMLEY Certainly, my dear sir, men of honour are—

COL. MOUNTFORT Too often the dupes of knaves, Mr Bromley.   50

BROMLEY (*aside*) I don't like him. [*To Woodley*] We'll talk over the
affair you hinted at in the next room. [*To Colonel Mountfort*] Command me, on all occasions. Ever, ever at your service. But I must
attend the ladies. The ladies and the coffee are powerful attractions
to me. You'll follow me, I presume, colonel?   55

    Exit [*Bromley*]

COL. MOUNTFORT Yes, with pleasure, through my whole regiment,
with a drum at your heels.° I am persuaded, Woodley, that fellow is
a knave, and I wish you would exclude both him and his flaunting°
wife from yours and Lady Mary's society. I can't conceive why you
are so partial to them.   60

WOODLEY The great civilities we received from them at Spa first
attached my wife to Mrs Bromley, who was there in the first sets,°

and even in London, where people are more nice.° She keeps very good company, I assure you, colonel.

COL. MOUNTFORT You'll pardon me, Woodley; she is seldom seen in public but with some damaged dowager of quality, who would be excluded from society if her title did not serve as a herald to make way for her ladyship.°—But enough of them! I am come to speak to you on a much more interesting subject, and to prove, what, however, I cannot doubt, your friendship to me.

WOODLEY Be assured, my dear Mountfort—

COL. MOUNTFORT I am so; you need not make professions. Therefore, with the frankness of a soldier, I venture to ask the highest proof of your regard, by consenting to make the fair Louisa mine.

WOODLEY My sister!

COL. MOUNTFORT You seem to hesitate, Mr Woodley! My fortune is—

WOODLEY As unexceptionable as your character, colonel; and as I truly love Louisa, and should rejoice in her happiness—

COL. MOUNTFORT You consent to mine. Is it so, my friend?

WOODLEY I know not how to answer you.

COL. MOUNTFORT You alarm me extremely, Mr Woodley! For heaven's sake, speak out! What can be your objections?

WOODLEY None in the world, to you; but circumstanced as I am at present, it would involve me in the greatest difficulties to be called upon so suddenly for ten thousand pounds.

COL. MOUNTFORT That shall not be the case, Woodley. I should think even Louisa too dearly purchased at the expense of distressing you. When I asked for your sister's hand, I did not demand her purse; nor shall I accept the one till I have signed a release for the other.

WOODLEY Mountfort, that must not, shall not be! I never will accept of such a sacrifice.

COL. MOUNTFORT Hark ye, Woodley! A soldier's character should be uniform; and if there could be one who was not liberal, I should suspect his courage to be of the mere animal kind. My fortune is sufficiently ample, and I would as soon mount my charger, cry stand and deliver,° as take money I don't want from a friend who does.

WOODLEY Your generosity, colonel—

COL. MOUNTFORT Is of too selfish a nature to merit praise. For I feel here (*laying his hand to his heart*) that the true luxury of fortune lies more in giving than in spending.

WOODLEY I will not lessen it by offering thanks. But have you opened

your trenches before the Knight of the Castle° yet? (*Pointing to the
middle door*) He used to speak well of you, and his opinion is of   105
some consequence in this business.

COL. MOUNTFORT My sentiments are even with° the good old
knight's, I assure you. I esteem his good qualities, and do not dislike
even his foibles, as they are truly natural and unsophisticate.° But
there, perhaps, you may see me play the usurer, like any Jew.° He   110
may double or treble Louisa's fortune, without the least impediment from any scruple or modesty of mine.

WOODLEY When do you purpose to make the essay?

COL. MOUNTFORT As soon as possible; for till I have paid the proper
respect due to him, I do not think myself entitled to throw myself   115
at Louisa's feet.

WOODLEY May success attend you, my generous friend!

COL. MOUNTFORT Fie, Woodley—no more of that! But adieu!
    Exeunt severally

4.1

Lady Mary's dressing-room
Lady Mary and Mrs Bromley

MRS BROMLEY And so that was all?

LADY MARY Every word, I assure you. But we shall soon make it up, for ours are but lovers' quarrels.

MRS BROMLEY Lovers! Talk of love after four years marriage! Believe me, Lady Mary, 'tis all a farce.   5

LADY MARY No, my dear Mrs Bromley, I cannot give you credit against the feelings of my own heart. I love Mr Woodley, and I am firmly persuaded that he has a sincere affection for me, notwithstanding the little peevishness of his behaviour today, which I own makes me apprehend that something must have ruffled him   10 extremely.

MRS BROMLEY How did you like his peremptory resolve of passing the whole summer in Dorsetshire?

LADY MARY Not at all, I confess. 'Tis frightful to think of it, though there is a tolerable neighbourhood—   15

MRS BROMLEY Of empty houses. No creature stays at their family seats nowadays, unless it be some antiquated dowager who, like an old gothic corner cupboard, remains fixed to the freehold.

LADY MARY I vow I won't go into the country—'tis quite *mauvais ton*°—except you'll come with us, and then we'll fly about to all the   20 bathing-places° and give a masquerade at one of them.

MRS BROMLEY I should like to pass a few weeks so well enough; and indeed, my dear, you'll be quite forgotten if you don't do something in that way. But are you sure that Mr Woodley would like it? For I must say, though I ask your pardon, Lady Mary, he is dull,   25 absolutely dull indeed, my dear.

LADY MARY Why, I own, of late he has been rather gloomy, but he is vastly good-natured, and never before refused any request of mine.

MRS BROMLEY That may be, but had Mr Bromley talked to me in the   30 same manner—

LADY MARY You would have loved him just as well as you do now.

MRS BROMLEY You are admirable at guessing, my dear; for as that same romantic notion of love never was the band of our connexion—   35

LADY MARY You startle me, Mrs Bromley. Marriage without love must
surely be a state of the greatest unhappiness.

MRS BROMLEY No, I don't feel in the least unhappy. Convenience is
the best matrimonial cement, and keeps many couples together for
years whose love did not outlast the honeymoon. But these are   40
mysteries into which you seem not yet initiated.

LADY MARY I hope I shall never know them by experience.

    Enter Louisa

LOUISA My dear sister—(*Sees Mrs Bromley*) I thought you were alone;
I had something in particular to tell you.

LADY MARY You alarm me vastly, Louisa! What is the matter, my dear?   45
You know I keep no secrets from Mrs Bromley.

LOUISA Another time, Lady Mary. Family affairs—

MRS BROMLEY Pray, my dear, make no stranger of me! (*Aside*) I hope
Mountfort has jilted her! I die to know. [*To Louisa*] Has the gallant
colonel deserted, my dear?   50

LOUISA Colonel Mountfort, madam, is no way concerned in the
present question.

MRS BROMLEY (*aside*) Then I would not give sixpence for the whole
story.

LADY MARY You look distressed, Louisa! What can have happened?   55
I'm all impatience.

LOUISA Though I had rather be excused, Lady Mary, yet, as you press
so earnestly to know, my uncle—

MRS BROMLEY (*aside*) Psha!

LOUISA Has insisted on my marrying—   60

MRS BROMLEY Not himself, I hope?

LADY MARY Giddy creature! Whom, my dear Louisa?

LOUISA Counsellor Belford.

MRS BROMLEY And is that all? I think it a monstrous good
match.   65

LADY MARY Monstrous, indeed! Why, he's fifty, at least.

MRS BROMLEY Fifty! Fiddlestick! What does that signify? He is rich
enough for threescore; and money, money, my dear, qualifies all
disproportions.

LADY MARY This is by much too serious a subject for jesting, Mrs   70
Bromley.—But Sir William is not your sole guardian, Louisa; and
your brother, I am certain, will never consent to sacrifice you to his
uncle's caprice.

LOUISA I would not on any account, my dear sister, have my brother
oppose Sir William in anything, as he is already but too much   75

offended with him. Besides, I am in hopes that there will not be any
occasion for his interposing.

MRS BROMLEY (*aside*) She's coming round, I find.

Enter Servant

SERVANT Mr Bromley, madam, has sent the carriage and desires to
speak with you, at home, immediately.   80

Exit [Servant]

MRS BROMLEY (*aside*) I'm glad of the release. (*To ladies*) What now
can he possibly want with me? But I am all obedience, though it
breaks my heart to leave you. But I shall return quickly, before
anyone sits down to loo. (*To Louisa*) And so, my dear, I leave you to
settle your important matters, which should be soon determined   85
were you my sister.

Exit [Mrs Bromley]

LOUISA Thank heaven, I am not! She is levity° itself.

LADY MARY Her lightness, Louisa, extends no farther than her manners; her morals are irreproachable. And when the mind is
untainted, its gaiety, like a coloured trimming to a grave suit, serves   90
only to enliven it.

LOUISA You are too partial, sister; for I much fear that you will one day
discover Mrs Bromley's manners and morals to be both of a piece.°

LADY MARY No more upon the subject at present! And in truth I wonder how you can have spirits to talk of anything else but your own   95
melancholy situation. Married to Belford! To your grandfather!

LOUISA I should be sad, indeed, if such a marriage was to take place,
but my 'intended' has generously consented to break off the match,
at my request, and to screen me from Sir William's displeasure at
the same time.   100

LADY MARY Then the old barrister° is charming, and I think I could
be a little in love with him myself. But I cannot submit to this new
insult from Sir William! What could he mean by disposing of you
without deigning to consult Mr Woodley? I shall insist upon an
explanation of his conduct.   105

LOUISA I again entreat you, Lady Mary, not to involve my brother
farther with Sir William. You do not know the consequences.

LADY MARY I am quite weary of all this temporizing, Louisa; and as
you are safe on shore, you must allow me to guide the helm for
myself at present. You'll permit me, at least, to acquaint Mr   110
Woodley with his uncle's contemptuous neglect of him in this
matter, which I shall go and do directly.

Exeunt

4.2

Sir William Woodley's apartments
Sir William and Waters

SIR WILLIAM Well, for once, Waters, I will acknowledge myself the happiest man in England.

WATERS I am proud to hear that your honour is so well pleased.

SIR WILLIAM Yes, yes, I am pleased, and I won't be pleased alone: they shall be pleased too! They shall have a noble service of plate!° 5
Louisa deserves everything; she behaved like an angel! I thought I should have had more trouble with her, but though it be strange, it is certainly true that all girls like to be married.

Enter Servant

SERVANT Colonel Mountfort, sir.

SIR WILLIAM I shall be glad to see him. Wait on him up, Waters. 10

Exeunt Waters and Servant

The colonel is a very good young man, as young men go at present, but nothing to compare to what his father was.

Enter Colonel Mountfort and Waters

I am very glad to see you, my young friend.—Set chairs, Waters.

[Waters brings chairs.] Exit Waters

COL. MOUNTFORT I am much obliged to you, Sir William, and happy 15
to perceive by your looks that all inquiries after your health must be superfluous.

SIR WILLIAM I thank you, sir! I fancy, indeed, I do look tolerably well, for serenity of mind goes a great way towards clearing up the coun-tenance; and I do not know when my spirits have ever been so 20
harmonized, as at this moment.

COL. MOUNTFORT (*aside*) How fortunate! [*To Sir William*] May I flatter myself, Sir William, that the present happy temper of your mind will assist my suit and render you propitious?

SIR WILLIAM Propitious? Nonsense! You are an idle young rogue!° 25
With such a noble fortune as yours—but I won't scold now. You have been on the turf, I suppose, or fleeced at the gaming-table? But I hope the *terra firma*° is safe. I should be grieved to see my old friend's estate in the hands of knaves or sharpers. What sum do you want? I know you to be a man of honour. 30

COL. MOUNTFORT You quite amaze me, sir, by suspicions which, I will be bold to say, are unworthy both of Sir William Woodley and me. I am no gambler, sir, nor have I dissipated the noble inheritance derived from my ancestors.

SIR WILLIAM I am heartily glad of it, sir! I ask your pardon, young man. (*Aside*) What the deuce, then, can he want from me? 35

COL. MOUNTFORT If I were so unfortunately weak, as you for a moment seemed to imagine, the respect I bear you would have prevented my applying to you upon such an occasion, as your good opinion, sir, is of the greatest consequence to my happiness. 40

SIR WILLIAM There you are wrong, colonel. You had much better apply to me, than to anyone else. I am no cent per cent man.° I never received a shilling interest from any friend in my life; and I have my doubts whether I should even take it from the funds° now that the nation is so poor.°—But come, colonel, if you don't want 45 money, in what other way can I possibly serve you? I have no interest at Court.

COL. MOUNTFORT You have an interest, sir, in what is far dearer to me than either wealth or preferment: your lovely niece, Louisa, sir— 50

SIR WILLIAM (*aside*) Thank heaven, she is better disposed of!

COL. MOUNTFORT You pause! Do not keep me on the rack, Sir William.

SIR WILLIAM I was only recollecting myself. Am much obliged to you, sir, for the honour—I think that's the phrase—you intend my 55 niece, but she's married, sir.

COL. MOUNTFORT Married, Sir William!

SIR WILLIAM Yes, sir, married, and settled in the country.

COL. MOUNTFORT This raillery is rather cruel, sir.

SIR WILLIAM I never joke, sir. I have passed my word that she shall be 60 married this day se'nnight; and if all the emperors, kings, princes, and potentates in Europe, nay the Great Mogul himself, were to demand her in marriage, William Woodley would not forfeit his promise. So that married she is, to all intents and purposes, my gay colonel. 65

COL. MOUNTFORT And has Miss Woodley consented, sir?

SIR WILLIAM Ay, to be sure; I force nobody.

COL. MOUNTFORT (*aside*) Confusion! [*To Sir William*] Impossible, sir!

SIR WILLIAM Why should you think so? She is a a modest, dutiful girl. It would be hard, indeed, if I was to have no comfort in my family. 70 But don't be disheartened, colonel! Many a gallant soldier has met with a repulse before now.

COL. MOUNTFORT If you could conceive of the tenderness of my

affection for Miss Woodley, sir, you would not treat my sufferings
so slightly.   75

SIR WILLIAM It may be a disappointment, to be sure, sir, for she is a
fine young woman, I confess; but my friend has her, sir, and you
must think of her no more.

COL. MOUNTFORT It is not in my power to obey your injunction.
(*Aside*) I wish it were, false and ungrateful girl! [*To Sir William*]   80
But pray, sir, who is the envied man so doubly blessed in your
friendship and Miss Woodley's love?

SIR WILLIAM That's a secret, colonel.

COL. MOUNTFORT That, I think, I have a right to know, sir.

SIR WILLIAM What! You want to exercise your valour a little [*pretend-*   85
ing to flourish a sword]—*sa, sa, sa*,°—by challenging your rival? But
keep your prowess for the common foe; we cannot spare a soldier at
present, colonel.

COL. MOUNTFORT This treatment is unlike yourself, Sir William. But
Miss Woodley, I suppose, will inform me; I presume she is not   90
bound to keep the secret.

SIR WILLIAM There you are wrong again, my young hero; for
she really is bound by the strongest of all possible ties: the not
knowing it.

COL. MOUNTFORT You cannot now be serious, sir; and I will try if   95
I have yet power enough over Louisa's heart to make her so—for I
will know my rival. Adieu, Sir William!

    Exit [*Colonel Mountfort*]

SIR WILLIAM Your servant, Colonel Huff-Cap.° What a hot-brained
boy! I am doubly glad Louisa has escaped him; I would have no
passionate man in the family, but myself. How lucky 'tis that Louisa   100
does not know her husband's name! Women should ever be kept in
ignorance to prevent mischief. I have conducted this business most
admirably! I have some doubts, however, whether my nephew
should not be made acquainted with it, but he does not deserve my
confidence and he shan't vex me now.   105

    Enter Mr Belford. Sir William runs and embraces him.

Are all things going on briskly and cleverly as they should do, my dear
nephew?

BELFORD The swiftest bowl does not always hit the jack,° Sir William;
and 'fair and softly'° is an established maxim in the law.

SIR WILLIAM Well, well, we must submit, but I hope you'll use as   110
much dispatch as possible.

BELFORD 'Dispatch' is a term, sir, not to be found in any law dictionary that I know of; and I fancy it will be a long time before the matters you talk of will be dispatched.

SIR WILLIAM Why, surely you have a mind to try my temper with your 'fair and softly'! But if you knew as much as I do, you would, perhaps, think it worthwhile to mend your pace a little; for 'many things fall out between the cup and the lip',° Mr Belford.   11

BELFORD (*aside*) So you'll find out presently. [*To Sir William*] The most material point in this important affair does not appear to be yet adjusted.   120

SIR WILLIAM Now, what can he mean?°

BELFORD There can be no marriage without the consent of parties; and I don't find that Miss Woodley—

SIR WILLIAM If I was not in the most heavenly temper, you would put me in a rage. Have I not told you, sir, that she had no consent, no choice, but what I please to give? And in twenty years acquaintance, have you ever known me say an untruth, sir? My niece is all compliance and gentleness, and you'll be a very happy man, my dear nephew.   12

BELFORD I should be unworthy of happiness if I could enjoy it on such terms, Sir William.   13

SIR WILLIAM Why, what's the matter, Belford? Your head seems to be turned with your good fortune, and you want to turn mine. No man that is unworthy can be happy—   13.

BELFORD In short, Sir William—

SIR WILLIAM Ay, ay, that's the thing! Now you talk sense! I like 'in short'—stick to that, my friend. If you want more clerks,° don't value expense, I'll clear all costs. You know I hate the law's delay.

BELFORD No law, but that of honour, has anything to do in this case, Sir William, and, however irksome the task, I must beg you will permit me to undeceive you.   14

SIR WILLIAM Then you acknowledge you have deceived me? I am thunderstruck!

BELFORD No, my good friend, 'tis you that have deceived yourself.   14

SIR WILLIAM Your proposition is false, sir. I never deceived myself, nor anyone else, since I was born, sir. I scorn and abhor deceit, Mr Belford. But come, sir, let me know what all this roundabout tends to? Despise the chicanery of your profession and speak as if you was a witness on the table,° not a lawyer at the bar, sir.   150

BELFORD I fear I shall rather appear a criminal at the bar to you, at present, Sir William.

SIR WILLIAM What, then, you are married, I suppose? Have a wife

already? Nay, don't smile, sir. There is no joke in this matter, and
you ought to have been hanged if you had married my niece.   155

BELFORD I think so too, though not upon the account you mention, as
I give you my honour I have no wife, and, if I continue in my
present mood, may venture to say that I never shall have one.

SIR WILLIAM Mighty well, mighty ill, Mr Belford! You have rewarded
my sincere friendly attachment—   160

BELFORD With true gratitude, sir.

SIR WILLIAM Don't offer to say so. What! To spurn my niece with
twenty thousand pounds! Let me tell you, sir—

BELFORD That she is much too good for me.

SIR WILLIAM Why, really I begin to think so.   165

BELFORD I rejoice, therefore, my dear friend—

SIR WILLIAM No, sir, don't rejoice. I am not your friend, nor ever will
be your friend. You have broke my heart—frustrated all my
schemes—disappointed my niece. Poor girl, I feel for her! Young
minds are easily broken by grief. You will have much to answer for   170
on her account, I assure you, Mr Belford.

BELFORD I should have much more to answer for to Miss Woodley, Sir
William, if I did not decline the match.

SIR WILLIAM Decline! Zounds, sir, I won't bear so contemptuous an
expression! (*Aside*) I wish I had not been quite so peremptory with   175
the colonel. [*To Belford*] If I could bring myself to unsay what I
have once uttered, I would give Louisa to Colonel Mountfort to vex
you.

BELFORD I agree with you, Sir William, that it would be a more
suitable match.   180

SIR WILLIAM Don't agree with me, Mr Belford, I won't suffer it.

BELFORD Allow me at least to say—

SIR WILLIAM No, sir, I won't allow you to say anything but 'yes' or
'no' to this simple question: do you accept or reject, my niece?

BELFORD The phrase is rather too strong, sir, but I have already told   185
you that, upon mature consideration, I decline the honour.

SIR WILLIAM Confound your honour, and your consideration, too!
And now, sir, I decline any further conversation, connexion, or
correspondence, with you. And so, sir, I am—no—I am not, your
humble servant.   190

    Exit [*Sir William*]

BELFORD His rage will soon subside, and we shall be as good friends as
ever. I am glad his resentment is entirely pointed at me, as 'tis
probable that, to make his niece amends for the loss of a husband

she did not like, he may give her one she does. And so ends, exactly
as it should, the matrimonial schemes of an old bachelor!°   19

Exit

4.3

Bromley's [*house*]
A dining-room
Enter Mr and Mrs Bromley

MRS BROMLEY I wish you would defer it till tomorrow! It will otherwise break up the assembly and make a monstrous bustle in the
family.

BROMLEY A fig for the assembly, and the bustle, too! No, no, my sweet
simpleton, business of some kinds brooks° no delay.

MRS BROMLEY You have no right to complain of my simplicity, Mr
Bromley. It is through me that you get this money from the
Woodleys.

BROMLEY Money, child! I have never touched above a thousand
pounds of their cash yet. This piece of paper is all I have got for   10
spending my time with a dull fool, and endeavouring to persuade
him that he was a Solomon° and his silly wife the Queen of Sheba.°
But I must be paid for my attendance and trouble, and in a few
minutes I shall convert this manuscript into the sum of seven thousand three hundred and fifty-three pounds, with costs. Costs must   15
be added.

MRS BROMLEY I can have no objection to your being paid for your
time and trouble, my dear. All I desire is that you may not lay on the
execution° till tomorrow. Let us devote this evening to pleasure, my
dear Brommy. I am to play gold loo° tonight, and I have a certain   20
presentiment° that I shall win considerably.

BROMLEY As to winning, I believe you are pretty secure in that point.
You don't leave much to chance, I imagine, my dove. But though
you might win, I shall lose considerably if this bond be not put in
force this very night. I have been with Woodley's attorney, Mr
Fleec'em, a very honest man,° and, for a small token of friendship,°   25
he has informed me that there will be six executions in the house
tomorrow.

MRS BROMLEY Six executions! Nay, then, they are done up, indeed,
and it does not signify much keeping any further terms° with them.   30

Yet I still wish you would postpone this ugly business till we are gone to the masquerade. Poor Lady Mary! It will be a sad disappointment to her not to show her finery.

BROMLEY Now you talk of finery, here, look at these! (*Showing Mrs Bromley Lady Mary's earrings*) 35

MRS BROMLEY Let me see! They are Lady Mary's earrings!

BROMLEY No; they were, my sweet innocent!

MRS BROMLEY But how came you by them? She told me they were gone to be new set.

BROMLEY Ask no questions, but take them and think yourself happy in such a provident husband. 40

MRS BROMLEY Thank you, my dear Brommy! They are beautiful indeed! I have long wished for them, I confess.

BROMLEY I must go and expedite this business directly. Don't be frightened, dove, when the bailiffs come in. They'll add to Lady Mary's squeeze, you know. But take a little hartshorn° in your pocket; it will be proper for you to faint, I think. 45

MRS BROMLEY Never fear my acting properly. But the carriage is at the door, and I have twenty places to call at. Shall I set you down at your lawyer's to save my dear the fatigue of walking? 50

BROMLEY How happy am I in such a discreet, tender wife! (*Aside*) A dissembling jade! [*To Mrs Bromley*] Come, dove.

MRS BROMLEY I follow, my dear Brommy. (*Aside*) Hateful wretch!
Exeunt

5.1

An ante-chamber, opening into a drawing-room
Forward, with a pencil and pocket-book. A Footman in the
drawing-room, placing card-tables for a rout°

FORWARD Four gold loo° tables, with monsters.°—Four pound four!—Two at half-crowns!°—Thrust them to the lower end of the room, James; they are seldom worth more than twelve shillings a-piece.°

JAMES Where shall I fix the whist tables, Mr Forward?

FORWARD Damn the whiskers!° Even the gold players never make it worth a gentleman's while to snuff their candles. I wish the parliament would put down all sneaking° games! A man can neither win or lose a fortune with any degree of credit at them. No! Faro,° faro's the sport.

JAMES Is this a pharaoh's table,° Mr Forward?

FORWARD No, but set that in the centre, in the best place in the room. That's a macao° table, and some of the *birds*,° I fancy, will be picked pretty bare that play at it.—Five pound five.—Do you hear, James? The moment the company's gone, pack up all the cards and candles, whether used or not, and carry them to my room. I may have occasion for them, if I should see company while I am out of place.°

JAMES What, you leave us a few packs to make merry with in the servants' hall, Mr Forward? I likes a game at all-fours,° dearly.

FORWARD Why, servants should have their amusements as well as their betters, James, so you may strip the whist-tables for your own use. The dons° always take snuff and sully their cards confoundedly.

JAMES Thank you, thank you, Mr Forward! Must I carry up the candles to your room that mayn't be lighted?

FORWARD Certainly; the others will only serve for my bedchamber or to dress by. I detest tallow.°

JAMES Well, well, I'll do as I'm bid. (*Aside*) What a thief it is! And as great a Jew to a poor fellow-servant as if he was not the same flesh and blood!

Exit [James]

FORWARD I shall make about twelve pieces packing penny.° I wish my master may win tonight, as I shall call upon him for my wages tomorrow; and, to do him justice, he is always ready to pay when he

has it. The funds° are low at present, and a prudent man should not
suffer his money to lie dead, especially in such hands where it may   35
be buried, too.

    Enter Lady Mary and Woodley

LADY MARY Let the ices° be brought before eleven, Forward, as I wish
the assembly to break up early. Are the bouquets come from the
King's Road?° Let there be a profusion of roses in all the rooms;
they are delicious at this season.   40

FORWARD Your ladyship shall be obeyed—(*aside*) for the last time by
your ladyship's most humble.

    Exit [Forward]

LADY MARY Your indifference upon this occasion really amazes me,
Mr Woodley! I thought you loved your sister.

WOODLEY I do, most tenderly, and shall therefore rejoice at seeing her   45
under the protection of a worthy man.

LADY MARY Bless me! Is there nothing but worth to be considered in
matrimony? No allowance to be made for liking? I vow, if you had
been fifty times as worthy as you are, I would never have married
you if you had not been agreeable also.   50

WOODLEY (*taking her hand*) Sweet flatterer!

LADY MARY But as the match is not to take place, his being agreeable
or not is of no consequence now.

WOODLEY I don't comprehend you.

LADY MARY You don't choose to comprehend me, Mr Woodley. But   55
still I must say that the indignity of Sir William's presuming to
dispose of your sister without your consent is not to be endured.

WOODLEY You are misinformed, my dear. Mountfort asked my
consent before he applied to Sir William. I did not see you since.

LADY MARY Mountfort is quite out of the present question, I tell you,   60
Mr Woodley.

WOODLEY You rave, my dear!

LADY MARY One of us does, that's certain.

WOODLEY (*with emotion*) I am not mad yet, madam—though I have
enough to make me so.   65

LADY MARY This is too much, Mr Woodley. Everyone takes notice of
your behaviour to me of late and wonder how I bear it.

WOODLEY (*looking gravely at her*) Did you know what I bear—

LADY MARY From me, Mr Woodley?

WOODLEY Not from, but for, you, Mary.   70

LADY MARY You terrify me! Explain your meaning, I intreat you.

WOODLEY It will too soon cease to be a mystery.

LADY MARY Then do not let me be the last to know it.

WOODLEY Could every pang I now endure be doubled to save you from the shock which you must feel, I'd bear them all without complaining. But ruin comes on apace, and that you must share it aggravates my distress. 75

LADY MARY Ungenerous Woodley! To think I would shrink from any misery that attends on you! But speak your meaning clearly. Suspense is torture. What misery awaits us? 80

WOODLEY Our fortune's gone, my Mary! We are undone!

LADY MARY Gone! Not all: my jointure° still is left. Dispose of that, and let me go into retirement with you. With pleasure I'll renounce all the fantastic gaieties of life and find true happiness in your society. 85

WOODLEY Your nobleness of mind but adds to my distress. Your jointure! No, I will live a beggar all my days, rather than leave you one when I must leave you. Somewhat may yet be done to save us from destruction. I have a dependence on Mr Belford's friendship.

LADY MARY So have I; but we must be our own friends, my dear. I will 90 go into Dorsetshire immediately. Let us discharge half our servants and become patterns of economy and conjugal happiness.

WOODLEY Generous, charming woman! Happiness must attend you everywhere.

LADY MARY 'Tis the inseparable companion of an upright heart. And 95 my dear Woodley shall soon be convinced from my conduct that cheerfulness can survive gaiety, and true love make ample amends for the loss of fortune.

WOODLEY Your sense and virtue have removed the heaviest weight that hung upon my heart. 100

LADY MARY Then clear your brow, my dear, and let us act the last scene of the farce with the same spirit as the first.
        Enter Servant

SERVANT Colonel Mountfort, sir.

WOODLEY Show him into my dressing-room. I'll wait on him instantly. 105
        Exit Servant

LADY MARY Don't let even Colonel Mountfort perceive your dejection, my dear Woodley. We should, in kindness to our friends, conceal our sorrows.

WOODLEY If Mountfort has succeeded with my uncle, Louisa's happiness will lighten my distress. 110

LADY MARY I have not time to ask an explanation of this matter now, but let me again entreat you to be cheerful. Something tells me that our situation is not so bad as you imagine. Let us not anticipate misfortune; 'tis always too soon to be wretched.

WOODLEY I will exert my utmost power, my dear, to emulate your fortitude.   115

Exit [Woodley]

LADY MARY My fortitude! Ah, Woodley! Little dost thou know the perturbation here. Ruin comes on apace! The shock was sudden and severe, but 'twas my love, not resolution, bore me through it. And now let me collect myself a little, and try, by Reason's stand-   120
ard, the value of those joys which I resign.—Dress! Won't my little person look as well in a plain silk as in all this finery? Vanity says, 'Yes.'—Grandeur. What is it? A magnificent sideboard,° a train of useless servants, gay furniture, crowded rooms, and blazing lights, which but oppress the spirits without affording enjoyment. Ele-   125
gance is not confined to state; her handmaid Neatness° shall pre-side at our board and render our rural fare delicious.—Operas! Ranelagh!° Plays! Masquerades! Assemblies! Company! Ay, there's the rub!° Society! Dear society! I shall not find a Mrs Bromley in Dorsetshire; but I shall have my Woodley there, and my endeavours   130
not to let him see I grieve will soon make me cease to do so. My resolution's fixed! I'll acquaint Louisa with it instantly.

Exit

5.2

Woodley's dressing-room
Woodley, Colonel Mountfort

WOODLEY Upon my honour, colonel, I am as unable to fathom Sir William's meaning as you can be. I am certain that no person ever proposed to me for Louisa but yourself, and she could not possibly give her consent before it was asked.

COL. MOUNTFORT This assurance has revived my hopes a little, but   5
'tis impossible my heart can be at ease till your sister has pro-nounced my doom.

WOODLEY If she consults her own heart, Mountfort, you will not, I fancy, have much reason to complain of her sentence. But as she is the only Oedipus that can expound this riddle,° let us apply to her   10
for the explanation. (*Rings [for Servant]*)

COL. MOUNTFORT You prevent my wishes, for you have an un-
doubted right to make the enquiry.

Enter Servant

WOODLEY Tell my sister I desire to speak with her immediately.

Exit Servant

COL. MOUNTFORT How my heart throbs at her approach!   15

WOODLEY For shame, my gallant friend!

COL. MOUNTFORT Oh, Woodley! When all one's happiness is staked
on the turn of a die, who would not tremble when he stood the
cast?°

Enter Servant

SERVANT Miss Woodley, sir, has just sent to let Sir William know she   20
wishes to pay her respects to him. At her return she will wait upon
you.

Exit [Servant]

COL. MOUNTFORT Inhuman girl! She trifles with my anxiety—
perhaps rejoices in it.

WOODLEY Lovers are of all beings the most irrational. I'd hazard my   25
life that Louisa has never heard of your proposal to Sir William,
and, of course, can know nothing of your anxiety.

COL. MOUNTFORT She will be soon acquainted with both. But have
not you informed her?

WOODLEY No, on my honour; I have not seen her since you left me.   30

COL. MOUNTFORT Your coolness on this subject, Mr Woodley, by no
means accords with my impatience.

WOODLEY You wrong me, Mountfort. Be assured, that your union
with Louisa is an object my heart is set on. But that heart is torn to
pieces at present.—I cannot speak—Louisa never stays long with   35
her uncle. She will return in a few minutes.

COL. MOUNTFORT They will be years to me.

WOODLEY Let us meet her then, before she goes into the drawing-
room.

Exeunt

5.3

Sir William Woodley's apartment
Enter Sir William

SIR WILLIAM Poor child! I am very sorry she is coming. I know not what excuse to make for Belford. I fear it will be a grievous disappointment to her.

Enter Louisa

LOUISA I come, sir, most joyfully to tell you something I am sure will give you pleasure.

SIR WILLIAM My poor dear! And I have something to tell you that I am sure will give you pain.

LOUISA Indeed, sir, I am so much rejoiced at present that there are but very few things that could render me unhappy.

SIR WILLIAM (*aside*) So much the worse. The shock will be the greater! I shall never have the courage to tell her. [*To Louisa*] The suddenness of this event, Louisa—

LOUISA Do you know it, sir?

SIR WILLIAM Ay, but too well, my dear.

LOUISA You quite surprise me, sir! It is not above five minutes since it was determined.

SIR WILLIAM Yes, yes, 'tis more than that—above half an hour. But though matters have taken an unexpected turn, I would not have you fret or grieve, my child!

LOUISA So far from it, sir, that I am quite rejoiced, and flattered myself that you would be so too, as I know it is a point you have long set your heart upon. And I must do Lady Mary the justice to declare the plan was entirely her own.

SIR WILLIAM Lady Mary! I guessed as much. How did she dare to thwart my schemes?

LOUISA Dear sir, have you not always wished that my brother and sister should live in Dorsetshire? And now that Lady Mary has, of her own accord, determined to quit London, you seem offended.

SIR WILLIAM Softly, softly, child; don't hurry me! For once in my life, I perceive I am left behind. (*Aside*) So, I find she knows nothing of Belford, and that work is all to do yet. [*To Louisa*] Go on, my dear! Lady Mary, you say—

LOUISA Has, unsolicited by anyone, resolved to give up all the gaiety and dissipation of this town and remain in Dorsetshire till my brother's affairs are entirely retrieved.

SIR WILLIAM (*aside*) She'll not return in a hurry, then, I doubt. [*To Louisa*] I am glad of it, my dear, for your sake, as well as your brother's. Air and exercise will be of great use to you. (*Aside*) I'm afraid she'll stand in need of them when she is acquainted with her misfortune.

LOUISA But, my good, dear uncle, won't you give Lady Mary credit

for her prudence? And won't you permit my brother and sister to
take leave of you before they go?

SIR WILLIAM I hate all forms and ceremonies, child! They have had
my leave to go into the country these three years past. And I am less   45
displeased with your sister for her prudent resolution. And so, at
your request, my dear, you may all breakfast with me before you
set out tomorrow. (*Aside*) I'll defer acquainting her till then with
Belford's behaviour.

LOUISA I don't believe, sir, that they can set out so immediately, but I   50
am certain they will not defer a moment to accept your kind invitation on that account.

SIR WILLIAM Stop, child, stop! I won't have them come to me till the
very hour they are going. If I were to see your brother often, I
might be weak enough to grow fond of him again. So don't let him   55
come, I charge you, till his boots are on. I have trouble enough on
my hands for others already. You don't know what I suffer on your
account, Louisa, at this moment. But you shall know all about it
when you are setting off for Dorsetshire.

LOUISA (*aside*) I wish I dare venture to make the good man's mind   60
easy with regard to me. [*To Sir William*] As I am perfectly resigned
to your commands, sir, on every occasion, I hope I shall never give
you cause for any real trouble.

SIR WILLIAM (*aside*) There now, she'll break my heart with her mild-
ness! [*To Louisa*] I hope for your own sake you'll be resigned, my   65
dear. But go, child, and tell your brother and Lady Mary that I shall
be glad to see them on the morning they are setting out, but not
before, upon any account whatever.

　　　Exit [*Sir William*]

LOUISA I rejoice to be the messenger of such glad tidings, for if he sees
my brother, I am certain he will serve him.   70

　　　[*Exit*]

5.4

　　　A drawing-room [*in Woodley's house*]
　　　Card-tables, with company at play.° *Lady Mary, Louisa, Mr*
　　　Belford, Colonel Mountfort

FIRST WHIST Fifty pieces on the rubber!°

SECOND WHIST A bet, my lord.

FIRST LOO A Pam flush!°

SECOND LOO You seldom deal, I think, without one, madam.°

FIRST LOO My Pam-box° can best answer that hint, madam, for this is   5
the first guinea I have been able to put into it this whole winter. But
you lose, at present, madam, and therefore have leave to speak.°
Please to mark the loo,° madam: 'tis just sixty guineas.

LOUISA (to Belford) How much am I obliged to you, my excellent
friend, for so generously saving me from the pain of offending the   10
best of uncles!

COL. MOUNTFORT And let me join my gratitude, sir, for your having
so kindly removed, I hope, the only obstacle to my happiness, by
releasing Sir William from his promise.

BELFORD I heartily wish he may be inclined to transfer his favour to   15
you, sir.

    Enter Mrs Bromley

FIRST LOO My dear cousin, here's a place for you! The monsters° must
come in with Mrs Bromley.

MRS BROMLEY I'll wait upon you, in a moment.

SECOND LOO The monsters positively shall not come in, till 'tis a   20
single stake.° And then I shall never have a flush after, I suppose.

LADY MARY My dear Bromley, I have a thousand things to say to you
of the utmost importance. I wish you would not play tonight.

MRS BROMLEY Not play! You must excuse me, indeed, Lady Mary!
Besides, we shall have time enough to talk over those same import-   25
ant matters, you know, at the masquerade.

LADY MARY I shall not go tonight, and have something so interesting
to tell you—

MRS BROMLEY (aside) 'Tis impossible she should suspect anything.
[To Lady Mary] Your ladyship knows I hate melancholy stories. (To   30
the table)° Is the loo over? (Aside) I can't help feeling a little awkward when I speak to her.

THIRD LOO Another flush, as I live! I don't believe we shall have a
single stake these two hours.°

FIRST QUADRILLE Your ladyship's basted:° you trumped the king of   35
diamonds.

SECOND QUADRILLE What then, madam? Here take the diamond; I
have my game without it.

THIRD QUADRILLE No, madam; a renounce is a beast.°

SECOND QUADRILLE I won't submit to it. Judgement!°   40

SEVERAL Your ladyship's a beast! A beast!

SECOND LOO What a racket they make, at this paltry play! Not above a crown a-fish,° I dare swear!—The loo is just two hundred and forty guineas! Deal, madam.

    Enter Woodley, and joins Louisa

LADY MARY Not keep your promise, Bromley?

MRS BROMLEY Why, no, indeed, madam! I cannot possibly think of rusticating myself with your ladyship.—But if any of the summer camps° should happen to lie near you, I may give you a call, *en passant,°* to see how love and a cottage° agree with you. [*To the table*] Will you never let me in, Mrs Henpeck?

THIRD LOO Dear madam, I wish you had been in my place the whole evening with all my heart! I have lost near three hundred pounds in it. Heigh-ho!

LADY MARY I had vainly flattered myself, it seems, that my company might have rendered the country passable, at least, to one who professed herself my friend.

MRS BROMLEY I always thought your ladyship very romantic.° (*Aside*) I wish she would not tease me so!

LADY MARY (*aside*) This shock is much severer to me than the first I felt, as friends were dearer to me than fortune. But let me rise above her worthlessness, nor let her see how her unkindness wounds me.

FIRST WHIST Lurched at four!° 'Tis confounded hard.

SECOND WHIST I bet you three to one.

LADY MARY (*to Mrs Bromley*) Will Mr Bromley be here tonight?

MRS BROMLEY Certainly. [*Aside*] Sooner than you wish, I fancy.

LADY MARY (*looking earnestly at Mrs Bromley*) Pray, Mrs Bromley, did you hire those earrings from my jeweller? I'm glad now he did not alter them.

MRS BROMLEY I have never yet been under the necessity of hiring jewels, madam, whatever other people may have been. But though the setting of these is not altered, madam, the property is; for they are mine, at present, I assure you.

LADY MARY You'll pardon me, Mrs Bromley.—Mr Woodley, pray are not those my earrings?

WOODLEY They were, my dear. (*Aside*) This is ungenerous of Bromley! [*To Lady Mary*] I will explain this matter another time, my dear.

MRS BROMLEY Nay, Mr Woodley, it requires but little explanation. Lady Mary is not so much a child as not to know that in this country, and in these times, property quickly changes hands, from those who have squandered their fortunes, and possibly that of others, to those who have been more prudent and less lavish.

HIRD LOO The loo is over,° Mrs Bromley.—Bring the monsters, sir.

IRS BROMLEY I thought it would never be a single stake! (*Sits down to the table*) 85

ADY MARY (*aside*) Her unkindness would be insupportable, did not the insolence of it render her despicable.

OL. MOUNTFORT Don't you think, Miss Woodley, that Lady Mary looks uncommonly grave this evening?

OUISA You will not be surprised at her seriousness when I tell you 90 that she has determined on quitting London immediately and retiring with my brother into Dorsetshire. I shall go with them, colonel.

OL. MOUNTFORT And I shall as certainly follow my leader. Sir William can have no objection to my being cantoned° in the neighbourhood of Woodley Park, I presume? 95

IRST WHIST Four by honours,° again! This is the fourth time you have dealt them in the rubber. Sixteen out of twenty are odds that de Moivre° could not play against. There's your money; there's your money, sir!

ECOND WHIST No—double or quit with your lordship. 100

IRST WHIST I know I am a bubble,° but I hate to cut a loser.° 'Tis a bet, sir.

IRST LOO Two Pams,° as I hope to be saved!

IRS BROMLEY Fie, madam, don't swear! 'Tis vastly ill-bred.

IRST LOO 'Tis much worse breeding to cheat, Mrs Bromley. 105

IRS BROMLEY Mean creature! I scorn your words.

IRST LOO You should begin by scorning mean actions, madam. But you shan't take up the loo, I assure you. I have long suspected you of such tricks.

ECOND LOO And so have I. Heigh-ho! She has got a deal of my 110 money. Heigh-ho!

HIRD LOO And of mine, too, I assure you; but her surprising luck is now accounted for.

IRS BROMLEY I won't touch another card with such vulgar, suspicious wretches. 115

IRST LOO We have renounced you first, madam; so if you please to rise from the table, madam. And I'll take care that you shall never sit down to any other wherever I am present, I assure you, madam.

ECOND LOO Put all the monsters out at once.° Heigh-ho!

IRS BROMLEY (*rising in a passion and addressing Lady Mary*) I did not 120 think your ladyship would stand tamely by and suffer me to be insulted in your house; but 'tis the last time I shall ever come into it, I promise you.

LADY MARY I shall take care that you shan't break that promise, if you should happen to forget it, Mrs Bromley.   12

MRS BROMLEY You speak like an oracle° without consciousness, madam, for this is the last night you shall have any authority here, believe me. And so I leave your ladyship to your future rural felicity.

Exit [Mrs Bromley]

LADY MARY (*to Louisa*) Was there ever so sudden and extraordinary a change in any human creature!   13

LOUISA 'Tis rather a discovery than a metamorphose,° my dear Lady Mary! I have long seen through Mrs Bromley's mask—'twas only made of gauze.°

Enter Forward, and speaks to Woodley

FORWARD There are some gentlemen below, sir, who, though not invited, insist upon coming up.   13

WOODLEY Admit them, directly. All gentlemen are welcome.

FORWARD I should have done so, sir, but that these gentlemen don't seem to be well enough dressed for my lady's assembly. They are but bailiffs, sir.   14

WOODLEY Distraction! My disgrace is public now!

BELFORD (*to Forward*) At whose suit do they come here?

FORWARD I think they mentioned Mr Bromley, sir.

WOODLEY Impossible! He is the very friend I thought of applying to in my present difficulties.   14

BELFORD Don't be too confident, Mr Woodley. I know that fellow to be a consummate knave.

COL. MOUNTFORT Don't let your spirits sink, my dear Woodley. We'll inquire into the matter, and accommodate it immediately.—I beg your ladyship not to be alarmed. Everything shall be settled, directly.—Try to support your sister's sinking heart, my dear Louisa.   15

Exeunt Colonel Mountfort, Woodley, and Belford. Louisa seems to comfort Lady Mary, who is in tears, and both go out together

SECOND WHIST Bailiffs, did the fellow say? Egad, I'll decamp in time. (*Rises*)

FIRST WHIST You must not stir, till the rubber is out,° sir.   15

SECOND WHIST Your lordship must excuse me! Such incidents are so common, to be sure, in the present times, that they cease to be scandalous, but that does not affect my being affected by them. I shall remember that seven to four are the points of our game,° and for debts of honour, my lord, you'll always find me solvent.   16

THIRD WHIST These scenes are apt to affect me, too, Charles! I never
could stand them. Peers are privileged° from such sympathies, so
let us countermarch down the backstairs together, or we may be
lurched, though we are seven.°

Exeunt Second and Third Whist Players

SECOND LOO I shall faint, if I see them! I must go, ladies.   165

FIRST LOO Let us have another round, madam! We are all married
women,° you know.

SECOND LOO My antipathy to these harpies° was contracted while I
was a widow, madam.—'Tis your deal, madam.°—Poor Lady
Mary! Heigh-ho!   170

FIRST LOO Ay, poor Lady Mary, I say too. Though, to be sure, one
cannot have any great compassion for such an extravagant woman.

THIRD LOO Compassion! No, truly! Such suppers after her routs!
—though I was never asked to one of them. That cheat Bromley was
one of her chief favourites, you know.   175

SECOND LOO She is gone out of the room, as I live, without making
the least apology. Did you ever hear of such rudeness! I'll never
visit her again. Heigh-ho!

FIRST LOO Nor I. 'Tis time to break up, indeed, when the lady of the
house has retired! I'll carry off this Pam, to triumph over that rude   180
wretch, Bromley. I shall have the honour of seeing you all tomorrow night.

ALL Certainly.

FIRST LOO My coach was not ordered till twelve. Will you carry me to
Lady Freakish's° rout? They never meet there till eleven.   185

THIRD LOO With pleasure. But I insist on telling the story of the
Woodleys.

FIRST LOO And I of Mrs Bromley.

SECOND LOO Then I have nothing left to do, but to count my losses.
Heigh-ho!   190

Exeunt

5.5

Sir William Woodley's apartment
Sir William and Waters

SIR WILLIAM Why didn't you say I was gone to bed? She'll break my
rest, for this night at least. She has heard of her misfortune, I fear.

Enter Louisa

LOUISA Oh, sir!—

SIR WILLIAM (*aside*) Yes, yes, 'tis all out, now. [*To Louisa*] Nay, my dear child, don't take on so; you'll break my heart, if you do. 'Twas not my fault, Louisa.

LOUISA Don't talk or think of faults, now, sir. You know that before this disgraceful event happened in the family—

SIR WILLIAM Don't you talk of it in such a melancholy strain, child. 'Tis no disgrace, I tell you.

LOUISA 'Tis too public to be concealed, sir. The bailiffs are but this moment gone out of the house.

SIR WILLIAM What house? This house? Your brother's house? What! Have they carried him to prison? I thought it would come to this.

LOUISA No, sir. Colonel Mountfort generously—

SIR WILLIAM What had he to do with it? Why should Colonel Mountfort, or anyone else? Why didn't they send to me?—But what have I to do with your brother, child? He should have gone to prison.

LOUISA He would not long have languished there, sir, believe me; a broken heart would soon have released him.

SIR WILLIAM Psha, psha, with your broken heart. You play the fool with me!—My nephew perish in a gaol! But he has brought it all on himself, you know, child.

LOUISA I grant that his imprudence, sir, has exceeded everything but your good nature.

SIR WILLIAM Confound my good nature! It is forever bringing me into scrapes—

LOUISA And bringing others out of them, my dear uncle.

SIR WILLIAM Well, well, well—I want Belford now, extremely! Every thing falls out unlucky!—But what of Colonel Mountfort, child?

LOUISA I was going to tell you, sir, that he became security° for my brother on the instant.

SIR WILLIAM That's noble! For he did not know that I would discharge the debt.—Nay, for that matter, I don't know that I shall—I promise nothing—but I like this action of the colonel.

LOUISA I rejoice to hear it, sir.

SIR WILLIAM Ay! Then perhaps you like the colonel? Be honest, speak out. I should be glad to make you some amends for a loss you don't know of—but I can conceal it no longer.—Belford has declared off! But he is unworthy your resentment. The colonel's father was my friend, and a noble fellow he was!

OUISA And his son is every way worthy of such a father!

IR WILLIAM (*aside*) I rejoice to find her so easily reconciled.—Well, that matter is settled, for the present. [*To Louisa*] But are you certain that your brother and Lady Mary will hold their resolution of retiring to Dorsetshire? 45

OUISA You know, sir, it was their determined purpose before this misfortune happened.

IR WILLIAM That's something in their favour, to be sure, and I'm glad you told me of it. One good act of choice is worth all the virtues of necessity in the world. I should be glad to make their minds easy tonight—but they'd thank me, and talk to me, and discompose me, and I should lose my night's rest, for I hate thanks. I should be glad to see Colonel Mountfort. His behaviour has shown a respect to me, and the family. 50 55

LOUISA You will meet him now at my brother's, sir, where your presence will make them all happy.

SIR WILLIAM Well, child, I can deny you nothing. I like to make people happy, when they'll assist me in doing so themselves; without which, the best endeavours are but labour in vain.—But the country is the place! You must settle in the country, Louisa! There is no safety for good folks in London, believe me, child. 60

LOUISA I should hope, sir, that with prudence and virtue one might be safe anywhere. 65

SIR WILLIAM A fig for your prudence—ay, and for virtue too, against example! Example, child, is the ruin of us all. We naturally strive to ape those that are called our betters, and so become worse than we otherwise would be.—But this is no time for moralizing. Do you step in and tell your brother I am coming. I'll just wrap my cloak around me and follow you. 70

Exeunt severally°

5.6

Woodley's dressing-room
Woodley, Belford, and Colonel Mountfort

BELFORD Fear not, my gallant colonel! Mr Woodley shall have ample vengeance upon that scoundrel Bromley, for as he has evidently altered the date of the bond, we shall find a way to reward his ingenuity.

WOODLEY I know not whether I am most astonished at his villainy or at my own weakness in being duped by it.

COL. MOUNTFORT The uprightness of your own heart, my dear Woodley, is the best excuse for your credulity.

Enter Lady Mary and Louisa

LOUISA I come the happy messenger of joyful tidings! My dear good uncle—but he's here.

Enter Sir William

SIR WILLIAM I'm glad to meet you here, all together, for I have business with every one of you, jointly and severally.—And first for you, colonel. I am very much obliged to you, sir, and I scorn to be obliged to any man, without making him some return for his kindness. I therefore make you a present I refused you a few hours ago, for the sake of Sir Doubtful Deliberation there.—But do you take Louisa, and, for aught I know, you may make her as good a husband as he would have done.

COL. MOUNTFORT I shall use my best endeavours, sir to deserve—

SIR WILLIAM That's right, stick to that. No thanks, but deserve as much as ever you can.—And as for you, Mr Belford, though I am confoundedly angry with you, I must get you to settle this young man's affairs: his debts of honour, his *post obits.*, *etc.*, though perhaps it may be only affording him an opportunity for *deranging* them again. That's the modern phrase, I think, for being over-head-and-ears in debt.

WOODLEY The sufferings my follies have brought upon me, sir, and the remembrance of your generosity, will remain too strongly impressed on my mind to admit of my relapsing into my former errors, as that would be adding ingratitude to extravagance, and vice to folly.

SIR WILLIAM Well, well, I hope so. Kindness should be the strongest tie to a generous mind, and I suspect you not of any baseness in your nature—though, to be sure, you have shown a plentiful lack of wisdom in your conduct. But misfortunes make Solomons of us all! (*To Lady Mary*) And now, madam, to show you that the merit of your voluntary retirement into the country is not lost upon me, I make you a present of this house, for your winter residence.

LADY MARY Your kindness, sir—

SIR WILLIAM Stop there—I won't be thanked. I wish to do as I would be done by, and as I should not like to be confined in the finest place in the world, not even Woodley Park, I would not impose such a restraint on one who I doubt not will hereafter merit my indulgence.

LADY MARY Gratitude overwhelms me, sir!—I cannot speak my sense
   of your goodness as it deserves.   45
SIR WILLIAM So much the better! There are nobler ways of showing
   one's sentiments.
LADY MARY They shall be demonstrated in my future conduct, sir; for
   the virtue that arises from the conviction of past errors, must be at
   once sincere, and permanent.   50
      [*Exeunt*]

EPILOGUE

Spoken by Miss Farren°

While grave-paced tragedy, with 'Oh's!' and starts,
Flies at high game to move and mend your hearts,
We merrier folks, with spirits blithe and jolly,°
Just perch upon some little sprig of folly.
For, in this age, so pious, chaste, and grave,   5
To rail at vice must surely be to rave!°
   Yet thanks to here and there a modish fool,
The comic muse may glean some ridicule.
Jews will be Jews, if dupes can yet be found,
And if one frail one's left on English ground,°   10
She'll find a phaeton and a pair of ponies
To elope—for all men are not macaronies:°
Those precious dears, at least, would make her wait—
'Twould be so vulgar, not to be too late.
   Our sex—but shall I charge the weaker kind?   15
Or can those fail to stray whose guides are blind!
Let men reform themselves, they're our examples—
And goods prove seldom better than their samples.
In former times the gallant British youth
Were famed for chivalry, and love, and truth.°   20
In such an age, in such a virtuous nation,
Love was in woman almost inspiration.
But now, alas, I speak without a jest,
Women are not inspired—they're but possessed.°
Men are our pilots! They should mark the shelves;°   25
For when they blame us, they reproach themselves.

THE BELLE'S STRATAGEM

HANNAH COWLEY

To
The Queen°

Madam,

In the following comedy, my purpose was to draw a female character, which, with the most lively sensibility, fine understanding, and elegant accomplishments, should unite that beautiful reserve and delicacy which, whilst they veil those charms, render them still more interesting. In delineating such a character, my heart naturally dedicated it to your majesty; and nothing remained but permission to lay it at your feet. Your majesty's graciously allowing me this high honour is the point to which my hopes aspired, and a reward of which, without censure, I may be proud.

Madam,
With the warmest wishes for the continuance of your majesty's felicity,
I am
Your majesty's
most devoted
and most dutiful servant,
H. Cowley

THE CHARACTERS OF THE PLAY

Doricourt°	*Mr Lewis*
Hardy°	*Mr Quick*
Sir George Touchwood°	*Mr Wroughton*
Flutter°	*Mr Lee Lewes*
Saville°	*Mr Aickin*
Villers°	*Mr Whitfield*
Courtall°	*Mr Robson*
Silvertongue°	*Mr W. Bates*
Crowquill°	*Mr Jones*
First Gentleman	*Mr Thompson*
Second Gentleman	*Mr L'Estrange*
Mountebank°	*Mr Booth*
French servant	*Mr Wewitzer*
Porter	*Mr Fearon*
Dick	*Mr Stevens*
Mask°]	
Folly]	
Letitia Hardy	*Miss Younge*
Mrs Racket°	*Mrs Mattocks*
Lady Frances Touchwood	*Mrs Hartley*
Miss Ogle°	*Mrs Morton*
Kitty Willis°	*Miss Stewart*
Lady	*Mrs Poussin*
Mrs Fagg°]	

Masqueraders, Tradesmen, Servants.

1.1

Lincoln's Inn°
Enter Saville, followed by a Servant, at the top of the stage,°
looking round, as if at a loss

SAVILLE Lincoln's Inn!—Well, but where to find him, now I am in Lincoln's Inn?—Where did he say his master was?

SERVANT He only said in Lincoln's Inn, sir.

SAVILLE That's pretty!° And your wisdom never enquired at whose chambers?

SERVANT Sir, you spoke to the servant yourself.

SAVILLE If I was too impatient to ask questions, you ought to have taken directions, blockhead!
     Enter Courtall singing
Ha, Courtall!—[*To Servant*] Bid him° keep the horses in motion, and then enquire at all the chambers round.
     Exit Servant
What the devil brings you to this part of the town? Have any of the long robes° handsome wives, sisters or chambermaids?

COURTALL Perhaps they have, but I came on a different errand. And had thy good fortune brought thee here half an hour sooner, I'd have given thee such a treat! Ha, ha, ha!

SAVILLE I'm sorry I missed it. What was it?

COURTALL I was informed a few days since that my cousins Fallow° were coming to town and desired earnestly to see me at their lodgings in Warwick Court, Holborn.° Away drove I, painting them all the way as so many Hebes.° They came from the farthest part of Northumberland,° had never been in town, and in course were° made up of rusticity, innocence, and beauty.

SAVILLE Well!

COURTALL After waiting thirty minutes, during which there was a violent bustle, in bounced five sallow damsels, four of them maypoles;° the fifth, Nature, by way of variety, had bent in the Æsop style.° But they all opened° at once, like hounds on a fresh scent:— 'Oh, cousin Courtall! How do you do, cousin Courtall! Lord, cousin, I am glad you are come! We want you to go with us to the park,° and the plays, and the opera, and Almack's,° and all the fine places!'—The devil, thought I, my dears, may attend you, for I am sure I won't. However, I heroically stayed an hour with them and discovered the virgins were all come to town with the hopes of leaving it wives: their heads full of knight-baronights,° fops, and adventures.

SAVILLE Well, how did you get off?

COURTALL Oh, pleaded a million engagements. However, conscience twitched me, so I breakfasted with them this morning and afterwards squired them to see the gardens here,° as the most private place in town, and then took a sorrowful leave, complaining of my hard, hard fortune that obliged me to set off immediately for Dorsetshire. Ha, ha, ha!

SAVILLE I congratulate your escape! Courtall at Almack's with five awkward country cousins! Ha, ha, ha! Why, your existence as a man of gallantry could never have survived it.

COURTALL Death and fire! Had they come to town, like the rustics of the last age, to see Paul's,° the lions,° and the waxwork,° at their service.° But the cousins of our days come up ladies—and, with the knowledge they glean from magazines and pocketbooks,° fine ladies—laugh at the bashfulness of their grandmothers and boldly demand their *entrées* in the first circles.

SAVILLE Where can this fellow be!—Come, give me some news. I have been at war with woodcocks and partridges° these two months, and am a stranger to all that has passed out of their region.

COURTALL Oh, enough for three gazettes! The ladies are going to petition for a bill that, during the war, every man may be allowed two wives.°

SAVILLE 'Tis impossible they should succeed, for the majority of both Houses know what it is to have one.

COURTALL Gallantry was blackballed° at the *coterie*° last Thursday, and Prudence and Chastity voted in.

SAVILLE Ay, that may hold till the camps break up.°—But have ye no elopements? No divorces?

COURTALL Divorces are absolutely out, and the commons-doctors° starving; so they are publishing trials of crim. con.° with all the separate evidences at large,° which, they find, has always a wonderful effect on their trade, actions tumbling in upon them afterwards like mackerel at Gravesend.°

SAVILLE What more?

COURTALL Nothing—for weddings, deaths, and politics I never talk of, but whilst my hair is dressing. But prithee, Saville, how came you in town, whilst all the qualified gentry are playing at pop-gun° on Coxheath,° and the country overrun with horses and foxes?

SAVILLE I came to meet my friend Doricourt, who, you know, is lately arrived from Rome.

COURTALL Arrived! Yes, faith, and has cut us all out!° His carriage, his liveries, his dress, himself are the rage of the day! His first appearance set the whole *ton* in a ferment, and his valet is besieged by *levées*° of tailors, habit-makers, and other ministers of fashion, to gratify the impatience of their customers for becoming *à la mode de*° Doricourt. Nay, the beautiful Lady Frolic t'other night, with two sister countesses, insisted upon his waistcoat for muffs;° and their snowy arms now bear it in triumph about town, to the heartrending affliction of all our *beaux garçons*.

SAVILLE Indeed! Well, those little gallantries will soon be over; he's on the point of marriage.

COURTALL Marriage! Doricourt on the point of marriage! 'Tis the happiest tidings you could have given, next to his being hanged. Who is the bride elect?

SAVILLE I never saw her; but 'tis Miss Hardy, the rich heiress. The match was made by the parents, and the courtship begun on their nurses' knees; Master used to crow at Miss, and Miss used to chuckle at Master.

COURTALL Oh, then by this time they care no more for each other than I do for my country cousins.

SAVILLE I don't know that; they have never met since thus high, and so, probably, have some regard for each other.

COURTALL Never met! Odd!

SAVILLE A whim of Mr Hardy's. He thought his daughter's charms would make a more forcible impression if her lover remained in ignorance of them till his return from the continent.

Enter Saville's Servant

SERVANT Mr Doricourt, sir, has been at Counsellor Pleadwell's, and gone about five minutes.

Exit Servant

SAVILLE Five minutes! Zounds! I have been five minutes too late all my lifetime!—Good morrow, Courtall; I must pursue him. (*Going*)

COURTALL Promise to dine with me today; I have some honest fellows. (*Going off on the opposite side*)

SAVILLE Can't promise; perhaps I may.—See there! There's a bevy of female Patagonians° coming down upon us.

COURTALL By the lord then, it must be my strapping cousins.—I dare
not look behind me.—Run, man, run.

    Exeunt, on the same side

1.2

    A hall at Doricourt's
    A gentle knock at the door. Enter the Porter

PORTER Tap! What sneaking devil art thou?

    Opens the door. Enter Crowquill

So! I suppose you are one of monsieur's° customers, too? He's above
stairs now, overhauling° all his honour's things to a parcel° of 'em.

CROWQUILL No, sir; it is with you, if you please, that I want to speak.

PORTER Me! Well, what do you want with me?   5

CROWQUILL Sir, you must know that I am—I am the gentleman who
writes the *tête-a-têtes*° in the magazines.

PORTER Oh, oh! What, you are the fellow that ties folks together in
your sixpenny cuts° that never meet anywhere else.

CROWQUILL Oh, dear sir, excuse me! We always go on *foundation*;°   10
and if you can help me to a few anecdotes of your master, such as
what marchioness he lost money to in Paris—who is his favourite
lady in town—or the name of the girl he first made love to at
college—or any incidents that happened to his grandmother, or
great aunts—a couple will do, by way of supporters°—I'll weave a   15
web of intrigues, losses, and gallantries between them that shall fill
four pages, procure me a dozen dinners, and you, sir, a bottle of
wine for your trouble.

PORTER Oh, oh! I heard the butler talk of you when I lived at Lord
Tinket's.° But what the devil do you mean by a bottle of wine? You   20
gave him a crown for a retaining fee.

CROWQUILL Oh, sir, that was for a lord's amours; a commoner's are
never but half. Why, I have had a baronet's for five shillings, though
he was a married man and changed his mistress every six weeks.

PORTER Don't tell me! What signifies a baronet or a bit of a lord, who,   25
maybe, was never further than sun and sun round London?° *We*
have travelled, man! My master has been in Italy, and over the
whole island of Spain, talked to the queen of France, and danced
with her at a masquerade. Ay, and such folks don't go to masquerades for nothing; but mum—not a word more. Unless you'll rank   30

my master with a lord, I'll not be guilty of blabbing his secrets, I assure you.

CROWQUILL Well, sir, perhaps you'll throw in a hint or two of other families where you've lived that may be worked up into something; and so, sir, here is one, two, three, four, five shillings.   35

PORTER (*pocketing the money*) Well, that's honest. To tell you the truth, I don't know much of my master's concerns yet. But here comes monsieur and his gang; I'll pump them. They have trotted after him all round Europe, from the Canaries to the Isle of Wight.

Enter several Foreign Servants and two Tradesmen. The Porter takes one of them aside

TRADESMAN Well then, you have showed us all?   40

FRENCHMAN All, *en vérité, messieurs!*° You *avez*° seen everything. *Serviteur, serviteur.*°

Exeunt Tradesmen

Ah, here comes one *autre*° curious Englishman, and dat's one *autre* guinea *pour moi.*°

Enter Saville

Allons, monsieur,° dis way; I will show you tings, such tings you   45
never see, begar, in England! Velvets by Le Mosse, suits cut by Verdue, trimmings by Grossette, embroidery by Detanville.°

SAVILLE Puppy, where is your master?

PORTER Zounds! You chattering frog-eating dunderhead, can't you see a gentleman? 'Tis Mr Saville.   50

FRENCHMAN Monsieur Saville! *Je suis mort de peur.*° Ten tousand pardons! *Excusez mon erreur,*° and permit me you conduct to Monsieur Doricourt; he be too happy *à vous voir.*°

Exeunt Frenchman and Saville

PORTER [*to Crowquill*] Step below a bit; we'll make it out somehow! I suppose a slice of sirloin won't make the story go down the worse.   55

Exeunt Porter

1.3

An apartment at Doricourt's
Enter Doricourt

DORICOURT (*speaking to a Servant* [*offstage*])I shall be too late for St James's°; bid him come immediately.

Enter Frenchman and Saville

FRENCHMAN Monsieur Saville.

    Exit Frenchman

DORICOURT Most fortunate! My dear Saville, let the warmth of this
    embrace speak the pleasure of my heart.   5

SAVILLE Well, this is some comfort after the scurvy reception I met
    with in your hall. I prepared my mind, as I came upstairs, for a
    bonjour,° a grimace, and an *adieu*.°

DORICOURT Why so?

SAVILLE Judging of the master from the rest of the family. What the   10
    devil is the meaning of that flock of foreigners below, with their
    parchment faces and snuffy whiskers? What? Can't an Englishman
    stand behind your carriage, buckle your shoe, or brush your coat?

DORICOURT Stale, my dear Saville, stale! Englishmen make the best
    soldiers, citizens, artisans, and philosophers in the world, but the   15
    very worst footmen. I keep French fellows° and Germans, as the
    Romans kept slaves, because their own countrymen had minds too
    enlarged and haughty to descend with a grace to the duties of such
    a station.

SAVILLE A good excuse for a bad practice.   20

DORICOURT On my honour, experience will convince you of its truth.
    A Frenchman neither hears, sees, nor breathes but as his master
    directs; and his whole system of conduct is comprised in one short
    word, *obedience!* An Englishman reasons, forms opinions, cogitates,
    and disputes. He° is the mere creature of your will; the other, a   25
    being conscious of equal importance in the universal scale with
    yourself, and is therefore your judge, whilst he wears your livery,
    and decides on your actions with the freedom of a censor.

SAVILLE And this in defence of a custom I have heard you execrate,
    together with all the adventitious° manners imported by our   30
    travelled gentry.

DORICOURT Ay, but that was at eighteen; we are always *very* wise at
    eighteen. But consider this point: we go into Italy, where the sole
    business of the people is to study and improve the powers of music;
    we yield to the fascination and grow enthusiasts in the charming   35
    science. We travel over France, and see the whole kingdom com-
    posing ornaments and inventing fashions; we condescend to avail
    ourselves of their industry, and adopt their modes. We return to
    England, and find the nation intent on the most important objects:
    polity, commerce, war, with all the liberal arts, employ her sons.   40
    The latent sparks glow afresh within our bosoms; the sweet
    follies of the continent imperceptibly slide away, whilst senators,

statesmen, patriots and heroes emerge from the *virtu*° of Italy and the frippery of France.

SAVILLE I may as well give it up! You had always the art of placing your faults in the best light; and I can't help loving you, faults and all. So, to start a subject which must please you: when do you expect Miss Hardy?

DORICOURT Oh, the hour of expectation is past. She is arrived, and I this morning had the honour of an interview at Pleadwell's.° The writings were ready, and, in obedience to the will of Mr Hardy, we met to sign and seal.

SAVILLE Has the event answered? Did your heart leap, or sink, when you beheld your mistress?

DORICOURT Faith, neither one nor t'other; she's a fine girl, as far as mere flesh and blood goes. But—

SAVILLE But what?

DORICOURT Why, she's *only* a fine girl; complexion, shape, and features, nothing more.

SAVILLE Is not that enough?

DORICOURT No! She should have spirit! Fire! *L'air enjoué*!° That something, that nothing, which everybody feels, and which nobody can describe, in the resistless charmers of Italy and France.

SAVILLE Thanks to the parsimony of my father that kept me from travel! I would not have lost my relish for true unaffected English beauty to have been quarrelled for by all the belles of Versailles and Florence.

DORICOURT Foh! Thou hast no taste. *English* beauty! 'Tis insipidity. It wants the zest; it wants poignancy, Frank! Why, I have known a Frenchwoman, indebted to nature for no one thing but a pair of decent eyes, reckon in her suite as many counts, marquises, and *petits-maîtres*,° as would satisfy three dozen of our first-rate toasts.° I have known an Italian *marquisina* make ten conquests in stepping from her carriage, and carry her slaves from one city to another, whose real intrinsic beauty would have yielded to half the little *grisettes*° that pace your Mall° on a Sunday.

SAVILLE And has Miss Hardy nothing of this?

DORICOURT If she has, she was pleased to keep it to herself. I was in the room half an hour before I could catch the colour of her eyes; and every attempt to draw her into conversation occasioned so cruel an embarrassment that I was reduced to the necessity of news, French fleets, and Spanish captures° with her father.

SAVILLE So Miss Hardy, with only beauty, modesty, and merit, is 85
doomed to the arms of a husband who will despise her.

DORICOURT You are unjust. Although she has not inspired me with
violent passion, my honour secures her felicity.

SAVILLE Come, come, Doricourt, you know very well that when the
honour of a husband is *locum-tenens*° for his heart, his wife must be
as indifferent as himself if she is not unhappy. 90

DORICOURT Foh! Never moralise without spectacles.° But, as we are
upon the tender subject, how did you bear Touchwood's carrying
Lady Frances?

SAVILLE You know I never looked up to her with hope, and Sir George
is every way worthy of her. 95

DORICOURT *A la mode anglaise*,° a philosopher even in love.

SAVILLE Come, I detain you; you seem dressed at all points, and of
course have an engagement.

DORICOURT To St James's. I dine at Hardy's, and accompany them to
the masquerade in the evening. But breakfast with me tomorrow, 100
and we'll talk of our old companions, for I swear to you, Saville, the
air of the continent has not effaced one youthful prejudice or
attachment.

SAVILLE With an exception to the case of ladies and servants.

DORICOURT True; there I plead guilty. But I have never yet found any 105
man whom I could cordially take to my heart and call friend who
was not born beneath a British sky, and whose heart and manners
were not truly English.

Exeunt

1.4

An apartment at Hardy's
Villers seated on a sofa, reading. Enter Flutter

FLUTTER Ha, Villers, have you seen Mrs Racket? Miss Hardy, I find, is
out.

VILLERS I have not seen her yet. I have made a voyage to Lapland
since I came in.° (*Flinging away the book*) A lady at her toilette is as
difficult to be moved as a Quaker.° (*Yawning*) What events have 5
happened in the world since yesterday? Have you heard?

FLUTTER Oh, yes; I stopped at Tattersall's° as I came by, and there I
found Lord James Jessamy,° Sir William Wilding, and Mr—— .

But now I think of it, you shan't know a syllable of the matter; for I
have been informed you never believe above one half of what I say.   10

VILLERS My dear fellow, somebody has imposed upon you most
egregiously!—Half! Why, I never believe one tenth part of what
you say; that is, according to the plain and literal expression. But, as
I understand you, your intelligence is amusing.

FLUTTER That's very hard now, very hard. I never related a falsity in   15
my life, unless I stumbled on it by mistake. And if it were otherwise, your dull matter-of-fact people are infinitely obliged to those
warm imaginations which soar into fiction to amuse you; for, positively, the common events of this little dirty world are not worth
talking about, unless you embellish 'em!—Hah! here comes Mrs   20
Racket. Adieu to weeds, I see! All life!°

Enter Mrs Racket

Enter, madam, in all your charms! Villers has been abusing your
toilette for keeping you so long, but I think we are much obliged to
it, and so are you.

MRS RACKET How so, pray? Good morning t'ye both. Here, here's a   25
hand a-piece for you.

Villers and Flutter kiss her hands

FLUTTER How so? Because it has given you so many beauties.

MRS RACKET Delightful compliment! What do you think of that, Villers?

VILLERS That he and his compliments are alike: showy, but won't bear
examining.—So you brought Miss Hardy to town last night?   30

MRS RACKET Yes, I should have brought her before, but I had a fall
from my horse that confined me a week. I suppose in her heart she
wished me hanged a dozen times an hour.

FLUTTER Why?

MRS RACKET Had she not an expecting lover in town all the time? She   35
meets him this morning at the lawyer's. I hope she'll charm him;
she's the sweetest girl in the world.

VILLERS Vanity, like murder, will out. You have convinced me you
think yourself more charming.

MRS RACKET How can that be?   40

VILLERS No woman ever praises another unless she thinks herself
superior in the very perfections she allows.

FLUTTER Nor no man ever rails at the sex unless he is conscious he
deserves their hatred.

MRS RACKET Thank ye, Flutter; I'll owe ye a bouquet for that. I am   45
going to visit the new-married Lady Frances Touchwood. Who
knows her husband?

FLUTTER Everybody.

MRS RACKET Is there not something odd in his character?

VILLERS Nothing, but that he is passionately fond of his wife. And so
petulant is his love that he opened the cage of a favourite bullfinch
and sent it to catch butterflies because she rewarded its song with
her kisses.

MRS RACKET Intolerable monster! Such a brute deserves—

VILLERS Nay, nay, nay, nay, this is your sex now! Give a woman but
one stroke of character, off she goes, like a ball from a racket; sees
the whole man, marks him down for an angel or a devil, and so
exhibits him to her acquaintance. This 'monster', this 'brute' is one
of the worthiest fellows upon earth: sound sense, and a liberal
mind, but dotes on his wife to such excess that he quarrels with
everything she admires, and is jealous of her tippet and nosegay.°

MRS RACKET Oh, less love for me, kind Cupid! I can see no difference
between the torment of such an affection and hatred.

FLUTTER Oh, pardon me, inconceivable difference, inconceivable; I
see it as clearly as your bracelet. In the one case the husband would
say, as Mr Snapper said t'other day, 'Zounds! Madam, do you suppose that *my* table and *my* house and *my* pictures!'—*A propos des
bottes*,° there was the divinest 'Plague of Athens'° sold yesterday at
Langford's!° The dead figures so natural, you would have sworn
they had been alive! Lord Primrose° bid five hundred.—'Six,' said
Lady Carmine.°—'A thousand,' said Ingot° the nabob.°—Down
went the hammer.—'A *rouleau*° for your bargain,' said Sir Jeremy
Jingle.° And what answer do you think Ingot made him?

MRS RACKET Why, took the offer.

FLUTTER 'Sir, I would oblige you, but I buy this picture to place in the
nursery. The children have already got "Whittington and his Cat";°
'tis just this size, and they'll make good companions.'

MRS RACKET Ha, ha, ha! Well, I protest that's just the way now! The
nabobs and their wives outbid one at every sale, and the creatures
have no more taste—

VILLERS There again! You forget this story is told by Flutter, who
always remembers everything but the circumstances and the person
he talks about. 'Twas Ingot who offered a rouleau for the bargain,
and Sir Jeremy Jingle who made the reply.

FLUTTER Egad, I believe you are right. Well, the story is as good one
way as t'other, you know. Good morning. I am going to Mrs
Crotchet's° concert, and in my way back shall make my bow at Sir
George's. (*Going*)

VILLERS I'll venture every figure in our tailor's bill, you make some
blunder there.   90

FLUTTER (*turning back*) Done! My tailor's bill has not been paid these
two years; and I'll open my mouth with as much care as Mrs
Bridget Button, who wears cork plumpers° in each cheek and never
hazards more than six words for fear of showing them.
      Exit Flutter

MRS RACKET 'Tis a good-natured insignificant creature: let in every-   95
where, and cared for nowhere.—There's Miss Hardy returned
from Lincoln's Inn. She seems rather chagrined.

VILLERS Then I leave you to your communications.
      Enter Letitia, followed by her Maid
Adieu! I am rejoiced to see you so well, madam! But I must tear
myself away.   100

LETITIA Don't vanish in a moment.

VILLERS Oh, inhuman! You are two of the most dangerous women in
town. Staying here to be cannonaded by four such eyes is equal to a
rencontre with Paul Jones,° or a midnight march to Omoa!° (*Aside*)
They'll swallow the nonsense for the sake of the compliment.   105
      Exit Villers

LETITIA (*gives her cloak to her Maid*) Order DuQuesne never to come
again; he shall positively dress my hair no more.
      Exit Maid
And this odious silk; how unbecoming it is! I was bewitched to
choose it. (*Throwing herself on a sofa and looking in a pocket-glass,
Mrs Racket staring at her.*) Did you ever see such a fright° as I am   110
today?

MRS RACKET Yes, I have seen you look much worse.

LETITIA How can you be so provoking? If I do not look this morning
worse than ever I looked in my life, I am naturally a fright. You
shall have it which way you will.   115

MRS RACKET Just as you please; but pray what is the meaning of all
this?

LETITIA (*rising*) Men are all dissemblers! Flatterers! Deceivers! Have I
not heard a thousand times of my air, my eyes, my shape—all made
for victory! And today, when I bent my whole heart on one poor   120
conquest, I have proved that all those imputed charms amount to
nothing; for Doricourt saw them unmoved. A husband of fifteen
months could not have examined me with more cutting indifference.

MRS RACKET Then you return it like a wife of fifteen months, and be
as indifferent as he.   125

224

LETITIA Aye, there's the sting! The blooming boy, who left his image
in my young heart, is at four and twenty improved in every grace
that fixed him there. It is the same face that my memory, and my
dreams, constantly painted to me, but its graces are finished, and
every beauty heightened. How mortifying, to feel myself at the   130
same moment his slave, and an object of perfect indifference to
him!

MRS RACKET How are you certain that was the case? Did you expect
him to kneel down before the lawyer, his clerks, and your father, to
make oath of your beauty?   135

LETITIA No, but he should have looked as if a sudden ray had pierced
him! He should have been breathless! Speechless! For, oh, Caroline,
all this was I!

MRS RACKET I am sorry you was such a fool! Can you expect a man,
who has courted and been courted by half the fine women in   140
Europe, to feel like a girl from a boarding-school? He is the petti-
est fellow you have seen, and, in course, bewilders your imagination; but he has seen a million of pretty women, child, before he
saw you, and his first feelings have been over long ago.

LETITIA Your raillery distresses me; but I will touch his heart, or never   145
be his wife.

MRS RACKET Absurd, and romantic! If you have no reason to believe
his heart pre-engaged, be satisfied; if he is a man of honour, you'll
have nothing to complain of.

LETITIA Nothing to complain of! Heavens! Shall I marry the man I   150
adore with such an expectation as that?

MRS RACKET And when you have fretted yourself pale, my dear, you'll
have mended your expectation greatly.

LETITIA (*pausing*) Yet I have one hope. If there is any power whose
peculiar care is faithful love, that power I invoke to aid me.   155
    Enter Hardy

HARDY Well, now; wasn't I right? Aye, Letty! Aye, Cousin Racket,
wasn't I right? I knew 'twould be so. He was all agog to see her
before he went abroad; and, if he had, he'd have thought no more of
her face, maybe, than his own.

MRS RACKET Maybe not half so much.   160

HARDY Aye, maybe so. But I see into things! Exactly as I foresaw, today
he fell desperately in love with the wench. He, he, he!

LETITIA Indeed, sir! How did you perceive it?

HARDY That's a pretty question! How do I perceive everything? How
did I foresee the fall of corn° and the rise of taxes? How did I know   165

that if we quarrelled with America, Norway deals would be dearer?° How did I foretell that a war would sink the funds?° How did I forewarn Parson Homily° that if he didn't some way or other contrive to get more votes than Rubric,° he'd lose the lectureship? How did I—but what the devil makes you so dull, Letitia? I thought to have found you popping about as brisk as the jacks° of your harpsichord.   170

LETITIA Surely, sir, 'tis a very serious occasion.

HARDY Foh, foh! Girls should never be grave before marriage. How did you feel, cousin, beforehand? Aye!   175

MRS RACKET Feel! Why, exceedingly full of cares.

HARDY Did you?

MRS RACKET I could not sleep for thinking of my coach, my liveries, and my chairmen; the taste of clothes I should be presented in distracted me for a week; and whether I should be married in white   180
or lilac gave me the most cruel anxiety.

LETITIA And is it possible that you felt no other care?

HARDY And pray, of what sort may your cares be, Mrs° Letitia? I begin to foresee now that you have taken a dislike to Doricourt.

LETITIA Indeed, sir, I have not.   185

HARDY Then what's all this melancholy about? A'n't you going to be married? And, what's more, to a sensible man? And, what's more to a young girl, to a handsome man? And what's all this melancholy for, I say?

MRS RACKET Why, because he *is* handsome and sensible, and because   190
she's over head and ears in love with him; all which, it seems, your foreknowledge had not told you a word of.

LETITIA Fie, Caroline!

HARDY Well, come, do you tell me° what's the matter then. If you don't like him, hang the signing and sealing, he shan't have ye.—   195
And yet I can't say that neither; for you know that estate that cost his father and me upwards of fourscore thousand pounds must go all to him if you won't have him; if he won't have you, indeed, 'twill be all yours. All that's clear, engrossed upon parchment,° and the poor dear man set his hand to it whilst he was a-dying.—'Ah!' said   200
I, 'I foresee you'll never live to see 'em come together, but their first son shall be christened Jeremiah after you; that I promise you.'— But come, I say, what is the matter? Don't you like him?

LETITIA I fear, sir—if I must speak—I fear I was less agreeable in Mr Doricourt's eyes than he appeared in mine.   205

HARDY There you are mistaken; for I asked him, and he told me he liked you vastly. Don't you think he must have taken a fancy to her?

MRS RACKET Why, really I think so, as I was not by.

LETITIA My dear sir, I am convinced he has not; but if there is spirit or invention in woman, he shall.

HARDY Right, girl; go to your toilette—

LETITIA It is not my toilette that can serve me; but a plan has struck me, if you will not oppose it, which flatters me with brilliant success.

HARDY Oppose it! Not I indeed! What is it?

LETITIA Why, sir—it may seem a little paradoxical—but as he does not like me enough, I want him to like me still less, and will at our next interview endeavour to heighten his indifference into dislike.

HARDY Who the devil could have foreseen that?

MRS RACKET Heaven and earth! Letitia, are you serious?

LETITIA As serious as the most important business of my life demands.

MRS RACKET Why endeavour to make him dislike you?

LETITIA Because 'tis much easier to convert a sentiment into its opposite than to transform indifference into tender passion.

MRS RACKET That may be good philosophy, but I am afraid you'll find it a bad maxim.°

LETITIA I have the strongest confidence in it. I am inspired with unusual spirits, and on this hazard willingly stake my chance for happiness. I am impatient to begin my measures.

Exit Letitia

HARDY Can you foresee the end of this, cousin?

MRS RACKET No, sir; nothing less than your penetration can do that, I am sure; and I can't stay now to consider it. I am going to call on the Ogles,° and then to Lady Frances Touchwood's, and then to an auction, and then—I don't know where, but I shall be at home time enough to witness this extraordinary interview. Good-bye.

Exit Mrs Racket

HARDY Well, 'tis an odd thing—I can't understand it—but I foresee Letty will have her way, and so I shan't give myself the trouble to dispute it.

Exit

2.1

Sir George Touchwood's
Enter Doricourt and Sir George

DORICOURT Married. Ha, ha, ha! You, whom I heard in Paris say such
things of the sex, are in London a married man.

SIR GEORGE The sex is still what it has been since *la petite morale°*
banished substantial virtues; and rather than have given my name
to one of your high-bred fashionable dames, I'd have crossed the   5
line in a fire-ship, and married a Japanese.°

DORICOURT Yet you have married an English beauty, yea, and a beauty
born in high life.

SIR GEORGE True; but she has a simplicity of heart and manners that
would have become the fair Hebrew damsels toasted by the   10
patriarchs.°

DORICOURT Ha, ha! Why, thou art a downright matrimonial Quixote.°
My life on't, she becomes as mere a town lady in six months as
though she had been bred to the trade.

SIR GEORGE (*contemptuously*) Common—common. No, sir, Lady   15
Frances despises high life so much from the ideas I have given her,
that she'll live in it like a salamander in fire.°

DORICOURT Oh, that the circle *dans la place Victoire°* could witness
thy extravagance! I'll send thee off to St Evreux° this night, drawn
at full length, and coloured after nature.   20

SIR GEORGE Tell him then, to add to the ridicule, that Touchwood
glories in the name of husband; that he has found in one English-
woman more beauty than Frenchmen ever saw, and more goodness
than Frenchwomen can conceive.

DORICOURT Well, enough of description. Introduce me to this   25
phoenix;° I came on purpose.

SIR GEORGE Introduce!—Oh, aye, to be sure—I believe Lady Frances
is engaged just now—but another time. (*Aside*) How handsome the
dog looks today!

DORICOURT Another time! But I have no other time. 'Sdeath! This is   30
the only hour I can command this fortnight!

SIR GEORGE (*aside*) I am glad to hear it, with all my soul. [*To Doricourt*]
So then, you can't dine with us today? That's very unlucky.

DORICOURT Oh, yes—as to dinner—yes, I can, I believe, contrive to
dine with you today.   35

228

SIR GEORGE Psha, I didn't think on what I was saying; I meant supper°—you can't sup with us?

DORICOURT Why, supper will be rather more convenient than dinner. But you are fortunate; if you had asked me any other night, I could not have come.

SIR GEORGE Tonight!—Gad, now I recollect, we are particularly engaged tonight. But tomorrow night—

DORICOURT Why, look ye, Sir George, 'tis very plain you have no inclination to let me see your wife at all; so here I sit. (*Throws himself on a sofa*) There's my hat, and here are my legs. Now I shan't stir till I have seen her, and I have no engagements. I'll breakfast, dine, and sup with you every day this week.

SIR GEORGE Was there ever such a provoking wretch! But, to be plain with you, Doricourt, I and my house are at your service. But you are a damned agreeable fellow, and ten years younger than I am, and the women, I observe, always simper when you appear. For these reasons, I had rather, when Lady Frances and I are together, that you should forget we are acquainted, further than a nod, a smile, or a how-d'ye.

DORICOURT Very well.

SIR GEORGE It is not merely yourself *in propria persona*° that I object to, but, if you are intimate here, you'll make my house still more the fashion than it is; and it is already so much so, that my doors are of no use to me. I married Lady Frances to engross her to myself; yet such is the blessed freedom of modern manners, that, in spite of me, her eyes, thoughts, and conversation, are continually divided among all the flirts and coxcombs of fashion.

DORICOURT To be sure, I confess that kind of freedom is carried rather too far. 'Tis hard one can't have a jewel in one's cabinet but the whole town must be gratified with its lustre. (*Aside*) He shan't preach me out of seeing his wife, though.

SIR GEORGE Well, now, that's reasonable. When you take time to reflect, Doricourt, I always observe you decide right, and therefore I hope—

    Enter Servant

SERVANT Sir, my lady desires—

SIR GEORGE I am particularly engaged.

DORICOURT Oh, lord, that shall be no excuse in the world. (*Leaping from the sofa*) Lead the way, John. I'll attend your lady.

    Exit [Doricourt], following the Servant

SIR GEORGE What devil possessed me to talk about her!—Here, Dori- 75
court! (*Running after him*) Doricourt!
[*Exit Sir George.*] *Enter Mrs Racket and Miss Ogle followed by
a Servant*

MRS RACKET Acquaint your lady that Mrs Racket and Miss Ogle are
here.
Exit Servant

MISS OGLE I shall hardly know Lady Frances; 'tis so long since I was
in Shropshire. 80

MRS RACKET And I'll be sworn you never saw her *out* of Shropshire.
Her father kept her locked up with his caterpillars and shells, and
loved her beyond anything—but a blue butterfly and a petrified
frog!

MISS OGLE Ha, ha, ha! Well, 'twas a cheap way of breeding her. You 85
know he was very poor, though a lord; and very high-spirited,
though a virtuoso.° In town, her Pantheons,° operas, and *robes de
cour*,° would have swallowed his seaweeds, moths, and monsters
in six weeks! Sir George, I find, thinks his wife a most extraordinary creature: he has taught her to despise everything like 90
fashionable life, and boasts that example will have no effect on
her.

MRS RACKET There's a great degree of impertinence in all that. I'll try
to make her a fine lady to humble him.

MISS OGLE That's just the thing I wish. 95
Enter Lady Frances

LADY FRANCES I beg ten thousand pardons, my dear Mrs Racket.—
Miss Ogle, I rejoice to see you. I should have come to you sooner,
but I was detained in conversation by Mr Doricourt.

MRS RACKET Pray make no apology. I am quite happy that we have
your ladyship in town at last. What stay do you make? 100

LADY FRANCES A short one! Sir George talks with regret of the scenes
we have left, and, as the ceremony of presentation° is over, will, I
believe, soon return.

MISS OGLE Sure he can't be so cruel! Does your ladyship wish to
return so soon? 105

LADY FRANCES I have not the habit of consulting my own wishes, but,
I think, if they decide, we shall not return immediately. I have yet
hardly formed an idea of London.

MRS RACKET I shall quarrel with your lord and master if he dares
think of depriving us of you so soon. How do you dispose of 110
yourself today?

LADY FRANCES Sir George is going with me this morning to the mercer's° to choose a silk; and then—

MRS RACKET Choose a silk for you! Ha, ha, ha! Sir George chooses your laces too, I hope, your gloves, and your pincushions!   115

LADY FRANCES Madam!

MRS RACKET I am glad to see you blush, my dear Lady Frances. These are strange homespun ways! If you do these things, pray keep 'em secret. Lord bless us! If the town should know your husband chooses your gowns!   120

MISS OGLE You are very young, my lady, and have been brought up in solitude. The maxims you learned among wood nymphs in Shropshire won't pass current here, I assure you.

MRS RACKET Why, my dear creature, you look quite frightened! Come, you shall go with us to an exhibition, and an auction. Afterwards,   125 we'll take a turn in the Park,° and then drive to Kensington.° So we shall be at home by four to dress, and in the evening I'll attend you to Lady Brilliant's masquerade.

LADY FRANCES I shall be very happy to be of your party, if Sir George has no engagements.   130

MRS RACKET What! Do you stand so low in your own opinion that you dare not trust yourself without Sir George! If you choose to play Darby and Joan,° my dear, you should have stayed in the country; 'tis an exhibition not calculated for London, I assure you!

MISS OGLE What, I suppose, my lady, you and Sir George will be seen   135 pacing it comfortably round the Canal,° arm and arm, and then go lovingly into the same carriage, dine *tête-a-tête*, spend the evening at piquet,° and so go soberly to bed at eleven! Such a snug plan may do for an attorney and his wife, but, for Lady Frances Touchwood, 'tis as unsuitable as linsey-woolsey° or a black bonnet° at the   140 *festino*!°

LADY FRANCES These are rather new doctrines to me! But, my dear Mrs Racket, you and Miss Ogle must judge of these things better than I can. As you observe, I am but young, and may have caught absurd opinions.—Here is Sir George!   145

Enter Sir George

SIR GEORGE (*aside*) 'Sdeath! another room full!

LADY FRANCES My love! Mrs Racket, and Miss Ogle.°

MRS RACKET Give you joy, Sir George. We came to rob you of Lady Frances for a few hours.

SIR GEORGE A few hours!   150

LADY FRANCES Oh, yes! I am going to an exhibition, and an auction, and the Park, and Kensington, and a thousand places! It is quite ridiculous, I find, for married people to be always together. We shall be laughed at!

SIR GEORGE I am astonished!—Mrs Racket, what does the dear   155
creature mean?

MRS RACKET Mean, Sir George? What she says, I imagine.

MISS OGLE Why, you know, sir, as Lady Frances had the misfortune to be bred entirely in the country, she cannot be supposed to be versed in fashionable life.   160

SIR GEORGE No; heaven forbid she should! If she had, madam, she would never have been my wife!

MRS RACKET Are you serious?

SIR GEORGE Perfectly so. I should never have had the courage to have married a well-bred fine lady.   165

MISS OGLE (sneeringly) Pray, sir, what do you take a fine lady to be, that you express such fear of her?

SIR GEORGE A being easily described, madam, as she is seen everywhere, but in her own house. She sleeps at home, but she lives all over the town. In her mind, every sentiment gives place to the lust   170
of conquest and the vanity of being particular.° The feelings of wife and mother are lost in the whirl of dissipation. If she continues virtuous, 'tis by chance; and if she preserves her husband from ruin, 'tis by her dexterity at the card table! Such a woman I take to be a perfect fine lady!   175

MRS RACKET And you I take to be a slanderous cynic of two-and-thirty. Twenty years hence, one might have forgiven such a libel! Now, sir, hear my definition of a fine lady: she is a creature for whom nature has done much, and education more; she has taste, elegance, spirit, understanding. In her manner she is free, in her   180
morals nice. Her behaviour is undistinguishingly polite to her husband and all mankind; her sentiments are for their hours of retirement. In a word, a fine lady is the life of conversation, the spirit of society, the joy of the public! Pleasure follows wherever she appears, and the kindest wishes attend her slumbers.—Make haste,   185
then, my dear Lady Frances, commence fine lady, and force your husband to acknowledge the justness of my picture!

LADY FRANCES I am sure 'tis a delightful one. How can you dislike it, Sir George? You painted fashionable life in colours so disgusting that I thought I hated it, but, on a nearer view, it seems charming. I have   190
hitherto lived in obscurity; 'tis time that I should be a woman of the world. I long to begin! My heart pants with expectation and delight!

MRS RACKET Come, then; let us begin directly. I am impatient to introduce you to that society which you were born to ornament and charm.   195

LADY FRANCES Adieu, my love! We shall meet again at dinner. (*Going.*)

SIR GEORGE Sure, I am in a dream!—Fanny!

LADY FRANCES (*returning*) Sir George?

SIR GEORGE Will you go without me?   200

MRS RACKET Will you go without me! Ha, ha, ha! What a pathetic address! Why, sure you would not always be seen side by side, like two beans upon a stalk. Are you afraid to trust Lady Frances with me, sir?

SIR GEORGE Heaven and earth! With whom can a man trust his wife in   205
the present state of society? Formerly there were distinctions of character amongst ye. Every class of females had its particular description: grandmothers were pious, aunts discreet, old maids censorious!° But now aunts, grandmothers, girls, and maiden gentlewomen are all the same creature; a wrinkle more or less is the   210
sole difference between ye.

MRS RACKET That maiden gentlewomen have lost their censoriousness, is surely not in your catalogue of grievances.

SIR GEORGE Indeed it is—and ranked amongst the most serious grievances. Things went well, madam, when the tongues of three or four   215
old virgins kept all the wives and daughters of a parish in awe. They were the dragons that guarded the Hesperian fruit;° and I wonder they have not been obliged, by act of parliament, to resume their function.

MRS RACKET Ha, ha, ha! And pensioned,° I suppose, for making strict   220
enquiries into the lives and conversations of their neighbours.

SIR GEORGE With all my heart, and empowered to oblige every woman to conform her conduct to her real situation. You, for instance, are a widow; your air should be sedate, your dress grave, your deportment matronly, and in all things an example to the young women   225
growing up about you! Instead of which, you are dressed for conquest, think of nothing but ensnaring hearts, are a coquette, a wit, and a fine lady.

MRS RACKET Bear witness to what he says! A coquette! A wit! And a fine lady! Who would have expected an eulogy from such an ill-   230
natured mortal! Valour to a soldier, wisdom to a judge, or glory to a prince is not more than such a character to a woman.

MISS OGLE Sir George, I see, languishes for the charming society of a century and a half ago, when a grave squire and a still graver dame, surrounded by a sober family, formed a stiff group in a mouldy old house in the corner of a park.   235

MRS RACKET Delightful serenity! Undisturbed by any noise but the cawing of rooks° and the quarterly rumbling of an old family coach on a state visit, with the happy intervention of a friendly call from the parish apothecary or the curate's wife.°   240

SIR GEORGE And what is the society of which you boast? A mere chaos, in which all distinction of rank is lost in a ridiculous affectation of ease, and every different order of beings huddled together as they were before the creation. In the same select party, you will often find the wife of a bishop and a sharper, of an earl and a fiddler.   245 In short, 'tis one universal masquerade, all disguised in the same habits and manners.

   [*Enter Servant*]

SERVANT Mr Flutter.

SIR GEORGE Here comes an illustration. Now I defy you to tell from his appearance whether Flutter is a privy counsellor or a mercer, a   250 lawyer or a grocer's 'prentice.

   Enter Flutter

FLUTTER Oh, just what you please, Sir George, so you don't make me a Lord Mayor.°—Ah, Mrs Racket!—Lady Frances, your most obedient; you look—now hang me, if that's not provoking! Had your gown been of another colour, I should have said the prettiest   255 thing you ever heard in your life.

MISS OGLE Pray give it us.

FLUTTER I was yesterday at Mrs Bloomer's.° She was dressed all in green; no other colour to be seen but that of her face and bosom. So says I, 'My dear Mrs Bloomer! You look like a carnation, just   260 bursting from its pod.'

SIR GEORGE And what said her husband?

FLUTTER Her husband! Why, her husband laughed and said a cucumber would have been a happier simile.

SIR GEORGE But there *are* husbands, sir, who would rather have   265 corrected than amended your comparison. I, for instance, should consider a man's complimenting my wife as an impertinence.

FLUTTER Why, what harm can there be in compliments? Sure they are not infectious, and, if they were, you, Sir George, of all people breathing, have reason to be satisfied about your lady's attachment. Every-   270 body talks of it: that little bird there, that she killed out of jealousy. The most extraordinary instance of affection that ever was given.

LADY FRANCES I kill a bird through jealousy! Heavens! Mr Flutter, how can you impute such a cruelty to me?

SIR GEORGE I could have forgiven you if you had.   275

FLUTTER Oh, what a blundering fool!—No, no; now I remember. 'Twas your bird, Lady Frances, that's it; your bullfinch, which Sir George, in one of the refinements of his passion, sent into the wide world to seek its fortune. He took it for a knight in disguise.°

LADY FRANCES Is it possible! Oh, Sir George, could I have imagined it   280
was you who deprived me of a creature I was so fond of?

SIR GEORGE Mr Flutter, you are one of those busy, idle, meddling people, who, from mere vacuity of mind, are the most dangerous inmates in a family. You have neither feelings nor opinions of your own, but, like a glass in a tavern, bear about those of every block-   285
head who gives you his; and, because you *mean* no harm, think yourselves excused, though broken friendships, discords, and murders are the consequences of your indiscretions.

FLUTTER (*taking out his tablets*°) Vacuity of mind!—What was the next? I'll write down this sermon; 'tis the first I have heard since my   290
grandmother's funeral.

MISS OGLE Come, Lady Frances, you see what a cruel creature your loving husband can be; so let us leave him.

SIR GEORGE Madam, Lady Frances shall not go.

LADY FRANCES *Shall* not, Sir George? (*Weeping*) This is the first time   295
such an expression—

SIR GEORGE My love! My life!

LADY FRANCES Don't imagine I'll be treated like a child! Denied what I wish, then pacified with sweet words.

MISS OGLE The bullfinch! That's an excellent subject; never let it   300
down.

LADY FRANCES I see plainly you would deprive me of every pleasure, as well as of my sweet bird, out of pure love! Barbarous man!

SIR GEORGE 'Tis well, madam. Your resentment of that circumstance proves to me what I did not before suspect: that you are deficient   305
both in tenderness and understanding. Tremble to think the hour approaches in which you would give worlds for such a proof of my love. Go, madam, give yourself to the public, abandon your heart to dissipation, and see if, in the scenes of gaiety and folly that await you, you can find a recompense for the lost affection of a doting   310
husband.

Exit Sir George

FLUTTER Lord! What a fine thing it is to have the gift of speech! I

suppose Sir George practices at Coachmakers Hall, or the Black
Horse in Bond Street.°

LADY FRANCES He is really angry; I cannot go.   315

MRS RACKET Not go! Foolish creature! You are arrived at the moment,
which some time or other was sure to happen, and everything
depends on the use you make of it.

MISS OGLE Come, Lady Frances! Don't hesitate! The minutes are
precious.   320

LADY FRANCES I could find in my heart—and yet I won't give up
neither. If I should in this instance, he'll expect it forever.
    Exit Lady Frances°

MISS OGLE Now you act like a woman of spirit.
    Exeunt Miss Ogle and Mrs Racket

FLUTTER A fair tug, by Jupiter, between duty and pleasure! Pleasure
beats, and off we go, *Iö triumphe!*°   325
    Exit

2.2

An auction room [filled with] busts, pictures, etc.
Enter Silvertongue with three Puffers° [*including Mrs Fagg and*
Mask]

SILVERTONGUE Very well, very well. This morning will be devoted to
curiosity; my sale begins tomorrow at eleven.—But, Mrs Fagg, if
you do no better than you did in Lord Filigree's° sale, I shall
discharge you. You want a knack terribly. And this dress—why,
nobody can mistake you for a gentlewoman.   5

FAGG Very true, Mr Silvertongue; but I can't dress like a lady upon
half-a-crown a day, as the saying is. If you want me to dress
like a lady, you must double my pay. Double or quits, Mr
Silvertongue.

SILVERTONGUE *Five shillings* a day! What a demand! Why, woman,   10
there are a thousand parsons in the town who don't make five
shillings a day, though they preach, pray, christen, marry, and bury,
for the good of the community. Five shillings a day! Why, 'tis the
pay of a lieutenant in a marching regiment, who keeps a servant, a
mistress, a horse; fights, dresses, ogles, makes love, and dies upon 15
five shillings a day.

FAGG Oh, as to that, all that's very right. A soldier should not be too

fond of life, and forcing him to do all these things upon five
shillings a day is the readiest way to make him tired on't.

SILVERTONGUE Well, Mask, have you been looking into the   20
antiquaries? Have you got all the terms of art in a string, aye?

MASK Yes, I have. I know the age of a coin by the taste, and I can fix the
birthday of a medal, *anno mundi*° or *anno domini*,° though the green
rust should have eaten up every character. But you know, the brown
suit and the wig I wear when I personate the antiquary are in limbo.°   25

SILVERTONGUE Those you have on may do.

MASK These! Why, in these I am a young travelled cognoscento:° Mr
Glib° bought them of Sir Tom Totter's° valet; and I am going
there° directly. You know his picture sale comes on today; and I
have got my head full of Parmegiano, Sal Rosa, Metszu, Tarbaek,   30
and Vandermeer. I talk of the relief of Woovermans, the spirit of
Teniers, the colouring of the Venetian School, and the correctness
of the Roman. I distinguish Claude by his sleep, and Ruisdael by his
water. The rapidity of Tintoret's pencil strikes me at the first
glance; whilst the harmony of Van Dyck, and the glow of   35
Correggio,° point out their masters.

Enter Company [of Ladies and Gentlemen]

FIRST LADY Hey-day, Mr Silvertongue! What, nobody here!

SILVERTONGUE Oh, my lady, we shall have company enough in a trice;
if your carriage is seen at my door, no other will pass it,° I am sure.

FIRST LADY (*aside*) Familiar monster! [*To Silvertongue*] That's a beau-   40
tiful Diana, Mr Silvertongue, but, in the name of wonder, how
came Actaeon° to be placed on the top of the house?

SILVERTONGUE That's a David and Bathsheba,° ma'am.

FIRST LADY Oh, I crave their pardon! I remember their names, but I
know nothing of their story.°   45

More Company enters, [Courtall among them]°

FIRST GENTLEMAN Was not that Lady Frances Touchwood coming
up with Mrs Racket?

SECOND GENTLEMAN I think so.—Yes, it is, faith. Let us go nearer.

Enter Lady Frances, Mrs Racket, and Miss Ogle

SILVERTONGUE Yes, sir, this is to be the first lot: the model of a city, in
wax.   50

SECOND GENTLEMAN The model of a city! What city?

SILVERTONGUE That I have not been able to discover; but call it
Rome, Peking,° or London, 'tis still a city. You'll find in it the same
jarring interests, the same passions, the same virtues, and the same
vices, whatever the name.   55

GENTLEMAN You may as well present us a map of *terra incognita*.°

SILVERTONGUE Oh, pardon me, sir! A lively imagination would convert this waxen city into an endless and interesting amusement.
For instance, look into this little house on the right-hand. There
are four old prudes in it taking care of their neighbours' reputa-   6
tions. This elegant mansion on the left, decorated with Corinthian
pillars—who needs to be told that it belongs to a court lord and is
the habitation of patriotism, philosophy, and virtue? Here's a City
Hall—the rich steams that issue from the windows nourish a
neighbouring work-house. Here's a church—we'll pass over that;   6
the doors are shut. The parsonage-house comes next; we'll take a
peep here, however. Look at the doctor! He's asleep on a volume
of Toland° whilst his lady is putting on rouge for the
masquerade.—Oh! Oh, this can be no English city; our parsons
are all orthodox,° and their wives the daughters of modesty and   7
meekness.

    Lady Frances and Miss Ogle come forward, followed by Courtall

LADY FRANCES I wish Sir George was here. This man follows me
about and stares at me in such a way that I am quite uneasy.

MISS OGLE He has travelled and is heir to an immense estate. So he's
impertinent by patent.°   7

COURTALL You are very cruel, ladies.—Miss Ogle, you will not let me
speak to you.—As to this little scornful beauty, she has frowned me
dead fifty times.

LADY FRANCES (*confused*) Sir—I am a married woman.

COURTALL (*aside*) A married woman! A good hint. [*To Lady Frances*]   8
'Twould be a shame if such a charming woman was not married.
But I see you are a Daphne° just come from your sheep and your
meadows, your crook and your waterfalls. Pray now, who is the
happy Damon° to whom you have vowed eternal truth and
constancy?   8

MISS OGLE 'Tis Lady Frances Touchwood, Mr Courtall, to whom you
are speaking.

COURTALL [*aside*] Lady Frances! By heaven, that's Saville's old flame.
[*To Lady Frances*] I beg your ladyship's pardon. I ought to have
believed that such beauty could belong only to your name—a name   9
I have long been enamoured of, because I knew it to be that of the
finest woman in the world.

    Mrs Racket comes forward

LADY FRANCES (*apart*) My dear Mrs Racket, I am so frightened!
Here's a man making love to me, though he knows I am married.

MRS RACKET Oh, the sooner for that, my dear; don't mind him.—Was   95
you at the casino° last night, Mr Courtall?

COURTALL I looked in. 'Twas impossible to stay. Nobody there but
antiques. You'll be at Lady Brilliant's tonight, doubtless?

MRS RACKET Yes, I go with Lady Frances.

LADY FRANCES (*to Miss Ogle*) Bless me! I did not know this gentleman   100
was acquainted with Mrs Racket. I behaved so rude to him!

MRS RACKET (*looking at her watch*) Come, ma'am; 'tis past one. I
protest, if we don't fly to Kensington, we shan't find a soul there.

LADY FRANCES Won't this gentleman go with us?

COURTALL (*looking surprised*) To be sure, you make me happy, madam,   105
beyond description.

MRS RACKET Oh, never mind him; he'll follow.

Exeunt Lady Frances, Mrs Racket, and Miss Ogle

COURTALL Lady *Touchwood* with a vengeance!° But, 'tis always so.
Your reserved ladies are like ice. Egad! No sooner begin to soften,
than they melt. (*Following*)   110

[*Exit*]

3.1

Hardy's
Enter Letitia and Mrs Racket

MRS RACKET Come, prepare, prepare; your lover is coming.

LETITIA My lover! Confess now that my absence at dinner was a severe mortification to him.

MRS RACKET I can't absolutely swear it spoilt his appetite: he eat° as if he was hungry, and drank his wine as though he liked it.   5

LETITIA What was the apology?

MRS RACKET That you were ill. But I gave him a hint that your extreme bashfulness could not support his eye.

LETITIA If I comprehend him, awkwardness and bashfulness are the last faults he can pardon in a woman, so expect to see me   10
transformed into the veriest mawkin.°

MRS RACKET You persevere then?

LETITIA Certainly. I know the design is a rash one, and the event° important: it either makes Doricourt mine by all the tenderest ties of passion, or deprives me of him forever. And never to be   15
his wife will afflict me less than to be his wife and not be beloved.

MRS RACKET So you won't trust to the good old maxim, 'Marry first, and love will follow'?

LETITIA As readily as I would venture my last guinea that good for-   20
tune might follow. The woman that has not touched the heart of a man before he leads her to the altar has scarcely a chance to charm it when possession and security turn their powerful arms against her.—But here he comes. I'll disappear for a moment. Don't spare me.   25

Exit Letitia. Enter Doricourt, not seeing Mrs Racket

DORICOURT (*looking at a picture*) So, this is my mistress, I presume. *Ma foi!*° The painter has hit her off. The downcast eye, the blushing cheek, timid, apprehensive, bashful. A tear and a prayer-book would have made her *La Bella Magdalena.°*—

Give *me* a woman in whose touching mien   30
A mind, a soul, a polished art is seen;
Whose motion speaks; whose poignant air can move.
Such are the darts to wound with endless love.

240

MRS RACKET (*touching him on the shoulder with her fan*) Is that an impromptu?   35

DORICOURT (*starting*) Madam! (*Aside*) Finely caught! [*To Mrs Racket*] Not absolutely. It struck me during the dessert, as a motto for your picture.

MRS RACKET Gallantry turned! I perceive, however, Miss Hardy's charms have made no violent impression on you. And who can   40 wonder? The poor girl's defects are so obvious.

DORICOURT Defects!

MRS RACKET Merely those of education. Her father's indulgence ruined her. *Mauvaise honte*,° conceit and ignorance all unite in the lady you are to marry.   45

DORICOURT Marry! I marry such a woman! Your picture, I hope, is overcharged.° I marry *mauvaise honte*, pertness and ignorance!

MRS RACKET Thank your stars that ugliness and ill temper are not added to the list. You must think her handsome?

DORICOURT Half her personal beauty would content me; but could   50 the Medicean Venus° be animated for me and endowed with a vulgar soul, *I* should become the statue, and my heart transformed to marble.

MRS RACKET Bless us! We are in a hopeful way then!

DORICOURT (*aside*) There must be some envy in this! I see she is a   55 coquette. [*To Mrs Racket*] Ha, ha, ha! And you imagine I am persuaded of the truth of your character?° Ha, ha, ha! Miss Hardy, I have been assured, madam, is elegant and accomplished—but one must allow for a lady's painting.°

MRS RACKET (*aside*) I'll be even with him for that. [*To Doricourt*] Ha,   60 ha, ha! And so you have found me out! Well, I protest I meant no harm; 'twas only to increase the *éclat*° of her appearance that I threw a veil over her charms.—Here comes the lady. Her elegance and accomplishments will announce themselves.

    Enter Letitia, running°

LETITIA La! Cousin, do you know that our John—oh, dear heart! I   65 didn't see you, sir. (*Hanging down her head, and dropping behind Mrs Racket*)

MRS RACKET Fie, Letitia! Mr Doricourt thinks you a woman of elegant manners. Stand forward, and confirm his opinion.

LETITIA No, no; keep before me. He's my sweetheart, and 'tis   70 impudent to look one's sweetheart in the face, you know.

MRS RACKET You'll allow in future for a lady's painting, sir. Ha, ha, ha!

DORICOURT I am astonished!

LETITIA Well, hang it, I'll take heart. (*Half apart*)° Why, he is but a
man, you know, cousin; and I'll let him see I wasn't born in a wood   75
to be scared by an owl. (*Advances and looks at Doricourt through her
fingers*) He, he, he! (*Goes up to Doricourt and makes a very stiff and
formal curtsey. Doricourt bows*) You have been a great traveller, sir, I
hear?

DORICOURT Yes, madam.   80

LETITIA Then I wish you'd tell us about the fine sights you saw when
you went oversea. I have read in a book that there are some countries where the men and women are all horses.° Did you see any of
them?

MRS RACKET Mr Doricourt is not prepared, my dear, for these enquir-   85
ies. He is reflecting on the importance of the question and will
answer you—when he can.

LETITIA When he can! Why, he's as slow in speech as Aunt Margery
when she's reading Thomas Aquinas°—and stands gaping like
mumchance.°   90

MRS RACKET Have a little discretion.

LETITIA Hold your tongue! Sure I may say what I please before I am
married, if I can't afterwards. D'ye think a body° does not know
how to talk to a sweetheart? He is not the first I have had.

DORICOURT Indeed!   95

LETITIA Oh, lud! He speaks!—Why, if you must know, there was the
curate at home. When Papa was a-hunting, he used to come a-
suitoring and make speeches to me out of books. Nobody knows
what a mort of fine things he used to say to me—and call me Venus,
and Jubah,° and Dinah!°   100

DORICOURT And pray, fair lady, how did you answer him?

LETITIA Why, I used to say, 'Look you, Mr Curate, don't think to
come over me with your flim-flams; for a better man than ever trod
in your shoes is coming oversea to marry me.'—But, ifags, I begin
to think I was out. Parson Dobbins° was the sprightfuller man of   105
the two.

DORICOURT Surely this cannot be Miss Hardy!

LETITIA Laws! Why, don't you know me? You saw me today, but I was
daunted before my father, and the lawyer, and all them, and did not
care to speak out; so, maybe you thought I couldn't. But I can talk   110
as fast as anybody, when I know folks a little. And now I have shown
my parts, I hope you'll like me better.

Enter Hardy

HARDY [*aside*] I foresee this won't do! [*To Doricourt*] Mr Doricourt,

maybe you take my daughter for a fool, but you are mistaken; she's
a sensible girl as any in England.   115

DORICOURT I am convinced she has a very uncommon° understanding, sir. (*Aside*) I did not think he had been such an ass.

LETITIA [*aside*] My father will undo the whole. [*To Hardy*] Laws!
Papa, how can you think he can take me for a fool, when everybody
knows I beat the potecary° at conundrums° last Christmastime?   120
And didn't I make a string of names, all in riddles, for the *Ladies'
Diary*?°—There was a little river, and a great house; that was
Newcastle.°—There was what a lamb says, and three letters; that
was Ba, and k-e-r, ker, Baker.—There was—

HARDY Don't stand ba-a-ing there. You'll make me mad in a   125
moment!—I tell you, sir, that, for all that, she's devilish sensible.

DORICOURT Sir, I give all possible credit to your assertions.

LETITIA Laws! Papa, do come along. If you stand watching, how can
my sweetheart break his mind and tell me how he admires me?

DORICOURT That would be difficult, indeed, madam.   130

HARDY I tell you, Letty, I'll have no more of this. I see well enough.

LETITIA Laws! Don't snub me before my husband—that is, is to be.
You'll teach him to snub me too, and I believe, by his looks, he'd
like to begin now. So, let us go. Cousin, you may tell the gentleman
what a genus° I have: how I can cut watch-papers,° and work   135
catgut;° make quadrille baskets° with pins, and take profiles in
shade°—ay, as well as the lady at No. 62, South Moulton Street,
Grosvenor Square.°

Exeunt Hardy and Letitia

MRS RACKET What think you of my painting, now?

DORICOURT Oh, mere water-colours, madam! The lady has carica-   140
tured your picture.

MRS RACKET And how does she strike you on the whole?

DORICOURT Like a good design, spoilt by the incapacity of the artist.
Her faults are evidently the result of her father's weak indulgence. I
observed an expression in her eye that seemed to satirize the folly   145
of her lips.°

MRS RACKET But at her age, when education is fixed, and manner
becomes nature, hopes of improvement—

DORICOURT Would be as rational as hopes of gold from a juggler's°
crucible. Doricourt's wife must be incapable of improvement; but it   150
must be because she's got beyond it.

MRS RACKET I am pleased your misfortune sits no heavier.

DORICOURT Your pardon, madam; so mercurial was the hour in which

I was born that misfortunes always go plump to the bottom of my
heart, like a pebble in water, and leave the surface unruffled. I shall   15
certainly set off for Bath, or the other world, tonight, but whether I
shall use a chaise with four swift coursers or go off in a tangent
from the aperture of a pistol° deserves consideration; so I make my
adieus. (*Going*)

MRS RACKET Oh, but I entreat you, postpone your journey till tomor-   16
row. Determine on which you will, you must be this night at the
masquerade.

DORICOURT Masquerade!

MRS RACKET Why not? If you resolve to visit the other world, you may
as well take one night's pleasure in this, you know.   16

DORICOURT Faith, that's very true; ladies are the best philosophers
after all. Expect me at the masquerade.

> *Exit Doricourt*

MRS RACKET He's a charming fellow! I think Letitia shan't have him.
(*Going*)

> *Enter Hardy*

HARDY What's° he gone?   17

MRS RACKET Yes, and I am glad he is. You would have ruined us! Now,
I beg, Mr Hardy, you won't interfere in this business; it is a little
out of your way.

> *Exit Mrs Racket*

HARDY Hang me, if I don't though. I foresee very clearly what will be
the end of it if I leave ye to yourselves; so, I'll e'en follow him to the   17
masquerade, and tell him all about it. Let me see, what shall my
dress be? A Great Mogul?° No. A grenadier?° No. No, that, I
foresee, would make a laugh. Hang me, if I don't send to my favourite, little Quick,° and borrow his Jew Isaac's dress.° I know the dog
likes a glass of good wine, so I'll give him a bottle of my forty-   18
eight,° and he shall teach me. Aye, that's it! I'll be cunning little
Isaac! If they complain of my want of wit, I'll tell 'em the cursed
duenna° wears the breeches and has spoilt my parts.°

> *Exit*

3.2

Courtall's
Enter Courtall, Saville, and three others, from an apartment in
the back scene.° (*The last three tipsy.*)

COURTALL You shan't go yet.—Another catch,° and another bottle!

FIRST GENTLEMAN May I be a bottle, and an empty bottle, if you catch me at that! Why, I am going to the masquerade. Jack—you know who I mean—is to meet me, and we are to have a leap at the new lustres.°

SECOND GENTLEMAN And I am going too—a harlequin. (*Hiccups*) Am not I in a pretty pickle to make harlequinades?° And Tony, here, he is going in the disguise—in the disguise—of a gentleman!

FIRST GENTLEMAN We are all very disguised;° so bid them draw up.° —D'ye hear!

    Exeunt the three Gentlemen

SAVILLE Thy skull, Courtall, is a lady's thimble—no, an eggshell.

COURTALL Nay, then you are gone too; you never aspire to similes but in your cups.

SAVILLE No, no; I am steady enough, but the fumes of the wine pass directly through thy eggshell and leave thy brain as cool as—hey! I am quite sober; my similes fail me.

COURTALL Then we'll sit down here, and have one sober bottle. [*Calling offstage*] Bring a table and glasses.

SAVILLE I'll not swallow another drop; no, though the juice should be the true Falernian.°

COURTALL By the bright eyes of her you love, you shall drink her health.

SAVILLE Ah! (*Sitting down*) Her I loved is gone. (*Sighing*) She's married!

COURTALL Then bless your stars you are not her husband! I would be husband to no woman in Europe who was not devilish rich, and devilish ugly.

SAVILLE Wherefore ugly?

COURTALL Because she could not have the conscience to exact those attentions that a pretty wife expects; or, if she should, her resentments would be perfectly easy to me—nobody would undertake to revenge her cause.

    [*Servant brings in table and glasses, then exits*]

SAVILLE Thou art a most licentious fellow!

COURTALL I should hate my own wife, that's certain, but I have a warm heart for those of other people. And so, here's to the prettiest wife in England: Lady Frances Touchwood.

SAVILLE Lady Frances Touchwood! I rise to drink her. (*Drinks*) How the devil came Lady Frances in your head? I never knew you give a woman of chastity before.

COURTALL (*sneeringly*) That's odd, for you have heard me give half the women of fashion in England. But, pray now, what do you take a woman of chastity to be?

SAVILLE Such a woman as Lady Frances Touchwood, sir.

COURTALL Oh, you are grave, sir. I remember you was an adorer of hers. Why didn't you marry her?

SAVILLE I had not the arrogance to look so high. Had my fortune been worthy of her, she should not have been ignorant of my admiration.

COURTALL Precious fellow! What, I suppose you would not dare tell her now that you admire her?

SAVILLE No, nor you.

COURTALL By the Lord, I have told her so.

SAVILLE Have? Impossible!

COURTALL Ha, ha, ha! Is it so?

SAVILLE How did she receive the declaration?

COURTALL Why, in the old way: blushed and frowned and said she was married.

SAVILLE What amazing things thou art capable of! I could more easily have taken the Pope by the beard than profaned her ears with such a declaration.

COURTALL I shall meet her at Lady Brilliant's tonight, where I shall repeat it. And I'll lay my life, under a mask, she'll hear it all without blush or frown.

SAVILLE (*rising*) 'Tis false, sir! She won't.

COURTALL She will! (*Rising*) Nay, I'd venture to lay a round sum that I prevail on her to go out with me—only to taste the fresh air, I mean.

SAVILLE Preposterous vanity! From this moment I suspect that half the victories you have boasted are false and slanderous, as your pretended influence with Lady Frances.

COURTALL Pretended! How should such a fellow as you, now, who never soared beyond a cherry-cheeked daughter of a ploughman in Norfolk,° judge of the influence of a man of my figure and habits? I could show thee a list in which there are names to shake thy faith in the whole sex! And, to that list I have no doubt of adding the name of Lady—

SAVILLE Hold, sir! My ears cannot bear the profanation. You cannot—dare not approach her! For your soul, you dare not mention love to her! Her look would freeze the word, whilst it hovered on thy licentious lips!

COURTALL Whu! Whu! Well, we shall see. This evening, by Jupiter, the trial shall be made. If I fail, I fail.

SAVILLE I think thou darest not! But my life, my honour on her purity.
    Exit Saville

COURTALL Hot-headed fool! (*Musing*) But since he has brought it to this point, by gad, I'll try what can be done with her ladyship. 85
    (*Rings [for Servant]*) She's frost-work, and the prejudices of education yet strong; ergo,° passionate professions will only inflame her pride and put her on her guard. For other arts then!
    Enter Dick
    Dick, do you know any of the servants at Sir George Touchwood's?

DICK Yes, sir; I knows the groom, and one of the housemaids. For the 90 matter o' that, she's my own cousin, and it was my mother that holped° her to the place.

COURTALL Do you know Lady Frances's maid?

DICK I can't say as how I know she.

COURTALL Do you know Sir George's valet? 95

DICK No, sir, but Sally is very thick with° Mr Gibson, Sir George's gentleman.

COURTALL Then go there directly and employ Sally to discover whether her master goes to Lady Brilliant's this evening, and, if he does, the name of the shop that sold his habit. 100

DICK Yes, sir.

COURTALL Be exact in your intelligence, and come to me at Boodle's.°
    Exit Dick
    If I cannot otherwise succeed, I'll beguile her as Jove did Alcmena, in the shape of her husband.° The possession of so fine a woman— the triumph over Saville—are each a sufficient motive; united, they 105 shall be resistless.
    Exit

3.3

The street
Enter Saville

SAVILLE The air has recovered me! What have I been doing? Perhaps my petulance may be the cause of *her* ruin whose honour I asserted. His vanity is piqued; and where women are concerned, Courtall can be a villain.

Enter Dick. Bows, and passes hastily
Ha! that's his servant!—Dick!

DICK (*returning*) Sir.

SAVILLE Where are you going, Dick?

DICK Going! I am going, sir, where my master sent me.

SAVILLE Well answered. But I have a particular reason for my enquiry, and you must tell me.

DICK Why then, sir, I am going to call upon a cousin of mine that lives at Sir George Touchwood's.

SAVILLE Very well. There. (*Gives him money*) You must make your cousin drink my health. What are you going about?

DICK Why, sir, I believe 'tis no harm, or elseways I am sure I would not blab. I am only going to ax° if Sir George goes to the masquerade tonight and what dress he wears.

SAVILLE Enough! Now, Dick, if you will call at my lodgings in your way back and acquaint me with your cousin's intelligence, I'll double the trifle I have given you.

DICK Bless your honour, I'll call. Never fear.

Exit Dick

SAVILLE Surely the occasion may justify the means. 'Tis doubly my duty to be Lady Frances's protector. Courtall, I see, is planning an artful scheme; but Saville shall out-plot him.

Exit

3.4

Sir George Touchwood's
Enter Sir George and Villers

VILLERS For shame, Sir George! You have left Lady Frances in tears. How can you afflict her?

SIR GEORGE 'Tis I that am afflicted; my dream of happiness is over. Lady Frances and I are disunited.

VILLERS The devil! Why, you have been in town but ten days; she can have made no acquaintance for a Commons affair° yet.

SIR GEORGE Foh! 'Tis our minds that are disunited; she no longer places her whole delight in me. She has yielded herself up to the world!

VILLERS Yielded herself up to the world! Why did you not bring her to town in a cage? Then she might have taken a peep at the world!

But, after all, what has the world done? A twelvemonth since, you was the gayest fellow in it. If anybody asked who dresses best?—Sir George Touchwood.—Who is the most gallant man?—Sir George Touchwood.—Who is the most wedded to amusement and dissipation?—Sir George Touchwood. And now Sir George is metamorphosed into a sour censor, and talks of fashionable life with as much bitterness as the old crabbed fellow in Rome.°

SIR GEORGE The moment I became possessed of such a jewel as Lady Frances, everything wore a different complexion. That society in which I lived with so much *éclat* became the object of my terror, and I think of the manners of polite life as I do of the atmosphere of a pesthouse. My wife is already infected; she was set upon this morning by maids, widows, and bachelors, who carried her off in triumph in spite of my displeasure.

VILLERS Aye, to be sure; there would have been no triumph in the case if you had not opposed it. But I have heard the whole story from Mrs Racket; and I assure you Lady Frances didn't enjoy the morning at all; she wished for you fifty times.

SIR GEORGE Indeed! Are you sure of that?

VILLERS Perfectly sure.

SIR GEORGE I wish I had known it. My uneasiness at dinner was occasioned by very different ideas.

VILLERS Here then she comes to receive your apology. But if she is true woman, her displeasure will rise in proportion to your contrition, and till you grow careless about her pardon, she won't grant it. However, I'll leave you. Matrimonial duets are seldom set in the style I like.

Exit Villers. Enter Lady Frances

SIR GEORGE The sweet sorrow that glitters in these eyes I cannot bear. (*Embracing her*) Look cheerfully, you rogue.

LADY FRANCES I cannot look otherwise if you are pleased with me.

SIR GEORGE Well, Fanny, today you made your *entrée* in the fashionable world; tell me honestly the impressions you received.

LADY FRANCES Indeed, Sir George, I was so hurried from place to place that I had not time to find out what my impressions were.

SIR GEORGE That's the very spirit of the life you have chosen.

LADY FRANCES Everybody about me seemed happy; but everybody seemed in a hurry to be happy somewhere else.

SIR GEORGE And you like this?

LADY FRANCES One must like what the rest of the world likes.

SIR GEORGE Pernicious maxim!

LADY FRANCES But, my dear Sir George, you have not yet promised to go with me to the masquerade.

SIR GEORGE 'Twould be a shocking indecorum to be seen together, you know.

LADY FRANCES Oh, no! I asked Mrs Racket, and she told me we might be seen together at the masquerade without being laughed at.

SIR GEORGE Really?

LADY FRANCES Indeed, to tell you the truth, I could wish it was the fashion for married people to be inseparable, for I have more heart-felt satisfaction in fifteen minutes with you at my side than fifteen days of amusement could give me without you.

SIR GEORGE My sweet creature! How that confession charms me! Let us begin the fashion.

LADY FRANCES Oh, impossible! We should not gain a single proselyte, and you can't conceive what spiteful things would be said of us. At Kensington° today, a lady met us whom we saw at Court when we were presented; she lifted up her hands in amazement! 'Bless me!' said she to her companion, 'Here's Lady Frances without Sir Hurlo Thrumbo!° My dear Mrs Racket, consider what an important charge you have! For Heaven's sake take her home again or some enchanter on a flying dragon will descend and carry her off.' 'Oh,' said another, 'I dare say Lady Frances has a clue at her heel, like the peerless Rosamond;° her tender swain would never have trusted her so far without such a precaution.'

SIR GEORGE Heaven and earth! How shall innocence preserve its lustre amidst manners so corrupt! My dear Fanny, I feel a senti-ment for thee at this moment, tenderer than love, more animated than passion. I could weep over that purity, exposed to the sullying breath of fashion, and the *ton*, in whose latitudinary vortex Chastity herself can scarcely move unspotted.

Enter Gibson

GIBSON Your honour talked, I thought, something about going to the masquerade?

SIR GEORGE Well.

GIBSON Isn't it?—Hasn't your honour?—I thought your honour had forgot to order a dress.

LADY FRANCES Well considered, Gibson. Come, will you be Jew, Turk, or heretic; a Chinese emperor or a ballad-singer; a rake or a watchman?

SIR GEORGE Oh, neither, my love; I can't take the trouble to support a character.°

ADY FRANCES You'll wear a domino° then. I saw a pink domino
trimmed with blue at the shop where I bought my habit. Would you
like it?

IR GEORGE Anything, anything.   95

ADY FRANCES Then go about it directly, Gibson. A pink domino
trimmed with blue, and a hat of the same.—Come, you have not
seen my dress yet. It is most beautiful; I long to have it on.

  Exeunt Sir George and Lady Frances

IBSON A pink domino trimmed with blue, and a hat of the same.—
What the devil can it signify to Sally now what his dress is to be?   100
Surely the slut has not made an assignation to meet her master!

  Exit

4.1

A masquerade°
A party dancing cotillons° in front. A variety of [Masks] pass
and repass
Enter Folly on a hobby-horse,° with cap and bells°

MASK° Hey! Tom Fool!° What business have you here?

FOLLY What, sir! Affront a prince in his own dominions!

[Folly] struts off. [Enter Mountebank]

MOUNTEBANK Who'll buy my nostrums?° Who'll buy my nostrums?

MASK What are they?

[Masks] all come round [Mountebank]

MOUNTEBANK Different sorts, and for different customers. Here's a
liquor for ladies—it expels the rage of gaming° and gallantry.
Here's a pill for members of parliament—good to settle con-
sciences. Here's an eye-water for jealous husbands—it thickens the
visual membrane, through which they see too clearly. Here's a
decoction for the clergy—it never sits easy, if the patient has more
than one living.° Here's a draught for lawyers—a great promoter of
modesty. Here's a powder for projectors°—'twill rectify the fumes
of an empty stomach and dissipate their airy castles.

MASK Have you a nostrum that can give patience to young heirs whose
uncles and fathers are stout and healthy?

MOUNTEBANK Yes; and I have an infusion for creditors—it gives
resignation and humility when fine gentlemen break their promises
or plead their privilege.°

MASK Come along! I'll find you customers for your whole cargo.

Enter Hardy in the dress of Isaac Mendoza°

HARDY Why, isn't it a shame to see so many stout, well-built young
fellows masquerading and cutting *courantas°* here at home instead
of making the French cut capers to the tune of your cannon—or
sweating the Spaniards with an English *fandango*?° I foresee the end
of all this.

MASK Why, thou little testy Israelite! Back to Duke's Place,° and
preach your tribe into a subscription° for the good of the land on
whose milk and honey ye fatten. Where are your Joshuas and your
Gideons,° aye? What, all dwindled into stockbrokers, peddlars, and
ragmen?

HARDY No, not all. Some of us turn Christians, and by degrees grow

252

into all the privileges of Englishmen!° In the second generation we
are patriots, rebels, courtiers, and husbands. (*Puts his fingers to his
forehead*)°

 Two other Masks advance

THIRD MASK What, my little Isaac! How the devil came you here?
Where's your old Margaret?° 35

HARDY Oh, I have got rid of her.

THIRD MASK How?

HARDY Why, I persuaded a young Irishman that she was a blooming plump beauty of eighteen; so they made an elopement. Ha,
ha, ha! And she is now the toast of Tipperary.° [*Aside*] Ha! 40
There's cousin Racket and her party. They shan't know me. (*Puts
on his mask*)

 Enter Mrs Racket, Lady Frances, Sir George, and Flutter

MRS RACKET Look at this dumpling° Jew! He must be a Levite° by his
figure. You have surely practised the flesh-hook° a long time,
friend, to have raised that goodly presence. 45

HARDY About as long, my brisk widow, as you have been angling for a
second husband. But my hook has been better baited than yours—
you have caught only gudgeons,° I see. (*Pointing to Flutter*)

FLUTTER Oh! This is one of the geniuses they hire to entertain the
company with their *accidental*° sallies. Let me look at your com- 50
monplace book,° friend; I want a few good things.

HARDY I'd oblige you, with all my heart, but you'll spoil them in
repeating; or, if you should not, they'll gain you no reputation, for
nobody will believe they are your own.

SIR GEORGE He knows ye, Flutter. The little gentleman fancies 55
himself a wit, I see.

HARDY There's no depending on what *you* see; the eyes of the jealous
are not to be trusted. Look to your lady.

FLUTTER He knows ye, Sir George.

SIR GEORGE (*aside*) What! Am I the town talk? 60

HARDY [*aside*] I can neither see Doricourt nor Letty. I must find them
out.

 Exit Hardy

MRS RACKET Well, Lady Frances, is not all this charming? Could you
have conceived such a brilliant assemblage of objects?°

LADY FRANCES Delightful! The days of enchantment are restored! 65
The columns glow with sapphires and rubies. Emperors and fairies,
beauties and dwarfs meet me at every stop.

SIR GEORGE How lively are first impressions on sensible minds! In

four hours, vapidity and languor will take place of that exquisite
sense of joy which flutters your little heart.   7

MRS RACKET What an inhuman creature! Fate has not allowed us these
sensations above ten times in our lives, and would you have us
shorten them by anticipation?

FLUTTER O lord! Your wise men are the greatest fools upon earth:
they reason about their enjoyments, and analyse their pleasures,   7
whilst the essence escapes. Look, Lady Frances! D'ye see that figure strutting in the dress of an emperor? His father retails oranges
in Botolph Lane.° That gypsy is a maid of honour,° and that
ragman a physician.

LADY FRANCES Why, you know everybody.   8

FLUTTER Oh, every creature. A mask is nothing at all to me. I can give
you the history of half the people here. In the next apartment
there's a whole family, who, to my knowledge, have lived on water-
cresses this month to make a figure here tonight; but, to make up
for that, they'll cram their pockets with cold ducks and chickens for   8
a carnival tomorrow.

LADY FRANCES Oh, I should like to see this provident family.

FLUTTER Honour me with your arm.
        Exeunt Flutter and Lady Frances

MRS RACKET Come, Sir George, you shall be *my* beau. We'll make the
tour of the rooms and meet them. Oh! Your pardon! You must   9
follow Lady Frances, or the wit and fine parts of Mr Flutter may
drive you out of her head. Ha, ha, ha!
        Exit Mrs Racket

SIR GEORGE I was going to follow her, and now I dare not. How can I
be such a fool as to be governed by the fear of that ridicule which
I despise!   95
        *Exit Sir George. Enter Doricourt, meeting a Mask [dressed as a
        Pilgrim]*

DORICOURT Ha! My lord! I thought you had been engaged at Westminster on this important night.

MASK So I am. I slipped out as soon as Lord Trope° got upon his legs.
I can badiner here an hour or two, and be back again before he is
down.°—There's a fine figure! I'll address her.   100
        Enter Letitia
Charity, fair lady. Charity for a poor pilgrim.

LETITIA Charity! If you mean my prayers, heaven grant thee wit,
pilgrim.

MASK That blessing would do from a devotee;° from you I ask other

charities, such charities as beauty should bestow: soft looks, sweet   105
words, and kind wishes.

LETITIA Alas! I am bankrupt of these, and forced to turn beggar
myself. [*Aside*] There he is! How shall I catch his attention?

MASK Will you grant me no favour?

LETITIA Yes, one: I'll make you my partner—not for life, but through   110
the soft mazes of a minuet. Dare you dance?

DORICOURT Some spirit in that.

MASK I dare do anything you command.

DORICOURT Do you know her, my lord?

MASK No. Such a woman as that would formerly have been known in   115
any disguise, but beauty is now common. Venus seems to have given
her cestus° to the whole sex.

A minuet. [*Letitia dances with the Mask*]

DORICOURT (*during the minuet*) She dances divinely.

When [*the dance has*] *ended,* [*exeunt Letitia and the Mask*]
Somebody must know her! Let us enquire who she is.

Exit Doricourt. Enter Saville [*dressed as a conjuror*]° *and Kitty*
Willis, habited like Lady Frances

SAVILLE I have seen Courtall in Sir George's habit, though he   120
endeavoured to keep himself concealed. Go and seat yourself in the
tea-room, and on no account discover your face. Remember too,
Kitty, that the woman you are to personate is a woman of virtue.

KITTY I am afraid I shall find that a difficult character. Indeed, I
believe, it is seldom kept up through a whole masquerade.   125

SAVILLE Of that, *you* can be no judge. Follow my directions and you
shall be rewarded.

Exit Kitty Willis. Enter Doricourt

DORICOURT Ha! Saville! Did you see a lady dance just now?

SAVILLE No.

DORICOURT Very odd. Nobody knows her.   130

SAVILLE Where is Miss Hardy?

DORICOURT Cutting watch-papers and making conundrums, I
suppose.

SAVILLE What do you mean?

DORICOURT Faith, I hardly know. She's not here, however, Mrs   135
Racket tells me. I asked no further.

SAVILLE Your indifference seems increased.

DORICOURT Quite the reverse; 'tis advanced thirty-two degrees
towards hatred.

SAVILLE You are jesting?   140

DORICOURT Then it must be with a very ill grace, my dear Saville, for I never felt so seriously. Do you know the creature's almost an idiot?

SAVILLE What?

DORICOURT An idiot. What the devil shall I do with her? Egad! I think I'll feign myself mad, and then Hardy will propose to cancel the engagements.

SAVILLE An excellent expedient. I must leave you; you are mysterious, and I can't stay to unravel ye. I came here to watch over innocence and beauty.

DORICOURT The guardian of innocence and beauty at three-and-twenty! Is there not a cloven foot° under that black gown, Saville?

SAVILLE No, faith. Courtall is here on a most detestable design. I found means to get a knowledge of the lady's dress° and have brought a girl to personate her whose reputation cannot be hurt. You shall know the result tomorrow. Adieu!

Exit Saville

DORICOURT (*musing*) Yes, I think that will do. I'll feign myself mad, see the doctor to pronounce me incurable, and when the parchments are destroyed—

As Doricourt stands in a musing posture, Letitia enters, [masked]

LETITIA (*sings*)°

> *Wake, thou son of Dullness, wake!*
> *From thy drowsy senses shake*
> *All the spells that Care employs,*
> *Cheating mortals of their joys.*
>
> *Light wingèd spirits, hither haste!*
> *Who prepare for mortal taste*
> *All the gifts that Pleasure sends,*
> *Every bliss that youth attends.*
>
> *Touch his feelings, rouse his soul,*
> *Whilst the sparkling moments roll.*
> *Bid them wake to new delight;*
> *Crown the magic of the night.*

DORICOURT By heaven, the same sweet creature!

LETITIA You have chosen an odd situation for study. Fashion and taste preside in this spot. They throw their spells around you; ten thousand delights spring up at their command. And you, a stoic, a being without senses, are rapt° in reflection.

256

DORICOURT And you, the most charming being in the world, awake me to admiration. Did you come from the stars?

LETITIA Yes, and I shall reascend in a moment.

DORICOURT Pray show me your face before you go. 180

LETITIA Beware of imprudent curiosity; it lost Paradise.

DORICOURT Eve's curiosity was raised by the devil; 'tis an angel tempts mine. So your allusion is not in point.°

LETITIA But *why* would you see my face?

DORICOURT To fall in love with it. 185

LETITIA And what then?

DORICOURT Why then—(*Aside*)—Aye, curse it! There's the rub.°

LETITIA Your mistress will be angry. But, perhaps, you have no mistress.

DORICOURT Yes, yes; and a sweet one it is! 190

LETITIA What! Is she old?

DORICOURT No.

LETITIA Ugly?

DORICOURT No.

LETITIA What then? 195

DORICOURT Foh! Don't talk about her, but show me your face.

LETITIA My vanity forbids it. 'Twould frighten you.

DORICOURT Impossible! Your shape is graceful, your air bewitching, your bosom transparent,° and your chin would tempt me to kiss it, if I did not see a pouting red lip above it, that demands— 200

LETITIA You grow too free.

DORICOURT Show me your face then. Only half a glance.

LETITIA Not for worlds.

DORICOURT What! You will have a little gentle force? (*Attempts to seize her mask*) 205

LETITIA I am gone forever.
        Exit [Letitia]

DORICOURT 'Tis false—I'll follow to the end.
        Exit [Doricourt.] [Enter] Flutter, Lady Frances, and Saville. They advance

LADY FRANCES How can you be thus interested° for a stranger?

SAVILLE Goodness will ever interest: its home is heaven; on earth, 'tis but a wanderer. Imprudent lady! Why have you left the side of your 210 protector? Where is your husband?

FLUTTER Why, what's that to him?

LADY FRANCES Surely it can't be merely his habit; there's something in him that awes me.

257

FLUTTER Foh! 'Tis only his grey beard. I know him; he keeps a lottery   215
office on Cornhill.°

SAVILLE My province, as an enchanter, lays open every secret to me.
Lady, there are dangers abroad. Beware!
    Exit [Saville]

LADY FRANCES 'Tis very odd. His manner has made me tremble. Let
us seek Sir George.   220

FLUTTER He is coming towards us.
    [Enter] Courtall, [who] comes forward, habited like Sir
    George

COURTALL [aside] There she is. If I can but disengage her from that
fool Flutter, crown me, ye schemers, with immortal wreaths!

LADY FRANCES Oh my dear Sir George! I rejoice to meet you! An old
conjuror has been frightening me with his prophecies. Where's   225
Mrs Racket?

COURTALL In the dancing room. I promised to send you to her, Mr
Flutter.

FLUTTER Ah, she wants me to dance. With all my heart.
    Exit [Flutter]

LADY FRANCES Why do you keep on your mask? 'Tis too warm.   230

COURTALL 'Tis very warm; I want air. Let us go.

LADY FRANCES You seem quite agitated. Shan't we bid our company
adieu?

COURTALL No, no; there's no time for forms. I'll just give directions to
the carriage and be with you in a moment. (*Going, steps back.*) Put   235
on your mask; I have a particular reason for it.
    Exit [Courtall.] [Enter] Saville with Kitty.

SAVILLE [aside to Kitty] Now, Kitty, you know your lesson.—Lady
Frances ([Saville] *takes off his mask*), let me lead you to your
husband.

LADY FRANCES Heavens! Is Mr Saville the conjuror? Sir George is   240
just stepped to the door to give directions. We are going home
immediately.

SAVILLE No, madam, you are deceived. Sir George is this way.

LADY FRANCES This is astonishing!

SAVILLE Be not alarmed. You have escaped a snare and shall be in   245
safety in a moment.
    Exeunt Saville and Lady Frances. Enter Courtall, who seizes
    Kitty's hand

COURTALL Now!

KITTY 'Tis pity to go so soon.

COURTALL Perhaps I may bring you back, my angel, but go now you
must.   250

    Exeunt [Courtall and Kitty Willis.] Music. [Enter] Doricourt
    and Letitia. [They] come forward

DORICOURT By heavens! I never was charmed till now. English
beauty—French vivacity—wit—elegance. Your name, my angel!
Tell me your name, though you persist in concealing your
face.

LETITIA My name has a spell in it.   255

DORICOURT I thought so; it must be *Charming*.

LETITIA But, if revealed, the charm is broke.

DORICOURT I'll answer for its force.

LETITIA Suppose it Harriet, or Charlotte, or Maria, or—

DORICOURT Hang Harriet, and Charlotte, and Maria! The name your   260
father gave ye!

LETITIA That can't be worth knowing; 'tis so transient a thing.

DORICOURT How, transient?

LETITIA Heaven forbid, my name should be *lasting* till° I am married.

DORICOURT Married! The chains of matrimony are too heavy and   265
vulgar for such a spirit as yours. The flowery wreaths of Cupid are
the only bands you should wear.

LETITIA They are the lightest, I believe, but 'tis possible to wear those
of marriage gracefully. Throw 'em loosely round, and twist 'em in a
true-lover's knot for the bosom.   270

DORICOURT An angel! But what will you be when a wife?

LETITIA A woman. If my husband should prove a churl, a fool, or a
tyrant, I'd break his heart, ruin his fortune, elope with the first
pretty fellow that asked me—and return the contempt of the world
with scorn, whilst my feelings preyed upon my life.   275

DORICOURT (*aside*) Amazing! [*To Letitia*] What if you loved him, and
he were worthy of your love?

LETITIA Why, then I'd be anything—and all! Grave, gay, capricious—
the soul of whim, the spirit of variety—live with him in the eye of
fashion, or in the shade of retirement—change my country, my sex,   280
feast with him in an Eskimo hut, or a Persian pavillion—join him in
the victorious war-dance on the borders of Lake Ontario, or sleep
to the soft breathings of the flute in the cinnamon groves of
Ceylon—dig with him in the mines of Golconda,° or enter the
dangerous precincts of the Mogul's° seraglio, cheat him° of his   285
wishes,° and overturn his empire to restore the husband of my
heart to the blessings of liberty and love.

DORICOURT Delightful wildness! Oh, to catch thee, and hold thee forever in this little cage! (*Attempting to clasp her*)

LETITIA Hold, sir! Though Cupid must give the bait that tempts me to   290
the snare, 'tis Hymen° must spread the net to catch me.

DORICOURT 'Tis in vain to assume airs of coldness. Fate has ordained you mine.

LETITIA How do you know?

DORICOURT I feel it *here*. I never met with a woman so perfectly to my   295
taste; and I won't believe it formed you so on purpose to tantalize me.

LETITIA (*aside*) This moment is worth a whole existence.

DORICOURT Come, show me your face, and rivet my chains.

LETITIA Tomorrow, you shall be satisfied.   300

DORICOURT Tomorrow! And not tonight?

LETITIA No.

DORICOURT Where then shall I wait on you tomorrow? Where see you?

LETITIA You shall see me in an hour when you least expect me.   305

DORICOURT Why all this mystery?

LETITIA I like to be mysterious. At present be content to know that I am a woman of family and fortune. Adieu!

    Enter Hardy

HARDY (*aside*) Adieu! Then I am come at the fag-end.

DORICOURT Let me see you to your carriage.   310

LETITIA As you value knowing me, stir not a step. If I am followed you never see me more.

    Exit [Letitia]

DORICOURT Barbarous creature! She's gone! What, and is this really serious? Am I in love? Foh! it can't be.

    Enter Flutter

Oh, Flutter, do you know that charming creature?   315

FLUTTER What charming creature? I passed a thousand.

DORICOURT She went out at that door, as you entered.

FLUTTER Oh, yes; I know her very well.

DORICOURT Do you, my dear fellow? Who?

FLUTTER She's kept by Lord George Jennet.°   320

HARDY (*aside*) Impudent scoundrel!

DORICOURT Kept!!!

FLUTTER Yes; Colonel Gorget° had her first, then Mr Loveill, then—I forget exactly how many—and at last she's Lord George's.

    [*Flutter*] *talks to other Masks*

DORICOURT I'll murder Gorget, poison Lord George, and shoot   325
myself.

HARDY [*aside*] Now's the time, I see, to clear up the whole. [*To Dori-court*] Mr Doricourt! I say, Flutter was mistaken; I know who you
are in love with.

DORICOURT [*aside*] A strange *rencontre*! [*To Hardy*] Who?   330

HARDY My Letty.

DORICOURT Oh! I understand your rebuke! 'Tis too soon, sir, to
assume the father-in-law.°

HARDY Zounds! What do you mean by that? I tell you that the lady
you admire is Letitia Hardy.   335

DORICOURT I am glad *you* are so well satisfied with the state of my
heart. I wish I was.
Exit [*Doricourt*]

HARDY Stop a moment. Stop, I say! What, you won't? Very well; if I
don't play you a trick for this, may I never be a grandfather! I'll plot
with Letty now, and not against her. Aye, hang me if I don't.   340
There's something in my head that shall tingle in his heart. He
shall have a lecture upon impatience that I foresee he'll be the
better for as long as he lives.
Exit [*Hardy*]. [*Enter*] *Saville* [*to Flutter and*] *other Masks*.
[*They come forward*]

SAVILLE Flutter, come with us. We're going to raise a laugh at
Courtall's.   345

FLUTTER With all my heart. 'Live to live', was my father's motto;
'Live to laugh', is mine.
[*Exeunt*]

4.2

Courtall's
Enter Kitty Willis and Courtall

KITTY Where have you brought me, Sir George? This is not our home.

COURTALL 'Tis *my* home, beautiful Lady Frances. (*Kneels, and takes
off his mask*) Oh, forgive the ardency of my passion, which has
compelled me to deceive you.

KITTY Mr Courtall! What will become of me?   5

COURTALL Oh, say but that you pardon the wretch who adores you.
Did you but know the agonizing tortures of my heart since I had

the felicity of conversing with you this morning—or the despair
that now—(*Knock*)

KITTY Oh! I'm undone!   10

COURTALL Zounds! My dear Lady Frances. [*Calling to Servant offstage*] I am not at home. Rascal! Do you hear? Let nobody in; I am
not at home.

SERVANT (*offstage*) Sir, I told the gentlemen so.

COURTALL Eternal curses! They are coming up. Step into this room,   15
adorable creature! *One* moment; I'll throw them out of the window
if they stay three.

> *Exit Kitty Willis, through the back scene.*° *Enter Saville, Flutter,
> and Masks*

FLUTTER Oh, Gemini!° Beg the petticoat's pardon. Just saw a corner
of it.

FIRST MASK No wonder admittance was so difficult. I thought you   20
took us for bailiffs.°

COURTALL Upon my soul, I am devilish glad to see you; but you
perceive how I am circumstanced. Excuse me at this moment.

SECOND MASK Tell us who 'tis then.

COURTALL Oh, fie!   25

FLUTTER We won't blab.

COURTALL I can't, upon honour. Thus far: she's a woman of the first
character and rank.—Saville, (*takes him aside*) have I influence, or
have I not?

SAVILLE Why, sure, you do not insinuate—   30

COURTALL No, not insinuate, but swear, that she's now in my bedchamber. By gad, I don't deceive you. There's generalship, you
rogue! Such an humble, distant, sighing fellow as thou art, at the
end of a six-months siege would have *boasted* of a kiss from her
glove. I only give the signal, and—pop!—she's in my arms.   35

SAVILLE What, Lady Fran—

COURTALL Hush! You shall see her name tomorrow morning in red
letters at the end of my list. [*Aloud, to the others*] Gentlemen, you
must excuse me now. Come and drink chocolate at twelve, but—

SAVILLE Aye, let us go, out of respect to the lady; 'tis a person of rank.   40

FLUTTER Is it? Then I'll have a peep at her. (*Runs to the door in the back
scene*)

COURTALL This is too much, sir. (*Trying to prevent him*)

FIRST MASK By Jupiter, we'll all have a peep.

COURTALL Gentlemen, consider—for heaven's sake—a lady of qual-   45
ity. What will be the consequences?

FLUTTER The consequences! Why, you'll have your throat cut, that's all; but I'll write your elegy. So, now for the door. (*Part opens the door, whilst the rest hold Courtall*) Beg your ladyship's pardon, whoever you are. (*Leads Kitty Willis out*) Emerge from darkness like the glorious sun, and bless the wondering circle with your charms. (*Takes off Kitty's mask*)   50

SAVILLE Kitty Willis! Ha, ha, ha!

ALL Kitty Willis! Ha, ha, ha! Kitty Willis!

FIRST MASK Why, what a fellow you are, Courtall, to attempt imposing on your friends in this manner! A lady of quality! An earl's daughter! [*To Kitty*] Your ladyship's most obedient. Ha, ha, ha!   55

SAVILLE Courtall, have you influence, or have you not?

FLUTTER The man's moonstruck.

COURTALL Hell, and ten thousand furies, seize you all together!   60

KITTY What! Me, too, Mr Courtall? Me, whom you have knelt to, prayed to, and adored?

FLUTTER That's right, Kitty; give him a little more.

COURTALL Disappointed and laughed at!

SAVILLE Laughed at and despised. I have fulfilled my design, which was to expose your villainy and laugh at your presumption. Adieu, sir! Remember how you again boast of your influence with women of rank, and when you next want amusement, dare not look up to the virtuous and to the noble for a companion.   65

    Exit Saville, leading Kitty Willis

FLUTTER And, Courtall, before you carry a lady into your bedchamber again, look under her mask, d'ye hear?   70

    Exeunt Flutter and Masks

COURTALL There's no bearing this! I'll set off for Paris directly.

    Exit

5.1

Hardy's
Enter Hardy and Villers

VILLERS Whimsical enough! Dying for her, and hates her; believes her a fool, and a woman of brilliant understanding!

HARDY As true as you are alive. But when I went up to him last night at the Pantheon, out of downright good nature to explain things, my gentleman whips round upon his heel and snapped me as short 5 as if I had been a beggarwoman with six children and he overseer of the parish.°

VILLERS Here comes the wonder-worker.

Enter Letitia

Here comes the enchantress who can go to masquerades and sing and dance and talk a man out of his wits!—But pray, have we morning 10 masquerades?°

LETITIA Oh, no; but I am so enamoured of this all-conquering habit that I could not resist putting it on the moment I had breakfasted. I shall wear it on the day I am married, and then lay it by in spices, like the miraculous robes of St Bridget.° 15

VILLERS That's as most brides do. The charms that helped to catch the husband are generally *laid by*, one after another, till the lady grows a downright wife, and then runs crying to her mother because she has transformed her *lover* into a downright husband. 20

HARDY Listen to me. I han't slept tonight for thinking of plots to plague Doricourt; and they drove one another out of my head so quick that I was as giddy as a goose and could make nothing of 'em. I wish to goodness you could contrive something.

VILLERS Contrive to plague him! Nothing so easy: don't undeceive 25 him, madam, till he is your husband. Marry him whilst he possesses the sentiments you laboured to give him of Miss Hardy; and when you are his wife—

LETITIA Oh, heavens! I see the whole! That's the very thing. My dear Mr Villers, you are the divinest man. 30

VILLERS Don't make love to me, hussy.

Enter Mrs Racket

MRS RACKET No, pray don't, for I design to have Villers myself in about six years. There's an oddity in him that pleases me. He holds

264

women in contempt; and I should like to have an opportunity of
breaking his heart for that.   35

VILLERS And when I am heartily tired of life, I know no woman whom
I would with more pleasure make my executioner.

HARDY It cannot be. I foresee it will be impossible to bring it about.
You know the wedding wasn't to take place this week or more, and
Letty will never be able to play the fool so long.   40

VILLERS The knot shall be tied tonight. I have it all here. (*Pointing to
his forehead*) The licence is ready. Feign yourself ill, send for
Doricourt, and tell him you can't go out of the world in peace
except° you see the ceremony performed.

HARDY I feign myself ill! I could as soon feign myself a Roman ambas-   45
sador. I was never ill in my life, but with the toothache. When
Letty's mother was a-breeding I had all the qualms.°

VILLERS Oh, I have no fears for *you*.°—But what says Miss Hardy?
Are you willing to make the irrevocable vow before night?

LETITIA Oh heavens!—I—I— 'tis so exceeding sudden, that   50
really—

MRS RACKET That really she is frightened out of her wits—lest it
should be impossible to bring matters about. But *I* have taken the
scheme into my protection, and you shall be Mrs Doricourt before
night. (*To Hardy*) Come, to bed directly. Your room shall be   55
crammed with phials° and all the apparatus of death; then hey
presto° for Doricourt!

VILLERS (*to Letitia*) You go and put off your conquering dress, and get
all your awkward airs ready. (*To Hardy*) And you practise a few
groans. (*To Mrs Racket*) And you—if possible—an air of gravity.   60
I'll answer for the plot.

LETITIA Married in jest! 'Tis an odd idea! Well, I'll venture it.
        Exeunt Letitia and Mrs Racket

VILLERS Aye, I'll be sworn! (*Looks at his watch*) 'Tis past three. The
budget's to be opened this morning.° I'll just step down to the
House. Will you go?   65

HARDY What! With a mortal sickness?

VILLERS What a blockhead!° I believe, if half of us were to stay away
with mortal sicknesses, it would be for the health of the nation.
Good morning. I'll call and feel your pulse as I come back.
        Exit [Villers]

HARDY You won't find 'em° over brisk, I fancy. I foresee some ill   70
happening from this making believe to die before one's time. But
hang it! A-hem! I am a stout man yet; only fifty-six. What's that? In

the last yearly bill° there were three lived to above an hundred. Fifty-six! Fiddle-de-dee! I am not afraid, not I.

Exit

5.2

Doricourt's
Doricourt in his robe-de-chambre. Enter Saville

SAVILLE Undressed so late?

DORICOURT I didn't go to bed till late. 'Twas late before I slept, late when I rose. Do you know Lord George Jennet?

SAVILLE Yes.

DORICOURT Has he a mistress?   5

SAVILLE Yes.

DORICOURT What sort of creature is she?

SAVILLE Why, she spends him three thousand a year with the ease of a duchess and entertains his friends with the grace of a Ninon.° Ergo, she is handsome, spirited, and clever.   10

Doricourt walks about disordered

In the name of caprice,° what ails you?

DORICOURT You have hit it: *Elle est mon caprice.*° The mistress of Lord George Jennet is my caprice—oh, insufferable!

SAVILLE What, you saw her at the masquerade?

DORICOURT *Saw* her, *loved* her, *died* for her—without knowing her.   15
And now the curse is, I can't hate her.

SAVILLE Ridiculous enough! All this distress about a kept woman, whom any man may have, I dare swear, in a fortnight. They've been jarring° some time.

DORICOURT Have her! The sentiment I have conceived for the witch is   20
so unaccountable that, in that line, I cannot bear her idea.° Was she a woman of honour, for a wife I could adore her; but, I really believe, if she should send me an assignation, I should hate her.

SAVILLE Hey-day! This sounds like love. What becomes of poor Miss Hardy?   25

DORICOURT Her name has given me an ague. Dear Saville, how shall I contrive to make old Hardy cancel the engagements! The moiety of the estate which he will forfeit shall be his the next moment by deed of gift.

SAVILLE Let me see. . . . Can't you get it insinuated that you are a   30

devilish wild fellow, that you are an infidel, and attached to wenching, gaming, and so forth?

DORICOURT Aye, such a character might have done some good two
centuries back, but who the devil can it frighten now? I believe it
must be the mad scheme, at last.—There, will that do for the grin?   35

SAVILLE Ridiculous! But, how are you certain that the woman who has
so bewildered you belongs to Lord George?

DORICOURT Flutter told me so.

SAVILLE Then fifty to one against the intelligence.

DORICOURT It must be so. There was a mystery in her manner   40
for which nothing else can account. (*A violent rap*) Who can this
be?

    Saville looks out

SAVILLE The proverb° is your answer: 'tis Flutter himself. Tip him a
scene of the madman and see how it takes.

DORICOURT I will—a good way to send it about town. Shall it be of   45
the melancholy kind, or the raving?

SAVILLE Rant! Rant!—Here he comes.

DORICOURT Talk not to me who can pull comets by the beard, and
overset an island!

    Enter Flutter

There! This is he! This is he who hath sent my poor soul, without   50
coat or breeches, to be tossed about in ether° like a duck feather!
[*To Flutter*] Villain, give me my soul again!

FLUTTER (*exceedingly frightened*) Upon my soul, I haven't got it.

SAVILLE Oh, Mr Flutter, what a melancholy sight! I little thought to
have seen my poor friend reduced to this.   55

FLUTTER Mercy defend me! What's° he mad?

SAVILLE You see how it is. A cursed Italian lady, jealousy, gave him a
drug, and every full of the moon—

DORICOURT Moon! Who dares to talk of the moon? The patroness of
genius, the rectifier of wits, the—oh! Here she is!—I feel her—she   60
tugs at my brain—she has it—she has it—oh!

    Exit [Doricourt]

FLUTTER Well! This is dreadful! Exceeding dreadful, I protest. Have
you had Monro?°

SAVILLE Not yet. The worthy Miss Hardy—what a misfortune!

FLUTTER Aye, very true. Do they know it?   65

SAVILLE Oh, no; the paroxysm seized him but this morning.

FLUTTER Adieu! I can't stay. (*Going in great haste*)

SAVILLE But you must. (*Holding Flutter*) Stay, and assist me. Perhaps

he'll return again in a moment, and when he is in this way, his
strength is prodigious.

FLUTTER Can't indeed—can't upon my soul. [*Going*]°

SAVILLE Flutter—don't make a mistake, now! Remember, 'tis
Doricourt that's mad.

FLUTTER [*Going*] Yes—you mad.

SAVILLE No, no; Doricourt.

FLUTTER Egad, I'll say you are both mad, and then I can't mistake.
   Exeunt severally

5.3

Sir George Touchwood's
Enter Sir George and Lady Frances

SIR GEORGE The bird is escaped: Courtall is gone to France.

LADY FRANCES Heaven and earth! Have ye been to seek him?

SIR GEORGE Seek him? Aye.

LADY FRANCES How did you get his name? I should never have told it
you.

SIR GEORGE I learned it in the first coffee-house I entered. Everybody
is full of the story.

LADY FRANCES Thank heaven, he's gone! But I have a story for you:
the Hardy family are forming a plot upon your friend Doricourt,
and we are expected in the evening to assist.

SIR GEORGE With all my heart, my angel, but I can't stay to hear it
unfolded. They told me Mr Saville would be at home in half an
hour, and I am impatient to see him. The adventure of last night—

LADY FRANCES Think of it only with gratitude. The danger I was in
has overset a new system of conduct that, perhaps, I was too much
inclined to adopt. But henceforward, my dear Sir George, you shall
be my constant companion and protector. And, when they ridicule
the unfashionable monsters, the felicity of our hearts shall make
their satire pointless.

SIR GEORGE Charming angel! You almost reconcile me to Courtall.
Hark! Here's company. (*Stepping to the door*) 'Tis your lively widow.
I'll step down the backstairs to escape her.
   Exit Sir George. Enter Mrs Racket

MRS RACKET Oh, Lady Frances! I am shocked to death.—Have you
received a card° from us?

LADY FRANCES Yes; within these twenty minutes.   25

MRS RACKET Aye, 'tis of no consequence. 'Tis all over: Doricourt is mad.

LADY FRANCES Mad!

MRS RACKET My poor Letitia! Just as we were enjoying ourselves with the prospect of a scheme that was planned for their mutual happiness, in came Flutter, breathless, with the intelligence. I flew here to know if you had heard it.   30

LADY FRANCES No, indeed; and I hope it is one of Mr Flutter's dreams.

Enter Saville

Apropos, now we shall be informed.—Mr Saville, I rejoice to see you, though Sir George will be disappointed; he's gone to your lodgings.   35

SAVILLE I should have been happy to have prevented Sir George. I hope your ladyship's adventure last night did not disturb your dreams?

LADY FRANCES Not at all, for I never slept a moment. My escape, and the importance of my obligations to you, employed my thoughts. But we have just had shocking intelligence. Is it true that Doricourt is mad?   40

SAVILLE (*aside*) So, the business is done. [*To Lady Frances*] Madam, I am sorry to say that I have just been a melancholy witness of his ravings. He was in the height of a paroxysm.   45

MRS RACKET Oh, there can be no doubt of it. Flutter told us the whole history. Some Italian princess gave him a drug, in a box of sweetmeats, sent to him by her own page, and it renders him lunatic every month. Poor Miss Hardy! I never felt so much on any occasion in my life.   50

SAVILLE To soften your concern, I will inform you, madam, that Miss Hardy is less to be pitied than you imagine.

MRS RACKET Why so, sir?

SAVILLE 'Tis rather a delicate subject, but he did not love Miss Hardy.   55

MRS RACKET He did love Miss Hardy, sir, and would have been the happiest of men.

SAVILLE Pardon me, madam; his heart was not only free from that lady's chains, but absolutely captivated by another.

MRS RACKET No, sir, no. It was Miss Hardy who captivated him. She met him last night at the masquerade and charmed him in disguise. He professed the most violent passion for her, and a plan was laid, this evening, to cheat him into happiness.   60

SAVILLE Ha, ha, ha! Upon my soul, I must beg your pardon! I have not

eaten of the Italian princess's box of sweetmeats, sent by her own   65
page, and yet I am as mad as Doricourt. Ha, ha, ha!

MRS RACKET So it appears. What can all this mean?

SAVILLE Why, madam, he is at present in his perfect senses, but he'll
lose 'em in ten minutes, through joy. The madness was only a feint,
to avoid marrying Miss Hardy. Ha, ha, ha! I'll carry him the intelli-   70
gence directly. (*Going*)

MRS RACKET Not for worlds. I owe him revenge now for what he has
made us suffer. You must promise not to divulge a syllable I have
told you, and when Doricourt is summoned to Mr Hardy's, prevail
on him to come, madness and all.   75

LADY FRANCES Pray do. I should like to see him showing off, now I am
in the secret.

SAVILLE You must be obeyed, though 'tis inhuman to conceal his
happiness.

MRS RACKET I am going home, so I'll set you down at his lodgings and   80
acquaint you, by the way, with our whole scheme. *Allons!*

SAVILLE I attend you. (*Leading Mrs Racket out*)

MRS RACKET [*to Lady Frances*] You won't fail us?
    Exeunt Saville and Mrs Racket

LADY FRANCES [*calling after Saville and Mrs Racket*] No; depend on
us.   85
    Exit

5.4

Doricourt's
Doricourt seated, reading

DORICOURT (*flings away the book*) What effect can the morals of fourscore have on a mind torn with passion? (*Musing*) Is it possible such
a soul as hers can support itself in so humiliating a situation? A
kept woman! (*Rising*) Well, well, I am glad it is so; I am glad it is so!
    Enter Saville

SAVILLE What a happy dog you are, Doricourt! I might have been mad   5
or beggared or pistoled myself, without its being mentioned; but
you, forsooth, the whole female world is concerned for! I reported
the state of your brain to five different women: the lip of the first
trembled; the white bosom of the second heaved a sigh; the third
ejaculated, and turned her eye—to the glass; the fourth blessed   10

herself; and the fifth said, whilst she pinned a curl, 'Well, now, perhaps, he'll be an amusing companion. His native dullness was intolerable.'

DORICOURT Envy!° Sheer envy, by the smiles of Hebe!° There are not less than forty pair of the brightest eyes in town will drop crystals 15 when they hear of my misfortune.

SAVILLE Well, but I have news for you: poor Hardy is confined to his bed. They say he is going out of the world by the first post and he wants to give you his blessing.

DORICOURT Ill? So ill? I am sorry from my soul. He's a worthy little 20 fellow—if he had not the gift of foreseeing so strongly.

SAVILLE Well, you must go and take leave.

DORICOURT What! To act the lunatic in the dying man's chamber?

SAVILLE Exactly the thing, and will bring your business to a short issue, for his last commands must be that you are not to marry his 25 daughter.

DORICOURT That's true, by Jupiter! And yet, hang it, impose upon a poor fellow at so serious a moment? I can't do it.

SAVILLE You must, faith. I am answerable for your appearance, though it should be in a strait waistcoat.° He knows your situation and 30 seems the more desirous of an interview.

DORICOURT I don't like encountering Racket. She's an arch little devil and will discover the cheat.

SAVILLE There's a fellow! Cheated ninety-nine women, and now afraid of the hundredth. 35

DORICOURT And with reason—for that hundredth is a widow.

Exeunt

5.5

Hardy's
Enter Mrs Racket and Miss Ogle

MISS OGLE And so Miss Hardy is actually to be married tonight?

MRS RACKET If her fate does not deceive her. You are apprised of the scheme, and we hope it will succeed.

MISS OGLE (*aside*) Deuce take her! She's six years younger than I am. [*To Mrs Racket*] Is Mr Doricourt handsome? 5

MRS RACKET Handsome, generous, young, and rich. There's a husband for ye! Isn't he worth pulling caps for?°

MISS OGLE (*aside*) I' my conscience, the widow speaks as though she'd
give cap, ears, and all for him. [*To Mrs Racket*] I wonder you didn't
try to catch this wonderful man, Mrs Racket?   10

MRS RACKET Really, Miss Ogle, I had not time. Besides, when I marry,
so many stout young fellows will hang themselves that, out of
regard to society, in these sad times, I shall postpone it for a few
years. (*Aside*) This will cost her a new lace.° I heard it crack.
        Enter Sir George and Lady Frances

SIR GEORGE Well, here we are.—But where's the Knight of the   15
Woeful Countenance?°

MRS RACKET Here soon, I hope, for a woeful night it will be without
him.

SIR GEORGE Oh, fie! Do you condescend to pun?

MRS RACKET Why not? It requires genius to make a good pun; some   20
men of bright parts can't reach it. I know a lawyer who writes them
on the back of his briefs and says they are of great use in a dry
cause.°
        Enter Flutter

FLUTTER Here they come! Here they come! Their coach stopped as
mine drove off.   25

LADY FRANCES Then Miss Hardy's fate is at a crisis. She plays a
hazardous game, and I tremble for her.

SAVILLE (*offstage*) Come, let me guide you! This way, my poor friend!
Why are you so furious?

DORICOURT (*offstage*) The House of Death—to the House of Death!   30
        Enter Doricourt and Saville
Ah, this is the spot!

LADY FRANCES How wild and fiery he looks!

MISS OGLE Now, I think, he looks terrified.

FLUTTER Poor creature, how his eyes work!

MRS RACKET I never saw a madman before; let me examine him. Will   35
he bite?

SAVILLE Pray keep out of his reach, ladies. You don't know your
danger. He's like a wild cat, if a sudden thought seizes him.

SIR GEORGE You talk like a keeper of wild cats. How much do you
demand for showing the monster?   40

DORICOURT [*aside*] I don't like this. I must rouse their sensibility.
[*Aloud*] There! There she darts through the air in liquid flames!
Down again! Now I have her.—Oh, she burns, she scorches!—Oh,
she eats into my very heart!

ALL Ha, ha, ha!   45

MRS RACKET He sees the apparition of the wicked Italian princess.

FLUTTER Keep her highness fast, Doricourt.

MISS OGLE Give her a pinch, before you let her go.

DORICOURT I am laughed at!

MRS RACKET Laughed at? Aye, to be sure! Why, I could play the 50
madman better than you.—There! There she is! Now I have her!
Ha, ha, ha!

DORICOURT (*aside*) I knew that devil would discover me. [*Aloud*] I'll
leave the house. I'm covered with confusion. [*Going*]

SIR GEORGE Stay, sir. You must not go. 'Twas poorly done, Mr Dori- 55
court, to affect madness rather than fulfill your engagements.

DORICOURT Affect madness!—Saville, what can I do?

SAVILLE Since you are discovered, confess the whole.

MISS OGLE Aye, turn evidence° and save yourself.

DORICOURT Yes; since my designs have been so unaccountably dis- 60
covered, I will avow the whole. I cannot love Miss Hardy, and I will
never—

SAVILLE Hold, my dear Doricourt! Be not so rash. What will the
world say to such—

DORICOURT Damn the world! What will the world give me for the loss 65
of happiness? Must I sacrifice my peace to please the world?

SIR GEORGE Yes, everything, rather than be branded with dishonour.

LADY FRANCES Though *our* arguments should fail, there *is* a
pleader whom you surely cannot withstand: the dying Mr Hardy
supplicates you not to forsake his child. 70

    Enter Villers

VILLERS Mr Hardy requests you to grant him a moment's conversation, Mr Doricourt, though you should persist to send him
miserable to the grave. Let me conduct you to his chamber.

DORICOURT Oh, aye, anywhere. To the antipodes. To the moon. Carry
me, do with me what you will. 75

MRS RACKET Mortification and disappointment, then, are specifics in
a case of stubbornness.° [*Aside to Sir George, Lady Frances, Saville,
and Flutter*] I'll follow and let you know what passes.

    Exeunt Villers, Doricourt, Mrs Racket, and Miss Ogle

FLUTTER Ladies, ladies, have the charity to take me with you, that I
may make no blunder in repeating the story. 80

    Exit Flutter

LADY FRANCES Sir George, you don't know Mr Saville.

    Exit Lady Frances

SIR GEORGE Ten thousand pardons, but I will not pardon myself for not observing you. I have been with the utmost impatience at your door twice today.

SAVILLE I am much concerned you had so much trouble, Sir George.   8₅

SIR GEORGE Trouble! What a word! I hardly know how to address you; I am distressed beyond measure, and it is the highest proof of my opinion of your honour and the delicacy of your mind that I open my heart to you.

SAVILLE What has disturbed you, Sir George?   90

SIR GEORGE Your having preserved Lady Frances in so imminent a danger. Start not,° Saville. To protect Lady Frances was my right. You have wrested from me my dearest privilege.

SAVILLE I hardly know how to answer such a reproach. I cannot apologize for what I have done.   95

SIR GEORGE I do not mean to reproach you; I hardly know what I mean. There is one method by which you may restore peace to me: I cannot endure that my wife should be so infinitely indebted to any man who is less than my brother.

SAVILLE Pray explain yourself.   100

SIR GEORGE I have a sister, Saville, who is amiable, and you are worthy of her. I shall give her a commission to steal your heart, out of revenge for what you have done.

SAVILLE I am infinitely honoured, Sir George, but—

SIR GEORGE I cannot listen to a sentence which begins with so   105
unpromising a word. You must go with us into Hampshire, and, if you see each other with the eyes I do, your felicity will be complete. I know no one to whose heart I would so readily commit the care of my sister's happiness.

SAVILLE I will attend you to Hampshire with pleasure, but not on the   110
plan of retirement. Society has claims on Lady Frances that forbid it.

SIR GEORGE Claims, Saville!

SAVILLE Yes, claims. Lady Frances was born to be the ornament of courts. She is sufficiently alarmed not to wander beyond the reach   115
of her protector; and, from the British court, the most tenderly-anxious husband could not wish to banish his wife. Bid her keep in her eye the bright example who presides there,° the splendour of whose rank yields to the superior lustre of her virtue.

SIR GEORGE I allow the force of your argument. Now for intelligence!   120
Enter Mrs Racket, Lady Frances, and Flutter

MRS RACKET Oh, heavens! Do you know—

FLUTTER Let me tell the story. As soon as Doricourt—

274

MRS RACKET I protest you shan't. Said Mr Hardy—

FLUTTER No, 'twas Doricourt spoke first. Says he—No, 'twas the
parson. Says he— 125

MRS RACKET Stop his mouth, Sir George; he'll spoil the tale.

SIR GEORGE Never heed circumstances!° The result, the result!

MRS RACKET No, no; you shall have it in form. Mr Hardy performed
the sick man like an angel. He sat up in his bed and talked so
pathetically that the tears stood in Doricourt's eyes. 130

FLUTTER Aye, stood! They did not drop, but stood. I shall, in future,
be very exact. The parson seized the moment; you know, they never
miss an opportunity.

MRS RACKET 'Make haste,' said poor Doricourt. 'If I have time to
reflect, poor Hardy will die unhappy.' 135

FLUTTER They were got as far as 'the Day of Judgement',° when we
slipped out of the room.

SIR GEORGE Then, by this time, they must have reached 'amazement',° which, everybody knows, is the end of matrimony.

MRS RACKET Aye, the reverend fathers ended the service with that 140
word, prophetically, to teach the bride what a capricious monster a
husband is.

SIR GEORGE I rather think it was sarcastically, to prepare the bridegroom for the unreasonable humours and vagaries of his helpmate.

LADY FRANCES Here comes the bridegroom of tonight. 145

*Enter Doricourt and Villers. Villers whispers [to] Saville, who
goes out*

ALL Joy! Joy! Joy!

MISS OGLE If *he's* a sample of bridegrooms, keep me single! A younger
brother, from the funeral of his father, could not carry a more
fretful countenance.

FLUTTER Oh! Now he's melancholy mad, I suppose. 150

LADY FRANCES You do not consider the importance of the occasion.

VILLERS No, nor how shocking a thing it is for a man to be forced to
marry one woman whilst his heart is devoted to another.

MRS RACKET Well, now 'tis over, I confess to you, Mr Doricourt, I
think 'twas a most ridiculous piece of Quixotism, to give up the 155
happiness of a whole life to a man who perhaps has but a few
moments to be sensible of the sacrifice.

FLUTTER So it appeared to me. But, thought I, Mr Doricourt has
travelled; he knows best.

DORICOURT Zounds! Confusion! Did ye not all set upon me? Didn't 160
ye talk to me of honour—compassion—justice?

SIR GEORGE Very true. You have acted according to their dictates, and I hope the utmost felicity of the married state will reward you.

DORICOURT Never, Sir George! To felicity I bid adieu; but I will endeavour to be content. Where is my—must speak it—where is my *wife*?   165

Enter Letitia, masked, led by Saville

SAVILLE Mr Doricourt, this lady was pressing to be introduced to you.

DORICOURT (*starting*) Oh!

LETITIA I told you last night, you should see me at a time when you least expected me, and I have kept my promise.   170

VILLERS Whoever you are, madam, you could not have arrived at a happier moment. Mr Doricourt is just married.

LETITIA Married! Impossible! 'Tis but a few hours since he swore to me eternal love. I believed him, gave him up my virgin heart—and now! Ungrateful sex!   175

DORICOURT Your virgin heart! No, lady, my fate, thank heaven, yet wants that torture. Nothing but the conviction that you was another's could have made me think one moment of marriage to have saved the lives of half mankind. But this visit, madam, is as barbarous as unexpected. It is now my duty to forget you, which, spite of   180 your situation, I found difficult enough.

LETITIA My situation! What situation?

DORICOURT I must apologize for explaining it in this company, but, madam, I am not ignorant that you are the companion of Lord George Jennet—and this is the only circumstance that can give me   185 peace.

LETITIA I—a companion! Ridiculous pretence! No, sir, know, to your confusion, that my heart, my honour, my name is unspotted as hers you have married; my birth equal to your own, my fortune large— that, and my person, might have been yours. But, sir, farewell.   190 (*Going*)

DORICOURT Oh, stay a moment. [*To Flutter*] Rascal! Is she not—

FLUTTER Who, she? Oh, lord! No, 'twas quite a different person that I meant. I never saw that lady before.

DORICOURT Then, never shalt thou see her more. (*Shakes Flutter*)   195

MRS RACKET Have mercy upon the poor man! Heavens! He'll murder him.

DORICOURT Murder him! Yes, you, myself, and all mankind. Sir George—Saville—Villers—'twas you who pushed me on this precipice; 'tis you who have snatched from me joy, felicity, and life.   200

MRS RACKET There! Now, how well he acts the madman! This is

something like! I knew he would do it well enough when the time came.

DORICOURT Hard-hearted woman! Enjoy my ruin, riot in my wretchedness. 205

Hardy bursts in

HARDY This is too much. You are now the husband of my daughter; and how dare you show all this passion about another woman?

DORICOURT Alive again!

HARDY Alive! Aye, and merry! Here, wipe off the flour from my face. I was never in better health and spirits in my life. I foresaw 'twould 210 do. Why, my illness was only a fetch, man, to make you marry Letty.

DORICOURT It was? Base and ungenerous! Well, sir, you shall be gratified. The possession of my heart was no object either with you or your daughter. My fortune and name was all you desired, and these 215 I leave ye. My native England I shall quit, nor ever behold you more. But, lady, that in my exile I may have one consolation, grant me the favour you denied last night: let me behold all that mask conceals, that your whole image may be impressed on my heart and cheer my distant solitary hours. 220

LETITIA This is the most awful moment of my life. Oh, Doricourt, the slight action of taking off my mask stamps me the most blessed or miserable of women!

DORICOURT What can this mean? Reveal your face, I conjure you.

LETITIA Behold it. [*Unmasks*] 225

DORICOURT Rapture! Transport! Heaven!

FLUTTER Now for a touch of the happy madman.

VILLERS This scheme was mine.

LETITIA I will not allow that. This little stratagem arose from my disappointment in not having made the impression on you I 230 wished. The timidity of the English character threw a veil over me you could not penetrate. You have forced me to emerge in some measure from my natural reserve and to throw off the veil that hid me.

DORICOURT I am yet in a state of intoxication; I cannot answer you. 235 Speak on, sweet angel!

LETITIA You see I *can* be anything. Choose then my character; your taste shall fix it. Shall I be an *English* wife? Or, breaking from the bonds of nature and education, step forth to the world in all the captivating glare of foreign manners? 240

DORICOURT You shall be nothing but yourself; nothing can be

captivating that you are not. I will not wrong your penetration by pretending that you won my heart at the first interview, but you have now my whole soul. Your person, your face, your mind, I would not exchange for those of any other woman breathing.   245

HARDY A dog! How well he makes up for past flights! Cousin Racket, I wish you a good husband with all my heart. Mr Flutter, I'll believe every word you say this fortnight. Mr Villers, you and I have managed this to a T.° I never was so merry in my life. Gad, I believe I can dance. (*Footing*)   250

DORICOURT Charming, charming creature!

LETITIA Congratulate me, dear friends! Can you conceive my happiness?

HARDY No, congratulate me, for mine is the greatest.

FLUTTER No, congratulate me, that I have escaped with life, and give   255
me some sticking plaster.° This wild cat has torn the skin from my throat.

SIR GEORGE I expect to be among the first who are congratulated, for I have recovered one angel, while Doricourt has gained another.

HARDY Foh! Foh! Don't talk of angels; we shall be happier by half as   260
mortals. Come into the next room; I have ordered out every drop of my forty-eight,° and I'll invite the whole parish of St George's,° but what we'll drink it out°—except one dozen, which I shall keep under three double locks, for a certain christening, which I foresee will happen within this twelvemonth.   265

DORICOURT My charming bride! It was a strange perversion of taste that led me to consider the delicate timidity of your deportment as the mark of an uninformed mind or inelegant manners. I feel now it is to that innate modesty English husbands owe a felicity the married men of other nations are strangers to. It is a sacred veil to your   270
own charms; it is the surest bulwark to your husband's honour, and cursed be the hour—should it ever arrive—in which British ladies shall sacrifice to foreign graces the grace of modesty!

[*Exeunt*]

EPILOGUE°

Nay, cease, and hear me. I am come to scold.°
Whence this night's plaudits to a thought so old?°
To gain a lover, hid behind a mask!
What's new in that? Or where's the mighty task?
For instance, now, what Lady Bab or Grace°   5
E'er won a lover in her *natural* face?
Mistake me not: French red or blanching creams°
I stoop not to, for those are hackneyed themes.
The arts I mean are harder to detect,
Easier put on, and worn to more effect,   10
As thus:°
Do pride and envy, with their horrid lines,
Destroy th' effect of nature's sweet designs?
The mask of softness is at once applied,
And gentlest manners ornament the bride.   15

   Do thoughts too free inform the vestal's eye,°
Or point the glance, or warm the struggling sigh?
Not Dian's brows more rigid looks disclose,°
And virtue's blush appears where passion glows.

   And you, my gentle sirs, wear vizors too;   20
But here I'll strip you and expose to view
Your hidden features:—First I point at you.°
That well-stuffed waistcoat and that ruddy cheek,
That ample forehead and that skin so sleek
Point out good nature and a generous heart.   25
Tyrant! Stand forth and, conscious, own thy part:°
Thy wife, thy children, tremble in thy eye,
And peace is banished, when the father's nigh.

   Sure, 'tis enchantment! See, from every side
The masks fall off! In charity I hide   30
The monstrous features rushing to my view.
Fear not there, grandpapa—nor you—nor you:
For should I show your features to each other,
Not one amongst ye'd know his friend or brother.

'Tis plain, then, all the world, from youth to age,   35
Appear in masks. Here, only, on the stage,
You see us as we are. *Here* trust your eyes;
Our wish to please admits of no disguise.

EXPLANATORY NOTES

The following abbreviations are used in the notes:

BB	*The Busybody*
Belle	*The Belle's Stratagem*
Boaden	*The Private Correspondence of David Garrick*, ed. James Boaden (London, 1831)
Bowyer	John Wilson Bowyer, *The Celebrated Mrs Centlivre* (Durham, NC, 1952)
Castle	Terry Castle, *Masquerade and Civilization: The Carnivalesque in Eighteenth-Century Culture and Fiction* (Stanford, 1986)
Clark	Constance Clark, *Three Augustan Women Playwrights* (New York, 1986)
Clubs	John Timbs, *Clubs and Club Life in London* (London, 1899)
Dryden	James Kinsley (ed.), *The Poems and Fables of John Dryden* (Oxford, 1962)
Holland	Peter Holland, *The Ornament of Action: Text and Performance in Restoration Comedy* (Cambridge, 1979)
IM	*The Innocent Mistress*
LS	*The London Stage 1660–1800*, 5 parts in 11 vols. (Carbondale, Ill., 1960–8)
Morgan	Fidelis Morgan, *The Female Wits* (London, 1981)
Nicoll I	Allardyce Nicoll, *A History of Early Eighteenth Century Drama 1700–1750* (Cambridge, 1929)
Nicoll II	Allardyce Nicoll, *A History of Late Eighteenth Century Drama 1750–1800* (Cambridge, 1937)
OED	*Oxford English Dictionary* (Oxford, 1971)
Parlett	David Parlett, *The Oxford Guide to Card Games* (Oxford, 1990)
Parsons	Mrs Clement Parsons, *Garrick and his Circle* (London, 1906)
Rochester	David M. Vieth (ed.), *The Complete Poems of John Wilmot, Earl of Rochester* (New Haven, 1968)
s.d.	stage direction
Tilley	Morris Palmer Tilley (ed.), *A Dictionary of the Proverbs in England in the Sixteenth and Seventeenth Centuries* (Ann Arbor, 1950)
Timbs	John Timbs, *Curiosities of London* (London, 1885)
TT	*The Times*
Williams I	E. N. Williams, *Life in Georgian England* (London, 1962)
Williams II	Gordon Williams, *Dictionary of Sexual Language and Imagery in Shakespearean and Stuart Literature* (London, 1994)
Wilson	F. P. Wilson (ed.), *The Oxford Dictionary of English Proverbs* (3rd edn.: Oxford, 1970)

1697   Mary Pix, *The Innocent Mistress* (London, 1697)
1709   Susanna Centlivre, *The Busie Body* (London, 1709)
1780   Elizabeth Griffith, *The Times* (London, 1780)
1782   Hannah Cowley, *The Belle's Stratagem* (London, 1782)

Act, scene, and line references for quotations from Shakespeare's plays in the notes are taken from William Shakespeare, *The Complete Works*, ed. Alfred Harbage (Baltimore: Penguin Books, 1969). Biblical references are to *The Holy Bible, King James Version, 1611* (New York, 1974).

The Innocent Mistress

THE CHARACTERS OF THE PLAY

Beauclair: a man associated with beauty and light—a good name for a lover.

Wildlove: a rake.

Beaumont: although the name directly translated from the French would mean 'beautiful mountain', it also sounds like *'beau amant'*, or 'handsome lover'.

Lywell: 'Ly' is a variant of 'lie'. The name emphasizes this con artist's deceitful nature as well as his sexual proclivities.

Cheatall: a man who tries to cheat, but in fact is cheated by others.

Gentil: a servant who foppishly imitates the language and behaviour of the gentry.

Flywife: a name that indicates this character's past actions.

Bellinda: a name created by pairing two words for beautiful: the French *belle* and the Spanish *linda*.

Mrs: an abbreviation of 'mistress', a term of respect for a woman, married or unmarried. Therefore, 'Mrs Beauclair' refers to Sir Charles Beauclair's unmarried niece (or to his daughter, were he to have one), while the baronet's wife bears the title 'Lady Beauclair'.

Arabella: another name indicating the beauty of the character it designates.

Peggy: nickname for Margaret; a name for a hoydenish girl.

Eugenia: a servant whose name reflects her sympathies with those of good breeding or high birth (from Greek 'eu' 'well' and 'genes' 'born').

Dresswell: a servant whose skill at dressing is of service to her mistress (and perhaps herself, too).

Drawers: tapsters at a tavern.

PROLOGUE

Mr Motteux: Peter Anthony Motteux (1663–1718), a successful play-wright, lyricist, and friend of Pix. Among his works are: *Loves of Mars and Venus* (1696), a masque; *Beauty in Distress* (1698), a tragedy; *Farewel Folly; or The Younger the Wiser* (1705), a farce; and the libretto for *Thomyris, Queen of Scythia* (1707), an opera.

1 *This season*: IM was first performed in June 1697, a disadvantageous time of year to introduce a new play. When fashionable society abandoned London for the country in the summer, theatres had to scramble to find enough ticket-buyers to meet their costs. Motteux's prologue elaborates the kinds of gimmicks used by different theatres to draw audiences.

both houses: IM was staged at Lincoln's Inn Fields by Thomas Bet-terton's company; the rival company, under the management of Christo-pher Rich, mostly performed at Drury Lane. Rich also had the rights to the immense Dorset Garden opera house, but the opera house was mainly reserved for spectacles. See Edward A. Langhans, 'The Theatres', in Robert D. Hume (ed.), *The London Theatre World, 1660–1800* (Carbondale, Ill., 1980), 42–4.

5 *Like wary . . . weather gauge*: like a pilot struggling to gain an advantage over another ship by keeping to its windward side.

7–8 *Nay, we've had . . . but half pay*: because of the difficulties of attracting audiences and meeting expenses during the summer season, theatres would change their offerings more frequently, bring new pieces to the stage with less rehearsal, and cut actors' pay. Actors therefore would need to learn more parts more quickly while being paid less than during the autumn/winter season.

9 *scaling*: climbing.

9–10 *We've scaling . . . and stands*: this passage offers a perhaps parodic glimpse of the bizarre scenic spectaculars the theatres were beginning to offer their audiences. Trained animals and dancing furniture (probably rigged to descend from the fly space above the stage) were modest offerings compared to some of the outlandish flying machines and water effects the theatres were trying out. For more detailed information on scenic spec-tacle, see Colin Visser, 'Scenery and Technical Design', in Robert D. Hume (ed.), *The London Theatre World, 1660–1800* (Carbondale, Ill., 1980), 90–107.

11 *There . . . here*: the prologue compares Rich's theatres at Drury Lane and Dorset Gardens to Betterton's at Lincoln's Inn Fields. The implied slight on Rich's theatres is that although they can offer spectacular scen-ery and theatrical machinery, Betterton's company has the superior performers.

13 *The World i'th'Moon*: a play by Elkanah Settle, produced at Dorset

283

Garden in June 1697. The piece called for spectacular effects such as chariots let down from above and a hanging silver moon, nearly fourteen feet in diameter. See Clark, 319, 322.

14 *you*: the audience.

17 *pit*: the audience area immediately in front of the forestage. The speaker laments that, despite the lavish spectacles, the theatres cannot attract many audience members.

20 *For*: because.

reformation: although Jeremy Collier's famous tract, *A Short View of the Immorality and Profaneness of the English Stage*, was not published until 1698, one year after the first staging of *IM*, the public sentiment against the licentiousness of Restoration drama that culminated in Collier's piece was already growing. The speaker of the prologue takes a mocking approach to the attempts to reform the contemporary stage, noting that comedies that follow the tendency for reform cannot attract audiences.

22 *looser*: more wanton, immoral, or dissolute.

24 *Drawcansirs*: Drawcansir is the name of a blustering, bragging character in *The Rehearsal* (1672), a burlesque by George Villiers, Second Duke of Buckingham, Samuel Butler, Thomas Sprat, and Clifford Martin, that viciously parodies rhyming, heroic drama, such as that written by Dryden. Drawcansir is made to enter a battle in the last scene and kill all the combatants on both sides.

29 *tickled*: sensually pleased or titillated, with a pun on the secondary meaning: whipped or lashed.

30 *lard*: garnish, enrich as if with fat; make juicy and delicious.

31–2 *No lady . . . i'th'gallery stays*: refined ladies of quality in the boxes will not be offended by the comedy, but the lower-class, more licentious inhabitants of the galleries may be bored by the innocent performance.

40 *No bawdy . . . woman's play*: Restoration women playwrights, such as Aphra Behn and Delarivière Manley, were often deemed even more licentious than their male counterparts.

41 *doubt*: fear or suspect.

42 *a deal cut out*: the prologue implies that some of the play's more risqué elements may have been cut by managers or actors who feared the reaction of theatrical reformers.

44 *maimed*: a pun suggesting a comparison between the censored text and a sexually incapacitated male spectator.

47 *Twice . . . usage found*: Mary Pix's previous successes were *Ibrahim, the Thirteenth Emperour of the Turks* (1696), a tragedy, and *The Spanish Wives* (1696), a farce.

48 *changed her ground*: Pix's first two dramatic works, *Ibrahim* and *The*

284

Spanish Wives, were premièred at Drury Lane. *IM* marked her début at Lincoln's Inn Fields.

1.1.3 *Langoon*: a kind of white wine, named for the French town of its origin located on the Garonne River.

5 *collegian*: Sir Francis and Sir Charles were students together at the same Oxford or Cambridge college.

12 *kidney*: (figurative) temperament, nature.

16 *from*: away from.

19 *Then*: in addition.

22 *in troth*: truly, indeed.

23 *run the career*: run the course, pursue the path.

25 *what humour's*: what oddity is; what style of behaviour is.

29–30 *three sorts . . . uppermost*: three types can be grouped together and are the most predominant.

31 *jilts will*: harlots or strumpets who will.

34–5 *She's a degree modester, if not kind to each*: the kept mistress is a slightly more virtuous kind of whore than the jilt because she reserves herself for one man at a time.

36 *quality*: person of rank or high social position.

40 *coquette*: a flirt; a woman who trifles with the affections of men for the satisfaction of her own vanity.

treating: being regaled with food, drink, or other entertainment.

41 *park*: St James's Park.

Windsor: Windsor Castle, located in the countryside 21 miles west of London, has been a principal residence of the British royal family since the eleventh century and has been a popular excursion from London at least since the time of *IM*.

46 *cit*: London shopkeepers or tradesmen, from 'citizen'.

46–7 *take compassion*: marry her, thus relieving her desperate plight.

49 *beau*: *1697* reads 'beaux', but since the rest of the list is in the singular, I have corrected what I assume was a printer's error.

53 *keeper*: a man who supports or maintains a mistress.

56–7 *her remembrance*: the memory of her.

61 *colic*: griping pains in the abdomen, or the temperamental irritability that such discomfort causes.

69 *doubt*: fear.

75 *Venturewell*: the name denotes a man who made his fortune through successful business speculations.

78 *this two-legged thing, his son*: an allusion to the description of Achitophel's son in Dryden's *Absalom and Achitophel* (1681) as 'that unfeathered two-legged thing, a son' (line 170). Dryden drew on a biblical story from 2 Samuel to create a mock heroic epic satirizing the Earl of Shaftesbury (Achitophel) and his exploitation of the Popish Plot. Shaftesbury's son, like Arabella's guardian's son Cheatall, possesses his father's ambition but lacks his talent for scheming and manipulation.

79 *contested with 'em*: disputed with them; challenged their legal position.

85 *modestly*: a pun on 'modestly' both as (1) in a reserved manner; and (2) chastely. Sir Francis is suggesting that Sir Charles and Lady Beauclair do not get along and live together celibately; the marriage has not been consummated.

91 *Indies*: West Indies.

94 *Even*: an intensifier; exactly, precisely, 'just'.

   interest: personal profit.

95 *younger brother*: Sir Charles's elder brother was to inherit the family title and estate while he was to make his own way in the world.

   Since: after Sir Charles's marriage, his elder brother apparently died without children and Sir Charles inherited his estate.

104 *a handsome fellow*: being a handsome fellow.

106 *platonic mistress*: mistress with whom he shares a purely spiritual, not carnal, love.

110 *Mrs Beauclair*: see note to *IM*, 'The Characters of the Play'.

127 *entailed*: Spendall claims that as a result of specific legal action his family has taken regarding the descent of their property, he must eventually inherit his father's estate.

129 *leave*: stop.

138 *chocolate-house*: like a coffee-house, where men gathered for refreshment, conversation, and gambling, except its focus was the serving of the fashionable beverage of chocolate rather than coffee. Chocolate-houses and coffee-houses were forerunners of the later gentlemen's clubs. The most famous chocolate-house at the time *IM* was written was the Cocoa Tree.

143 *Mrs Bantum, the Indian woman*: non-fictional owner of a coffee-house near Guildhall.

147 *civil*: polite, courteous, decent.

153 *knight errant*: a knight of medieval romance who sought adventures, especially those that served fair ladies.

160 *of my side*: on my side.

163 *fell upon*: happened into the company of; also 'fall to' means start to eat. Mariamne became an eager devourer of romance.

167 *Scudéry's*: Mariamne is an *aficionado* of romance literature, the most prominent writer of which was Madeleine de Scudéry (1607–1701), whose best-known novels in English include *Artamenes, or the Grand Cyrus* (1653–5) and *Clelia: An excellent new Romance* (1661). In her tales of chivalry, the heroes are always handsome, strong, and gifted with poetic language, and the heroines are always beautiful and persecuted by tyrannical guardians and loathsome, unscrupulous suitors. Mariamne is a stock comic heroine who expects life to mirror romance.

169–70 *populous wilderness*: Beaumont mocks Mariamne by comparing her to heroines of romance who would have escaped parental tyranny by fleeing to a desolate landscape beyond civilization. Instead, Mariamne escapes to London where civilization itself hides her from prying eyes.

175 *Allons*: let us go.

1.2.1 *tuneful numbers*: lyrical verses.

4 S.D. *[and Betty]*: Betty's entrance is not marked in *1697*, but she is present in the scene. It is logical that she would enter when she shows Mrs Beauclair into the room.

6–7 *'My anxious hours . . . peace by day'*: no source has been found for this couplet. It may well be of Pix's own invention.

17 *Bedlam*: Hospital of St Mary of Bethlehem, rebuilt in 1676 near the London Wall and known as an asylum for the mentally ill.

ere this: *1697* prints 'o're this'. I have amended for sense.

32 *masked*: ladies of high rank had begun appearing in public masked as early as the reign of Elizabeth as a fashionable way to protect their faces from wind and the elements as well as from the bold glances of gallants. These vizard masks, which covered the whole face and were generally made of black velvet, came into more general use during the reign of Charles II. As Pepys records, high-ranking ladies began the custom of wearing masks to the theatre: 'Abroad with my wife by water to the Royall Theatre. . . . Here I saw my Lord Falconbridge, and his Lady, my Lady Mary Cromwell, who looks as well as I have known her, and well clad; but when the House began to fill she put on her vizard, and so kept it on all the play; which of late is become a great fashion among the ladies, which hides their whole face. So to the Exchange, to buy things with my wife; among others, a vizard for herself' (*The Diary of Samuel Pepys*, 12 June 1663). The vizard became popular for ladies to wear to the theatre, especially when a new comedy was being shown because it concealed their reactions to bawdiness on the stage; their blushing or their enjoyment could be kept private. As private masquerades began to gain popularity, the carnivalesque aspects of appearing masked began to become more prevalent, and masking became associated with sexual freedom. The fashion of appearing in public masked began to filter down from the social élite to those who wished to imitate them, including, and perhaps

especially, prostitutes, for whom the anonymity of the mask had decided benefits. One could not always easily tell whether a masked woman was a lady of quality or a prostitute for hire, and the uncertainty provided a good deal of titillation. Prostitutes in masks became so common that the epithet 'vizard' became synonymous with '*bona roba*'. For more on the custom of appearing masked see William B. Boulton, *The Amusements of Old London* (London, 1901), 82–91; Montague Summers, *The Restoration Theatre* (New York, 1964), 85–91; and Castle.

36 *generously*: genteelly.

38 *wait upon me*: pay his respects to me.

39 *nicely*: punctiliously.

52–3 *thought to have stood the fairest pattern of my sex*: believed I would have held fast to being an impeccable example of the most scrupulous female behaviour.

53 *blotted*: wiped out.

63 *relation*: story.

72 *little more*: an odd construction, apparently meaning 'a few more'.

74 *Flywife*: the gentleman has chosen an odd pseudonym that reveals what he is trying to hide: that he has run away from his wife.

81 *Cassandra rules*: Cassandra, the daughter of Priam of Troy, was a chaste prophetess who rejected the advances of Apollo. Apollo took his revenge by making no one believe her prophecies. Mrs Beauclair suggests that Bellinda and Sir Charles, with their platonic affection, imitate Cassandra's strict chastity.

84 *rambler*: rake.

89–90 *comely as rising day . . . eminently known*: Mrs Beauclair quotes from Thomas Otway's tragedy, *The Orphan* (1680). In Otway's play, the despairing heroine, Monimia, seeks her husband, whom she calls 'My wishes' lord, comely as rising day; | Amidst ten thousand eminently known' (5.197–8).

91 *heroic*: heroic verse; in this case, two lines of high-flown iambic pentameter.

96 *Cousin*: used as a generic term for collateral kin, niece or nephew.

97 *abroad*: out of doors.

101 *MRS BEAUCLAIR*: in *1697* this speech is mistakenly ascribed to Bellinda.

104 *conduct*: safe-conduct; guidance of one safely or blamelessly.

105 *extend innocent favours*: exaggerate polite social intercourse in order to suggest greater intimacy than exists.

109 *wildest*: although *1697* prints this word as 'mildest', the sense of the line suggests that this is a typographical error.

126 *hospital*: a charitable institution.

133 *she-wit*: a woman of intellect or cleverness.

blazing star: comet.

137 *adroit*: clever; to the point.

had like to: had almost, were in danger of.

137–8 *had like to have hanged yourself ?*: 1698 reads 'had like to hanged yourself.' Edited for grammatical sense.

140 *take pet*: take offence and become ill-humoured or sulky.

145 *assembly*: the company assembled.

146 *Stuff*: nonsense; rubbish.

151 *Court*: Sir Charles could be referring to any of three possible royal households: Whitehall had been the official residence of the Stuart monarchs, but since William III found its location irritated his asthma, he and Mary II (d. 1694) spent little time there. Kensington House (later called Kensington Palace) became their preferred residence, but they also held occasional councils at St James's Palace. (After Whitehall burnt to the ground in 1698, St James's Palace became the official Court.) Official Court functions were open only to persons of high social rank (such as Sir Charles), foreign statesmen and their guests, but at Whitehall anyone appropriately dressed could stand in the stone gallery of the palace to watch the king pass. Additionally, visitors to Kensington might walk and meet in its fine gardens. William III would hold *levées* in the morning, at which time foreign dignitaries and other men of high rank might be presented to him, but, due to William III's sober tastes, these were sparsely attended compared to the *levées* of other monarchs. Evening Court assemblies consisted mostly of card playing, gossip, seeing and being seen. For further description of the social gatherings at the Court of William III, see Abel Boyer (ed.), *Letters of Wit, Politics and Morality* (London, 1701), 210–15 (reprinted with an introduction by Holger M. Klein, Hildesheim, 1982).

155 *Tower*: the Tower of London, the famed fortress and prison. After the coronation of Charles II, parts of the Tower began to be open to visitors, many of whom were willing to pay a small fee to the Deputy-Keeper to see the king's new regalia. The Tower continued to serve as a prison until 1820. (See Charles G. Harper, *The Tower of London: Fortress, Palace, and Prison* (London, 1909, pp. v–vi).) Sir Charles may be suggesting that Spendall tell Lady Beauclair that he is visiting at the Tower, or Sir Charles may be flippantly suggesting that he doesn't care if Spendall tells Lady Beauclair he has been sent to the Tower as a prisoner.

163 S.D. *Lywell*: the first edition reads, '*Enter Lady Lyewell*', but the list of characters in the play has only 'Lywell', and he is played by a Mr Freeman. I have therefore assumed that 'Lady' is an error and have altered the name accordingly.

289

166–7 *when I was in my Lord Worthy's family*: Lywell may mean either, 'when I was employed by Lord Worthy and lived in his household' or 'when I had gained the trust of Lord Worthy and had influence in his household'.

168 *crown*: a coin worth five shillings.

180 *perquisite*: profit; thing to which one has sole right.

1.3 S.D. [*Flywife's apartment*]: *1697* does not indicate a scene break or change here. The setting may well be the same as that described in *IM* 1.2 as Bellinda's apartment, a stock sitting-room. See 'Introduction', p. xvi and 'The Restoration and Eighteenth-Century Stages', p. lii n. 2, in this volume.

7–8 *refuse of Newgate*: discards from Newgate prison, sentenced to transportation to the West Indies.

11 *faith*: loyalty.

13 *portion*: dowry.

14 *forward*: precocious; presumptuous.

15–17 *bartering what . . . pleasure*: forfeiting my good name, which I had not the sense to value, by becoming someone's kept mistress.

26 *great*: intimate; good friends.

27 *Fubby*: Mrs Flywife's pet name for Flywife. It means 'short and squat'.

29–30 *'twas a courted favour*: in Jamaica, Mrs Flywife only dressed formally when Mr Flywife beseeched her to do so.

32–3 *spite of my oath and strong aversion*: Flywife had wished to remain in Jamaica and not return to England.

33 *high road of hell*: Flywife's opinion of the multiple temptations of London for an attractive woman.

35–6 *courted . . . lawful way*: wooed me to marry them.

38 *only on your protested love*: on the basis of the love you proclaimed for me. Mrs Flywife reveals that her relationship with Flywife was never formalized by a legal marriage.

40–1 *if you lived . . . believe you dead*: Flywife convinced Mrs Flywife that he could only live with her if his family in England believed him dead.

43 *your cargo was sunk so low*: you had so little money.

44 *topping*: garnish. Mrs Flywife could not have afforded any new fashionable item of dress arriving from London to repair her appearance and make her able to attract another man.

45 *lock for life*: marriage.

47 *a separate fortune*: Flywife made Mrs Flywife financially independent.

50–2 *Well, well . . . I will*: Mr and Mrs Flywife often engage in a kind of baby talk as love play.

56 *sackcloth*: a coarse material worn to display humility, penitence, or mourning.

64 *A sonnet*: Flywife first assumes he has discovered a sonnet written to his wife by a potential seducer.

65 *hand*: handwriting.

.1.10 *Never . . . . wife*: a popular song, possibly by Motteux. Airy, a character in Motteux's *Love's a Jest* (1696) is said to sing a song titled 'Never let her be your wife' (4.1), but the lyrics of the song are not quoted in full in the published edition, nor is credit given to a lyricist or composer. The song appears again in the work of another friend of Pix and Motteux, Catharine Trotter. In *Love at a Loss* (1701), Trotter has the character Beaumire sing, 'Wou'd you, wou'd you love the Nymph forever | Never, never, never, never, never let her be your wife.'

14 *make shift*: succeed with difficulty; bestir myself.

15 *tease*: irritate; annoy.

22–3 *Having no occasion . . . my pocket*: if he doesn't argue with her, there will no need to buy her an expensive present to make up.

31 *So seal it and carry it*: this order is directed to Jenny.

32 *post-house*: post office.

36 *Puggy*: Flywife's pet name for Mrs Flywife, a term of endearment for a woman or child.

2.2 S.D. *[Sir Charles Beauclair's house]*. *1697* records no defined scene break here. The text simply indicates that Mrs Flywife exits and Lady Beauclair and Cheatall enter. While it is possible that *1697* left out a scene change, it is also possible that the audience accepted the generic sitting-room as different locations depending upon who populated the scene. See 'Introduction', p. xvi, and 'The Restoration and Eighteenth-Century Stages', p. lii n. 2 See also Holland, 35–6.

3–4 *accessories have been hanged . . . principal*: Lady Beauclair would have her brother risk committing a rape even though those merely assisting or having foreknowledge of such a crime may be hanged for it.

5 *What*: an intensifier; 'I'll have you know.'

8 *necessaries*: Lady Beauclair is prone to malapropisms. Here she means 'niceties', mocking what she considers Cheatall's fastidious concern about committing a crime. She may also be confusing 'necessaries' with Cheatall's alarm about 'accessories'.

9 *the craft will be in catching, as the saying is*: the proverb to which Cheatall alludes is, 'All the craft is in the catching' (Tilley, 127).

10–11 *lily-white hand, as the poet has it*: Cheatall would seem to be misquoting, 'At ev'ry Turn, she made a little Stand, | And thrust among the Thorns her Lilly Hand' (Dryden, *Palamon and Arcite*, I. 191–2).

21–2 *Sir John Empty . . . Noisy*: the names indicate the characters of Peggy's suitors. They are empty-headed (if not empty-pocketed), gibbering fools.

27 *rout*: fuss. Lady Beauclair believes her daughter to be the observed of all observers.

31 *Mark the end on't*: observe how it turns out.

34 *citizen*: a tradesman (as opposed to a gentleman).

34–5 *Lord Mayor's son*: the Lord Mayor is still a tradesman despite his prosperity and position.

39 *this young fellow*: my current husband, Sir Charles Beauclair.

46 *primer*: a book for teaching children to read. Arabella mocks Peggy for her ignorance.

53 *horn-fair*: literally, a fair once held in Kent for the sale of horn goods, metaphorically, a reference to being made a cuckold. 'The summons to horn-fair' would be a proclamation of one's cuckoldry.

58 *chair*: a sedan chair.

64 *at our dispose*: under our management; at our disposal.

69 *corectors*: Lady Beauclair's malapropism for 'characters'.

75 *nor such as you are*: Lady Beauclair wishes to keep all beautiful young women away from her husband.

76 *vather-in-law*: Peggy refers to her stepfather. The substitution of the 'v' for the 'f' sound reveals her as a country girl from the south, probably Dorset.

85–6 *neither attendance nor conveniency*: neither servant to attend me nor sedan chair for me to travel in.

92 *Hug– Uggun–* : Lady Beauclair can't pronounce 'Eugenia', a name that means 'well-bred'.

94 *Flippant*: voluble, impertinent.

114 *leaw*: Lady Beauclair mispronounces 'law'.

119–20 *My injuries. . . my eyes*: the source for Cheatall's quotation or proverb has not been identified.

140 *Cobblecase*: the aptly named lawyer clumsily patches together his cases.

153 *make out*: demonstrate the truth of.

165–6 *Oh, give . . . . lips no more*: part of the fifth verse of a song from John Crowne's *The Married Beau* (1694), 2.1.412–13. *LS* records that the song is attributed to John Eccles (1668–1735), who also wrote original music for *IM*. Eccles originally composed songs for Rich's company but followed Betterton to Lincoln's Inn Fields.

168 *varses*: dialect for 'verses'.

173 *expose myself*: lay myself open to ridicule.

74 *madam*: the following song is described in *1697* as 'A Song by Mr ——'. The author has not been identified.

78 *Pastora*: name for a shepherdess; from pastoral.

folded: shut in their pen for the night.

79 *Her garland . . . scrip*: the stock accessories of a shepherdess: her wreath of flowers for her head, shepherd's staff, and small satchel.

81 *Loose*: unrestrained; laces untied.

undressed: unkempt; not fully or properly dressed.

82 *myrtle*: evergreen tree with white sweet-scented flowers, symbolic of love.

83 *conscious*: knowing; privy to secrets.

90 *contain*: restrain himself.

95 *humour*: this might be a misprint. In context the word that seems to have been meant is 'honour'. However, considering the tone of the song, the word 'humour', meaning 'whim', 'bent of disposition', might be meant as a deliberate slight on Pastora's honour.

97 *expiring*: playing on the contemporary double meaning of 'dying' = experiencing sexual climax.

200 *died away*: a continuation of the sexual joke.

201 *blessed*: Pastora is the understood subject of this verb.

209 *I han't seen him these two days*: this lie is part of Spendall's plan to win Lady Beauclair's confidence and free himself from suspicion that he is the source of the letter that is about to arrive.

210 *take up*: take myself in hand; start afresh.

222–3 *to go the ready way to lose 'em*: to take the most direct route to losing them.

229–30 *my— my Lady Beauclair*: Lady Beauclair can barely read.

Mrs Banter's . . . house: Lady Beauclair misreads 'Mrs Bantum's, The India House'.

240–1 *I've often told him his own with tears*: I've often told him, with tears in my eyes, the full, unpleasant truth about himself.

241 *forsworn*: denied.

247 *they'd watch and turn him back*: those at Mrs Bantum's would watch out for Sir Charles and prevent him from entering and encountering his wife.

271 *tuition*: custody; protection.

2.3 S.D. *St James's Park*: the transition from the stock drawing-room set to the specific scene of the real park was probably achieved by drawing apart the shutters that created the back wall of the room and revealing several pairs of shutters creating the park scene. A pair of open shutters painted with trees would provide a place for Bellinda and Sir Charles to withdraw to, and a pair of closed shutters further upstage and painted to resemble a real location in the park could create the impression of depth and open space. Such a scene would have been able to be used for many different plays. See 'The Restoration and Eighteenth-Century Stages', in this volume, p. lii n. 2.

10–11 *we'll be . . . the title*: possibly referring to the saying 'As merry as the maids'. Perhaps Mrs Beauclair leaves the phrase unfinished to tease her uncle about his platonic affair with Bellinda, or perhaps even to tease him about his celibate marriage. See Wilson, 527.

11 *sticks ahand*: comes readily to mind.

13 *Rosamond's Pond*: an oblong pond by the Long Avenue in St James's Park. Known as a place for lovers' suicides, it also figured as a site for romantic assignations in Restoration and early eighteenth-century dramas by such playwrights as Congreve, Otway, and Farquhar

27 *pickeer for a particular prize*: 'to pickeer' means to scout or to practise piracy as well as to skirmish playfully or amorously. There is a further pun on 'prize' as a ship captured at sea during war and as a token of victory or superiority.

29 *pinnace*: a small, light vessel, generally two-masted, and schooner-rigged; figuratively a mistress or prostitute. Mrs Beauclair continues the naval *double entendre* and teases Sir Francis with this gender reversal.

30 *freight*: more naval *double entendres*. 'Freight' refers to both the cargo of a ship and the weight of Sir Francis's body in an embrace.

33 *this hour*: it is too early for fashionable people to be strolling in the park. The fashionable time to be seen in St James's Park was after dinner.

34 *lady of quality*: woman of rank or high social position.

miss: a kept mistress.

36 *credit out*: credit exhausted.

37 *SIR FRANCIS*: in the first edition, this line is misassigned to Sir Charles, who has previously exited with Bellinda.

42 *side face*: profile.

46 *buds*: young women, who are about to blossom into female perfection, except, as Sir Francis goes on to complain, they are too virtuous.

56 *A match*: Agreed! Done!

57 *With arms across*: the conventional posture of a woebegone lover pleading with his mistress or lamenting in solitude.

81 *stays*: waits.

89–90 *accept my acknowledgement*: Sir Francis most likely gives her money for her service.

98–9 *as your affairs . . . the ceremony*: since you have so much business on your hands, you may well wish to omit these time-consuming courtesies.

2.4 S.D. *A house*: the downstage shutters probably closed on the park at this moment, returning the audience to the generic house scene.

7 *masks*: women wearing masks.

11 *shy*: cautiously reserved; chary.

14 *housed 'em*: saw them enter the house.

15 *Locket's*: a very fashionable tavern near Charing Cross, founded by Edward Locket in 1693, and celebrated by, among others, Susanna Centlivre, in the Prologue to *Love's Contrivances* (1703): 'At Locket's, Brown's, and at Pontack's enquire | What modish kickshaws the nice beaux desire, | What famed ragouts, what new invented sallad, | Has best pretensions to regain the palate.' Centlivre is said to have died on the premises in 1723 (*Clubs*, 441).

20 *the banquet o'er*: after their lovemaking.

3.1.8 *headclothes*: head covering or cap for wearing indoors.

15 *go snacks with*: share in, enjoy part of.

20 *writings of my estate*: legal documents controlling the ownership of my estate.

25 *let me alone*: trust me. Gentil is claiming a proprietary interest in Eugenia's affairs.

28–9 *cut my apron . . . bib on't*: an apron is a garment worn by an adult and a slobbering bib is a piece of cloth worn by a baby under its chin, to protect their clothes. Eugenia is saying that if she can't manage Cheatall she is no adult but a mere baby.

30 *ARABELLA*: this line is assigned to Gentil in the first edition, but in Eugenia's next speech she addresses the speaker of this line, referring to the scheme to make it appear that Cheatall has murdered 'ye', that is, Arabella. I have changed the assignment of the line to reflect the sense of Eugenia's speech.

32 *make all fast*: lock the room, make everything secure.

35 *Very indifferent*: the slightest of.

3.2.2 *Indian queen*: an allusion to the title character of the heroic drama of the same name (1664), by John Dryden and Robert Howard, punning on 'quean' (= whore). Mrs Flywife is the harlot from the Indies.

14 *as*: as if.

15 *look a needle in a bottle of hay*: proverbial; to engage in a hopeless search. A bottle of hay is a bundle of hay.

18 *for*: for being.

20 *Ah lard*: a fashionable distortion of 'Ah lord'. Searchwell imitates the affected pronunciation of a fop.

24 S.D. *Mrs Beauclair*: the first edition lists a non-existent Mrs Beaumont entering with the other characters. Clearly Mrs Beauclair was intended.

25 *regalo*: an elegant repast or entertainment (*OED*).

26 *Sir Charles*: Mrs Beauclair has a rather informal relationship with her uncle. Although she usually refers to him as 'sir' or 'uncle', in this scene she addresses him by name.

29–30 *are not so free of their company*: may not socialize with young men as freely as town ladies.

33 *summer season*: the season in which fashionable people abandon London for the country. It is also the season in which *IM* was first performed. See note to *IM*, Prologue 1.

41 *granting one . . . the rest*: granting that there exists one of these who is.

42 *power*: mental vigour, force of character; also power to attract men.

43 *consumption*: a wasting disease of the lungs; in this case the decay is emotionally induced by her longings for refined pleasures.

51 *thoughtful*: contemplative; absent-minded; melancholy.

52 *brisker*: more lively, also more pert or unpleasantly sharp-witted.

56 *Dryden*: John Dryden (1631–1700), one of the most renowned writers of poetry and prose in the late seventeenth century and a celebrated playwright. Dryden's eloquence shone in both comedy and tragedy in such plays as *The Indian Queen* (1664), *Marriage à la Mode* (1671), *The Spanish Friar* (1680), and *Amphitryon* (1690).

57 *Congreve*: William Congreve (1670–1729), given early encouragement by Dryden, became one of the best-known writers of Restoration comedy. Some of his most famous works are *The Old Bachelor* (1693), *Love for Love* (1695), and *The Way of the World* (1700). Congreve was devoted to the great comic actress Anne Bracegirdle, who played Mrs Beauclair in the original production of *IM*, and wrote some leading female roles in his comedies specifically for her.

64 *railing*: jesting; playfully mocking.

65 s.d. *[Enter Musicians and Singers]*: *1697* makes no mention of the entrance of either musicians or singers. The heading of the song given is 'A Song by Mrs P ——, sung by Mr Hodgson.' Mr Hodgson is the name of the actor who plays Mr Beaumont. *LS* (part 1, 481) records that the song is sung by a 'Mrs' Hodgson, another performer in Betterton's company. This would solve the problem of Mr Hodgson being both the entertainer and the entertained, but it does seem that this first song is sung by a man. *The Catalogue of Printed Music in the British Library* records that Pix herself wrote the lyrics to this song and Eccles (see note to *IM*, 2.2.165–6) composed the music.

75 *hug each apocryphal text*: cherish my false declarations of devotion.

77 s.d. *A dance*: there is no record as to whether this dance was performed by the characters or by the performers brought to entertain them.

18 *HE*: this song is described in *1697* as 'A DIALOGUE, BETWEEN TWO PLATONIC LOVERS: THE WORDS BY MR MOTTEUX, AND SET BY MR ECCLES.' According to the *Catalogue of Printed Music in the British Library* (vols. 18 and 60), the lyricist is Peter Motteux (see note to *IM*, Prologue) and the composer is Eccles, who also composed the previous song. It is not known who performed this song.

32 *Strephon*: name sometimes used by Restoration poets (Rochester among others) to speak of unfulfilled ardour or to be a spokesman for erotic inconstancy.

35 *improve*: become purer or more refined.

45 *linen*: linen clothes, specifically an undergarment or shirt.

51 *carriage*: conduct; behaviour.

55 *estate*: wealth; fortune.

one has fell: an estate or title, and the wealth accompanying it, has fallen into your possession.

60 *you have still commanded*: you always had, and continue to have, at your disposal.

64–5 *ugly black . . . for nothing*: Lady Beauclair's description of Shakespeare's *Othello*.

65 *Metride, King o' the Potecaries*: Lady Beauclair refers to *Mithridates, King of Pontus* (1678), a tragedy by Nathaniel Lee.

66 *Timon the Atheist*: Lady Beauclair incorrectly refers to Thomas Shadwell's *Timon of Athens* (1678), a reworking of Shakespeare's tragedy of the same name.

Man in the Moon: Lady Beauclair is most likely referring to *The Emperor of the Moon* (1687), a comedy-farce by Aphra Behn.

68–9 *shown yourself*: exposed your true colours.

74–5 *take such courses*: follow such ways of action; proceed in such a way.

75 *varsal*: ungenteel abbreviation of 'universal'; meaning 'whole, entire'.

202 *nicely jealous*: fastidiously concerned lest; overly fearful that.

3.3.5 *racks*: acute pains or sufferings.

9–10 *rising damps and falling dews*: sighs and tears.

20–1 *None but . . . boldness*: Morgan treats this line as an aside, and it is conceivable that it could be played as such. However, it is equally possible that Beaumont addresses it directly to Bellinda, who responds negatively, forcing Beaumont to present her with the picture as his evidence.

40 *upon the rack*: suffering intensely. A figurative reference to the pain caused by the instrument of torture, the rack.

49 *Tell*: *1697* records this word as 'Till'. Although Morgan retains this spelling, the syntax is very confusing. I have altered the spelling both for sense

and because Bellinda repeats several times, in this and her following speech, 'tell him', apparently referring back to an original, 'Tell that dear man.'

69 S.D. *Enter Gentil*: *1697* indicates that Searchwell enters here, but this would appear to be an error. Searchwell is involved with arranging Sir Francis Wildlove's assignation with Mrs Flywife, while Gentil is the one helping Eugenia to arrange Arabella's escape from Cheatall's mercenary grasp.

71 *Rarely*: splendidly.

3.4 In the *Errata* to the first edition of *IM*, the printer notes that his placement of this scene was incorrect, 'By a mistake in the Copy, which was false Folio'd, in the Scene in Sir Charles Beauclair's House ... should have came in in the latter part of the the third Act, which ends with,

CHEATALL Oh, that ever I should live to see my self hang'd.'

I find the printer's comments clear and consistent with the sense of the comedy, and so, as Fidelis Morgan did in an earlier edition of *IM*, I have followed the printer's instructions for the correct placement of the scene. Constance Clarke disputes Morgan's correction, saying that there is no proof of where this scene was placed, how it was staged, or what Pix's preferences were. My primary dispute with Morgan is that, although I understand her frustration with the plethora of printing errors in *1697*, she seems to suggest more errors than there are. See Morgan, 263–4 and Clark, 259.

22 *I doubt*: I suspect.

22–3 *speak one word . . . as the saying is*: a proverbial saying that first appears in a literary context in John Lacy's (1600–81) posthumously produced comedy, *Sir Hercules Buffoon* (1682). Innocentia, a provincial heiress, comments to her sophisticated and conniving cousin Fidelia, 'but I doubt, cousin, thou'll speak ean word for me, and twea for thyself' (5.4).

37 *merry*: slightly drunk; in the mood to make jokes (with the implication that the speaker is not).

39 *cargo*: burden, freight, weight.

40–1 *Am not I damnable ingenious*: Cheatall's wit is laboured rather than ingenious. He may perhaps be making a poor pun on 'cargo' as an arcane oath in itself (Shakespeare had Caliban use it in *The Tempest)* or he may be punning on 'lies' by suggesting that the strength of bullies is limited to their swearing, or that bullies' seeming strength is deceptive. Regardless of what he intends, Cheatall is alone in finding his efforts amusing.

41–2 *Live and learn . . . the saying is*: the proverb is 'One may live and learn, and be hang'd and forget all' (Wilson, 473).

43 *qualm*: a sudden feeling of sickness.

45 *the witch . . . ballad*: the witch whose image is displayed above the latest ballad. Broadside ballads, or simply broadsides, so called because they were printed on one side of a large folio sheet, were the equivalent of today's tabloid newspapers. These cheap publications, frequently decorated with woodcut prints, were used to spread accounts of lurid crimes, executions, sensational current events, and political propaganda among the general populace. Cheatall is referring to the illustration of a witch that preceded the text of the ballad on the most recent broadside. For more information on broadside ballads, see Leslie Shepard, *The Broadside Ballad: A Study in Origins and Meaning* (London, 1962).

65 *scattered my rough image*: left many illegitimate children.

74 *Kentish ague*: a type of illness associated with seafaring people, such as those of Kent on England's south-eastern coast. Perhaps a reference to a malarial fever found in sailors who had been to the tropics.

92 *hold laughing*: prevent myself from laughing.

93–4 *I cannot keep it!*: I must speak out; I cannot remain silent.

97–8 *All the water in the sea . . . stains out*: a parodic echo of *Macbeth*, 'Will all great Neptune's ocean wash this blood | Clean from my hand?' (*Macbeth* 2.2.58–9). In similar vein, the previous mention of 'at least a pailful of blood' may echo Lady Macbeth in the sleepwalking scene, 'Yet who would have thought the old man to have had so much blood in him?' (5.1.36–7).

10 *the first atoms that huddled up*: the tiniest particles that originally came together to form your body. Beaumont is trying to convey that he will unmake Cheatall; reduce him to the smallest primary particles of matter.

16 *What made him . . . to be denied*: Eugenia wonders why Cheatall denied Arabella was in the house when she was supposed to be there. Eugenia is suggesting Cheatall knew Arabella wasn't there because he murdered her.

49–50 *make it up*: reconcile matters; come up with a plan of action.

57–8 *quibble*: pun; play word games.

4.1.1 *cross*: obstinately contrary; perverse.

18 *put to an attorney*: apprenticed to a lawyer.

19 *to turn beau*: to turn myself into a beau.

20 *actions*: legal prosecutions for debt.

21 *sempstress*: seamstress.

peruke-maker: wig-maker.

hosier: one who sells or makes socks or woven undergarments.

24–5 *dressing up a fop*: dressing like a fop; providing the accoutrements which qualify a man as a fop.

25 *unwelcome*: *1697* reads 'unwelcoming'. Sense dictates the correction.

35 *The devil's in the dice today*: 'Everything is turning out unlucky for me today!'

54 *ordinaries*: public meals served at fixed prices at taverns or eating-houses.

Blue Posts: a fashionable tavern in the Haymarket.

62 *solacing*: entertaining.

69 *have*: should have.

76 *park*: St James's Park.

95 *Jacobite*: an adherent of James II and his descendants after his abdication in 1688. Such a political position was a dangerous one in 1697 since it was adversarial to the reigning monarch, William III, and his late wife, James II's daughter, Mary II.

113 *gang*: Sir Francis's fellow rakes.

116 *Good lack*: exclamation, meaning, 'Good Lord!'

canting sot: hypocritical fool or drunk.

118–21 *Trim tram . . . 'Like mistress, like maid'*: a parody of a rhyming jingle, 'Trim-tram, like master, like man', referring to the similar treatment of two people of different ranks.

4.2 S.D. *[Outside Mrs Beauclair's lodging]*: *1697* does not supply a location for this scene, but outside of Mrs Beauclair's lodging is the logical setting. Mrs Beauclair apparently does not live in her uncle's household.

S.D. *Mrs Beauclair*: *1697* has '*Mrs Beaumont*', a non-existent character.

11 *gave the maid the drop*: (slang), lost the maid; parted from the maid before she was aware.

4.3.10 *those green years*: your youth.

28 S.D. *(Mrs Beauclair puts up her ring)*: Mrs Beauclair shows Sir Francis her own ring.

34 *plastered*: vulgarly or excessively adorned. Mrs Beauclair refers to women Sir Francis pursues.

36–7 *the painted tribe*: the cosmetically enhanced; the prostitutes or fallen women of the town.

40 *loving*: flirting; love-making.

42 *unrig*: to undress; Mrs Beauclair wants to get rid of her male costume and reassume her own appearance. The sexual tension between Mrs Beauclair and Sir Francis, heightened by Mrs Beauclair's leg-revealing male garb, is further intensified as she calls attention to her inappropriate dress and announces her wish to remove her clothing.

4.4 S.D. *[Outside Mrs Beauclair's lodgings]*: Pix does not specify this scene location, but since Arabella, later on, in what is not designated as a new scene, observes that she is outside Mrs Beauclair's house, I have assumed that Spendall and Lywell are also conversing there.

3 *chymical*: alchemical; referring to the pursuit or science of transmuting base metals to gold; magic or mysterious illusion.

4 *projection*: alchemical term referring to the casting of the powder of the philosopher's stone into the crucible in which a base metal is in the process of being transmuted to gold.

9 *daughter-in-law*: stepdaughter.

14 *Templar's chamber*: barrister's chamber or office in the Inner or Middle Temple Inns of Court.

15 *long robe*: barrister or lawyer; referring to their official garb.

27 *lusty*: merry; tasty.

42 *your worship's . . . to direct*: your name is not sufficiently well known that, by giving it, someone would know how to direct me to your chambers.

49 *clutter*: turmoil; bustle; confusion.

4.5 S.D. *Temple*: one of two Inns of Court: the Middle Temple or the Inner Temple. The Temple extends from Fleet Street to the Thames and was originally the seat of the Order of Knights Templars.

2 *to boot*: in addition, as well.

4–5 *Coke upon Littleton*: one of the most important commentaries on British law. Sir Thomas Littleton (d. 1481) wrote *Les Tenures*, the basis of real property law in England. Sir Edward Coke (1551/2–1632) wrote *The Institutes of the Laws of England*, a four-part work, the first of which contains the 'Commentary on Littleton's Tenures' (1628), often called 'The Bible of the Law'. Coke was Attorney-General under Elizabeth I and knighted under James I. He also conducted the proceedings against Sir Walter Raleigh in 1603.

10 *with a wet finger*: old saying, meaning 'with the utmost ease' (Wilson, 881). Possibly deriving from wetting a finger to turn pages more easily.

15 *Zed*: dialect for 'said'.

15–16 *I'll vaw*: dialect for 'I'll vow'.

16 *waundily*: dialect for 'woundily'.

17 *not unfit for you*: who were suitable marriage prospects for you.

18 *never free you should be seen*: always strict about how and where you could be seen in public.

45 *such offers don't stick o' hand now-a-days*: such marriage proposals are not likely to remain available for long. Lywell is suggesting that if Peggy doesn't accept Spendall's offer quickly, he'll find someone else who will.

53 *Noverint, etc.*: the beginning of the opening phrase of a legal writ, meaning, 'Let all men know'.

54 *lay*: dialect for 'law'.

59–60 *I'd willingly . . . face will bear it*: Lady Beauclair asserts that her daughter's beauty is worth her husband's displaying in an expensive coach drawn by six horses.

69 *cannick hour*: canonical hour; hours between 8 a.m. and 3 p.m. during which time marriages could be performed at a parish church. There were places in London, such as within the precincts of Fleet prison, where clandestine marriage transactions could be made outside of canonical hours. The Marriage Act of 1753 sought to eliminate such ceremonies, which enabled fortune hunters of either sex to marry before their partner or their partner's parents had time to reflect.

76 *trinkets*: sweet foods, dainties.

4.6.3 *none*: (baby-talk) your own.

32 *some perdu devil of hers*: some hireling of hers set to spy for her.

4.7.19 *within*: in my heart.

5.1.25–6 *I am not to be moved . . . all pleasures*: I will neither be persuaded to change my mind about renouncing you (the most difficult sacrifice) nor about renouncing all other of life's lesser pleasures.

34–5 *the air*: enjoying the unpolluted country air.

35–6 *create new . . . country o'er*: feign friendships among the neighbouring gentry, claim as bosom acquaintances all the inhabitants of the county.

43 *fragrancy*: sweet smell of good repute.

44 *I do not use*: I am not accustomed to.

49 *not worth*: (understood) you behave as if I am not worth.

no regard of tenderness: no tender look.

72 *It is a guilty thought*: Bellinda has been suggesting that Lady Beauclair might die and that she and Sir Charles might then marry.

5.2.2–3 *a dose of rhubarb*: East Indian or Chinese rhubarb was used medicinally as a purgative.

3 *vaulter*: a performer, such as a tumbler, acrobat, or juggler, who jumps high.

9 *You leave me alone and*: i.e. if you leave me alone.

13 *the glimpse on't*: a flash of it; a brief glimmer of it.

21 *A full and true relation*: the boy offstage is pretending to hawk a new broadside ballad or pamphlet written about Cheatall's supposed murder of Arabella. In this case, the boy is clearly part of the plot to frighten Cheatall into believing he will be hanged for Arabella's murder. See note to *IM*, 3.4.45.

25–6 *Chelsea Reach*: Chelsea, on the north bank of the Thames, was a fashionable riverside community in the seventeenth and eighteenth centuries. A reach is a bay or harbour.

40 *Pin-up petticoats*: pinned-up petticoats.

43 *peach*: accuse formally; impeach; inform against (her) to the authorities.

49–50 *greasing in the fist*: a bribe.

53 *make her hands white*: turn her rough servant's hands into the smooth white hands of a lady.

54 *spark it with quality*: dress or display herself so that she may mix with those of high social position.

3.3.17 *canting trade*: habit of using affected religious or pious language.

50 *down*: falling downstairs.

riding post: riding with great speed; riding with the speed of post-horses.

58 *Much of passion . . . love*: there are different interpretations possible to this line. Perhaps Mrs Flywife believes that jealousy over her escapade with the disguised Mrs Beauclair has driven Sir Francis to distraction, and her confusion is a source of comedy for the audience. Or, perhaps she is jealous over what she correctly understands to be Sir Francis's passion for another. In either case the audience is in suspense over what action this volatile woman might take.

5.4 S.D. *Enter Mrs Beauclair [and] Dresswell*: the original stage direction reads, *Enter Mrs Beauclair, Dresswell and a woman*, but this mysterious, anonymous woman neither speaks nor is mentioned again. It may be that this is a printing error that should have read, *Enter Mrs Beauclair and Dresswell, her woman*.

12 *Give me a glass, you*: Peggy's incivility to her husband is probably the result of her drunkenness. Either that or she believes over-familiarity to a spouse is fashionable behaviour

21 *green pease at Christmas*: since peas are a spring crop, Peggy is using a rather rustic way of saying she will want expensive luxuries.

83 *have been pleased abroad*: have been out having a romantic interlude with some other woman.

89 *romantic style*: Mrs Beauclair warns Sir Francis that he seems to be altering his rakish style in favour of the language used by heroes of romances, such as those written by Mme de Scudéry and favoured by Bellinda.

110 *bride-folk*: those celebrating a wedding.

115 *what*: why.

134 *I went no further*: I never consummated the marriage.

139 *beside*: besides.

147 *Ask Mrs Peggy that*: Spendall replies ribaldly to Lady Beauclair's question and implies that he and Peggy have already consummated their union, perhaps prematurely.

152 *what's matter*: so it doesn't matter; it makes no difference.

153–4 *Doctor's Commons*: the College of Doctors of Civil Law in London. Marriage licences, divorce proceedings, and probate of wills were among the business conducted there until the society was dissolved in 1858.

162 *leave this counterfeiting ... lose your ears*: false personation could fall under the category of a 'cheat', a misdemeanour at common law, which could be punishable by 'fine, imprisonment, and other corporal punishment' (Edward Hyde East, *Pleas of the Crown* (1803; repr. London, 1972), 814). Or Sir Charles could be referring to an old Tudor statute regarding vagrancy which required that vagabonds 'calling themselves serving men, but having no masters' be whipped and 'have the upper part of the gristle of the right ear cut clean off' (Sir James Fitzjames Stephen, *The Criminal Law of England*, vol. 3 (London, 1883), 271).

164 *smock-faced*: having a pale smooth face; effeminate-looking.

168 *what a puff the old lady's in*: how Lady Beauclair looks as if she were about to explode with rage.

176 *gentiles*: heathens or pagans; also a variant spelling of 'gentles'. Perhaps Cheatall is trying to offer a civil greeting, but his dialect variant becomes a joke.

180 *underhead*: a person of inferior intelligence; dunderhead; blunderhead. There is extra space around the word 'underhead' in *1697*. Morgan believes this space indicates a printer's error that should read 'blunderhead'. I believe Pix may have intended any of these three possibilities: underhead, dunderhead, or blunderhead.

187 *paying my club*: paying my share of the joint bill.

195 *pared*: shaved.

198–9 *Much good may d'ye*: may much good come to you.

206–7 *it does not ... own head*: one day she does not make cuckold's horns grow upon his head.

207 *I am friends*: I will be a friend to you.

208 *something towards housekeeping*: a wedding present.

228 *next fair wind*: the wind is suitable to set sail back to the Indies. Flywife is already planning his escape from his rediscovered wife.

240 *scarce a pin to choose*: scarcely anything to choose between you.

242 *natural*: Flywife is punning on the word. Lady Beauclair is his natural spouse both because the force of circumstances requires that he recognize his relationship to her and because he views her as foolish or half-witted, a contemporary meaning of 'natural'.

247 *friend*: *double entendre* on friend meaning 'lover'. Mrs Beauclair reminds Sir Francis that she was the beau who seduced Mrs Flywife away from him.

250 *private pocket*: a secret reserve of funds.

252 MRS BEAUCLAIR: this line, and many others in the rest of the scene, were mistakenly assigned in the first edition to a non-existent Mrs Beaumont.

261 SIR CHARLES : this line was mistakenly assigned in *1697* to Sir Francis.

262–3 *That kept it some time private*: for that reason we kept the marriage a secret for some time.

263 *before we came together*: before we consummated the marriage.

265 *conveniency's*: convenience's; for the sake of saving trouble.

268 *date of*: beginning of; starting-point for.

272 *go to my house*: there is some confusion inherent in this line. The characters are already assembled at Sir Charles's house, the one that he shares with Lady Beauclair. Perhaps Sir Charles means to go into the other rooms of his house.

290 *hopeful*: promising. Lady Beauclair is being sarcastic.

299 *once escaped*: who has once escaped and is then caught.

301 *loose*: set free; release; also a pun on 'lose'.

5.5.15 *pangs of death*: either (1) the death-like pangs of childbirth; or (2) a transcription slip for 'pangs of birth'.

16 *Mine*: my clinging.

52 *that black gentleman*: the clergyman, wearing black, who will perform the marriage ceremony, with a *double entendre* on the devil—as most men fear the devil, Sir Francis fears the clergyman.

55 *till*: that.

61 *these*: these men.

62 *ding-dong*: in good earnest.

64 *scarce risings*: Cheatall crudely posits that after seven years of marriage, the wives will scarcely inspire an erection in their husbands.

67 *would*: thought it good to.

68 *good-humoured to this lady*: Mrs Beauclair credits Cheatall for behaving generously toward Arabella, especially after having been tricked by her.

EPILOGUE

Mr Scudamore: Barnabas Scudamore, a member of Betterton's company. It was not unusual to have an actor with no other speaking role in a play perform the epilogue.

Mr Motteux: see note to *IM*, Prologue.

1 *Scribbler*s: petty authors; writers without worth.

1 *huff*: scold; storm at; speak insolently about.

2 *feigned courage . . . ague fit*: faking the bravery to confront the audience in this way often gives them nervous spasms, making them shiver and shake as if taken with a fever.

3 *their condition*: their true position as supplicants for the audience's favour.

5 *Mr Bayes his notion*: Mr Bayes's notion.

6 *If thunder cannot save them, halters must*: in *The Rehearsal* (see note to Prologue 24), Mr Bayes, the character of the dramatist whose play is being rehearsed (and a parody of John Dryden), proposes to win his audience's sympathy through pity by bringing out a hangman to stand behind him during the prologue and informing the audience, 'That if, out of good nature, they will not like my Play, why Igad, I'l e'en kneel down, and he shall cut my head off' (London, 1672, p. 7). He alternatively tries the efficacy of terror to win the audience's applause by having the epilogue performed by thunder and lightning (pp. 9–10). The speaker of the epilogue says that mediocre dramatists follow the lead of Mr Bayes and try both pity and terror, not knowing which is the better method, to move the audience to approve their play.

9 *the middle way*: the speaker is about to suggest that between pity and terror lies flattery.

13 *If so*: if you think you are one of the qualified judges of wit to which I have just addressed myself.

16 *reformation*: see note to Prologue 20.

18 *sparks with broad-brim hats and little bands*: a sarcastic reference to more strait-laced playgoers, who are not sparks or fops at all but wear hats and collars similar to those of Quakers or clergymen.

21 *but not to ogle you*: the epilogue refers to the numerous contemporary comic/satiric accounts of ogling behaviour in church, such as Lord Foppington's speech in Sir John Vanbrugh's *The Relapse* (1696) in which he describes the attractions of church for him: 'There is my Lady *Tattle*, my Lady *Prate*, my Lady *Titter*, my Lady *Leer*, my Lady *Giggle*, and my Lady *Grin*. These sit in the Front of the Boxes, and all Church-time are the prettiest Company in the World, stap my Vitals' (2.1.269–81) (Sir John Vanbrugh, *Four Comedies*, ed. Michael Cordner (London, 1989), 74). The 'nice dames' in question treat the theatre as they do church: as a place to socialize and be part of the spectacle rather than as a place to listen and be instructed. For a more extensive discussion of the subject, see Michael Cordner, 'Time, the Churches, and Vanbrugh's Lord Foppington', *Durham University Journal*, NS 46 (1984), 11–17.

22 *sweeter*: more genial, more charming, less austere than those in the broad-brim hats.

23 *chains*, *gowns and coifs*: men of high-ranking professions. Chains were worn as symbols of civic office; specific gowns indicated that their wearers were members of the legal and clerical professions; white caps were worn by lawyers as a mark of their profession. These items of dress stand for well-to-do and sober-minded members of these professions who are viewed as desirable prospective husbands by ladies in the boxes.

have their places: shall prevail with them.

24 *stockjobbing*: the buying and selling of stocks by a member of the Stock Exchange; speculative dealing in stocks and shares.

25 *middle-fry*: middle-class people sitting in the middle gallery who, in this case, are assumed to take a fastidiously high moral tone in relation to a play.

gall'ry: the upstairs, less costly seating in the theatre. There were two levels of galleries: the middle was generally occupied by tradespeople, while the upper, and even less costly, was occupied by a mixed group ranging from servants to rakes and prostitutes.

26 *humh*: a grunt of approval.

27 *lectures*: sermonizing orations by dissenting preachers, i.e. those not conforming to the Church of England.

29 *Lambeth Wells*: the parish of Lambeth runs along the south bank of the Thames and includes Vauxhall. Lambeth has a long history as a centre for public amusements and beautiful gardens. In the late seventeenth century Lambeth Wells was known for its mineral waters, sold for a penny a quart, and was located in Three Coney Walk (now Lambeth Walk). See Timbs, 498.

this weather: this season. See note to Prologue 1.

30 *stored*: well stocked. The audience is well-stocked with the people just described.

31 *beau-crowded stage*: until the mid-eighteenth century, fashionable men were allowed to pay for the privilege of being admitted backstage during the performance of a play. There they were able to visit the actors in the green room, flirt with the actresses, and watch the performance from the wings. Sometimes they roamed the stage and chatted with their friends or were otherwise disruptive. See Allardyce Nicoll, *The Garrick Stage: Theatres and Audience in the Eighteenth Century* (Athens, Ga., 1980). The speaker suggests that, although the theatre could use their money, with such a high-toned audience, the performance is unlikely to attract these beaux.

33 *So . . . we'll change*: we will change the content of our plays to suit our new audience. (The implication is we have to change for lack of a better audience.)

34 *doily-stuff*: an inexpensive but genteel light woollen material for summer wear developed in the late seventeenth century and named for its inventor, Doiley or Doyley (*OED*).

The Busybody

TITLE PAGE

Quem tulit . . . reficit: 'He whom Ambition conveys to the stage in her breeze-fickle car is | Wilted by audience listlessness, given new breath at their laughter. | That is how little it takes to tear down or build up any spirit | Lusting at all costs for fame.' *The Letters of Horace, Book 2, Letter 1*, in Charles E. Passage (trans.), *The Complete Works of Horace* (New York, 1983).

1 *John, Lord Somers*: Baron Somers of Evesham, Worcestershire (1651–1716), a jurist and Whig leader. He served as Lord High Chancellor in the reign of William III and as President of Queen Anne's Privy Council from 1708 to 1710.

7 *heathenish poets*: ancient Greek and Roman poets.

10 *consent*: agreement.

13 *to*: upon.

that council: the Privy Council, the body of the sovereign's closest advisers.

14 *at this critical juncture, overrules the fate of all Europe*: see note to Prologue 13, below.

15 *Lelius*: Laelius Gaius (*c.*190–after 129 BC), a close friend of Scipio and noted orator. He was the central figure in Cicero's *De amicitia*.

Scipio: Cornelius Scipio Aemilianus (born 185/4 BC), warrior, diplomat, orator, and patron of the arts. Cicero depicts him as the ideal statesman in *De republica*.

18 *Terence's*: Publius Terentius Afer (d. 159 BC), born a slave probably in Carthage, gained freedom and became a Roman playwright who was patronized by prominent Romans such as Lelius and Scipio. In his comedies, mostly based on Greek sources, he introduced a naturalistic style, close to everyday language. Terence also began the practice of using prologues to argue with his critics.

19 *unbinding*: relaxing; freeing; opening up.

20 *put my . . . with those*: rank my plays with those.

23 *best and fairest*: most elegant; highest ranking; most beautiful, i.e. ladies of the highest social rank.

25 *nicer*: more refined; more fastidious.

THE CHARACTERS OF THE PLAY

Airy: someone with a light, sprightly, vivacious disposition.

Gripe: a good name for a miser, it indicates skill in grasping and clutching things or one who will not let go his grip.

Sir Jealous Traffick: the name indicates both the character's suspicious nature and his involvement in trade. The word 'traffic' is sometimes used to refer to trade that is somewhat shady or illicit, perhaps even of a sexual nature.

Marplot: a name that forewarns us that the character meddles in the lives of others and disrupts all their schemes—especially their 'mar'riage plots, perhaps.

Whisper: this servant's secretiveness aids his master's intrigues.

Miranda: an admirable character whose name has its roots in the Latin mirari, 'to wonder' (*OED*).

Isabinda: a combination of the Spanish names 'Isabella' and 'Linda', both of which comment on the beauty of their holders.

kept up: locked away.

Patch: a false beauty mark, sometimes used to accentuate a feature on a woman's face, or to hide a blemish.

Scentwell: a servant whose name refers to a lady's perfumes.

PROLOGUE

Tunbridge-Walks: a 1703 comedy by Thomas Baker in which Baker creates the homosexual character of Maiden, described in the list of dramatis personae as 'a Nice-Fellow, that values himself upon his Effeminacies'. For more information on Baker and the connection of *Tunbridge-Walks* to *The Busybody*, see Introduction, pp. xxiii–xxiv.

1 *modern prophets were exposed*: The Modern Prophets: or, New Wit for a Husband, a new comedy by Thomas D'Urfey (1653–1723), opened at Drury Lane in May 1709 and was poorly received. D'Urfey used the preface of his play to criticize Baker's recent comedies. D'Urfey attacked Baker's *Hampstead-Heath* (Drury Lane, Oct. 1705) for being a mere reworking of Baker's unproduced piece, *An Act at Oxford* (1704). *An Act at Oxford* had been suppressed because it offended the University authorities at Oxford. Baker eliminated the cause for offence by changing the location and the names of the characters. D'Urfey also denounced Baker's *The Fine Lady's Airs* (Drury Lane, Dec. 1708) as an 'abuse of the fair sex . . . and deservedly hist' (*The Modern Prophets*, Preface*)*, but

other critics report that Baker's comedy was a success. Baker uses the prologue to *BB* to take some revenge on D'Urfey. See Nicoll I, 21–2, 175–6.

2 *author*: Thomas D'Urfey. See previous note.

3 *If . . . an audience had been fired*: Baker is casting aspersions on D'Urfey's comedy. He claims that such a poorly crafted piece would have required a more gifted poet than D'Urfey to make it worthy of the enthusiasm of an audience.

11 *camps*: military camps. These camps had become tourist attractions. See notes to *Belle* 1.1.62 and 73.

13 *the wished-for peace*: the end to hostilities between England and her allies and France and hers. When Charles II of Spain, the last of the Spanish Habsburgs, died childless in 1700, he left his throne to Philip of Anjou, grandson of Louis XIV. The accession of Philip to the Spanish throne would have shifted the balance of power in Europe enormously toward France. England, therefore, made a Grand Alliance with the Holy Roman Empire and the Netherlands to support the claim of Archduke Charles, son of the Holy Roman Emperor Leopold I, to the Spanish throne. The result was the War of the Spanish Succession, which was fought from 1701 to the signing of the Treaty of Utrecht (1713–14), which recognized Philip's claim to the Spanish throne while transferring substantial territory in Canada from France to England. In 1708 there seemed to be a chance for peace after the English commander, John Churchill, first Duke of Marlborough, and Eugene, Prince of Savoy, won a great victory at Oudenarde that led Louis XIV to sue for peace. Negotiations broke down and Marlborough and Savoy won an even bloodier victory in 1709 at Malplaquet.

15–16 *The grand monarch . . . lose his own*: the king will not engage his forces on his son's behalf if it means risking his own throne. Most likely this would be a reference to Louis XIV and his *grand*son, Philip of Anjou. In the spring of 1709, France was in such dire straits economically that it would have seemed unlikely for Louis XIV to do much to aid Philip in Spain. It was only due to the later bunglings of the English and their allies' negotiators that France was able to obtain a favourable settlement.

17 *This season . . . face*: because of England's martial successes, most of the populace is happy.

18 *But players in . . . case*: actors have a hard time trying to drum up an audience in the heat of the summer. Fashionable people generally left London for the summer, and therefore theatrical audiences were so meagre that actors might have to perform for reduced pay. See note to *IM*, Prologue 7–8.

19 *our act of grace*: a formal pardon for us; our only hope of a reprieve from penury.

21 *great*: expensively; in the style a great man is expected to sustain.

22 *basset*: 'an obsolete game at cards, resembling Faro' (*OED*).

24 *city-wives*: wives of tradesmen or shopkeepers who live in the City (the financial and business centre) of London as opposed to gentlewomen or ladies.

   Tunbridge: Tunbridge Wells. A fashionable watering place where visitors drank rather than bathed in the waters.

27 *by the waters . . . conceive*: the city-wives credit the waters of Tunbridge Wells with restoring their fertility. The writer of the prologue, however, intimates it is their dalliances with courtiers at the resort that deserve the true credit, and makes overt reference to the Earl of Rochester's poem, 'Tunbridge Wells' (1674), with its images of the promiscuous social intermingling at the spa (Rochester, 73–80). The prologue specifically echoes Rochester's description of the gigolos, Cuff and Kick, 'Who more substantially will cure thy wife, | And on her half-dead womb bestow new life. | From these the waters got the reputation | Of good assistants unto generation' (ll. 145–8).

28 *Fleet Street*: one of the most ancient and important thoroughfares in London, it housed many types of businesses, taverns, coffee houses, and two of the Inns of Court: the Inner Temple and Middle Temple. The sempstress in question apparently makes a good living for herself catering to lawyers and law students, and enjoys their attentions.

29 *runs*: quickly stitches up.

30 *Cupid's Gardens*: Cuper's Gardens, commonly known as 'Cupid's Gardens', a pleasure garden with good bowling greens, was opened by Boyder Cuper in the early 1690s. It was located on the south side of the Thames, opposite Somerset House, on the waterfront and was popular with apprentices and sempstresses. In the later part of the century, the gardens became more elaborate and attracted more people of fashion. A waterside tavern, called 'The Feathers', was part of the garden.

31 *'Fair Dorinda'*: 'Fair Dorinda, happy, happy | Happy may'st thou ever be', a song from the opera *Camilla*, music by Marc Antonio Bononcini and libretto by Owen MacSwiney (translated from Silvio Stampiglia's *Il Trionfo di Camilla*, 1697). Centlivre's contemporary, George Farquhar (1677–1707), also referred to this popular song in his last comedy, *The Beaux' Stratagem* (1707). Many seventeenth-century-songs and poems were written to or about 'Dorinda'. The name was used frequently in pastoral poetry to characterize a chaste maiden who spurns one who loves her.

   bottled ale: an inexpensive alternative to imported wine. London ale would be transported in bottles from the country rather than brewed on the premises. In the country, ale was generally drunk at its place of production, and therefore no bottling was necessary.

34 *Should I . . . fate today*: should I proclaim the author will have a success today.

35 *cry down*: publicly condemn or disparage.

37 *'Tis tattling . . . Isaac Bickerstaff*: a character invented by Jonathan Swift in 1708 to attack the scurrilous astrologer, John Partridge. Bickerstaff was supposed to be a rival astrologer who comically predicted Partridge's imminent demise. The character took on a life of his own, and not only did Swift write a number of items in Bickerstaff's name but other writers wrote pamphlets attributed to him as well. Bickerstaff became so popular that after Swift had finished with the character, Sir Richard Steele chose to continue him in his new journal as *The Tatler*.

38 *Since war . . . that write*: since war and political place-seeking and faction-fighting claim the attention of the male writers.

1.1. S.D. *The Park*: St James's Park, a fashionable place to walk, to see and to be seen. The reference to birding is especially apt as the park had a famous Bird-Cage Walk, where, in the time of Charles II, cages of an aviary were hung from the trees. The park was often referred to as a place for trysts in the dramatic works of Congreve, Farquhar, Otway, and Southerne. See Timbs, 652–3.

1 *A-birding*: 'the action or sport of bird-catching or fowling' (*OED*). The *OED* cites Charles's line as an example of the figurative use of 'birding': Charles is suggesting that Sir George is hunting women, not birds.

3 *figure*: high rank or social position.

unfashionable hours: fashionable people took their turn in St James's Park after dinner. As this scene takes place early in the morning, Charles jokingly suggests that Sir George must be engaged in some form of hunting, an early morning activity, and for forbidden prey, since he is at the park at a time when he would expect not to be observed by people of fashion.

13 *whimsical*: uncertain, fluid.

calculation of my nativity: drawing up of my horoscope.

16 *midnight councils*: secretest, most covert meetings or conspiracies.

18 *below*: on earth.

38 *the Jew my father*: my tightwad of a father. Because Jews in England were prohibited from working in government institutions or universities and restricted in other professions and in land-holding, they were mostly to be found earning their livings in business, and often in one of the less savoury aspects of business, money-lending. The stereotype of the Jewish money-lender, as exemplified in Shakespeare's Shylock, lived on, and the

term 'Jew' became a byword for someone grasping; a money-grubber who lives off the financial misfortunes of others.

39 *her and thirty thousand pound*: Miranda's personal fortune of thirty thousand pounds is in the hands of Sir Francis Gripe. When she marries, her husband will assume that control.

45 *Not a souse*: not even one small coin.

46 *wildnesses of youth*: gambling, drinking, and wenching (most likely).

50 *Prester John's dominions*: the lands of the legendary Christian king and priest who ruled a great land somewhere in the east, possibly in India, Ethiopia, or Abyssinia.

55 *a brown musket*: a burnished musket. Charles is threatening to join the army.

63 *ingeniously*: frankly; 'used by confusion, for "ingenuously"' (*OED*).

73 *for that contempt*: because I do not consider her beautiful.

89 *A good assurance!*: what impudence! Charles rebukes Marplot for addressing him so familiarly as 'dear boy'.

99 *the rout of the world*: the more vulgar classes. Marplot seems to suggest that his more common acquaintance will accord him greater status if he is admitted to the company of Sir George.

100 *Whigs*: members of the political party opposed to the Tories. The Whigs originated with those who opposed the succession of James II because of his allegiance to the Roman Catholic Church.

Jacks: Jacobites; adherents of the deposed James II or of his descendants.

101 *High-Flyers*: Tories, or High Church adherents; members 'of the Church of England holding opinions which give a high place to . . . those points of doctrine, discipline, and ritual, by which the Anglican Church is distinguished from the Calvinistic churches of the Continent, and the Protestant Nonconformist churches in England' (*OED*).

Low-Flyers: Low Church adherents; members 'of the Church of England holding opinions which give a low place to the authority and claims of the episcopate and priesthood, the inherent grace of the sacraments, and to matters of ecclesiastical organization' (*OED*).

Levellers: members of a political party that came to prominence in the mid-1640s. The Levellers held that legislatures drew their power from and were accountable to the people, and that therefore sole sovereignty should be accorded to the House of Commons. They also advocated fuller protection of the individual's rights at law, broadening suffrage, and greater religious tolerance for dissenting Protestant sects. For a more complete account of the Leveller movement, see G. E. Aylmer (ed.), *The Levellers in the English Revolution* (Ithaca, 1975).

104 *without*: unless.

107 *mourning nose*: a red and running nose that requires frequent mopping with a handkerchief. Marplot's nose appears to weep.

112 *Spain or Portugal*: while it is not certain which battles of the War of Spanish Succession are being referred to, the British were involved in various indecisive campaigns in Spain between 1708 and 1710, and in 1708 the British conquered Minorca, thus gaining control of the Mediterranean.

114 *Groom Porters*: officers 'of the English Royal Household, abolished under George III; [their] principal functions, at least from the sixteenth century, were to regulate all matters connected with gaming within the precincts of the court, to furnish cards and dice, etc., and to decide disputes arising at play' (*OED*).

118 *North Briton*: Scotsman.

121–2 '*Now the deel a ma sol, sir, gin ye touch yer steel, Ise whip mine through yer wem*': the antagonist speaks with a Scots dialect. Roughly translated: 'Now, the devil take my soul, sir, if you touch your sword, I'll thrust mine through your belly.'

130–1 *a bow . . . ever yours*: Marplot is anxious not just for Sir George's friendship but for others to know of it. He therefore pledges eternal service to Sir George if only Sir George will acknowledge him publicly by bowing to him from his box at the theatre or will allow Marplot to be seen in his carriage.

135 *reigning toasts of the town*: the season's celebrated beauties.

139 *air of business*: attitude of seriousness or industry; as if you were not delivering a letter concerning romantic intrigue.

163 *to make the compliment*: to perform this exceedingly civil action to my social inferior.

183–4 *I'll make one*: I'll be one of the drinking party.

185 S.D. *[aside to Charles]*: Centlivre does not provide this stage direction, but, given Whisper's name and Marplot's reaction to not being able to hear what Whisper has said to Charles, it seems that Whisper is whispering, or at least speaking confidentially, to Charles.

186 *Spanish*: Spanish-mannered.

198 S.D. *([as if] coming out of a chair)*: Centlivre does not specify whether Miranda is now carried in in a sedan chair or whether she enters from a door behind the proscenium and calls aback *as if* to a chairman. If the chair makes an entrance too, it and its attendants must either exit after Miranda dismisses them or wait for her in the upstage scenic area. It is possible that when she makes her escape at the end of the scene she retreats to the waiting chair and is carried off. A chair is a sedan chair, a private and fashionable means of transportation; 'an enclosed vehicle, to seat one person, and borne on two poles by two bearers, one in front and one behind' (*OED*).

199 *dogged*: tracked (like a hunting dog).

213 *Sir Jealous*: *1709* records this instance as 'Sir Jealousie'. Perhaps this was a version of the name Centlivre considered using, but as it only occurs here and at l. 230, I therefore have treated it as an error.

216–17 *Spanish customs*: Patch refers to the custom of sequestering women made much of in the *comedias de capa y espada* (cape and sword plays) of Spanish Golden Age (sixteenth- to seventeenth-century) literature. For a further description of such 'Spanish manners', see 'Introduction' to this volume, p. xxv. See also John Loftis, *The Spanish Plays of Neoclassical England* (New Haven, 1973).

244 *that she wants*: that is the thing which she lacks/desires.

245 *in this deshabille*: dressed in a fashionably relaxed or revealing style.

250 *Argus*: a mythological creature with a hundred eyes; a vigilant person, watcher or guardian.

253 S.D. *Miranda and Patch withdraw*: Miranda and Patch hide themselves either behind the proscenium or in the scenic area, so that Miranda can watch, unobserved by Sir George and Sir Francis, and still be close enough to the forestage and the audience to make her asides. See 'The Restoration and Eighteenth-Century Stages' in this volume for more physical description of the early eighteenth-century stage.

256 *vicious*: full of vices.

257 *In sober sadness*: truly.

258 S.D. *(peeping)*: Miranda peers out from where she has withdrawn and addresses these comments as asides to Patch and the audience.

267 *first night's lodging*: the opportunity to be the first to sleep with a virgin. Patch and Miranda suspect that Sir George and Sir Francis are negotiating the price of the prostitution of Miranda.

270 *The favour!*: Miranda mistakes Sir George's request to speak with her without charge as a request to sleep with her without charge.

288 *Imprimis*: in the first place.

290 *let*: impediment.

296 *fit*: punish; be even with.

312 *incognita*: unknown one.

322 *the lady*: the lady of whom he was previously speaking.

324 *the other lady . . . a set meal*: I plan to make a full formal meal of the other lady. Sir George opposes a dish of chocolate to a set meal to contrast light flirtation with marriage.

337 *cloud*: mask.

315

338 *Remember . . . the park*: remember, the park is a dangerous place to be when no respectable people are around to protect you.

351 *the lady*: the masked incognita with whom Sir George is currently conversing.

388 *gypsy*: a playful term for a woman, especially a brunette.

2.1.4 *pieces*: pieces of gold; guineas.

8 *Gardee*: Miranda's nickname for Sir Francis, from 'guardian'.

12–13 *Thou shalt outshine . . . night*: the jewellery I will shower you with will make you outshine that of all the ladies in the queen's box at the opera.

14 *ring*: a circular racecourse in Hyde Park where it was fashionable to be seen riding on horseback or in one's carriage.

28 *Chargee*: Sir Francis's nickname for Miranda, from 'charge', or ward.

28–9 *settle it upon thee for pin-money*: make a legal arrangement for that estate to be turned over to you as a private fund for your own personal expenses after our marriage. Pin-money was a woman's allowance for her private expenditures.

54–5 *ought to have sent before they entered*: ought to have sent in the servant to announce them and to discover whether or not the person whom they hoped to see would receive them, rather than charged in unannounced.

67 s.d. *[Aside]*: Miranda's final line would not be for Sir Francis's ears. Although she has expressed eager anticipation for the interview with Sir George so that she and Sir Francis can carry out their joke, Miranda does not call her guardian 'old gentleman' to his face. Miranda is reminding the audience that her expectations of the interview are beyond what Sir Francis suspects.

75 *to set upon a card*: to gamble away at cards.

77 *To fine for sheriff*: to pay in order to escape performing the duties of sheriff.

78 *put up for parliament-man*: to try to win a seat in the House of Commons.

88 *the pox*: syphilis. Sir Francis reinforces the hint Charles has dropped (see note to 1.1.46) that the young man has led a wild youth.

104–6 *[Aloud] . . . help thee*: Centlivre's lack of stage directions and odd punctuation create confusion in this speech. The original is: 'Guardian, —your servant *Charles*, I know by that sorrowful countenance of thine. The old man's fist is as close as his strong box—But I'll help thee.' Perhaps 'your servant' is directed to Sir Francis as a courtesy, or perhaps to Charles, or perhaps it refers to Charles as Sir Francis's servant. It is logical that Marplot's recognition of Charles would be addressed so that Sir Francis would hear it—it would be odd should he not acknowledge Charles's presence—but I do not believe even Marplot would be outrageous enough to intend for his guardian to overhear his comment to

Charles about Sir Francis's stinginess. There are other directorial possibilities, however, which would involve Sir Francis's response to overhearing Marplot's indiscreet comment.

141 *you think . . . father*: you don't think this is a match a thoughtful father would propose for his son.

168–9 *vary a thousand shapes*: experiment with, or deploy, a thousand different styles of wooing.

174 S.D. *(Salutes Miranda)*: Sir George kisses Miranda.

176 *Mammon*: personification of wealth, riches. Used as a term of opprobrium, indicating someone who hoards riches and is covetous of them.

178 *young Timon*: the eponymous character of Shakespeare's *Timon of Athens*, as well as of Thomas Shadwell's 1678 adaptation of the same name, known for being a misanthrope. Although, in the early part of the play, Timon is beneficent to a fault, losing his own wealth by helping all who come to him, his faith in mankind is lost when all abandon him in his need. Sir Francis compares Sir George to the young Timon: he squanders his money, believing that his free-spending can buy love, and will be disillusioned when his affections are not returned

one hour: when the bargain was first struck in the previous act, only ten minutes were stipulated. See 1.1.290.

179–80 S.D. *(Retires to the bottom of the stage)*: the stage at the Theatre Royal, Drury Lane was raked, or angled, so that the 'bottom' of the stage truly describes a lower point than 'upstage'. Sir Francis retires to the front part of the forestage so that he can more easily direct his asides to the audience as well as become an audience to Miranda and Sir George, who either play their dumb show in the scenic area or further up on the forestage framed by the proscenium. See 'The Restoration and Eighteenth-Century Stages' in this volume, p. liii.

193–4 S.D. *(Running up)*: running upstage to where Miranda and Sir George are playing the scene. This scene, including Sir Francis's intrusions upon the interview, has a source in Ben Jonson's *The Devil is an Ass*, 1.6 (1616). Some critics have unjustly accused Centlivre of plagiarizing Jonson's scene (see Introduction, p. xxii n. 29), but she has rather used her source creatively as a point of departure. Whereas Jonson's passive Mistress Fitzdottrel is forced into the interview with Wittipol by her husband, who has commanded her to be silent, Miranda chooses silence as a deliberate strategy to play her suitor and her guardian against each other. Jonson's lady is the object of the men's manipulations; Miranda manipulates the action herself. For further discussion of this scene, see 'The Restoration and Eighteenth-Century Stages', p. liii.

194 *palming*: (1) touching palms; (2) trickery, fraud.

234 *fit*: match.

262–3 *apprehensive of the promise*: sensitive to the need to keep the promise.

265 S.D. *(Turns on her side)*: Miranda and Sir George are facing each other during this scene. When Sir George plays at speaking for Miranda, he turns to face the direction she is facing, and probably increases the comic effect by acting and speaking as he would have her react to him.

277 *assurance*: self-confidence; impudence.

280 *Now for a quick . . . extempore!*: Now, let's hope I have a quick imagination and can create a long, clever, improvised letter.

286 *numbers*: verses.

302 *just in the nick*: at the critical moment.

304 *nicked*: beaten at a game of hazard, such as dice. Sir Francis is punning on Sir Charles's use of 'just in the nick'. See previous note.

307 *fleering*: grimacing; mocking; laughing scornfully.

309 *snuff*: powdered tobacco; something of small value.

324 *Beelzebub*: i.e. devil.

329 *Actaeon's horns*: the young hunter Actaeon accidentally came across Diana bathing in the woods. The goddess was so angry that she turned Actaeon into a stag. His own hounds hunted and killed him. Sir George refers to the stag's horns as a symbol of the cuckold.

335 *at large*: unsettled or unrestrained lives. Sir Francis puns on 'at large' as meaning both inconstancy and living beyond one's means.

2.2. S.D. *[and the doorway leading to the street]*: the location of 2.2 moves between a room in Sir Jealous's house and the threshold to the house. The conventions of the scenic stage, with its generalized settings, allowed for such fluidity without violating the audience's credulity. See 'The Restoration and Eighteenth-Century Stages', pp. lii–liii.

1 *balcony*: in *1709*, this word is printed as 'balcone'. It may be that Centlivre wishes Sir Jealous to use the Spanish word *balcon*, but since there is no pattern of Sir Jealous using Spanish words in English contexts, I have regularized the English spelling here and at line 20 below.

2 *bill*: written advertisement.

3 *passengers*: passers-by.

7 *Spanish rules*: Sir Jealous seems to be referring to Roman Catholic strictures on mortification of the flesh. His fanaticism on these matters could easily have been regarded as an anti-Jacobite lampoon. His suspicion of both the religion and the women of his own country would hardly have the sympathy of his creator, who was a supporter of Protestant Queen Anne and an opponent of those who would restore the Catholic descendants of James II to the throne. See 'Introduction' to this volume, pp. xxiv–xxv.

taste: physical sense of taste; faculty of discernment of what is beautiful or appropriate; inclination. Sir Jealous is punning on the various meanings.

8 *flesh*: meat; sensual appetites. Sir Jealous is playing with both meanings.

10 *close*: closed; shut up; confined.

13 *rampant*: violent and extravagant; lustful, vicious.

13–14 *ratafia . . . claret*: Sir Jealous lists a variety of spirits popular among fashionable ladies and suggests that these ladies are drunkards. Ratafia is flavoured with the fruit or kernels of peaches, apricots, or cherries, or almonds. Persico is prepared by macerating peach or apricot kernels in spirits. Cinnamon water derives its aromatic properties from the spice. Citron is a brandy flavoured with citron- or lemon-peel. Spirit of claret is probably a sweet cordial made from clary flowers (a type of salvia or sage) rather than a spirit made from claret wine.

15–16 *carries many a guinea . . . doctor*: makes money flow, as if being carried on the high tide, to the doctor. Sir Jealous continues the high-water metaphor that alcoholic spirits flood a lady's brain so that it swims, and the illness caused is a current that carries riches away to the attending doctor.

26 *Asgill's translation*: John Asgill (1659–1738) wrote the unorthodox tract, 'An argument proving that according to the covenant of the Scripture, man may be translated from hence into that eternal life, without passing through death, altho the humane nature of Christ himself could not be thus translated till he has passed through death' (1700), and was expelled from the House of Commons in 1707.

32–3 *If we had but the ghostly helps . . . Spain*: Isabinda privately remarks that if her father had his wish and England were conducted as Spain, she would be able to enlist such Spanish Catholic assistance as crafty priests or friars who would have access to confined young women for their confessions. Such 'ghostly' or spiritual characters who act as go-betweens are common in drama and fiction since before Shakespeare, as are those more secular characters who make use of clerical robes to gain access to sequestered women.

43 *Change*: the Exchange; 'a place where merchants meet for the transaction of business' (*OED*).

43–4 *some sauntering coxcomb . . . a feather*: i.e. a dandyish officer.

46 *Senior Barbinetto's*: although Centlivre's Spanish is not always accurate or consistent, Sir Jealous's Spanish seems consistently and deliberately bad. (See 5.2.11 where Sir Jealous confesses he has lost much of his Spanish.) It would be especially comic for Sir Jealous, with all his admiration of Spanish culture, to speak the language blatantly poorly. I have therefore kept *señor* misspelled (although I have standardized the misspelling to 'senior') when Sir Jealous speaks, and restored the spelling to *señor* when it is used by those who, presumably, speak Spanish well. Centlivre is also inconsistent with the name of Isabinda's Spanish suitor. Sometimes he is

Barbinetto and sometimes Babinetto. The names are closer to Italian than to Spanish and I have decided to favour 'Barbinetto' for its resemblances to the Spanish *'barba negra'* or 'blackbeard' as well as to the Italian colloquialism *barbino*, meaning 'second rate'. *Barbinetto* might therefore be a diminutive form.

52–3 *If I can but . . . blown upon*: if I can but keep her from tarnishing her reputation. The *OED* uses this line as an example of the phrase 'blow upon'. It defines it as 'To take the bloom off; to make stale or hackneyed; to bring into discredit, defame'. Sir Jealous is also playing with a more sexually suggestive meaning of being blown up, inflated, that is to say, made pregnant.

55 *has a pregnant wit*: has a fertile mind; is quick-witted; resourceful. When speaking of his daughter, Sir Jealous cannot restrain the sexual double meanings in his language.

56 *Grand Signior's*: the Sultan of Turkey's.

62 *confabulation*: a familiar chat (perhaps with a hint of more intimacy).

64 s.d. *Patch goes in and shuts the door*: Patch retreats through a door, located either on the proscenium façade or on one of the shutters that make up the back wall of the scene.

71 *he-bawd*: a procurer or pander. Since a bawd was assumed to be female, the gender specification is used.

75 *set in the stocks*: placed in a wooden instrument of punishment, made up of two planks, the upper one moveable, with half-circle holes cut in the edges, which allowed the ankles of a seated person to be inserted between them. The planks were then locked together, and the person thus confined was subject to public ridicule. Sometimes, stocks had a pair of cut planks contrived to confine the neck and wrists as well.

86 *Lady Love-puppy*: Whisper invents a rather lame name for his fictional lady. A puppy is not only a little dog but a term designating an empty-headed young man; a fop. Sir Jealous picks up on this meaning to berate Whisper.

89–90 *pressed into the service*: forcibly enlisted in, or press-ganged into service in the army or navy.

2.3.2 *take up*: borrow at interest.

34 *Thatched House*: a celebrated tavern on St James's Street, noted for its large public room and for being the meeting place of many prominent clubs. A favourite resort of Swift. See *Clubs*, 450–2.

49 *civil*: polite; well-bred.

3.2 s.d. *Scene draws*: the shutters representing the outside of Sir Jealous's house open to reveal Charles, Isabinda, and Patch in the acting space behind them. I have given this scene a new number since the stage had been left empty and the setting changed. An argument could be made for making it a continuation of 3.1.

17–18 *taken a thousand pound upon*: borrowed a thousand pounds against.

31 *Fortune generally assists the bold*: proverbial, 'Fortune favours the bold' (Wilson, 282).

35–6 *write in characters*: use a cipher for secret correspondence.

45 *full in the teeth*: in direct confrontation.

3.3.2–3 *That fellow's . . . door*: the strange appearance of Whisper hovering about my door (in 2.2).

4 *St Iago*: a Spanish name for St James. St James the Great is the patron saint of Spain. Sir Jealous's love of all things Spanish even extends to his oaths.

15 *myrmidons*: hired thugs. From the nation of Thessalian warriors Achilles led to the Trojan War.

23 *flea*: flay.

24 *I'll equip him for the opera*: I'll castrate him. Sir Jealous threatens to make Charles a eunuch, like one of the famed castrati whose soprano or alto voice was preserved through castration before puberty.

58 *into*: on; at.

69 *without*: unless.

72 *Don Carlo*: Patch tries to render Charles's name in Spanish, but succeeds in making it Italian. It should be 'Don Carlos'.

3.4.4 *muzzle*: fondle with the mouth.

tuzzle: variant of 'tussle'. The word means 'to wrestle or struggle'. Sir Francis means a more gentle and amorous contention.

5 *lavish*: unrestrained; wild.

ride post: ride with great speed; ride with the speed of post-horses.

8 *delicate*: pleasing to the senses.

26 *excuse*: offer an apology for.

34 *licence*: marriage licence.

41–2 *If . . . eating gold . . . can make thee happy*: Wilson (214) gives the following as a source of the saying, which may derive from a proverb from the sixteenth century, 'If she would eat gold, he would give it her.'

46 *Temple*: see note to *IM*, 4.5 S.D.

49 *writings*: financial documents.

51 *thought on*: formed an idea of; anticipated; imagined.

52 *make a bonfire of your own act and deed*: cancel out your action of giving me control of my own money, because, by marrying me, you regain control of my estate.

59 *dry stubble*: Miranda may be remarking literally on the dry stubble of Sir Francis's beard, which she has just felt against her face as he fondled her while telling her how he burns, or she may be commenting on him as a dried-up old man, like the desiccated stubble of grain that remains after harvest, past fertility or vitality, ready to be ploughed into the earth.

60 *What's*: what, is.

75 *conscionable*: conscientious; scrupulous; in a negative sense, over-scrupulous.

83 *quotha!*: said he (with a sarcastic overtone).

97 *fine*: Marplot uses 'fine' to mean excellent or admirable; Miranda puns on an alternative and disparaging meaning: smartly or showily dressed.

99 *valet de chambre*: a gentleman's personal attendant.

109 *Jew*: see note to 1.1.38.

116–17 *to have and to hold, and so forth*: as in the promises made in the Anglican marriage service.

122 *eighteen*: Miranda is 18 years old.

123 *leather bag*: pouch of skin. Marplot points out how Sir Francis's muscles have withered from age.

buckram: a coarse, stiffened fabric; someone pompous or stiff like buckram fabric

124 *canvas*: coarse, unbleached fabric used to make sails and tents, or for use by artists for oil-painting.

scrub you to repentance: constantly chafe you. Marplot suggests that Miranda's marriage to Sir Francis will result in perpetual physical and spiritual penance for her.

131 *blunderbuss*: 'a short gun with a large bore, firing many balls or slugs, and capable of doing execution within a limited range without exact aim' (*OED*).

134 *MIRANDA*: the first edition mistakenly attributes this speech to Marplot.

144 *Mr Saucebox*: contemptuous appellation for a man given to impertinent remarks.

149 *the Exchange*: see note to 2.2.43.

150 *the son of a whetstone*: the *OED* cites this line as an example of an allusion to the old custom of hanging a whetstone around the neck of a liar.

158–9 *the market lasts all the year*: Miranda reminds Sir Francis that he doesn't have to hoard up kisses and hugs from her; when they are married, they will be available to him every day.

166 *at dispatching an heiress*: when marrying off an heiress whose fortune they hold in trust.

167 *O! Mihi praeteritos referet si Jupiter Annos*: Dryden translates this, 'Would Heav'n . . . my strength and youth recall' (Virgil, *Aeneid*, 8.742).

3.5 S.D. *Discovers Sir George . . . waiting*: these stage directions indicate that the shutters that serve as the backdrop for the scene in Sir Francis's house open, after Sir Francis's exit, to reveal this tavern scene. Sir George, Charles, and Whisper are already in place with their conversation in progress.

5 *transport him*: carry him away (figuratively).

8 *lash*: by its own violence exhaust itself.

21 *huffs*: speaks insolently to.

26 *Desire him*: ask him; with a play on Marplot's 'desire to know' at line 23.

27 *chagrin*: vexation; annoyance.

36 *eat up with spleen*: melancholy; sullen. The spleen was once believed to be the seat of melancholy, and therefore Sir George jokingly attributes Charles's dejection to the overactivity of this organ.

43 *get*: beget.

44 *possessed*: married. Also, mad; possessed by demons or spirits. This is the meaning Marplot uses to pun on in l. 45.

61 *assignation*: invitation; appointment, tryst.

66 *bumper*: 'a cup or glass of wine, etc., filled to the brim, *esp.* when drunk as a toast' (*OED*).

70 *pledge this health*: reciprocate this toast.

78–9 *Along, huzza!*: come, drink!

87–8 *en cavalier*: in such a free and easy way; like a brave cavalier.

96 *give him the drop*: slip away from him; lose him.

4.1.18 *Puts it besides*: (accidentally) lays it outside of the pocket.

20 *utensil*: instrument; article necessary for the running of a household.

33 *of*: on.

44 *cloth*: table-cloth.

48 *Argus*: see note to 1.1.250.

4.2.3 *clapped*: placed, with a suggestion of the action being performed with energy and promptness.

31 *easy chair*: 'a chair adapted for sitting or half reclining in an easy posture, often furnished with arms and padded back' (*OED*). The first record of the usage of this term in the *OED* is in 1707 in George Farquhar's *The Beaux' Stratagem*.

35 *event*: outcome, consequence.

40 S.D. *coats*: petticoats; skirts of her dress.

48 *owning it*: confessing it to be hers.

323

84 *spinet*: 'a keyed musical instrument, common in England in the eighteenth century, closely resembling the harpsichord, but smaller and having only one string to each note' (*OED*).

90 *sing*: Patch may be punning on 'sing' as 'cry out', to warn Charles.

90–1 *Humph, humph*: Patch is clearing her throat.

94 *would the key . . . once*: Patch puns on Sir Jealous's use of the musical term 'key', wishing she could turn the key of the door on him and lock him out of the room.

103–4 *atop of the house . . . down in the cellar*: there is no musical concord between the two women. Isabinda is playing very high; Patch is singing very low.

116 *sound*: swoon.

122 *Here lies the charm*: Isabinda, lying here, is the charm.

129 *smell to this*: breathe this in. Patch holds hartshorn or salts of ammonia to Isabinda's nose to revive her from her swoon.

138 *Mrs Pander*: Mrs Pimp.

139 *troop!*: be off!

151 *looked up*: searched for. Perhaps this is an error and Patch means 'locked up', meaning, packed up.

4.3 S.D. *[Outside . . . house] Enter [Sir Jealous Traffick and Patch] at the lower door*: since the location of the action changes from inside the house to outside, I have broken this section into a separate scene. Apparently, a pair of shutters is drawn closed on the interior of Sir Jealous's house, and Sir Jealous and Patch re-enter at the lower door, creating the illusion they are emerging from Sir Jealous's house and into the street before it.

4 *posture*: condition, situation.

5 *inured*: accustomed to. The original text has 'immured'. I assume this is an error.

20 *Policy*: a prudent or politic course of action; contrivance.

21 *apprehend*: understand.

22 *personating*: impersonating.

27 *how attended*: what servants he brings with him.

29 *Don Pedro Questo Portento Barbinetto*: a nonsensical Spanish-sounding name.

31 *conceive*: understand.

33 *concert*: arrange; plan.

4.4 S.D. *Scentwell waiting offstage:* Scentwell is apparently visible, though partially concealed behind one of the proscenium doors. She is watching for Sir George, but does not wish to be seen.

2 *ditty*: song; ballad.

12 *For aught you know*: for all you know things may not be as simple as you expect. Patch does not seem especially taken with Sir George's mental quickness.

4.5.3 *But then*: but, on the other hand.

28 *so*: if.

39 *Doctors' Commons*: see note to *IM* 5.4.153–4.

42 *Epsom*: a town in Surrey known for its mineral springs, hence, 'Epsom salts'.

43 *his executor*: the one, upon his death, appointed to ensure his will is carried out. There is sometimes a monetary benefit to the executor, which is why Sir Francis covets the position.

45 *instruments*: agents, or written documents from such agents. Miranda has arranged for Sir Francis to receive some kind of confirmation that the man is dying.

46 *he*: Sir Francis.

54 *his*: Sir Francis's.

69 *chimney-board*: 'a board used to close up a chimney in the summer' (*OED*).

71 *close*: hidden.

74 *desperate to*: desperate as to.

80 *to come*: asking me to come.

81 *Squeezum's*: an appropriate name for a usurer, who squeezes his clients dry

92 *green pip*: green sickness: an illness that turns the complexion green or pale, primarily affecting young women, and often characterized by strange appetites.

95 *monkey*: besides the name for a small primate, a playful term for a young person. Monkeys are also traditionally used to represent lasciviousness, and a chained monkey historically has been used as an emblem of subjection to lust. Miranda's references to the monkey thus contain a number of *double entendres*. Gordon Williams records a number of seventeenth-century literary references to monkeys both as homoerotic images and as male substitutes (either literal or likened to a dildo) for single or otherwise unsatisfied women. See Williams II, ii. 900–2.

95–96 *the man comes that is to tame it*: Miranda means for Sir Francis to understand this phrase to refer to an animal tamer but for the rest of her audience to understand her reference to the clergyman who is to perform the marriage ceremony (and thus tame the 'monkey's' lasciviousness).

96 *'twill break all my china*: an allusion to the famous 'china closet' scene from William Wycherley's *The Country Wife* (1675), in which the word

325

'china' becomes a code word for the supposed eunuch Horner's actual sexual potency. Just as Lady Fidget and Horner engage in ribald banter with each other and Sir Jasper Fidget about how Lady Fidget is determined to get a piece of Horner's 'china', so Miranda, Marplot, and Sir Francis banter on several levels of meaning regarding Miranda's 'monkey', which takes on increasing phallic connotations as the comic business develops.

98 *next thee*: next to thee.

102–3 *miniatures of man*: an echo of Rochester's 'A letter from Artemisia in the Town to Chloe in the Country', in which Artemisia recounts the story of a 'fine lady' who exclaims passionately to her pet monkey, 'Kiss me, thou curious miniature of man! | How odd thou art! How japan! | Oh, I could live and die with thee!' (Rochester, 108, ll. 143–5).

112 *bamboo*: a cane made of bamboo.

114 *rout*: uproar or clamour. Marplot doubts that the monkey let loose would have made as much of a tumult as Sir Francis defending the chimney-board.

130 S.D. *Sir George Airy runs off . . . some china*: Sir George most likely exits through a door in the proscenium, throwing some pieces of china as he goes. It seems as if Marplot scratches his own face, or perhaps Sir George injures him when Marplot discovers him behind the chimney-board.

139 *look it*: look for it.

150 *serviceable*: ready to be of assistance.

155 *converse*: talk or have dealings with, with play on another meaning of 'converse', i.e. 'have sexual intercourse with'.

5.1.7 *find your account in*: discover a profit or advantage with.

8–9 *indued with*: who is possessed of.

46 *look them*: look for them.

68 *great Mogul*: an emperor, with a kingdom centred on Delhi.

69 *all the potentates that are not in wars*: Sir Francis would only consider envying the rich and powerful whose wealth is safe.

78 *Hymen*: Greek god of marriage.

5.2.5–6 *Senior, beso . . . esta tierra*: 'Sir, I kiss your hands. Your honour is most welcome to this country.' I have regularized Centlivre's Spanish in this and the other Spanish speeches in the rest of the scene. The translations are my own.

7–10; *Señor, soy el muy humilde . . . su yerno*: 'Sir, I am your honour's most humble and obliged servant. My father conveys his most profound repects to your honour, and has commissioned this English merchant to conclude an affair that makes me the happiest man in the world, by making me your son-in-law.'

11 *I am glad on't*: Sir Jealous is glad to have the presence of the supposed English merchant to translate for him. Despite his admiration of Spanish culture, Sir Jealous does not speak the language well and speaks only the most basic sentences.

19 S.D. *(Seems to read)*: a further suggestion that Sir Jealous does not really speak or understand much Spanish.

39 *hawking females*: prostitutes.

40 *put off their damaged ware*: sell their sexual favours, since they have already lost their virginity; make a profit on their lack of virtue.

42 *Kentish men*: Men on the coast of Kent were said to watch for shipwrecks, in order to carry off the victims' goods.

52 *his last but one*: the letter I received from him before the last one.

53 *by way of jointure*: to serve as a provision in the case of widowhood.

57 *lodge it in some of our funds*: invest it in some of the government stocks that fund the national debt.

58 *return for*: return to.

70–1 *with all expedition*: with all possible speed.

77 *Mr Tackum*: the name indicates someone who attaches or fastens things together; an appropriate name for someone who performs marriages.

81 *five thousand pounds*: this is an inconsistency in the text. At 5.2.53, the sum is said to be only five thousand crowns, or one thousand, two hundred and fifty pounds..

83 *rubs*: obstacles.

88–92 *Oh, hear me . . . How's that?*: from her own point of view, Isabinda's story is becoming a tragedy, and thus she adopts heroic style by switching to blank verse. This abrupt stylistic change, aside from the content of the speech, may contribute to Sir Jealous's rather unheroic response.

106–8 *Could I suspect . . . the treacherous part*: *1709* prints this passage as prose, but clearly Isabinda is returning to her heroic flight of blank verse.

114 *Have patience, madam, and look at him!*: the dialogue suggests the possibility for much stage business as Sir George tries to get Isabinda to look at Charles, she avoids looking, and the audience wonders how far things will go before she recognizes her lover. Perhaps Sir George nearly succeeds in this speech, or even physically moves her toward Charles, before Sir Jealous joins the urging, and Isabinda flings herself away in defiance.

117 *Senior, pase usted adelante*: 'Sir, step forward.'

119–20 *Señora, obligue me, vuestra merced, de su mano*: 'My gracious lady, please favour me with your hand.'

132 *that*: Sir Jealous points out a case or box.

137 S.D. *(Walks off)*: Sir Jealous walks away from the lovers to a distant part of the set, but remains on stage.

149 *my own hand . . . Gordian knot*: the intricate knot referred to was tied by King Gordius in Phrygia. It had been foretold that whoever could loosen this knot would rule Asia. Alexander the Great simply cut through the knot with his sword. 'Cutting the Gordian knot' means evading difficulties to come to a swift conclusion. Isabinda threatens to evade the Gordian knot of her arranged marriage by ending her life.

183–4 *Senior, tome usted su esposa; este momento les junta las manos*: 'Sir, take your wife; this moment joins your hands.' In *1709* this line reads: *'Senior, tome vind sueipora; cete moment les junta las manos.'* Perhaps the incomprehensibility of the original is intentional, but I doubt that the audience would have been able to distinguish the mistakes. I have therefore assumed that the most egregious errors are the compositor's and have adjusted the Spanish accordingly. This sentence is one that Sir Jealous has long waited to pronounce and could be played as a laboriously rehearsed line. His problems with the language could still be conveyed by an actor using selected mispronunciations. Other directorial choices are of course possible.

185–6 *Señor, yo la recibo como se debe un tesoro tan grande*: 'Sir, I accept her as one ought to receive such a great treasure.'

5.3 S.D. *The street . . . door*: most likely, the shutters are drawn across the previous scene. See 4.3 S.D. and note.

5.4 S.D. *Inside [Sir Jealous Traffick's] house*: the shutters reopen to discover the inside of the house.

12 *Heyday! . . . understand you*: Marplot's response to Sir Jealous suggests that Sir Jealous has been speaking in some odd way. Perhaps Sir Jealous assumes that, as a friend of Señor Barbinetto's, Marplot does not speak English, and so Sir Jealous is trying to sound as if he is speaking Spanish.

23 *exalt*: lift up; raise.

29 *rogue*: rogue who.

41 S.D. *between the scenes*: from the wings between two pairs of shutters.

48 *act and deed*: marriage and the disposal of the estate.

73 *Get out with your bags*: take out your purses or money-bags.

84 *Does not your hundred pound stick in your stomach?*: doesn't the memory of losing that hundred pounds make you sick to your stomach?

106–8 *'Tis well it's no worse . . . bless you both*: many critics have reacted negatively to Sir Jealous's sudden reversal as being inconsistent with his character. Sir Jealous may well be reading Charles's papers and reacting to the size of the estate Charles has inherited. His new friendliness to Charles may be due to discovering that his son-in-law is quite rich! See 'Introduction', p. xxv.

114 *this gentleman:* Sir Jealous.

122 *poor Pilgarlic:* poor me. Pilgarlic is a pitying term for one's self.

151 *By my example, let all parents move:* from the behaviour I now exhibit, let all parents take the pattern for their own behaviour.

EPILOGUE

Neither the author of this epilogue nor its speaker has been identified. Although John Wilson Bowyer ascribes the epilogue to Centlivre (Bowyer, 96), *LS* offers no corroboration.

5 *sessions:* judicial sessions; sittings of judges or justices of the peace to hear causes. A metaphor for the audience sitting in judgement on the play.

half-condemned ere tried: pre-opening gossip regarding *BB* had been negative. John Mottley reports that during rehearsal, Robert Wilks, who played Sir George Airy, threw his script into the pit and swore that 'no body would bear to sit to hear such Stuff'. Furthermore, reports were circulating that branded the comedy as 'a silly thing wrote by a Woman' (Bowyer, 96). Sir Richard Steele came to Centlivre's aid after *BB* had opened. He defended the play and attacked those critics who had derided it before it had been performed: 'In old times, we used to sit upon a play here after it was acted; but now the entertainment is turned another way.' See Steele, *The Tatler*, nos. 15, for 14 May, 1709, and 19 for 24 May, 1709.

6 *Some, in three days . . . and died:* some plays, after a run of three days, are dismissed from the stage and never played again. The judicial wordplay is continued here with the use of 'turned off', which is the term used to describe the action by which the condemned is pushed off the ladder at the gallows to meet his fate.

7 *parties:* factions; bodies of partisans. Here the author refers to organized groups in an audience who cheer the play and try to encourage further positive audience response.

8 *false prophets:* a false messiah who cannot be raised from the dead. Perhaps an allusion to D'Urfey's *Modern Prophets*. See note to Prologue 1.

9 *cast:* irretrievably cast, like the throw of a die, and doomed or defeated.

10 *execution speeches:* speeches addressed by one about to be executed to those gathered to watch the execution, and frequently printed after the execution. Such addresses could be used to ask forgiveness, create a sense of martyrdom, or cast the speaker in a heroic light.

17–18 *would have a peace . . . bravely fight:* call for an end to the War of the Spanish Succession, which is disloyal to the brave fighting English troops. These mercenary and whining members of the opposition are foolish still to fear an enemy who is now demoralized and on the run.

The prologue interprets these busybodies from Centlivre's Whig perspective.

22 *still*: the opposite of busy. The epilogue continues to pun on various meanings of this word: ever; always; to be motionless; abstaining from action.

28 *his brows adorns*: makes him a cuckold.

31 *quirks*: quibbles; arguments.

32 *physic*: the practice of medicine.

33 *mobbed up*: muffled, with a cloak over one's head (to conceal one's identity).

fry: large number of insignificant persons, like a swarm or the innumerable spawn of fish. Here the prologue refers to anonymous quacks, numerous as spawn, who practise their trade in every neighbourhood, fashionable as well as common, secretly treating syphilis victims with horrific mercury 'cures', whose side effects are at least as bad as the disease itself.

neighbouring curse: curse found in every neighbourhood; also, curse which operates by seeming to perform neighbourly actions.

34 *Love's pain*: syphilis.

35 *meddling tribe*: busybodies.

37–8 *Let none but . . . crown the night!*: the epilogue tries to flatter the audience into applauding the play by asking that none but busybodies condemn it.

The Times

ADVERTISEMENT

7 *Mr Garrick*: David Garrick (1717–79), the celebrated actor and playwright, was also the manager of Drury Lane from 1747 to 1776. He had had a stormy professional relationship with Elizabeth Griffith that had culminated in his production of her adaptation of Beaumarchais's *Eugénie*, *The School for Rakes* (1769). Their conflicts had proven so arduous to him that he seemed resolved not to work with Griffith again. She, however, was extremely anxious to patch up their disputes and regain his support. *TT* was produced at Drury Lane, but during Richard Brinsley Sheridan's reign as manager and shortly after Garrick's death. Despite Griffith's grateful tribute to the late Garrick and her wish to be remembered as one of his circle, it is highly unlikely that Garrick would have offered any assistance to her in producing another play.

Goldoni's Bourru bienfaisant: Carlo Goldoni (1707–93), an Italian dramatist who had moved to Paris, had created a new form of farcical intrigue comedy out of the old *commedia dell'arte* form. His innovations were watched by English playwrights, including Griffith, with great interest, and Griffith's *Double Mistake* may have been an earlier attempt to imitate Goldoni's style. *Le Bourru bienfaisant* was written in 1771.

10 *how far I have profited by Goldoni's work*: Griffith's comedy remains rather close to her source play with a few significant differences. First, Griffith shifts the focus of Goldoni's comedy from the difficulties of the young lovers attempting to win the old uncle's consent to their marriage to the difficulties of the young married couple on the brink of financial ruin. Second, her portrait of Sir William Woodley is considerably harsher than Goldoni's portrait of Geronte, whose gruffness merely covers up a very soft heart. *Le Bourru bienfaisant* is actually an adaptation of an earlier play written by Goldoni in Italian, *La casa nova* (1758), and, although Griffith never acknowledges this earlier comedy, some of Griffith's revisions of Goldoni's French comedy appear to have had their origin in this Italian source. For a discussion of *La casa nova* as a possible source for *TT*, see 'Introduction' to this volume, pp. xxxi–xxxii.

11–14 *had Mr Garrick lived . . . it has been honoured*: *TT* played nine or ten times, a very respectable run, in 1780 at Drury Lane, and was very well received by its audiences. Its reviews were mixed. The *London Packet* (Wednesday, 1 December to Friday, 3 December 1779) and the *London Evening Post* (Thursday, 2 December to Saturday, 4 December 1779) praised the comedy for the merits of its dialogue, wit, and polite satire. The *General Advertiser* (3 December 1779) considered it a good play for a female writer. For a more detailed account of the critical reception of the comedy, see Dorothy Hughes Eshleman, *Elizabeth Griffith* (Philadelphia, 1949).

14–15 *'with all its imperfections on its head'*: a reference to *Hamlet*, 1.5.78–9, where the ghost of Hamlet's father explains how Claudius murdered him without giving him a chance to be absolved of his sins: 'No reck'ning made, but sent to my account | With all my imperfections on my head.'

16 *into the closet*: in its reception by its readers. *TT* was first performed at Drury Lane on 2 December 1779, and published in early 1780.

20 *Mr Sheridan, senior*: Thomas Sheridan, a prominent Irish actor, playwright, and theatre manager, who moved to London at about the same time as Griffith. She probably knew him from her acting days in Dublin when he managed Smock Alley. He was the father of Richard Brinsley Sheridan, the more celebrated playwright and the manager of Drury Lane when *TT* was first performed. His wife, Frances Sheridan, was also a well-known playwright and novelist.

22–3 *not of modern growth*: and therefore trustworthy and sincere.

25 *Mrs Abington*: Frances Abington, an actress of lowly origins who rose to

become a trendsetter among modish society. She started a fashion of loose, flowing robes, and her gestures were widely copied. Mrs Abington's popularity was rising at the end of Garrick's career. He was not a supporter of hers and referred to her once as 'the worst of bad women'. See Parsons, 124 and Boaden, II. 141 (a note written by Garrick at the bottom of a letter received from Mrs Abington on 4 March 1776). Mrs Abington created the role of Lady Teazle in Richard Brinsley Sheridan's *School for Scandal*.

26 *Miss Pope*: Jane Pope, a disciple of the celebrated comic actress Kitty Clive, and a leading comic actress at Drury Lane during the reigns of both Garrick and Sheridan.

28 *Mr King*: Thomas King, a leading comic actor at Drury Lane during the tenures of both Garrick and Sheridan. Upon his retirement, Garrick bequeathed King his stage sword as a token of their long friendship.

31 *The Critic*: a burlesque by Richard Brinsley Sheridan, first performed 30 October 1779, just two months before the première of *TT*. Mr King played the character of Puff, 'a practitioner of panegyric'. Griffith here has found a way to pay tribute to the manager of Drury Lane, Sheridan, junior.

31–4 *'But it is impossible . . . judicious audience'*: Griffith has slightly paraphrased the line which reads, 'But it is not in the power of language to do justice to Mr King! Indeed, he more than merited those repeated bursts of applause which he drew from a most brilliant and judicious audience!' (1.2.173–6, in Richard Brinsley Sheridan, *The School for Scandal and Other Plays*, ed. Michael Cordner (Oxford, 1998)). The joke here pertains to Mr King playing Puff, a character who writes praises for, among other things, theatrical productions. Puff is demonstrating how he can write such praises without having seen the play. He gives an example, using the name of the well-known actor Mr King, whom the audience knows is himself!

THE CHARACTERS OF THE PLAY

Woodley: the Woodley family's name indicates they are all characters who 'would' do or act other than they do in fact. Sir William likes to appear harsher than he is; his nephew, Mr Woodley, 'would' be more responsible than he has been able to be; Lady Mary 'would' be a model wife if only she knew how.

Mountfort: the colonel's name literally means 'mountain of strength'. He is a responsible man of firm judgement, and his unswerving loyalty may be relied on.

Belford: the name may be a combination of *belle* and 'ford', and thus might mean a beautiful or good place to cross safely. Counsellor Belford leads his friends through the difficult waters of stubbornness and misunderstanding to the security of reconciliation.

Bromley: this name may come from 'broma', a worm that feeds on the wood of ships. If allowed to, these worms can destroy a ship. The *OED* also records that 'brombille' is an archaic form of 'bramble'. Thus, Mr and Mrs Bromley may be like worms feeding off and destroying an otherwise sound ship, or like brambles that clutch at and catch such innocents as the Woodleys.

Forward: a name indicating this servant's presumptuousness and ambition.

Waters: a name perhaps signalling that the servant is very emotional and often tearful, even when expressing gratitude.

PROLOGUE

2 *public weal*: community; welfare of the public.

4 *Attic salt*: refined or poignant wit; referring to the style of classical Athens.

6 *sores*: vices of society.

4–6 *And though . . . sharpest pickle*: and although the comic muse may season moral messages with sharp wit, and, with her art, will apply her rod to scour society of its vices. The prologue plays with the contemporary phrase, 'keeping a rod in pickle', that is, keeping the rod ready for inflicting a flogging.

6 *pickle*: salt or acid brine used to preserve foods. A rod soaked in pickle would inflict an especially painful wound.

7 *divine*: member of the clergy.

8 *Methodist*: an adherent of the evangelical movement led by John and Charles Wesley and George Whitefield. Methodists used itinerant preachers who would often speak out in the fields to the common people. Their sermons were characterized by great enthusiasm and emotion.

13 *Congreve or Wesley, Whitfield or Molière*: Griffith is suggesting common ground between comic playwrights such as William Congreve (1670–1729) and Molière (Jean Baptiste Poquelin, 1622–73) and leading preachers of the Methodist movement, John Wesley (1703–91) and George Whitefield (1714–70). All encourage their audiences to laugh and weep at their own and others' follies.

15 *or in himself*: either in himself.

17 *descried*: discovered.

20 *all Newmarket's hopeful knowledge*: a full knowledge of horse racing. Newmarket, close to Cambridge, was a town known for horse racing. The

333

college youth has imbibed the knowledge of Newmarket rather than that of Cambridge.

24 *jail*: debtors' prison.

26 *gives*: provides.

30 *small fry*: small fish; young fish; insignificant beings.

1.1.1 *involved*: beset with difficulties; entangled; enwrapped in embarrassing circumstances.

5–6 *Heigh-ho!*: an audible sigh; an expression of yawning or languor.

17 *tripping*: stumbling, figuratively. Forward has never observed any adulterous tendencies in Woodley.

18 *of business*: regarding finances.

21 *Jews*: moneylenders. See note to *BB* 1.1.38.

27–8 *The executions will therefore immediately be laid on*: your creditors will be allowed to seize upon your personal property immediately.

28 *prevail on Lady Mary to release her jointure*: obtain Lady Mary's permission to use her jointure to settle your debts. In order to protect a woman from penury if she were widowed, a legal provision could be made to allow her a life interest in designated property upon her husband's death. Lady Mary has such a jointure, and therefore since she holds this property jointly with him, her husband does not have the right to dispose of it himself, even if he is in debt.

29 *Duke's Place*: the first place Cromwell allowed Jews to settle in 1650, and the site of the first synagogue (1656). Duke's Place remained the centre for Jewish life in London throughout the eighteenth century. See Timbs, 483–4.

31 *Fleec'em*: the attorney's name indicates that he is out to strip Woodley utterly of all he possesses, much as if he were fleecing a sheep of its wool.

32 *small bill of costs*: list of expenses I have incurred in handling your business affairs. Forward's reaction to them suggests, as does Fleec'em's name, that the attorney is out to secure as much of Woodley's money as he can for himself.

33 S.D. *Enter Woodley*: Woodley's entrance suggests several possibilities for stage business. Has Forward hastily replaced the letter on the table when he hears Woodley enter, and is he pretending to straighten the rest of the papers? Or does Woodley catch him in the act of reading Fleec'em's letter?

39 *provide yourself*: secure another servant to replace me.

post-obit: a document promising payment of a debt after the debtor's death.

46 *Newmarket*: see note to Prologue 20.

48 *matches*: horse races; wagers on races.

49 *meeting*: assembly for a set of horse races, such as the Derby or the Westminster Races.

56 *incident to*: relating to; naturally appertaining to.

58 *That is selon*: that all depends.

60–1 *They are surest to win who carry least weight*: the horse who carries the least weight is the likeliest to win the race. Woodley suggests that, like the horse who carries the least weight, those who come to the track unencumbered with a fortune are the more likely to win their wagers.

75 *Charles Surface*: a character in Richard Brinsley Sheridan's *The School for Scandal* who, in 4.1, raises money by auctioning off the portraits of his ancestors. Colonel Mountfort goes on to imitate Charles Surface's high style of auctioneering when he demonstrates to Woodley how he would proceed with a horse he names Bucephalus. When *TT* was first staged at Drury Lane, Sheridan was the manager of the theatre and therefore responsible for producing the comedy. Griffith may well be demonstrating her gratitude to him with this small tribute.

76 *Bucephalus*: the famous horse of Alexander the Great. His name means 'ox-head', and Alexander was the only person who was capable of mounting him. The horse adored his master so that he knelt down each time Alexander wished to ride.

77 *right line*: direct line.

82 *Tattersall*: Richard Tattersall, a famous equine auctioneer who established an eponymous horse auction market and sporting rendezvous at Hyde Park Corner in 1766. In 1779, the year *TT* was written, Tattersall made his fortune by purchasing Highflyer, a celebrated stud horse, from Lord Bolingbroke. He is also mentioned by Hannah Cowley in *The Belle's Stratagem*. For more information see Timbs, 769–70.

89–90 *calculating, not their nativities, but their deaths*: figuring out how much time remains to them instead of calculating their horoscopes. Colonel Mountfort means for Woodley to think that Knightly and Careless are approaching their physical demise, but he is really only referring to the deaths of their fortunes.

91 *Boodle's*: one of the principal, fashionable, private gambling clubs in London. It was located at No. 28 St James's Street.

98–9 *granting annuities for this twelvemonth past*: for this past year, they have been setting up legal provisions for annual payments, for either a set term of years or in perpetuity, to various parties in order to get those parties to lend them money. What is unusual about an annuity is that it is chargeable not against the grantor's land but directly against the grantor or his heirs personally.

102–3 *compounding the terms and running together for three months each*: pooling their resources in order to hold out collectively for three months.

109 *visible*: disposed to be visited.

140 *Lady Mushroom's*: the name denotes someone *nouveau riche*; an upstart. Mushrooms appear full-blown seemingly out of nowhere, and so a person or family of obscure background that suddenly springs into the social scene with only their money to establish their place is referred to as a mushroom.

157 *Setwell*: a name that indicates a fine jeweller; one who sets stones well.

158–9 *this bar ... the drop*: parts of an earring. The bar is most likely a band of precious metal that Lady Mary wants removed to make room for larger stones. The drop is a pendant, in this case a diamond, that is the most eye-catching element of the earring.

160–1 *I must positively wear them at Court next Sunday*: Lady Mary is probably referring to her plans to attend a drawing-room held by the queen. These were usually held on Sundays.

179 *Christie's*: a famed auction house.

194 *filigree dressing-plate*: toiletry articles wrought of delicate threads and beads of silver.

195 *Gothic*: Lady Mary uses this term not to describe something truly in the Gothic style or medieval in design, but rather to suggest something so extremely old-fashioned that it has the aura of barbarity about it.

198 *Sèvres*: a costly porcelain manufactured in that city.

204 *doubtful*: Colonel Mountfort, Louisa, and Lady Mary play with various meanings of the word 'doubtful' in order to avoid being frank about Mrs Bromley. Colonel Mountfort tries to get away with dismissing Mrs Bromley's character as indistinct or uncertain, but Lady Mary understands that he believes her friend's character to be decidedly worse than questionable. When Louisa comes to her lover's aid, Lady Mary turns the word on her, asking if there is anything 'doubtful' about Louisa, either in terms of her opinion of Mrs Bromley or in terms of her own character. While denying that she herself is a doubtful character, Louisa teasingly equivocates by declaring she has no doubts about Mrs Bromley's character, but without revealing her true opinion of her sister-in-law's friend.

216 *cicisbeo*: recognized gallant; admirer of a married woman, possibly her lover. Lady Mary misuses the term at 2.2.47 when she refers to Colonel Mountfort as Louisa's 'cicisbeo' since Louisa is unmarried.

227 *mandarin*: the generic title for any Chinese official, but used as a term of derision for someone obese and pompous.

228 *dejeuner*: set of breakfast china.

239 *three hundred pieces*: three hundred and fifteen pounds. See note to *BB* 2.1.4.

243 *T. Knightly*: Knightly was previously referred to as 'Jack'. See 1.1.88.

259 *bon ton*: good style or breeding; fashionable society.

286 *drug*: a commodity no longer in demand and therefore difficult to sell.

298 *pocket-book*: a book-like case for holding papers, banknotes, or bills.

301 *Does the wind sit in that point?*: ah, are his financial straits as difficult as that?

302 *cut and dry*: all prepared, ready for use. The *OED* attributes this phrase to herbalist shops which displayed their herbs cut and dried, as opposed to fresh growing.

307 *The knowing ones are taken in*: even my wife and myself have been deceived by appearances about the extent of the Woodleys' wealth.

320 *memorandum*: record of a monetary transaction or debt.

325 *that's rather early*: five was the very earliest fashionable people would dine in the late eighteenth century. Later hours were more the *ton*. Bromley's comment is a slight criticism.

325–6 *Nay, no ceremony*: Woodley has moved to accompany Bromley out, but Bromley protests that there is no need for such formality and encourages Woodley to remain.

333–4 *what a hand . . . made of them*: how the other servants have been stealing from the Woodleys.

338 *ruffles*: gathered, ornamental frills for a garment. Ruffles were commonly worn by men at their wrists in the late eighteenth century.

345 *smokes a little*: has a fireplace that is producing a little smoke.

349 *old Square-Toes*: tight-laced old-fashioned person.

363 *college*: at university (at Oxford or Cambridge).

365 *quality*: high rank. Lady Mary comes from a noble family.

374 *Counsellor*: lawyer.

380 *gammoned*: beaten in backgammon. A gammon is a special type of victory in which one player has removed all his pieces before his opponent has removed one. Sir William wants to show how Belford was able to achieve a stunning victory over him.

2.1.5 *discriminating*: singling out.

24 *family-compact*: treaty between family members. Belford thinks he can achieve a peace between the two branches of the Woodley family, but only if Lady Mary is left out.

30 *Spa*: a Continental resort town (in Germany in Cowley's day, now in Belgium) famous for its mineral springs. Its name has become a generic term for luxurious, health-focused resorts.

38 *to have preserved such a gem pure and entire*: to have kept your wife free of

the taint of sexual scandal. Belford's comment reveals that although Lady Mary has a reputation for extravagance, she has no reputation for dishonour. Lady Mary's delicacy has helped her escape the snares being set for her, as becomes apparent in her later discussions with Mrs Bromley about Sir Harry Granger.

49 *Temple Coffee-house*: because of its proximity to the Inns of Court, a place where lawyers would gather.

54–5 *Do not distrust . . . to the suit*: trust me to do my best for you, but I can't guarantee my labours will succeed.

56 *proud*: gratified, pleased, glad.

68–9 *apprenticed my eldest boy*: found a position for my son as an apprentice, thus enabling him to learn a trade and eventually earn a living for himself.

2.2 s.d. *toilet*: dressing-table.

1 *dressing plate*: articles for a dressing-table made of silver, such as combs, brushes, small boxes, and mirrors.

4 *Mrs Stockwell*: her name suggests that Mrs Stockwell's husband has done well brokering stock and has acquired a good amount of stock / capital of his own.

8 *stalking show-glass*: person who serves as a living display case.

11 *done-up*: bankrupted.

13–14 *her chariot . . . since*: she has been able to maintain her style of living thanks to the wealth she had hidden away.

19–20 '*You'll look a goddess, and you'll move a queen!*': Mrs Bromley misquotes Pope's translation of *The Iliad*, III. i. 208: 'She moves a goddess, and she looks a queen.' Her butchery of Pope's poetry suggests she is only a pretender to knowledge and culture.

28–9 *the throne of Delhi*: the epitome of exotic luxury.

32–5 *in these days . . . lively regimental*: the fashion of the day was for women's dress to resemble military uniforms.

39 *Corydon*: a generic proper name for a shepherd or rustic. The source of the name is in Theocritus and Virgil and it was commonly used in English pastoral poetry.

47 *Louisa's cicisbeo*: Lady Mary uses the term 'cicisbeo' incorrectly, since it refers to the admirer of a married woman. Perhaps she misunderstands it or perhaps she is so flustered by Mrs Bromley's hints about Sir Harry that she stumbles over her response.

75 *toys*: trifles.

82 *If it should take wind*: if word of this should get out.

92 *Duke's Place*: see note to 1.1.29.

91–9 *Borrow, then . . . .a reproach to their sex, perhaps*: although she passes it off as a joke, Mrs Bromley appears to be trying to tempt Lady Mary to borrow money from Sir Harry Granger. Lady Mary is extremely sensitive to the improprieties of the suggestion: it would be assumed that a lady who obtained money from a gentleman had paid for it with sexual favours. It is likely that Mrs Bromley wishes to see Lady Mary compromised in order to be better able to blackmail her.

102 *finest*: most admirable; most ornamented; smartest dressed.

110 *adio, mia cara*: Italian for 'Good-bye, my dear.'

2.3.2–3 *Cinque ace*: five one. Sir William calls out the result of his dice roll, a five and a one. In backgammon, one rolls two dice.

9 *Hastily*: uttered in a suddenly irritable or angry manner.

10 *box*: box used for shaking the dice in backgammon. Sir William is impatient for Belford to take his turn.

66 *party*: game.

109 *Ruined!*: any loss of stature in society can be called ruin, whether a loss of means or honour. In order to escape embarrassment, Sir William plays with several meanings of the word. Initially he means to convey that Woodley and Lady Mary have lost all their money, but he tries to dilute his meaning by saying that the word has become such a fashionable commonplace that it is meaningless. See 2.3.117–18, where Sir William uses it to refer to losing his dignity by giving in to Lady Mary's tears.

110–11 *lords, and commons*: nobility and commoners.

2.4.3 *impose upon*: deceive by false representations.

34–5 *Don Choleric*: irascible man whose temperament is tolerated only because of his rank; a stereotype from Spanish plays, which were known for their hot-headed characters.

68 *en Turc*: dressed in Turkish style.

80–1 *a hundred and ninety-one excuses within these two days*: it would appear that rumours of the Woodleys' ruin are abroad and people of fashion are beginning to drop their acquaintance.

83 *Lady Sitfast*: a woman whose name indicates how difficult it is to remove her from a card table.

86 *Mrs Henpeck*: her name indicates that she dominates her husband despite her drooping demeanour at the card table.

87–8 *the after-game*: a second game played in order to reverse or improve the issues of the first.

94 *tempers a salad*: adjusts the seasonings of a salad. Bromley plays with several meanings of the word 'temper'. To temper a salad would be to bring it into culinary balance, but Bromley is also reacting to Lady Mary's refusal to allow Sir Harry into her house. He is apparently trying

to reassure Lady Mary that despite her reasons for banishing him, Sir Harry is a restrained man, a harmonious influence on company.

95 *compendium*: epitome; an embodiment in miniature.

97 *Hannah Glasse*: (1708–70) author of a popular cookbook, *The Art of Cookery*.

98 *Most excellent ... fashion!*: Lady Mary is being facetious, although Bromley chooses to take her remark seriously in the next line.

103 *I attend Mrs Bromley*: it is notable that Lady Mary rejects Bromley's arm in to dinner. Her interactions with Bromley in this scene are characterized by a subtle distrust that might be highlighted by an actor's choice. Although taken in by Mrs Bromley's professions of friendship for her, Lady Mary has a clear sense of propriety when it comes to relationships between the sexes. Lady Mary is lukewarm in her reception of any flattery by Bromley, and (see note to 2.2.91–9) there also seems to be more than Sir Harry Granger's 'being out of fashion' in question in Lady Mary's marked exclusion of him from her house and her strong reaction to Mrs Bromley's professions of Sir Harry's affection for Lady Mary. Mrs Bromley appears to push both her own husband and Sir Harry on Lady Mary as admirers. Given the Bromleys' blatant immorality, it seems plausible that another of their hopes is to entrap Lady Mary in an illicit relationship, or at least the appearance of one, in order to gain more from her through blackmail. There is a continuing tension in the play regarding how far the con artists can lure their innocent prey. Lady Mary seems to have more resistance than her hapless husband. In the version of *TT* performed on its opening night, Sir Harry Granger does appear and, bribed by Mrs Bromley, makes an unsuccessful attempt on Lady Mary's chastity. Griffith subsequently cut the character, banishing Sir Harry from both the stage and published edition of the comedy as Lady Mary banished him from her home. See Dorothy Hughes Eshleman, *Elizabeth Griffith* (Philadelphia, 1949), 99–100, and the Larpent manuscript of *TT*.

3.1.29 *macaronies*: young men who affect the styles and fashions of the Continent; fops. The designation derives from the Macaroni Club, whose name may have indicated its members' preference for foreign food.

hearts of oak: true-bred Englishmen; men of courageous spirit; men capable of endurance.

30 *aspens*: men who are timorous. Aspen trees are known for their quivering leaves.

33 *the oak and the laurel*: courage and artistic achievement. The oak is a symbol of strength and the laurel is the emblem of distinction in poetry.

112 *pin-money*: see note to *BB* 2.1.28–9.

128 *sister*: sister-in-law.

130–1 *questions nor commands, but cross-purposes*: these games were favourite eighteenth-century pastimes. In 'questions and commands', each person takes a turn at addressing ludicrous questions and commands to each of the other members of the party. In 'cross-purposes', each individual or team has a different idea of the subjects and arguments at stake and so, while attempting to work towards the same goal, they interfere with one another due to misconceptions. Without realizing it, Sir William is about to begin playing both games at once with Louisa by commanding her to marry without knowing who her prospective husband is and and by working at cross-purposes with her by assuming he understands Louisa's attitude towards this prospective marriage while she fruitlessly tries to clarify the matter.

132–3 *Come nearer . . . afraid of?*: note how Sir William complains that both Louisa and Lady Mary keep their distance from him in the scenes in which they enter his presence. This may give a clue to Sir William's physical mannerisms. His blustery language would seem to be a counterpart to his movements and gestures. Sir William's use of large quantities of space may be the source of a good deal of comic business in his scenes. Other characters need to give him ample room or risk being knocked over, hit by flying objects, or swept off their feet. By this point of the play, the audience would know very well what the ladies are afraid of, and so, unbeknownst to Sir William, his question is comical. See 'Introduction' to this volume, pp. xxxii–xxxiii, for more on the *commedia* origins of Sir William's actions.

136–7 *what favourable dispositions I have towards you*: Sir William employs two meanings of 'disposition' at once: he is both favourably disposed towards Louisa, and he is making favourable dispositions for her, that is, he is making preparations to settle her financial affairs to her benefit.

161 *kites*: birds of prey; figuratively, rapacious people.

173 *separate maintenance*: support given by a husband to a wife when they have separated.

209 *benchers*: senior members of the Inns of Court.

214 *brief*: summary of the facts of a legal case with references to relevant points of law written for the instruction of the legal counsel who is to argue the case in court. Belford uses the term metaphorically: his hope of attaining Louisa is a brief, and Louisa's delight in greeting him is the first argument in its favour.

3.2.3 *give out*: abandon play.

17 *clear*: settle accounts; discharge debts.

41 *Gamesters, like lovers*: gamblers are as quick to forget their vows as lovers.

45–7 *But while there are such things . . . bonds*: while Bromley tries to insinuate himself with Colonel Mountfort by suggesting that they are both men of honour, Colonel Mountfort employs a number of double meanings to intimate that he understands what Bromley is about. By reminding Bromley that there are knaves in the world, Colonel Mountfort suggests that Bromley is one of them and not a man of honour. The references to bars and bonds are not solely to courts of law and legal obligations. In addition to the bar signifying the place in court where criminals are arraigned, bars are both the false dice the colonel suspects Bromley has been using and an objection to a legal action so forceful that it breaks off the action. The revelations of Bromley's criminal activity might be sufficient bars to any attempt on Bromley's part to bring legal action against Woodley. Colonel Mountfort's choice of words may even imply a threat since a bar is also an instrument for breaking criminals on the rack. Bonds also suggest images of confinement and prison as well as legal commitments to paying sums of money. Bromley indeed responds to Colonel Mountfort's speech as if it were a veiled threat and hastily retreats.

56–7 *through my . . . at your heels*: I would have you publicly disgraced and expelled from society by having you paraded through my regiment with a drum banging behind you.

58 *flaunting*: impudent; extravagant; ostentatious.

62 *in the first sets*: in the most exclusive of social circles.

63 *nice*: scrupulous in matters of reputation.

66–8 *damaged dowager . . . her ladyship*: widowed noblewoman whose reputation is so tarnished that only her rank saves her from social exile.

97 *stand and deliver*: the cry of a highwayman.

103–4 *opened your trenches . . . Knight of the Castle*: begun your assault on a castle to rescue the fair damsel from the tyrannic knight who imprisons her; that is to say, approached Sir William about your intentions towards Louisa. Woodley is being slightly sarcastic regarding Sir William's tight hold on the money and people he controls.

107 *even with*: equal to. Colonel Mountfort's goodwill towards Sir William is equal to Sir William's good opinion of him.

109 *natural and unsophisticate*: uncorrupted and genuine.

110 *like any Jew*: see note to *BB* 1.1.38.

4.1.19–20 *mauvais ton*: something not done in fashionable society; gauche; bad form.

21 *bathing-places*: fashionable spas.

87 *levity*: unbecoming frivolity; taking serious issues too lightly.

93 *of a piece*: cut from the same piece of cloth.

101 *barrister*: a legal counsellor who has been granted the privilege of serving as an advocate in the superior courts.

4.2.5 *service of plate*: a set of silver serving pieces for the table.

25 *You are an idle young rogue!*: Sir William jumps to the conclusion that Colonel Mountfort is about to apply to him for monetary assistance. In typical fashion, Sir William gets carried away with an idea before he knows the facts.

28 *terra firma*: property in the country.

42 *cent per cent man*: usurer; literally someone who charges interest equal to the amount of the principal.

44 *funds*: see note to *BB* 5.2.57.

44–5 *now that the nation is so poor*: at the time *TT* was written and performed, England was continuing to be impoverished by the high cost of the war with the American colonies, which followed the treasury depletions caused by the wars with France between 1754 and 1763 in Europe and North America.

86 *sa, sa, sa*: from French, 'ça, ça, ça', used by fencers when delivering a thrust.

98 *Huff-Cap*: swashbuckler; swaggerer.

108 *The swiftest . . . jack*: careful aim and thought are more likely to attain their goal than brisk, but reckless, action: a bowling metaphor.

109 *'fair and softly'*: Belford is referring to two proverbs that advise taking a slow and careful path to one's goal: 'Fair and softly goes far' and 'Fair and softly, as lawyers go to heaven'. See Wilson, 238.

117–18 *'many things fall . . . lip'*: this popular proverb can be traced back to ancient Greece. It has been repeated in Latin, Italian, and English throughout the centuries. See Wilson, 160.

122 *Now, what can he mean?*: it is not clear whether this line is an aside or is directed to Belford.

138 *want more clerks*: i.e. to expedite the drafting of the financial documents for the marriage.

150 *witness on the table*: witness under oath to speak the truth.

195 *old bachelor*: perhaps a reference to the Restoration comedy *The Old Batchelour* (1693) by William Congreve, in which an old man's love for a young woman leads him into humiliation. There may be some ambiguity in Belford's remark: is he referring to Sir William's schemes or to his own concealed affection for Louisa?

4.3.5 *brooks*: *1780* records 'brook', which is grammatically incorrect.

12 *Solomon*: biblical king of Israel, the son of David, renowned for his wisdom.

Queen of Sheba: beautiful and wise queen who came to Solomon's court to test his wisdom (1 Kings 9:1–13).

19 *execution*: seizure, by sheriff's order, of the goods or person of a debtor in default of payment.

343

20 *gold loo*: a form of lanterloo, a card game related to whist. A player who fails to take a trick or who breaks any of the rules is 'looed' and must pay into the pool. Loo has a myriad of varieties and therefore it is difficult to be certain what varieties are played at Lady Mary's party. In 'limited loo' the stakes are fixed; in 'unlimited loo' they are not and can escalate quickly. 'Gold loo' suggests a high stakes game, but whether it refers to stakes of gold pieces that are limited or whether it refers to unlimited stakes is not clear. For more information on eighteenth-century card games, see Parlett.

21 *presentiment*: a vague expectation; a premonition. In Mrs Bromley's case, this expectation is based on her skill as a cheat rather than a premonition of good luck.

26 *a very honest man*: Bromley means that Fleece'em will live up to the promise he has been bribed to make.

small token of friendship: bribe.

30 *keeping . . . terms*: continuing to have dealings.

46 *hartshorn*: smelling salts. The chief source of ammonia at the time was the horn or antler of a hart sliced or rasped.

5.1 S.D. *An ante-chamber . . . for a rout*: the setting for this scene makes especial use of the depth of the late eighteenth-century stage. One pair of shutters, in a partially open position, serves to mark the division between the ante-chamber and the drawing-room beyond it. That drawing-room must be, or must give the appearance of being, sizeable, as it will need to hold the large cast of card players and other guests at Lady Mary's assembly (5.4). The action that takes place in the ante-chamber, which is closer to the forestage and audience, is of a more intimate nature than what will occur in the more spectacular scene of the rout upstage: we hear servants gossiping, Woodley and Lady Mary discussing their family affairs, and Lady Mary's soliloquy. The festivities that take place later in the upstage space framed by open shutters are more public and emotion- ally at a greater remove from the audience and serve as a backdrop and counterpoint to the intimate action occurring downstage.

1 *gold loo*: see note to 4.3.20.

monsters: an obscure loo term, but it seems possibly to derive from a seventeenth-century multi-player version of *triomphe*, a precursor to games like loo. According to Parlett, there was a version of Triomphe known originally as *l'homme* ('man'), and which later became known as *la bête* ('beast'). As in the game of ombre, a player who attempted to win three tricks thereby became 'the man' or lone bidder, but if he were to be challenged and then failed to make his tricks, he was 'beasted' and no longer a 'man' and had to pay a double stake or *bête*. It appears likely that the 'monsters' of the loo games at Lady Mary's party are closely related to the double stakes 'beasts' of *la bête*.

2 *Two at half-crowns!*: Forward calculates that the two regular loo tables he has been instructed to set up will have low stakes of only a half-crown, or two shillings and sixpence.

3–4 *they are . . . a-piece*: Forward is attempting to calculate how much he is likely to take in from the players at each table. He estimates that he will receive a guinea from each gold loo table, but only twelve shillings from those who play for half-crown stakes. The higher stake tables therefore are assigned the better locations in the room.

6 *whiskers*: whist players; whisters. Whist is a trick-taking game and a precursor of bridge.

8 *sneaking*: niggardly; paltry. Forward is critical of whist because even when the stakes are high, one doesn't win or lose money quickly at the game. Because whist players are characteristically more cautious with their money, they are also likely to be less generous with the servants.

9 *Faro*: a game in which players bet on the order in which certain cards will appear when cards are drawn from the top of the deck. According to Forward, faro is played for very high stakes.

11 *a pharaoh's table*: James obviously is unfamiliar with the high stakes game of 'faro'. He therefore makes an unintentional pun when he asks whether this card table is intended for a king of Egypt. Forward picks up on the pun in the next line, according the faro players the best place in the room, for one must be nearly as rich as a pharaoh to play the game.

13 *macao*: a one-card version of baccara.

birds: Forward is making a play on words: 'macao' is also a variant spelling of 'macaw', a tropical bird similar to a parrot.

17–18 *out of place*: unemployed.

20 *all-fours*: a gambling card game played mostly by the lower orders.

23 *dons*: upper-class men. In this case it might refer to distinguished men who are not loose with their money since Forward has already sneered at the low stakes in whist. The various card games are associated with different sorts of players.

27 *tallow*: a material derived from animal fat which could be used to make inexpensive candles.

31 *packing penny*: money given to an employee upon dismissal. Forward estimates he will earn twelve gold pieces on his last night serving the Woodleys.

34 *funds*: Forward employs a double meaning: personal funds/the national funds.

37 *ices*: ice-creams and water ices.

39 *King's Road*: a fashionable shopping area.

82 *jointure*: see note to 1.1.28.

123 *sideboard*: a piece of furniture in a dining-room used for holding side-dishes, wine, and silver. Often with cupboards and drawers for storage.

126 *Neatness*: elegance of form characterized by simplicity or freedom from embellishment.

128 *Ranelagh!*: a public pleasure garden with a rococo rotunda in Chelsea where one could go to hear music, to take tea or wine, or to view art, sculpture, and lighting displays.

128–9 *Ay, there's the rub!*: although the sentiments of Lady Mary's soliloquy are admirable, they are expressed in a comically overly-dramatic way. The exaggeration is emphasized by mourning the loss of fashionable pleasures with an allusion to Shakespeare's *Hamlet*: To die, to sleep— | To sleep—perchance to dream: ay, there's the rub, | For in that sleep of death what dreams may come | When we have shuffled off this mortal coil, | Must give us pause' (3.1.64–8).

5.2.10 *Oedipus . . . riddle*: by solving the riddle of the Sphinx, Oedipus put an end to the curse plaguing Thebes; likewise Colonel Mountfort is plagued by Sir William's conundrum about Louisa's marriage and only her explanation can put an end to his suffering.

17–19 *When all . . . he stood the cast?*: the colonel, carried away by his passion, seems to have forgotten that he recently caught Woodley literally staking his happiness on the turn of a die and trembling before casting it.

5.4 S.D. *A drawing-room . . . company at play*: the shutters that partially revealed this drawing-room in 5.1 are now fully opened to display the party scene in all its grandeur. This scene presents the greatest challenge for directors and designers. It involves a very large speaking cast, the suggestion of many more people, and a great deal of activity on several levels. Although Forward has indicated that there will be a number of other games played at Lady Mary's party, there are only three card games being played by characters who speak: whist, loo, and quadrille. The players at each table have their own conversations going regarding the game being played and their language provides a metaphoric background for the actions of the major characters. Each game is further characterized by the people playing: the whist players are noblemen and high-stakes gamesters, the loo players are women playing for high stakes, and the quadrille players are women playing for lower stakes. How and whether to suggest more people is left to the director and designer's imagination. Margaret Anne Doody has suggested that the card players may be dressed for the masquerade that is to follow Lady Mary's party. Masquerade costumes would add a surrealistic quality to the scene.

1 *Fifty pieces on the rubber!*: I bet fifty pieces of gold that I will win two out of the next three games of whist.

3 *A Pam flush!*: in loo, a natural four-card flush topped by the jack of clubs (Pam). It is the highest hand in the game.

4 *You seldom . . . madam*: the second loo player suggests that the first loo player cheats.

5 *Pam-box*: a container for holding one's winnings at loo.

7 *lose, . . . have leave to speak*: proverbial, 'give losers leave to speak'. See Wilson, p. 485.

8 *Please to mark the loo*: the first loo player, who has just won with a Pam flush, reminds the second loo player that her loss means she owes a sixty-guinea loo to the betting pool. A player who has failed to take a trick or who has broken a rule is said to be 'looed' and must pay a sum or 'loo' into the pool.

17 *monsters*: although not identical to the *bête* discussed in the game of *homme*, in the note at 5.1.1, the monsters seem to bear some relationship to when penalties are to be doubled in the version of loo being played at Lady Mary's party. They are also a *double entendre* that calls attention to the beastliness of Mrs Bromley.

20–1 *The monsters . . . single stake*: see note to 5.1.1.

30–1 S.D. *(To the table)*: it is not clear whether Mrs Bromley goes to the loo table or turns to look at the state of the play in order to try to disengage herself from Lady Mary. If she does go to the table, Lady Mary follows her because the two women continue their conversation aside while the audience listens to the card players chat. When the audience is allowed to rejoin Mrs Bromley and Lady Mary's conversation, Lady Mary has revealed her plans to Mrs Bromley.

33–4 *I don't believe . . . two hours*: it is not clear what must occur before the stakes may revert from double to single and the loo can end. Perhaps the stakes remain double until someone wins a hand without a flush.

35 *basted*: a variant of 'beasted'; to have failed to have made one's tricks in a card game and to be subject to a double stake.

39 *a renounce is a beast*: a renounce is the failure to follow suit on a trick, to revoke a card, or to renege. It is subject to the double stakes of being beasted. The language of being beasted and renouncing also reflects on Mrs Bromley's renunciation of Lady Mary.

40 *Judgement!*: a formal call for a decision on the play.

42–3 *a crown a-fish*: each betting chip is worth only a crown. A small flat piece of bone or ivory used as a betting chip is called a fish. The loo players, who play for guineas, scorn the low stakes of the quadrille players.

47–8 *summer camps*: military camps that have become tourist attractions. See notes to *Belle* 1.1.62, 73.

48–9 *en passant*: in passing.

49 *love and a cottage*: Mrs Bromley, as usual, mangles her allusions. She means to say 'love in a cottage', a phrase by which she sneeringly refers to a marriage without sufficient means, but she also uses it to cast doubt on whether Lady Mary and Mr Woodley will be able to maintain their love exiled from society in their country 'cottage'.

57 *romantic*: a style found characteristically in romance novels: tending towards the noble or chivalric; exaggeratedly picturesque; placing a high emphasis on loyalty, friendship, and love enduring through all difficulties.

62 *Lurched at four!*: I lost after scoring four. To lose a game of whist without scoring five is said to be a lurch. The first whist player is frustrated because he had scored four. Also, Lady Mary has been metaphorically lurched by Mrs Bromley.

83 *The loo is over*: this particular game of loo is finished. Also, Mrs Bromley's duplicity has been understood by Lady Mary, and therefore, that particular game is over now too.

94 *cantoned*: quartered.

96 *Four by honours*: you have scored four by being dealt all four top trump cards. Being dealt all four top trump cards, or honours, results in scoring an additional four points. Also, the whist player's language calls attention to Colonel Mountfort's honourable attentions to Louisa.

98 *de Moivre*: Abraham de Moivre (1667–1754), the author of *The Doctrine of Chances or a Method of Calculating the Probability of Events in Play* (1718) and *Annuities on Lives* (1743).

101 *a bubble*: someone empty-headed; a dupe.

cut a loser: break off the game while losing.

103 *Two Pams*: Pam is the knave of clubs and the highest trump in the game of five-card loo. Mrs Bromley has been discovered to be holding two Pams at once, either in her hand or perhaps concealed on her person, and is thus revealed to be a cheat. How this revelation occurs is left to the play's modern director.

119 *Put all the monsters out at once*: this would seem to refer to clearing all penalties and restoring the game to its normal state. It also refers to putting out Mrs Bromley. See note to 5.4.17.

126 *oracle*: one divinely inspired to reveal the future, sometimes in language not immediately understood.

132 *metamorphose*: transformation.

134 *gauze*: light, transparent fabric.

155 *till the rubber is out*: until someone has won two out of three games in a series.

159 *the points of our game*: the score.

162 *privileged*: exempted; immune.

163–4 *or we may be lurched . . . seven*: or we may lose decisively, even though we outscore our opponent. The second and third whist players appear to be in the process of cheating the first whist player, a lord. Not only has the second whist player been dealing a series of remarkably lucky hands to himself (see ll. 96–8 above), but now he and the third whist player are anxious to escape before being discovered by the bailiffs.

166–7 *We are all married women*: the first loo player intimates that since married women have a fuller knowledge of men, they are more hardened to the world and various social indiscretions than their virginal sisters.

168 *harpies*: ministers of divine vengeance resembling birds of prey with women's faces from Greek mythology; rapacious, vengeful, grasping people that prey on others.

169 *'Tis your deal, madam*: the drawing power of the loo game is strong enough to tempt the second loo player into another deal even though she claims she will faint if she sees the bailiffs.

185 *Lady Freakish's*: the name denotes Lady Freakish's capricious nature.

5.5.32 *security*: pledged to guarantee Woodley's debts with his own property or money.

71 S.D. *severally*: separately; through different doorways or exits.

EPILOGUE

Miss Farren: Elizabeth Farren (1759?–1829) was a rising young actress performing at Drury Lane when *TT* opened. She became one of the theatre's leading actresses, succeeding to Mrs Abington's roles upon that lady's retirement in 1782. Farren attracted the attention of the Earl of Derby and, in 1797, she retired from the stage to marry him and become Countess of Derby.

3 *We merrier folks*: those of us who portray comedy.

6 *For, in this age . . . surely be to rave!*: the speaker mockingly suggests that contemporary society is so virtuous that there is no vice to be railed at.

10 *one frail one's left*: any morally weak woman who is unable to resist temptation remains.

12 *macaronies*: see n. to 3.1.29 above.

20 *famed*: in *1780*, this word appears as 'formed'. In the copy I have used, however, Griffith herself has crossed out 'formed' and written 'famed' above it. I have followed her correction.

24 *possessed*: Griffith here puns on the word 'possessed', meaning both controlled by a demonic spirit, as opposed to being divinely inspired, and owned, as a piece of property.

25 *shelves*: submerged sandbanks or ledges of rock that can damage a ship; also slang for women with no prospects of marrying. Griffith plays with the nautical metaphor: women are the ships, men the pilots. The men must guide their womenfolk away from hidden dangers; it is the men's fault if women become morally weak.

The Belle's Stratagem

DEDICATION

2 *The Queen*: Charlotte Sophie of Mecklenburg-Strelitz (1744–1818), wife of George III. Queen Charlotte was known for her domestic virtues and, as the mother of fifteen children, was an emblem of devoted motherhood.

THE CHARACTERS OF THE PLAY

Doricourt: a name possibly meaning 'golden courtship', from *d'or*, ('golden'), and 'court'.

Hardy: physically robust; courageous, daring. These first qualities pertain to the father; the latter to his daughter Letitia.

Touchwood: any woody substance that catches fire easily; tinder. Sir George easily blazes with jealousy.

Flutter: make an ostentatious display; create perpetual meaningless chatter or noise.

Saville: perhaps a combination of *savoir*, 'to know', and *ville*, 'town'. Saville is thus knowing in the ways of the town and therefore able to defuse Courtall's plots.

Villers: also from *ville*. Villers is the consummate man of the town, a sophisticate.

Courtall: a name indicating a character with no discrimination. Courtall pursues all women for the sport of it.

Silvertongue: sweet-spoken; eloquent. The name indicates the character's success in his profession: he is an auctioneer.

Crowquill: a type of quill used for a writing implement.

Mountebank: 'an itinerant quack who from an elevated platform appealed to his audience by means of stories, tricks, juggling, and the like' (*OED*).

Mask: one who earns his living by impersonation.

Racket: indicating one who lives a gay, busy social life.

Ogle: flirt or coquette.

Kitty Willis: 'Kitty' is a term used to describe a sexually loose woman.

The last name perhaps indicates someone 'willess'. Kitty is a loose woman who is used as an instrument in the plots of others.

Fagg: a name that comes from 'fag': weary, fatigued from drudgery. Mrs Fagg is worn down by her hard work and meagre pay puffing for Silvertongue.

1.1 s.d. *Lincoln's Inn*: one of the four Inns of Court located near St Paul's Cathedral. The inns housed law students, young barristers, and the offices of senior lawyers.

s.d. *at the top of the stage*: see note to *BB* 2.1.179–80. This staging allows Saville to enter the stage at a position which immediately commands the attention of the audience. He then meanders, as if lost, downstage, losing the power of his original position, but drawing the audience into a more intimate relationship with him as he confesses his confusion.

4 *pretty*: excellent, admirable (ironic).

9 *him*: the stableman or hosteller watching their horses.

12 *long robes*: lawyers.

17 *Fallow*: a ploughed field that is not planted. The name indicates the rusticity of the cousins as well as their readiness to be 'planted', or married.

19 *Holborn*: an unfashionable and inexpensive neighbourhood, both business and residential, located between the City and the more fashionable Bloomsbury, and containing within it the Old Bailey, Newgate Prison, and Lincoln's Inn.

20 *Hebes*: beautiful, innocent country maidens. Hebe, goddess of youth and spring, was the daughter of Zeus and Hera.

21 *Northumberland*: most northern county in England, located on the Scottish border and known primarily for its ports, heavy industry, and mining.

in course were: of course one would therefore expect them to be.

26 *maypoles*: painted tall poles decked with flowers to be danced around on May Day; very tall, thin people.

26–7 *Æsop style*: hunchbacked, like Æsop, the Roman fabulist.

27 *opened*: began speaking.

30 *park*: Hyde Park. Sir John Fielding advises that Hyde Park was 'the usual place of exercise in a morning for fine gentlemen and ladies, who resort thither to see and be seen' (*Guide to London*, 1776).

Almack's: Almack's assembly rooms in King Street, St James's. Balls were held there once a week during the London season for subscription holders. A fashionable club, that became open to both sexes, was founded in 1770 at Almack's and was known for high-stakes gambling.

34 *knight-baronights*: a nonsense title. Perhaps Courtall is mocking his cousins who can't tell a knight from a baronet, especially since both are addressed as 'Sir', and their wives as 'Lady', a title to which they aspire.

38 *the gardens here*: the gardens at the Inns of Court were considered worth visiting.

46 *Paul's*: St Paul's Cathedral.

lions: the most famous of the animals held in a small menagerie at the Tower of London, one of the sights country visitors felt required to see when in town.

waxwork: while there were several collections of waxworks in eighteenth-century London, Courtall is most likely referring to the most renowned, Mrs Salmon's Moving Waxwork on Fleet Street.

46–7 *at their service*: then I would have been happy to escort them.

48 *pocketbooks*: small guidebooks, easily carried about in one's pocket.

52 *at war with woodcocks and partridges*: hunting in the country.

52–7 *during the war . . . two wives*: in 1780, when *Belle* was first performed, England was at war with the American colonies and with the colonies' chief ally, France. The war carried large numbers of young men off to North America and to the West Indies to serve as soldiers. The result was that the number of marriageable men at home was palpably reduced.

60 *blackballed*: voted against, outlawed. Traditionally such voting was done by casting a white ball into a ballot box to signify 'yea' or a black ball 'nay'.

coterie: i.e. the most exclusive of exclusive gatherings.

62 *camps break up*: military camps disperse. Britain responded to France's recognition of the independence of Britain's American colonies and declaration of war against Britain in 1778 by establishing military camps in southern England along the routes of a possible French invasion. These camps attracted tourists from all classes who came to observe the soldiers practising military manœuvres. Saville contends that prudence and chastity won't stand much of a chance once the military camps disperse and the licentious soldiers, as well as their libidinous followers, return to town.

64 *commons-doctors*: divorce lawyers. See note to *IM* 5.4.153–4.

65 *crim. con*: criminal conversation; 'adultery, in the legal aspect of a *trespass* against the husband at common law' (*OED*). Such cases were widely publicized via the newspapers, with correspondents named, thus having the 'wonderful effect' of increasing business for the commons-doctors.

66 *at large*: fully written out or described.

68 *Gravesend*: part of the London port system, located on the Thames in north-west Kent. Fishing was its major industry.

72–3 *playing at pop-gun*: playing at being soldiers like children with pop-guns.

73 *Coxheath*: see note to l. 62 above. Courtall is remarking that all the gentry who would usually be spending this time of year foxhunting are at Coxheath, a military camp near Maidstone that had become a phenomenal tourist attraction. Spectators, ranging from the lower classes to the most exclusive sets, flocked to Coxheath to watch the troops. Coxheath quickly expanded into a miniature city with its own merchants, tailors, and purveyors who catered to the needs of its transient population. Coxheath became so fashionable that plays were written about it and staged in London for enthusiastic audiences who couldn't get enough of the camp. One of these pieces was Richard Brinsley Sheridan's *The Camp*, which, after opening on 15 October 1778, played at Drury Lane for a fabulously successful fifty-six performances in its first season. For more information on Coxheath, see Gillian Russell, *The Theatres of War: Performance, Politics, and Society, 1793–1815* (Oxford, 1995), 33–51.

77 *cut us all out*: outclassed us all.

80 *levées*: receptions for people of high rank held in a nobleman's bedroom upon his arising. In this case Doricourt's valet is treated like a nobleman by tradespeople who want to attend him upon his arising to procure his favour with Doricourt.

81–2 *à la mode de*: in the fashion of.

83 *insisted upon his waistcoat for muffs*: demanded that Doricourt's valet give them Doricourt's recognizable waistcoat so they could have it made into muffs for them.

111 *Patagonians*: South American Indians who were reputed to be the tallest known people; therefore, giants.

1.2.2 *monsieur's*: Doricourt's French valet's.

3 *overhauling*: displaying in detail, pulling around.

parcel: crowd, pack.

7 *tête-a-têtes*: gossip columns concerning romantic encounters and scandals.

9 *sixpenny cuts*: inexpensive engravings used for magazines.

10 *foundation*: i.e. basis of fact.

15 *supporters*: the kind of details which will lend circumstantial probability to the sensational claims about him my article will make.

19–20 *Lord Tinket's*: this nobleman's name seems to be drawn from the 'tinking' sound of a bell and the proverb, ' "As the fool thinketh, the bell tinketh", i.e. to the fool the bell seems to say what he wants it to say; referring to the superstitious notion that the tinkling of a bell sometimes gives an oracular monition or answer' (*OED*). Lord Tinket's name would seem to suggest that many fools listen with grave seriousness to his

353

words, although these words contain no more meaning than the tinking sound of a bell.

26 *sun and sun round London*: a day's journey from London.

41 *en vérité, messieurs!*: in truth, gentlemen!

avez: have.

42 *Serviteur, serviteur*: your servant, your servant (said as a means of dismissing those addressed).

43 *autre*: other.

44 *pour moi*: for me.

45 *Allons, monsieur*: come, sir.

46–7 *Le Mosse . . . Verdue . . . Grossette . . . Detanville*: these Parisian fine apparel makers were presumably real people known to Cowley's audience.

51 *Je suis mort de peur*: literally, 'I am dead from fear'. The Frenchman is startled to recognize Saville.

52 *Excusez mon erreur*: forgive my mistake.

53 *à vous voir*: to see you.

1.3.2 *St James's*: Doricourt is probably referring to attending a *levée* for the king at court.

8 *bonjour*: hello, good day.

adieu: good-bye, farewell.

16 *fellows*: men; servants.

25 *He*: the Frenchman.

30 *adventitious*: extraneous.

43 *virtu*: love of the fine arts. It is the root of 'virtuoso', one who collects art, antiquities, or other curios.

50 *Pleadwell's*: an appropriate name for an attorney.

61 *L'air enjoué!*: a certain aura of playfulness or spriteliness.

73 *petits-maîtres*: fops; dandies; effeminate men.

toasts: reigning beauties to whom a company is requested to drink.

77 *grisettes*: working-class girls, such as shop assistants. The name comes from an inexpensive grey fabric worn by such girls in France.

Mall: a tree-bordered promenade in St James's Park, fashionable in the seventeenth and eighteenth centuries.

83 *French fleets, and Spanish captures*: the French became allies of Britain's American colonies and joined their war for independence from Britain in 1778. In return, the American colonies agreed to support French territorial gains in the West Indies. In 1780 French fleets, with the assistance

of Spain, who joined the alliance with the American colonies in 1779, were keeping British forces well engaged in the West Indies. It is not clear whether Doricourt is referring to Spanish captures of British vessels or Britain making captures of Spanish vessels.

89 *locum-tenens*: one who fills the role of another in the absence of the proper office-holder.

91 *Never . . . spectacles*: you are too young to moralize.

96 *A la mode anglaise*: such Englishness!

1.4.3–4 *voyage to Lapland since I came in*: Villers has read an entire book on Lapland while waiting for Mrs Racket.

4–5 *as difficult to be moved as a Quaker*: as unwilling to hurry as a Quaker waiting to be inspired by the divine spirit. Quakers were known to wait patiently for the divine spirit to move them before they spoke or acted.

7 *Tattersall's*: an equine auctioneer's. See note to *TT*, 1.1.82.

8 *Jessamy*: jasmine, a flower used in making perfumes. The name suggests that the nobleman is a fop.

21 *Adieu to weeds, I see! All life!*: good-bye to mourning attire, I see. The widow has re-embraced life by dressing in the gayest fashion.

61 *tippet and nosegay*: a tippet is a garment with hanging ends that drapes around the shoulders, usually made of fur or wool; a nosegay is a bunch of sweet-smelling flowers, a small bouquet.

67–8 *A propos des bottes*: literally, 'talking of boots', but meaning 'speaking of that' or 'that reminds me'.

68 *'Plague of Athens'*: a painting portraying the horrific plague that afflicted Athens during the second year of the Peloponnesian War. Thucydides records the details of the virulence of the disease, the high level of contagion, the despair of the populace, and the streets filled with the dead and dying in Book II, 47–55 of *The Peloponnesian War*.

69 *Langford's*: Langford and Son, an art auctioneering house in London.

70 *Primrose*: a pale greenish yellow or lemon colour; prime, first bloom. The nobleman is named for his stage in life as well as for a colour used by painters in the art he covets.

71 *Carmine*: a red or crimson pigment obtained from cochineal, an insect. This lady is also named for a colour found in the paintings she admires, and also perhaps for a colour she uses on her own cheeks.

Ingot: mass, generally in the shape of a brick, of precious metal.

nabob: an Englishman who has returned from India with a large fortune and is very ostentatious. A pejorative term.

72 *rouleau*: a roll of coins.

73 *Jingle*: the sound the coins make as they strike each other in the gentleman's pocket or purse.

76 *"Whittington and his Cat"*: Richard (Dick) Whittington (d. 1423), a historical figure who was four times (not three as legend has it) Mayor of London, was the son of a successful merchant from Gloucestershire and attained his wealth and prominence due to a combination of family connections and hard work. According to an early seventeenth-century ballad, however, Whittington's cat helped make his fortune. While a scullion to the cook of a well-to-do merchant, the legendary Whittington supposedly sent his cat, his only possession, on one of his master's trading ventures. A king with a terrible rodent problem bought the cat for a huge sum of money. Before he learned of his good fortune, however, Whittington ran away from the merchant's home because of his ill treatment by the cook. He returned to his master after he heard church bells and imagined they told him, 'Turn again, Whittington, thrice Lord Mayor of London'.

86–7 *Mrs Crotchet's*: this musical lady is named for a quarter note, or a note half the length of a minim.

93 *cork plumpers*: balls or pads made of cork worn inside the mouth to fill out the hollow of the cheek.

104 *Paul Jones*: John Paul Jones (1747–92), Scottish sea captain with a chequered history on British ships. After killing a crewman in self-defence on *The Betsy* on a trip to the West Indies, Jones fled to America. He obtained an appointment in the American Navy and rose to the rank of captain. Jones captured many British ships, including the man-of-war HMS *Drake*, and over 500 prisoners of war, and raided the British coast. In 1781 Jones certainly had a fierce reputation in England. Although he had the best record of any American naval commander, Jones never received the promotions or rewards he felt his due, and he abandoned the United States for Europe in 1788. He accepted a major-generalship from Russia, but after disappointments and scandal, he resigned and settled in Paris, where he died in 1792.

Omoa: fabled city of the legendary El Dorado, an enormously wealthy chief in South America. The legend was begun by sixteenth-century Spanish explorers, and European adventurers continued to seek Omoa for two centuries, generally with catastrophic results. Most who sought it found death from disease. Villers says to stay with Mrs Racket and Letitia is like courting certain death by pursuing unattainable riches.

110 *a fright*: a person grotesque in appearance.

165 *fall of corn*: fall of the price of corn.

166–7 *if we quarrelled . . . would be dearer?*: in 1780 Norway was a province of Denmark, and Denmark was an ally of France. Trade, therefore, between Norway and England would be hampered by France's alliance with the American colonies and state of war against England, and goods from Norway would be scarcer and more expensive.

167   *funds*: see *BB* 5.2.57.

168   *Homily*: serious religious discourse addressed to a congregation; a sermon.

169   *Rubric*: direction for the conduct of divine service in liturgical books, and properly written or printed in red.

171   *jacks*: upright pieces of wood attached to the back of the harpsichord's key levers for holding the quills that pluck the strings when a key is depressed.

183   *Mrs*: see note to *IM*, The Characters of the Play.

194   *do you tell me*: tell me (imperative).

199   *parchment*: the skin of a sheep or goat prepared for writing; an official document.

228   *maxim*: rule of conduct.

235   *Ogles*: although the Ogles are mentioned here, and in *1782*, 2.1, Lady Frances says, 'Mrs Racket and the Miss Ogles', only one Ogle, Miss Ogle, makes an appearance in the play and speaks. See note to 2.1.147.

2.1.3   *la petite morale*: the contemporary obsession with minor matters of etiquette and propriety, as opposed to a concern with the more 'substantial virtues' to which Sir George refers.

5–6   *I'd have crossed the line in a fire-ship . . . Japanese*: I would rather have faced the purgatorial double heat of crossing the equator in a ship on fire in order to marry a Japanese wife, who, though culturally alien, would be properly submissive.

10–11   *the fair Hebrew damsels toasted by the patriarchs*: Sir George is probably referring to the encomium on the 'virtuous woman' in Proverbs 31:10–31 whose 'price is far above rubies': 'The heart of her husband doth safely trust in her. . . . She will do him good and not evil all the days of her life. . . . Strength and honour are her clothing. . . . She openeth her mouth with wisdom; and in her tongue is the law of kindness'.

12   *matrimonial Quixote*: overly romantic idealist, like Don Quixote, on the subject of matrimony whose fantasies have no basis in reality.

17   *like a salamander in fire*: like the legendary salamander, who lives in fire and does not burn. A metaphor for 'a woman who (ostensibly) lives chastely in the midst of temptation' (*OED*). Sir George's frequent use of fire imagery when speaking of marriage and his wife betokens his burning jealousy.

18   *place Victoire*: la place des Victoires. A fashionable square in Paris near the Palais Royale. It was designed by Jules Hardouin Mansart (1646–1708), royal architect to Louis XIV, in 1685, and became a model for other squares built in France. *La place des Victoires* was noted for its harmonious, homogeneous buildings that created a jewel-box effect around a statue of Louis XIV on horseback.

19 *St Evreux*: Comte d'Evreux, whose family originally built the Hôtel d'Evreux (1718–26) in what was then the outskirts of Paris, as a town home. This residence was the foundation of the fashionable Faubourg Saint-Honoré district in Paris. Hôtel d'Evreux was considered one of Paris's finest homes and, at the time of *Belle*, was owned by the financier Nicolas Beaujon. The building was expanded and renovated over time and eventually became the Elysées Palace. Doricourt is threatening to write a letter to the Comte d'Evreux revealing Sir George's metamorphosis from man of the world to jealous spouse.

26 *phoenix*: paragon. Note how Doricourt plays along with Sir George's fire imagery. The phoenix is a legendary bird of great beauty, which, as the only one of its kind, would reproduce itself by rising reborn from the ashes of its own funeral pyre.

37 *supper*: in fashionable society of the latter half of the eighteenth century, supper was a light late-evening meal. Dinner, the most substantial meal of the day, was served between 4 and 7 p.m.

56 *in propria persona*: in your own self; in your own person.

87 *virtuoso*: collector of curios and antiquities; dilettante. Often, but not always, someone more interested in collecting for collecting's sake than out of real knowledge.

Pantheons: excursions to the Pantheon. From 1772 until it was destroyed by fire in 1792, the Pantheon was a locus of fashionable indoor evening entertainments such as masquerades, concerts, and assemblies. It was located on Oxford Street.

87–8 *robes de cour*: gowns to be worn at Court.

102 *the ceremony of presentation*: my ceremonial presentation to the monarch. This ritual marked a person's official entrance into fashionable society. It could serve as a 'coming out' for a young person of rank or could mark a marriage or other special event. One could not attend any Court function until such a presentation had taken place, and so the ceremony also served to certify one's acceptability to society. Women were presented at drawing-rooms, while men were presented at *levées*. The ceremony itself was very formal and required elaborate and expensive costuming.

113 *mercer's*: fabric shop; '*esp.* a dealer in silks, velvets, and other costly materials' (*OED*).

126 *Park*: Hyde Park, most likely. The Mall in St James's Park was also a fashionable place to visit of a morning.

Kensington: a fashionable district bordering Hyde Park near Kensington Palace. Mrs Racket is probably referring to the royal gardens at Kensington.

132–3 *play Darby and Joan*: be inseparable. A humorous term for a husband and wife, especially in the lower classes.

136 *Canal*: canal in St James's Park.

138 *piquet*: a two-person card game.

140 *linsey-woolsey*: a coarse material originally made of wool and flax, later of inferior wool and cotton.

black bonnet: hat indicative of mourning.

141 *festino*: a feast or entertainment.

147 *Miss Ogle*: both the Larpent manuscript and *1782* record ' . . . and the Miss Ogles', but only Mrs Racket and one Miss Ogle are mentioned entering at line 76, and there is no mention of any other woman having entered the room. No other Miss Ogle speaks or appears in the list of characters. The review of the play in *London Magazine* (vol. 49, January 1780, 55), however, does mention that Mrs Racket is accompanied by *two* ladies when she calls upon Lady Frances. I have chosen to make the text consistent by eliminating this mysterious, silent lady, but certainly a director could choose to reinstate her.

171 *particular*: remarkable; individual, unique.

209 *censorious*: fault-finding; severely critical.

217 *the Hesperian fruit*: the golden apples of the Isle of the Blessed. The daughters of Hesperus, with the aid of a dragon, were said to guard the garden where they grew.

220 *pensioned*: awarded a governmental stipend.

238 *rooks*: crows, of a kind known especially for their raucousness.

237–40 *Undisturbed by any noise . . . or the curate's wife*: Mrs Racket seems to be referring to George Etherege's well-known comedy *The Man of Mode* (1676) in which, at 5.2.471–81, the heroine, Harriet, speaks resignedly of returning to life in the country, 'There you'll find my mother, an old lame aunt, and myself, sir, perched up on chairs at a distance in a large parlour; sitting moping like three or four melancholy birds in a spacious volar . . . Methinks I hear the hateful noise of rooks already—kaw, kaw, kaw' (George Etherege, *Plays*, ed. Michael Cordner (Cambridge, 1982), 331).

253 *Lord Mayor*: title held by the mayor of London, who is annually elected to preside over the Corporation of the City of London.

258 *Mrs Bloomer's*: this lady's name seems to comment on her appearance as a blooming flower.

279 *He took it . . . disguise*: like Don Quixote, Sir George mistook an innocent object for a dangerous figure from the world of romance.

289 *tablets*: small sheaf of paper for making notes, sometimes bound in ivory or simply in wax; notebook.

313–14 *Coachmakers Hall, or the Black Horse in Bond Street*: the editor has not been able to identify these locations.

322 S.D. *Exit Lady Frances*: *1782* has the stage direction, '*Exeunt Lady Frances and Mrs Racket*'. At line 323, however, Mrs Racket exits again in the company of Miss Ogle. It is not clear whether this is an oversight or if Mrs Racket returns for Miss Ogle. There are a variety of ways in which this could be staged, but I think it logical that Lady Frances would storm off in a passion after her speech to be followed by the other women, who approve her decision. The Dublin edition of 1781 of *Belle* (as performed at Smock Alley) gives the stage directions differently. Where *1782* has Lady Frances exit, the Dublin edition indicates she is '*going*'. All the ladies exit at the point at which the first edition indicates that Mrs Racket exits with Miss Ogle. Although the Dublin edition is pirated, in this instance its version seems more logical.

325 *Iö triumphe!*: O, triumph! A Latin invocation of triumph.

2.2 S.D. *Puffers*: people hired to inflate the prices of objects at auction either by bidding for them to run up the price or by extolling them in the presence of would-be buyers.

3 *Filigree:* a name that reflects its holder's love of delicate decorative work made of threads and beads of gold or silver, generally used on jewellery or fine decorative objects.

23 *anno mundi*: calculation of date from the year of creation in accordance with Jewish chronology. Traditionally, the date of creation was set at 7 October 3761 BC.

anno domini: in the year of Our Lord; date calculated from the year in which Christ is reputed to have been born.

25 *in limbo*: pawned (slang).

27 *cognoscento*: *cognoscente*; connoisseur of fine arts.

27–8 *Mr Glib*: another auctioneer. 'Glib' and 'Silvertongue' both indicate characters whose skill with words can be dangerous.

28 *Totter's*: the gentleman's name indicates that he is financially on the skids.

29 *there*: to Mr Glib's auction house.

30–6 *my head full of Parmegiano . . . glow of Correggio*: Mask does indeed seem to have a head full of Parmesan cheese as he mistakes many of the artists he is supposed to recognize. He is most likely referring to Parmigianino (1503–40); Salvator Rosa (1615–73), known for his wild landscapes; five Dutch painters: Gabriel Metszu (1629/30–67), known for his intimate scenes of middle-class life; Gerard Terborch the Younger (1617–81), who studied under his father and was famous for his interiors and small portraits; Jan Vermeer (1632–75), Philips Wouwerman (1619–68), known for his hilly countrysides and horses, and whose works commanded high prices in the eighteenth century; and David Teniers (there were three artists by this name: father (1582–1649), son (1610–90), and grandson (1638–85)); the French painter Claude Lorrain (1600–82), known for his serene landscapes (often contrasted with Rosa); Jacob Van Ruisdael (1628–82), Jacopo Robusti Tintoretto (1518–94), Anthony Van Dyck (1599–1641), and Antonio Allegri Correggio (1489–1534).

39 *pass it*: i.e. without coming in. Her presence recommends the auction.

41–2 *Diana . . . Actaeon:* see note to *BB* 2.1.329.

43 *David and Bathsheba*: in the biblical story, King David was walking upon his rooftop, and from there caught a glimpse of Bathsheba, the beautiful wife of Uriah the Hittite, as she bathed below. He lusted after her, seduced her, and arranged for Uriah to be killed in battle. David married Bathsheba and she later became the mother of Solomon. David's actions earned him the wrath of God.

44–5 *I remember . . . story*: a comment upon the morality of town life: the lady knows only the pagan, not the Old Testament, stories.

45 S.D. *[Courtall among them]*: Cowley does not specify when Courtall enters the scene. It is also possible he may enter with the earlier company or follow Lady Frances, Mrs Racket, and Miss Ogle.

53 *Peking*: now Beijing.

56 *terra incognita*: unknown land. It is not clear whether Cowley is commenting on the ignorance of the gentleman or of Silvertongue or on the poor quality of the model. Either the model is such a generalized city that recognition is impossible or the viewers lack the knowledge to be able to identify the city in question. A director of the scene would have many possibilities from which to choose.

68 *Toland*: John Toland (1670–1722), an Irish freethinker who became famous for his book, *Christianity not Mysterious* (1696), which began the Deist controversy. Toland also wrote a biography of Milton (1698).

70 *are all orthodox*: all conform to the doctrines of the established church.

75 *impertinent by patent*: entitled to be rude because of his wealth and social standing. Miss Ogle intends for Courtall to hear this cutting remark.

82 *Daphne*: a virgin shepherdess with whom Apollo fell in love. When unable to outrun Apollo, Daphne prayed to the gods to escape his advances and was transformed into a laurel tree.

84 *Damon*: a stock name for a shepherd.

96 *casino*: public room used for social gatherings, especially for music or dancing.

108 *Lady Touchwood with a vengeance!*: Courtall believes Lady Frances lives up to her name, that is, that she can be easily kindled with passion. He takes her embarrassment at discovering him to be one of Mrs Racket's friends and her subsequent courteous invitation to him, on Mrs Racket's account, as favourable notice of him.

3.1.3 *eat*: ate; a past tense form of 'eat'.

11 *mawkin*: 'an untidy female, especially a servant or country wench' (*OED*).

13 *event*: outcome.

27 *Ma foi!*: a mild oath, literally meaning, 'my faith!'

29 *La Bella Magdalena*: a standard portrayal of a magdalen, a reformed or contrite prostitute.

44 *Mauvaise honte*: artificial shame, false bashfulness.

47 *overcharged*: exaggerated.

51 *Medicean Venus*: nude sculpture of Venus dating from the first century BC that became part of the collection of Ferdinando I de' Medici. It is now housed in the Uffizi Gallery in Florence.

57 *character*: portrayal of Letitia's character.

59 *painting*: (1) (bias or inaccuracy in) sketching another woman's character; (2) application of make-up (to hide the effects of age). The latter meaning of Doricourt's double-edged cut explains Mrs Racket's needled response.

62 *éclat*: dazzling effect, perhaps in this case with the double meaning of ostentation or public exposure.

64 S.D. *Enter Letitia, running*: from her very entrance in the scene, Letitia plays the role of ignorant, ill-bred country wench. Instead of entering with the elegance and grace befitting a fashionable woman of her status, she runs. She flagrantly exhibits *mauvaise honte* by hiding behind Mrs Racket and then dashing out to flirt with Doricourt. Her language is indiscreet (when she alludes to Parson Dobbins) and uncouth (a-suitoring, sprightfuller, flim-flams, etc.). Every word she utters and move she makes is designed to reveal her defects.

74 S.D. *(Half apart)*: Letitia pretends to be talking aside to Mrs Rackett, but she intends for Doricourt to overhear her.

83 *men . . . horses*: in Jonathan Swift's tale of the land of the Houyhnhnms in his satire, *Gulliver's Travels* (1726), horses, or Houyhnhnms, are the rational beings, and humans, or yahoos, are the savage beasts. Letitia pretends to be so ignorant as to take this fiction for fact.

89 *Thomas Aquinas*: leading Roman Catholic theologian who lived 1225–74. Aquinas reconciled the philosophies of St Augustine and Aristotle. He was canonized in 1323. His writings would clearly prove difficult for a rustic, uneducated woman.

89–90 *gaping like mumchance*: with his mouth hanging open. Doricourt is so stunned by Letitia's seeming ignorance that he stands speechless. Letitia further increases her display of bad manners by calling attention to Doricourt's astonishment and comparing him to a mute or someone acting in a dumb show.

93 *a body*: a person.

100 *Jubah*: unidentified reference. Maybe mistaken pronunciation of 'Juno', or 'Julia'. 'Jubal' is the only biblical possibility, but rather bizarre since he is male and a warrior.

Dinah: biblical daughter of Jacob and Leah. Shechem, son of the Hivite prince, saw her, desired her, and took her. He then begged his father to ask Jacob to give Dinah to him as his wife. Dinah's brothers deceitfully agreed, on the condition that all Hivite men were circumcised. While the Hivite men were recovering from this procedure, two of Dinah's brothers came and slew them all (Genesis 34). An odd choice for Letitia to make for her fictitious parson to call her as a love tribute. Possibly Letitia deliberately mistakes Dinah for 'Diana', chaste Roman goddess of the hunt.

105 *Parson Dobbins*: the fictitious good parson's name reflects his rusticity: a dobbin is a farm horse.

116 *uncommon*: remarkably great or rarely to be met with. Doricourt makes use of a *double entendre* to veil his contempt for Letitia's understanding.

120 *potecary*: a countrified variant of 'apothecary'.

conundrums: a game of riddles involving puns and plays on words.

121–2 *Ladies' Diary*: The Ladies' Diary: or Woman's Almanack. an annual journal containing calendars, astronomical observations, mathematical questions, enigmas, rebuses, and puzzles.

123 *Newcastle*: the River Tyne empties into the port of Newcastle upon Tyne; the Duke of Newcastle wielded much political power. Letitia may also be making a strained pun upon Tyne/tiny ('a little river').

135 *genus*: Letitia is mispronouncing 'genius'.

watch-papers: ornamental discs of paper or silk used to line the outer case of a watch.

136 *catgut*: coarse cloth woven widely, used for lining and stiffening skirts or sleeves or for working handkerchiefs.

quadrille baskets: small worked baskets to hold winnings from the card game quadrille

136–7 *profiles in shade*: silhouettes.

137–8 *the lady . . . Grosvenor Square*: unidentified lady. It sounds as if Letitia is quoting an advertisement from a newspaper.

145–6 *expression in her eye . . . her lips*: perhaps Doricourt has caught Letitia signalling her own amusement with her performance to either Mrs Racket or the audience. Mrs Racket is quick to steer Doricourt away from this observation.

149 *juggler's*: a magician's or trickster's; alchemist's.

157–8 *go off . . . pistol*: suddenly diverge from this path and go off to the other world by way of a pistol shot.

363

170 *What's*: what, is.

177 *Great Mogul*: Emperor of Delhi.

 grenadier: member of 'a company of the tallest and finest men in the regiment' (*OED*).

179 *little Quick*: John Quick, one of the favourite actors of George III, created the role of Isaac Mendoza in Richard Brinsley Sheridan's popular comic opera, *The Duenna*—as well as the role of Hardy in *Belle*! He was one of the leading comic actors at Covent Garden, and so his audience would have been especially appreciative of the joke about his borrowing a costume from himself to wear in the next act's masquerade. Hardy would certainly be well informed regarding Quick's predilection for good wine!

 Jew Isaac's dress: the very costume worn by John Quick in his portrayal of the character of Isaac Mendoza in Richard Brinsley Sheridan's *The Duenna* (1775). 'Little Isaac', a mercenary Portuguese Jew, intends to marry a young Spanish lady of fortune. He believes himself to be very cunning, but he is outfoxed by the lady and her duenna into marrying the duenna instead. *The Duenna* was one of the most popular comic pieces of the eighteenth century and it made Sheridan's career. Its success attracted the attention of David Garrick, who approached Sheridan about purchasing a share in Drury Lane. Garrick retired from the management of the theatre in 1776 and Sheridan assumed his position. Although *Belle* opened at Covent Garden, Cowley's extended allusion to Sheridan's most successful work may be considered a shrewd tribute. Several of her earlier works, such as *The Runaway* (1776) and *Who's the Dupe?* (1779), were performed at Drury Lane, and she returned to Drury Lane in 1786 with *The School for Greybeards*.

180–1 *forty-eight*: according to Michael Broadbent, Master of Wine and founder of Christie's auction house's wine department, the German vintage of 1748 was 'a great vintage, and as it happens, the *first vintage* of any wine sold by James Christie (in July 1772)'. See Broadbent, *The Great Vintage Wine Book* (London, 1980), 301.

183 *duenna*: the character Isaac Mendoza is tricked into marrying in Sheridan's *The Duenna*.

 parts: talents or cleverness, with a pun on 'private parts'.

3.2 S.D. *Enter Courtall . . . in the back scene*: two pairs of shutters are used to create the setting for this scene: the first pair serves as the back wall of the room in which the action of this scene is to take place and contains a door to the room from which the characters enter, while another pair of shutters, behind the first, create the back wall of the suggested room beyond.

 1 *catch*: musical round, often humorous, for three or more singers.

4–5 *a leap at the new lustres*: a try at jumping up to reach the new chandeliers; a try at seducing some of the new beauties.

7 *make harlequinades*: perform as if I were a clown from a pantomime.

9 *disguised*: drunk, inebriated.

so bid them draw up: bid the carriages to draw up to take them to the masquerade.

20 *Falernian*: name of a celebrated wine from the region of Campania in Italy.

73 *Norfolk*: a county on the east coast of England known for its agriculture.

87 *ergo*: therefore.

92 *holped*: helped.

96 *thick with*: intimate with.

102 *Boodle's*: see note to *TT* 1.1.91.

103–4 *Jove did . . . husband*: Zeus came to Alcmena disguised as her husband, Amphitryon, and slept with her. She bore him Heracles.

3.3.16 *ax*: ask.

3.4.6 *Commons affair*: matter to be handled at Doctor's Commons; *i.e.* Lady Frances has not had time to find a lover for Sir George to prosecute for crim. con. See notes to 1.1.64 and 65.

18 *the old crabbed fellow in Rome*: the Pope.

67 *Kensington*: see note to 2.1.126.

69–70 *Sir Hurlo Thrumbo*: the title character in the burlesque *Hurlothrumbo* (1729), by Samuel Johnson (1691–1773), a dancing master from Cheshire.

73–4 *clue at her heel . . . Rosamond*: Rosamond Clifford was mistress to Henry II in 1174. He supposedly kept her in a house so labyrinthine that only he could find her. Henry's queen, Eleanor of Aquitaine, foiled him by following Rosamond by way of a ball of thread attached to her heel. See Joseph Addison's opera, *Rosamond* (1705), 1.3.

90–1 *support a character*: play a role for the entire night.

92 *domino*: masquerade garment consisting of a loose hooded cloak worn by someone not dressing as a particular character.

4.1 S.D. *masquerade*: masked ball. Such events were popular throughout most of the eighteenth century, though often deplored for the mixing of classes and the sexual liberty they permitted. Masquerades are often used in the literature of the century as a device to explore issues of self-concealment and revelation (as in the Letitia/Doricourt plot) and also as an occasion to lead the heroine into sexual dangers (as in the Courtall/Lady Frances plot). For further explanation of the masquerade tradition and its use in *Belle*, see 'Introduction' to this volume, pp. xliv–xlvii, and Castle.

s.d. *cotillons*: types of dances, originating in France, that are made up of intricate steps and figures

s.d. *hobby-horse*: lightweight horse figure designed to be worn around the waist of a dancer or other performer. It would be used in morris dances or other theatrics to imitate the moves of a skittish horse.

s.d. *with cap and bells*: the traditional insignia of the jester or comic fool.

1 *Mask*: a masquerader. A different character than the puffer given the proper name 'Mask' in 2.2.

Tom Fool!: mentally deficient person. Here used as a proper name for someone acting the fool.

3 *nostrums*: homemade remedies; especially quack remedies made by their hawker.

6 *gaming*: gambling.

11 *living*: benefice; posting in the Church of England as vicar or rector of a parish. The mountebank suggests that a clergyman holding more than one living is doing so out of greed; one man cannot minister well to the needs of more than one flock.

12 *projectors*: dreamers or schemers; promoters of (often fraudulent) schemes and projects.

18 *plead their privilege*: plead their immunity as members of parliament from prosecution for debt.

19 s.d. *Isaac Mendoza*: see note to 3.1.179.

21 *courantas*: variant or mispronunciation of courants or courantes; dances characterized by gliding or running steps.

23 *fandango*: lively dance popular in Spain. Mr Hardy jokes of an *English* fandango—not a dance but a military attack.

25 *Duke's Place*: see note to *TT* 1.1.29.

26 *a subscription*: levy, financial contribution.

27–8 *Joshuas and your Gideons*: warrior heroes of the Old Testament: Joshua led the Israelites in bringing down the walls of Jericho (Joshua 6); Gideon struck down the altar of Baal and, with a very small army, defeated the Midianites (Judges 6–7).

30–1 *Some of us turn Christians . . . Englishmen!*: those Jews who habituate themselves to English ways, naturally lose their warrior capacities and dwindle into the kind of patriots that Samuel Johnson had in mind when he said, 'Patriotism is the last refuge of a scoundrel' (Boswell, *Life of Johnson* (New York, 1952), *Aetat.* 66, 7 Apr. 1775, p. 251), rebels to authority, back-stabbing courtiers, and cuckolds.

32–3 S.D. *(Puts his fingers to his forehead)*: Hardy puts his fingers up to signify horns, the sign of cuckoldry.

35 *Margaret*: the title character in Sheridan's *The Duenna* who attempts to trick Isaac into marriage.

40 *Tipperary*: county in southern Ireland; the name of a district within that county and near its county town, Clonmel.

43 *dumpling*: short and dumpy or rotund.

Levite: contemptuous term for clergy; the name is derived from the Hebrew tribe of Levi, whose descendants assisted the priests in the temple. Mrs Racket suggests that clergymen indulge in gluttony.

44 *flesh-hook*: a hook to remove meat from a pot or to hang meat upon. Mrs Racket observes that Hardy's rotundity is a good indicator of his skill in providing himself with good food.

48 *gudgeons*: small freshwater fish used for bait; gullible people. Hardy makes a pun at Flutter's expense.

50 *accidental*: improvised. Flutter is being sarcastic.

50–1 *commonplace book*: 'a book in which one records passages or matters to be especially remembered or referred to' (*OED*). Flutter is sneering that the alleged improvisations are all in fact stale and learned by rote from his recording of others' writings and conversation.

64 *objects*: sights to be gazed on, both animate and inanimate.

78 *Botolph Lane*: a street in the heart of the City; an unfashionable location.

maid of honour: young unmarried woman, usually of high rank, who attends the queen or princess.

98 *Lord Trope*: since a trope is a type of figurative language in which a word is used in another way than in its original sense, Lord Trope's name indicates his verbosity and flights of rhetoric.

99–100 *is down*: has concluded his speech and resumed his seat.

104 *devotee*: devout person, religious enthusiast.

117 *cestus*: a belt or girdle belonging to Venus that inspires love.

119 S.D. *[dressed as a conjuror]*: Saville's costume is commented upon as being that of 'an enchanter' (l. 217) and 'an old conjuror' (l. 225), therefore it must be easily recognizable as that of a wizard or other commander of magic.

152 *cloven foot*: mark of the devil.

154 *a knowledge of the lady's dress*: an inconsistency in the text. Saville only asked for information on Sir George's costume. See 3.3.16–17.

159 S.D. *(sings)*: lyrics by Cowley; music by composer, actor, and singer, Michael Arne (1740–86).

176 *rapt*: *1782* prints this word as 'wrapt'. It might also possibly be rendered 'wrapped', although 'rapt' seems preferable.

183 *in point*: apposite, well targeted.

187 *rub*: obstacle, hindrance. Possibly an allusion to *Hamlet*, 3.1.64–8. See note to *TT* 5.1.128–9.

199 *transparent*: seeming to transmit light.

208 *interested*: personally concerned, solicitous.

216 *Cornhill*: located in one of London's financial districts and site of the Royal Exchange, Cornhill is the former site of a grain market.

264 *till*: only until.

284 *Golconda*: old Muslim kingdom located in the central Hyderabad state of India; legendary for its diamond mines, treasury, and diamond market.

285 *Mogul's*: see note to 3.1.177.

him: the Mogul.

285–6 *his wishes*: his desire to possess me.

291 *Hymen*: Greek god of marriage.

320 *Jennet*: name taken from a small Spanish horse, considered an emblem of lust. See Williams II, ii. 732–3. Also, variant of 'genet', an animal related to the civet cat and mongoose or the fur or skins from such an animal, used like such luxury furs as sable or mink.

323 *Gorget*: name taken from a neck ornament, either military or decorative; collar or necklace. Perhaps the name is a *double entendre* suggesting an impressive part of the colonel's uniform as well as the gifts he employed to win the young woman.

333 *assume the father-in-law:* presume to act as if you were already my father-in-law.

4.2.17 S.D. *Exit ... back scene*: the set of Courtall's house was probably created by closing shutters that had been open in the previous scene to extend the depth of the setting of the masquerade. Two pair of shutters could be used to create the illusion of a drawing-room and bedchamber beyond by creating a doorway in the downstage pair and having the upstage pair provide a back wall to the bedchamber beyond the doorway. See note to 3.2 S.D. and 'The Restoration and Eighteenth-Century Stages' in this volume, pp. li–lii.

18 *Gemini*: used as an oath, corrupted from *Jesu domine*.

21 *bailiffs*: officers who would seize items of Courtall's property in lieu of debts unpaid. See *TT* 5.4.141–52. The Mask jokes that he suspects Courtall of having money problems.

5.1.6–7 *overseer of the parish*: overseer of the poor, a parish administrator whose duties are connected to the relief of the poor. Hardy's description of such a character suggests that these administrators are more bureaucratic than charitable.

10–11 *have we morning masquerades?*: Letitia is wearing her masquerade costume.

14–15 *lay it by . . . the miraculous robes of St Bridget*: treating her gown as a holy relic. St Bridget was considered, along with St Patrick, as the patron saint of Ireland. Her origins can be traced back to the Celtic goddess Brid. Neither the Catholic nor Celtic histories refer to miraculous robes.

44 *except*: unless.

47 *qualms*: feelings of faintness or illness, generally of the stomach. Hardy seems sympathetically to have suffered his wife's morning sickness.

48 *I have no fears for you*: I have no fears about your being able to perform the role well.

56 *phials*: small glass bottles for holding liquids, especially medicine; vials.

56–7 *hey presto*: language of a conjuror or magician, a command for something to happen immediately.

64 *budget's to be opened this morning*: Villers notes that this day in the House of Commons the Chancellor of the Exchequer will present his annual statement of the revenues and expenditures expected for the coming year as well as the financial proposals relating to them. In the late eighteenth century, morning hours referred to the period between breakfast and dinner. The fashionable dined late, often between three and six, and therefore when Villers looks at his watch and exclaims that the budget will be opened this morning and he wishes to step over to the House, he has not necessarily missed the event although it is past three.

66 *What a blockhead!*: addressed to himself. Villers has already forgotten that Hardy is to let it be known that he is mortally ill.

69 *'em*: my pulses.

72 *yearly bill*: annual official report of deaths and births.

5.2.9 *Ninon*: Anne de Lenclos (1620–1705), celebrated Frenchwoman renowned for her wit and beauty. Her salon was frequented by such luminaries as Molière.

11 *caprice*: sudden, arbitrary turn of mind; fancy, whim.

12 *Elle est mon caprice*: she is my caprice. If Doricourt is quoting another source, it remains unidentified.

19 *jarring*: quarrelling.

21 *in that line . . . idea*: I cannot bear to think of possessing her as a bought mistress.

43 *the proverb*: the proverb being referred to is 'Speak of the devil', i.e. the man of whom we were just speaking.

51 *ether*: mythical subtle fluid said to fill the regions of space beyond the moon and to be the substance breathed by the gods.

56 *What's*: what, is.

63 *Monro*: John Monro (1715–91) was the physician to Bethlehem hospital (Bedlam). He devoted himself to the study and treatment of insanity.

71 S.D. *[Going]*: although the stage directions in *1782* indicate that Flutter exits at this point, they also indicate he exits at line 74, and again at the end of the scene. Flutter repeatedly tries to escape while Saville repeatedly detains him—probably physically. It is also likely that each attempt at escape is more desperate than the one before.

5.3.24 *card*: a card inviting them to Letitia and Doricourt's wedding.

5.4.14 *Envy!*: Doricourt jokingly accuses Saville of feeling envy over Doricourt's popularity and therefore falsely portraying society women as being unconcerned for his supposed madness.

Hebe: see note to 1.1.20.

30 *strait waistcoat*: laced garment for the upper body used to restrain the arms of violent lunatics; straitjacket.

5.5.7 *worth pulling caps for*: quarrelling over, especially in an undignified manner.

14 *lace*: string, ribbon, or cord used to pull together opposite sides of a piece of clothing. In this case Mrs Racket refers to the cord tying Miss Ogle's bodice or stays.

15–16 *Knight of the Woeful Countenance*: title mockingly given to Cervantes's mad Don Quixote.

23 *cause*: legal action, case in court.

59 *turn evidence*: become a witness for the prosecution in order to be treated with leniency for one's own crimes.

76–7 *specifics . . . stubbornness*: especially efficacious remedies against the ailment of stubbornness.

92 *Start not*: be not startled.

118 *the bright example who presides there*: Queen Charlotte, wife of George III, had borne fifteen children and was an emblem of domestic virtue and motherhood. See note to Dedication 2.

127 *Never heed circumstances!*: don't bother about the details.

136 *'the Day of Judgement'*: phrase used near the beginning of the Anglican marriage ceremony at the point at which the priest asks if either of the couple knows of any reason the marriage should not take place.

138–9 *'amazement'*: the final word of the Anglican marriage ceremony. It concludes the portion that explains the subjection of wives to their husbands.

240 *to a T* : perfectly; precisely.

256 *sticking plaster*: sticky substance on a piece of muslin used to apply to a wound to help close it.

262 *forty-eight*: see note to 3.1.180–1.

parish of St George's: probably referring to the neighbourhood around St George's, Hanover Square, a fashionable district, suitable for the residence of the Hardy family.

262–3 *I'll invite . . . but what we'll drink it out*: we'll drink all of it even if I have to invite the whole parish of St George's to help us do it.

EPILOGUE

The first edition does not indicate who speaks the epilogue, but context would suggest it is the actress who plays Letitia (Miss Younge, in the original production).

1 *cease*: the actress asks the audience to hold their applause while she speaks.

2 *plaudits*: rounds of applause.

5 *Lady Bab or Grace*: characters from popular afterpieces who use disguise to win lovers, at least temporarily. Lady Bab is actually Lady Bab's maid who dresses up as her mistress in Revd James Townley's immensely popular *High Life Below Stairs* (1759). Lady Bab herself does not appear. Grace also dresses as her mistress, in Charles Dibden the Elder's burletta *Poor Vulcan* (1778), to take her mistress's place with a lover.

7 *French red . . . creams*: cosmetics to redden cheeks or lighten the complexion.

11 *As thus*: for example.

16 *vestal's*: virgin's, like those of the priestesses of Vesta in ancient Rome.

18 *Dian's*: Diana's, chaste Roman goddess of the hunt.

22 *First . . . at you*: the actress singles out individual spectators several times during the epilogue.

26 *conscious, own thy part*: guiltily aware, confess your true behaviour.

GLOSSARY

abroad out of doors

ad a mild intensifying oath, from 'Gad', or 'God'

Adod a mild oath, meaning 'Oh, God!'

adroit clever; to the point

Adsheart an oath meaning God's heart

advance move swiftly

Agad a mild oath expressing strength of feeling and meaning 'Oh, God!'

agitation commotion; scheming; contrivance

ague a violent fever that causes shivering

allons let us go

amour love affair

anotherguess another sort or kind

a'n't aren't

Apollo Greek and Roman god of poetry, music, and light

apology explanation; excuse; expression of regret

aqua mirabilis a spirit or cordial made from wine with mace, cardamom, ginger, nutmeg, and other spices

assembly a festive social gathering; the company assembled

assignation a lovers' meeting; 'the arrangement of the time and place for an interview; an appointment, tryst' (*OED*)

attend accompany, wait upon

avaunt be off!

badiner banter

baggage playful term for a saucy young woman, or a contemptuous term for a disreputable one.

bailiffs officers who execute writs of judgment against debtors

balk frustrate; hinder; put obstacles in the way of something

band collar or neck band, specifically for a Puritan or Quaker

banter jest; trick

bark a small ship; a sailing or rowing vessel

basilisk mythical reptile whose breath or glance was lethal

basset 'an obsolete game at cards, resembling Faro' (*OED*)

bate abate; omit

bawdy-house brothel

beaux fops; ones who give excessive or particular attention to dress, mien, and social etiquette

beaux garçons fops

Bedlam Hospital of St Mary of Bethlehem, rebuilt in 1676 near the London Wall and known as an asylum for the mentally ill

begar an oath, from 'by God', a variant of 'begad'

bill a written advertisement; bank-bill, authorizing the bearer to draw on funds

billet a short note, letter

billet-doux love letter

black bonnet a hat indicative of mourning

blotted wiped out

blunderbuss 'a short gun with a large bore, firing many balls or slugs, and capable of doing execution within a limited range without exact aim' (*OED*)

bona robas (Latin) prostitutes

booby a lubber; a coarse fool

bubble someone empty-headed; a dupe

buckram a coarse, stiffened fabric; someone pompous or stiff like buckram fabric

buds young ones; children

bugbear object of fear or dread

bully (n.) fine fellow, gallant, bravo

bumper 'a cup or glass of wine, etc., filled to the brim, esp. when drunk as a toast' (*OED*)

business commercial or financial

transactions; mischievous or impertinent activity; matter of concern; euphemism for sexual intercourse

buss kiss

busy constantly occupied; exerting oneself diligently; meddlesome; officious; sexually active

buxom yielding; unresisting to pressure; lively; blithe

buzz murmur, whisper busily

B'w'y abbreviation of 'God be with you'

camps military camps. These could also be gathering places for fashionable people to watch the military exercises

cantoned to be quartered

canvas coarse, unbleached fabric used to make sails and tents, or for use by artists for oil-painting

caper high leap in dancing

caperer someone who performs frisky leaps while dancing, or who acts in a frolicsome, lively, carefree manner

cargo freight, burden; contemptuous term for a person

carriage behaviour

cast (n.) throw of the dice

cast (vb.) to throw dice; to form into a final shape, as in pouring molten metal into a mould; to stamp with an impression

censorious fault-finding; severely critical

chagrin vexation; annoyance

chain a personal neck ornament worn as an emblem of office

chair a light vehicle drawn by one horse; or a sedan chair

chairmen men whose occupation is to carry riders in sedan chairs

chaise a carriage for travelling, a post-chaise

chambers law offices

Change 'a place where merchants meet for the transaction of business, an exchange' (*OED*)

chap cheek

charge one for whom one is responsible

charm (n.) talisman or amulet; anything

worn that supposedly has the magical ability to ward off evil

chicken someone young, inexperienced, and defenceless

chimney-board 'a board used to close up a chimney in the summer' (*OED*)

chops jaws and mouth

chouse cheat

cicisbeo the recognized gallant or admirer of a married woman, possibly her lover

cit contemptuous term for town shopkeepers or tradesmen, from 'citizen'

citizen a tradesman (as opposed to a gentleman)

civil polite, courteous, decent; well-bred

clack senseless, continuous chatter

clap (1) place, with great energy and promptness; (2) close with a bang

closet 'a room for privacy or retirement; a private room; an inner chamber' (*OED*)

cloth tablecloth

clutter turmoil; bustle; confusion

cockade a knot of ribbons or a rosette worn as a badge of office on a hat

coif a white cap worn by lawyers as a mark of their profession, especially the cap worn by a serjeant-at-law; sometimes used to refer to a serjeant-at-law

colic griping pains in the abdomen, or the temperamental irritability that such discomfort causes

complaisance desire to please; obligingness, courtesy

complaisant obliging; disposed to please; yielding

composures musical, literary, or artistic compositions

conceive understand

concert (vb.) arrange; plan

condition rank, status, social position; nature, state of being

conduct (n.) safe-conduct; guidance of one safely or blamelessly

confabulation a familiar chat (perhaps with a hint of more intimacy)

confounded something strongly objected to; cursed

conjure appeal solemnly; implore, beseech

conscionable conscientious; scrupulous; in a negative sense, over-scrupulous

conscious knowing; privy to secrets

consent agreement

constitution the make-up of one's physical nature in respect to health and strength

consumption a wasting disease of the lungs; phthisis

conundrums a game of riddles involving puns and plays on words

convince give proof

coquet, coquette a flirt, primarily a woman who trifles with the affections of men for the satisfaction of her own vanity. Before 1720 the male spelling was used for both sexes

cotillon one of several types of dances of French origin, characterized by intricate steps and figures

counsellor counsellor-at-law; barrister

course a way of action; personal conduct or behaviour

courser a swift horse, a racer

cousin used as a generic term for collateral kin, niece or nephew

coxcomb fop; fool

cribbing pilfering

crown a coin worth five shillings

cuff miserly old man

cully a dupe; one easily taken in

curmudgeon an avaricious, churlish fellow

damosels young, unmarried women

debar deprive; exclude from; prevent access to

debauchee person (of either gender) who is in the habit of freely indulging in sensual pleasures and vice

decamp make a quick exit

decoction a medicinal agent made by boiling an animal or vegetable substance in liquor to extract its potent qualities

dejeuner set of breakfast china

delicate pleasing to the senses; discriminating

descry declare; make known; discover

deshabille dressed in a negligent or careless style; in a state of partial undress

design (vb.) plan; intend

deuce bad luck, mischief, plague, devil; often used as an imprecation

devotee a zealously religious woman

dickens slang for the devil, used in interjections

die dice

direction the address of a letter; instruction

discreet discerning, prudent, of good judgement, civil, courteous

dispose (n.) under the management of; subject to the disposal of

disposition temper or attitude; settlement of affairs

distracted mad, insane, out of one's wits

divert entertain

divine (n.) member of the clergy

dogged (vb.) tracked like a dog

doit half a farthing; a trifling sum

don a Spanish gentleman or nobleman; a distinguished man, especially one in an academic profession

done up financially ruined

doubt suspect, fear

dowager widowed woman of property

drawer 'one who draws liquor for customers; a tapster at a tavern' (*OED*)

dross impurities

duenna 'any elderly woman whose duty it is to watch over a young one; a chaperon' (*OED*)

dunner one looking to collect money

éclat brilliancy or public display

ecod mild oath, variant of 'egad'

egad mild oath, from 'God'

elseways otherwise

emblazon extol publicly; make illustrious

en cavalier in such a free and easy way; like a brave cavalier

encomiums panegyrics

encumbrance burden; impediment

engross monopolize

engrossed drawn up

en groupe as a group; as a party

en passant in passing

entail the fixed or prescribed line of descent for an estate that cannot be altered by any one possessor

entrée entrance; right of admission

equipage furnishings; carriage, horses, and footmen

ere before

errant itinerant, travelling (especially in quest of adventure)

essay trial; test; attempt

essence perfume; essential oil of a fragrance

estate status; position; wealth

even an intensifier; exactly, precisely, 'just'

event outcome, consequence

excuse (vb.) to offer an apology for something

executor one appointed to ensure the will of one deceased is carried out. There is sometimes a monetary benefit to the executor

exigence pressing state of affairs

expectation anticipation

expedite clear away difficulties

expose hold up to ridicule

extend widen the scope or meaning

fag-end a remnant of anything, although specifically of cloth; what is left of something after the best part of it has been used

fain gladly

fair appropriate, right; elegant; beautiful; of spotless reputation

faith loyalty

fame reputation

fancy imagination; invention; taste

farce a short theatrical piece whose sole aim is laughter; a hollow pretence; a mockery

fatal fraught with destiny

favour kindness or friendly action

fell upon happened into the company of

festino a feast or entertainment

fetch (n.) trick, ruse

fetch (vb.) cause to come; subdue, win

feth dialect variant of 'in faith'

flammed deceived by a shammed story or trick

flea flay

fleece strip a person of money or property

fleering grimacing; laughing in either a scornful or flattering manner

flesh meat; sensual appetites

flim-flams nonsense; humbug

flippant voluble, impertinent

fluttering making an ostentatious display; noisy; making a spectacle of oneself

forward precocious; presumptuous

freehold an estate held for a life term

friends near relations

frippery old clothes; cheap ornaments

frisk gambol, frolic, dance

froppish froward, fretful, peevish

fubsy fat and squat

Fury one of the avenging Greek goddesses from Tartarus who punished crimes; an angry, vengeful woman

gad (vb.) to wander about with no serious object, stopping here and there

gad (exclamatory) a mild oath, from 'God'

Gadso variant of 'catso', a word of interjection or exclamation. Also, a rogue or scamp

Gadzooks an oath based on 'God's hooks', referring to the crucifixion

gaol prison, jail

garb distinctive dress or costume

gauze a light, transparent fabric

gazette periodical, newspaper

Gemini used as an oath, from a corruption of *Jesu domine*

gillflirt a wanton young woman

Good your honour Please, good sir

gown a flowing outer robe indicating the wearer's profession; most often worn by those holding clerical, legal, or parliamentary offices

Grand Signior the Sultan of Turkey

grannam grandmother; old woman

gratis freely, without cost

gravity the quality of being grave, serious, solemn

great (adj.) intimate; good friends

great (adv.) expensively

Great Mogul the emperor of Delhi, a potentate living in luxury

greatness intimacy, friendship

guinea gold coin valued at twenty shillings from 1663 until 1717; after 1717, valued at twenty-one shillings

gypsy a playful term for a woman, like 'hussy' or 'baggage', especially a brunette

habiliment attire; accoutrement

habit apparel; mode of dress

hackney-coach carriage for hire

halter a rope with a noose, generally used for hanging criminals

hand handwriting

hanger a kind of short sword

hangings draperies or tapestries with which the walls of a room are hung

han't have not

harkee listen to me

harpy in Greek mythology, a divine agent of vengeance resembling a bird of prey with a woman's head; a rapacious, grasping, vengeful person

hartshorn smelling salts, so called because the chief source of the ammonia used to make them was the horn or antler of a hart

hey-dey exclamation of surprise or excitement

honest chaste, sexually virtuous; honourable, true to one's word

hosier one who sells or makes socks or woven undergarments

house boarding house, inn, house in which rooms are let

housewife hussy; a term of contempt; a pert woman

huff to scold; to storm at; speak insolently to or about someone

humour character, sentiment, caprice

huswife houswife

huzza shout of exultation

Hymen Greek and Roman god of marriage

ices ice-creams and water-ices

I doubt I fear

ifags an unsophisticated, if mild, oath meaning 'in faith'

imprimis in the first place

implement (n.) instrument; person doing one's bidding

impose deceive by false representations; intrude; presume; lay a burden upon someone

improve prove; demonstrate the truth or worth of something

indifferent euphemistically, rather unfavourable

Indies West Indies

indued with possessed of

infidel libertine, rake

in fine in conclusion

instrument written document; a thing used to accomplish an action

interest personal profit; a right to share in something; a stake or claim upon something

in troth in faith

involved beset with difficulties; enwrapped in embarrassing circumstances; entangled

Iö triumphe! Latin exclamation of triumph

jackanapes one who is like an ape or monkey; impudent fellow

Jacobite after 1688, an adherent of James II or his descendants

jade 'a term of reprobation applied to a woman' (*OED*)

jilts harlots, strumpets

Jove another name for Jupiter, highest of the Roman deities

juggler a magician or trickster; an alchemist

Jupiter Roman name for Zeus, the highest of the Greek gods

kidney (figurative) temperament, nature

knight errant a knight of medieval romance who wandered in search of adventures

Langoon a kind of white wine, named for a town on the Garonne River in France

lard (interjection) a dialect version for the mild oath, 'O lord'

lard (vb.) garnish, to enrich as if with fat; make juicy and delicious.

lash (vb.) move suddenly or quickly

latitudinary lax in religious matters

Laws a vulgar exclamation of astonishment

leave (vb.) stop

legerdemain sleight of hand; trickery; hocus-pocus

lett impediment

levée a reception for visitors upon one's rising from bed; the collection of visitors gathered for such a reception

levity unbecoming frivolity; moral lightness

liberal generous; open-hearted

licence formal written permission from the appropriate legal authority

limbo slang for pawned

linen garments made of linen; often referring to undergarments

list enlist

loo short for 'lanterloo'; a fashionable card game related to whist

loose (adj.) unrestrained; wanton; dissolute; with laces untied

loose (vb.) set free, release; lose

lubberly coarse; loutish; lazy; stupid

Lud a mild oath; a careless pronunciation of 'lord'.

lustre (1) radiance; (2) chandelier

macaroni young man who affects the styles and fashions of the Continent; a fop.

Ma foi! My word!

mal a-propos inopportune

Mammon personification of wealth, riches. Used as a term of opprobrium, indicating someone who hoards riches and is covetous of them

management prudence, ingenuity

mantua-makers dressmakers

manuscript a handwritten document

marquisina young Italian marchesa, marchioness

masks women wearing masks

masquerade costume or disguise such as one would wear to a masquerade or masked ball

matches horse race or wagers on races

mauvais ton gauche; bad form. Referring to someone whose ignorance of proper social decorum leads them to affect false modesty or shame. The term may also refer to someone painfully shy. In either case, the person in question behaves inappropriately in society.

merry slightly drunk

metamorphose (n.) transformation

mien aspect of countenance, expression of face

milksop a weak, effeminate youth or man

milliner someone who sells ribbons and dresses for women; a maker of hats, from 'Milan', a city known for its exquisite bonnets, gloves, and other articles of female apparel

minion lover, mistress

minx pert girl; hussy

miscreant vile wretch

modest unassuming; scrupulously chaste in feeling, language, and conduct

mort a great quantity

mum lips sealed, not a word

mummy a pulpy substance; dead flesh

murther murder

muzzle 'to fondle with the mouth close' (*OED*)

myrtle evergreen tree with white sweet-scented flowers, symbolic of love

nice fastidious, refined; scrupulous in matters of reputation

nicely punctiliously

nonage minority; the time of being legally under age

North Briton a Scotsman

Od! an oath from the name 'God'

Ods heart an oath from 'God's heart'

Ods precious oath from 'God's precious blood'

off-settings embellishments; ornamentation

overplus excess

overreached outwitted, outmanœuvred

oversea overseas

overset conquer, overwhelm; overturn

own admit, confess

panegyric a formal encomium or praise of a person

paraphernalia personal property or belongings

parts talents, wits, cleverness; also, private parts

party game; also a faction or body of partisans

passengers passers-by

pate skull; head

Peking Beijing

perquisite profit; thing to which one has sole right

personating impersonating

peruke wig

pesthouse house infected with plague

phaeton a light, open, four-wheeled, horse-drawn carriage

phiz face

phlegmatic not easily roused to action or shows of emotion

physic the practice of medicine

pickle plight, state

piece a guinea (twenty-one shillings)

piquet a two-person card game

place position, either at court or with a wealthy patron

plagued bothered; tormented

plaguily exceedingly; confoundedly

plaudit round of applause

plum-cake cake containing raisins, orange peel, and other preserved or dried fruits; fruitcake

poignancy piquancy; piercing quality of words or looks; ability to provoke and attract

policy a prudent or politic course of action; contrivance

poniard dagger

portion dowry

pos. unconditionally; absolutely

post obit sum of money owed that is to be paid after the death of the debtor

posture (n.) condition, situation

potecary a countrified varient of 'apothecary'

power mental vigour; force of character

pox syphilis, plague; *a pox*, an exclamation of irritation or impatience

prate (n.) idle chatter

prentice apprentice; someone in the early stages of learning a trade or profession

presentiment premonition; a vague expectation

pretend lay claim

pretension unwarrantable assumption; claim put forth

prithee archaic colloquialism for 'I pray thee'; please

privileged exempted; immune

prole prowl

proper handsome

proselyte a convert

proviso condition; stipulation

pshaw exclamation expressing rejection, contempt, or impatience

pugh a blowing sound; an expression of contempt

pump attempt to elicit information by persistent effort

puppy a term of contempt meaning an empty-headed young man; a coxcomb

purblind almost blind; dim-sighted

quality rank; high social position

quean strumpet; harlot

quirks quibble; argument

quotha said he or she (with a sarcastic overtone)

rack an instrument of torture for stretching bodies; often used in a figurative sense; (pl.) intense pain or suffering, such as one would experience on a rack

railing jesting; using abusive language

rake abbreviation of rakehell, 'an idle dissipated man of fashion' (*OED*)

rally tease; banter with, make fun of

rambler one who wanders unrestrained

randy aggressive, loud, scolding

rattle lively, thoughtless chatterer

receipts recipes

recommend bring forward as worthy of notice; introduce

redress restore to the proper condition; to put something right

regalio erroneous form of *regalo*, an elegant repast or entertainment

regard esteem

relation tale, narrative

relish taste, connoisseurship

rencontre encounter, skirmish

ride post ride with great haste or great speed

robe-de-chambre dressing-gown

robes de cour gowns to be worn at Court

rogue rascal, imp; sometimes a term of endearment

rook a kind of crow, known for its raucousness

rouleau a roll of coins

rout a large evening party; a fashionable gathering

sackcloth a coarse material worn to display humility, penitence, or mourning

saloon reception room; room used for assemblies or entertainments; salon

scaling climbing

scribbler 'a petty author; a writer without worth' (*OED*)

'sdeath an oath from 'God's death'.

seat residence; country estate

se'nnight week (from this day)

select exclusive; choicest; group chosen for the superiority of its individual members

sempstress seamstress

sense (n.) rationality, understanding, wisdom

serviceable ready to be of assistance

sessions sittings of judges or justices of the peace to hear causes

settlement particular legal term regarding conferring property, usually upon a woman when she marries

severally stage direction meaning 'separately or in different directions'

sham deceit

sharper swindler

she-wit a woman of intellect or cleverness

shown to have exposed oneself to public contempt

shy cautiously reserved; chary

singular unique; idiosyncratic

sirrah a term of disrespect used to address a boy or man. It indicates an assumption of authority on the part of the speaker

slattern slovenly girl or woman

slut a loose woman; a hussy

small beer weak beer; beer of inferior quality

smock (n.) a chemise or shift worn as a woman's undergarment

smock-faced having a pale smooth face; effeminate looking

sneaking niggardly; paltry

snivelling making sniffling or snuffling sounds; mean-spirited

snuff powdered tobacco; something of small value

solace comfort, cheer, entertain

sound swoon

spark fop; one who affects smartness and display in dress and manners

spinet 'a keyed musical instrument, common in England in the eighteenth century, closely resembling the harpsichord, but smaller and having only one string to each note' (*OED*)

spite of notwithstanding

spruce dapper; lively

spurn to strike with the foot; to kick

squeeze a crowded social gathering

state (n.) high rank; exalted position; splendour

stay (vb.) wait

still (adj.) to be motionless; abstaining from action

still (adv.) ever

stockjobbing the buying and selling of stocks by a member of the Stock Exchange; speculative dealing in stocks and shares

store accumulate; stock up in reserve

strict holding oneself to an austere, virtuous code of conduct

stuff nonsense; rubbish

sublime lofty, having grandeur; referring to a high moral, intellectual, or spiritual level

subscribe agree; concur; acquiesce

subtle having keen penetration; sly

suite band of wooers

sultana female sultan

superscription the address on a letter

sweet powder scented cosmetic powder used on the skin or hair

swingeing huge, immense

take up take one's self in hand; start afresh; borrow at interest

tarpaulin a nickname for a sailor, taken from a sailor's waterproof hat made from canvas covered or impregnated with tar

taste inclination; faculty of discernment of the beautiful, appropriate, or harmonious; the sense of perceiving flavour

tawdry cheaply adorned; slovenly

tease worry, irritate, annoy

temporizing conforming to time and circumstance; waiting for a more propitious occasion

termagant overbearing, violent, quarrelsome

testy irascible, sour-tempered

tête-à-tête private interview between two people

thoughtful contemplative; absent-minded; melancholy

throughly thoroughly

toasts reigning beauties to whom a company is requested to drink

toilet a dressing-table

token an expression of affection; a sign or presage of something to come;

ton fashion, mode, vogue; fashionable society

train group of people following or waiting upon someone

transport (vb.) figuratively, to carry away by passion

treating being regaled with food, drink, or other entertainment

trepanned inveigled

trice instant, moment

troop (vb.) go away

tuition custody; protection

turf race track

tuzzle variant of 'tussle'

twinklers sparkling eyes

udsbores oath or expletive based on 'Ud', a corruption of possessive form of 'God'

unconscionable unscrupulous; having no conscience

underhead a person of inferior intelligence; dunderhead

valet de chambre a gentleman's personal attendant

vapours a nervous disorder, primarily ascribed to women, supposedly caused by exhalations of bodily organs; depressed spirits

Venus Roman goddess of love

verily truly

vestal virgin, chaste as the priestesses of Vesta in ancient Rome

vizor mask

votary a devout worshipper, bound by vows

wag someone mischievous; a joker

warrant assure

what an intensifier; 'I'll have you know'

wheedling persuading by the use of soft flattering words; cajoling; gently coaxing

whim caprice; freakish idea

whoreson bastard son; sometimes used coarsely as term of reprobation or jocular familiarity

without unless, except; (stage direction) offstage

woundy extremely; very

wry-necked having a crooked neck

zounds oath, from 'God's wounds'